ON POLITICS, HISTORY AND IDEOLOGY

ON POLITICS, HISTORY AND IDEOLOGY

JOHN E. BEERBOWER

P.J.Bear

First Edition May 2023
Fourth Edition, Decenber 2024

CONTENTS

PREFACE

The four books in my *Wanderings* series contain many essays on politicized topics. I decided to collect them in one place, arranged by related subjects, with a few "tweaks" and updates. I called it "*Politics*," based on an unusual definition attributed to the late Christopher Boehm, formerly the Director of the Jane Goodall Research Center.

> "[T]he essence of politics:
> the ability to reflect consciously
> on different directions one's society could take,
> and to make explicit arguments why
> it should take one path rather than another."
>
> David Graeber and David Wengrow
> *The Dawn of Everything: A New History of Humanity*
> (2021), p. 86.

I would clarify by adding "attainable" before "directions" and "rational" before "arguments," making it less Utopian but also more aspirational. It seems silly to do more than dream about societies that can never exist; and we can still hope for rational argument about ours. I believe that these essays meet both criteria.

In May 2023, I became concerned again that I would run out of time and, frankly, was feeling worn out. So, I wrapped up my writing projects and published them. Then, during that summer, I resumed reading. Then writing. The book *Politics* became longer, as I revised and expanded it. It seems one cannot discuss politics without considering history and ideology. And, I felt the original title was now too narrow.

With a subsequent (modest) burst of renewed energy, I continued reading, then writing, producing my fifth set of essays in my *Wanderings* series, which I titled *Disappointments*. About half of the essays involved scientific issues. So, I revised, supplemented and repackaged them into a new volume as a second addendum to *Important Things We Don't Know*. Much of the remainder seemed to be useful additions to *Politics, History and Ideology*.

While adding that material, I decided on a substantial restructuring. The essays consisting essentially of book reviews (really, critiques) have been moved to the last chapter. I think that this change makes it much easier to follow the themes of the and, for anyone interested, to find my comments on particular books referenced.

Here is the new, new, expanded edition.

Visions of Reality

"The views of political commentators or writers
on social issues often range across a wide spectrum,
but their positions on these issues are seldom random.
...There is usually **a coherence to their beliefs,**
based on a particular set of underlying assumptions
about the world—a certain vision of reality.
Visions differ of course from person to person,
from society to society, and from one era to another.
Visions also compete with one another, whether for
the allegiance of an individual or of a whole society."

Thomas Sowell
The Vision Of The Annointed
(1995), p.ix.
(Emphasis added.)

The effects of personal perspectives or biases are pervasive. This, of course, is something that I had previously recognized, as I discussed at length in my first book. The theme of that book, *Limits of Science: Important Things We Don't Know* (2016), was the importance of recognizing our ignorance and our limitations. I carried that skepticism of experts and expertise throughout my *Wanderings*, where I expressed criticisms of the views, conclusions and reasoning of several social commentators, as well as of some scientists.

The role of biases in political and policy conclusions is paticularly significant. I have discussed Jonathan Haidt's *The Righteous Mind: Why Good People Are Divided by Politics and Religion* (2012), which attributes differences in political views to value systems, and Arthur Brooks' *Who Really Cares: The Surprising Truth About Compassionate Conservatism: Who Gives, Who Doesn't, and Why It Matters* (2006), which approaches the same question from a different perspective (focused on who actually behaves how, finding that those who believe in individual responsibility, give of their own money and time; those who believe in collective responsibility, give of other people's money and time). As a result of this realization, I try to set out clearly the beliefs and opinions that underlay my world view in the following section of this chapter before addressing the various subjects of controversy.

Interestingly, neuroscientist Steven Pinker credits economist Thomas Sowell with first propounding the assertion that people's differing visions of reality determine their politics: "Thomas Sowell's theory of the contrasting theories of human nature that underlie right-wing and left-wing political ideologies has been joined by several other attempts to distill out the essence of each one." Steven Pinker, *The Blank Slate: The Modern Denial of Human Nature* (2002, 2016), 2016 Afterword, p.434. Seems obvious. Perhaps. I was just early (or late) to the party.

In The *Vision Of The Annointed: Self-congratulation As A Basis For Social Policy* (1995), Sowell starts out neutrally enough, and so continues for one page. Then, he directs most of his commentary to a critique of "the intelligentsia of the United States and much of the Western world." He is often eloquent (and humorous) and generally insightful, but his writing is also often repetitive and his jargon, sometimes confusing or (to me) counterproductive.

A rather remarkable (but frustrating) book: Scathing, hard-hitting, relentless, sarcastic, cutting, and a little bitter. My kind of commentary. It was written almost 30 years ago. It is probably good that I did not read it then. It could have derailed my 40 year effort to be open minded, to see all sides and points of view (an effort somewhat at odds with my professional activities).

Contrasting Worldviews

The key differences in the visions arise from contrasting views of human nature, human life and human capabilities and, to some extent, of nature itself. Thomas Sowell, *The Vision Of The Annointed: Self-congratulation As A Basis For Social Policy* (1995). "The[re] are systematic differences that follow logically from fundamental differences in underlying assumptions, beginning with assumptions about the nature of human beings and the range of possibilities open to them." *Id.*, p.105.

Sowell claims that:

"[I]n some eras one vision so predominates over all others that it can be considered the prevailing vision of that time and place. ...It is not that these views are especially evil or especially erroneous. Human beings have been making mistakes and committing sins as long as there have been human beings. The great catastrophes of history have usually involved much more than that." *Id.*, p.2.

Sowell uses many words discussing the differences in the two visions. The result is pretty repetitive, but my main dissatisfaction is with the names he adopts—the "tragic" vision and the vision of the "anointed." I found neither sufficiently descriptive nor sufficiently objective. Unfortunately, I am challenged in searching for adequate substitutes. (Pinker notes: "[In *A Conflict of Visions* (1987),] Sowell calls them the Constrained Vision and the Unconstrained Vision; I will refer to them as the Tragic Vision (a term he uses in a later book) and the Utopian Vision." *The Blank Slate*, p.287). I use "pragmatist" and "utopianist" below.

The pragmatist recognizes the imperfection and imperfectability of humankind. People will be lazy, selfish, greedy, manipulating, shortsighted, violent and easily tempted. The humble pragmatist recognizes how much we do not know, do not understand, cannot foresee or predict and are unable to control. The unsentimental, humble pragmatist recognizes the importance of chance, of luck (good and bad), the unpredictability of the world, that shit happens, that miracles occur, that resources are limited, that unpalatable tradeoffs are inevitable and that often the only alternatives are "the bad" and "the worse." And, he or she believes that improvements must be incremental, sometimes individual by individual.

In contrast, the utopianist believes the myth of the "Noble Savage," that most evils are the result of civilization and society, of corrupt and corrupted social institutions perpetuated by bad people, and that the human condition can be cured only through the intervention. The arrogant utopianist believes that he or she and the like-minded few have the skills and insights successfully to reform human institutions, as well as humanity, and to tame nature. The self-righteous, arrogant utopianists believe that they are the enlightened and blessed and are, therefore, endowed with a mission to change others. Both groups can be elitists and view the common man with distain, but for only the second group is that a necessary component of the view. And, only the second group denies him the right to be who he is. The anointed do not simply happen to have a disdain for the public. Such disdain is an integral part of their vision, for the central feature of that vision is preemption of the decisions of others." *Id.*, p.123.

And,

> "One of the most important questions about any proposed course of action is whether we know how to do it. ...With these and innumerable other issues, the question for the anointed is not knowledge but compassion, commitment, and other such subjective factors which supposedly differentiate themselves from other people. ...Intractable problems with painful trade-offs are simply not part of the vision ... ."

Id., p.109.

Truth or "Truth"?

**"[W]hy ...is [it] so necessary to believe in a particular vision
that evidence of its incorrectnessis ignored,
suppressed, or discredited—ultimately,
why one's quest is not for reality but for a vision.
What does the vision offer that reality does not ... ?**

Thomas Sowell
The Vision Of The Annointed, p.2.

The interesting question is why do people doggedly prefer their own "truth" to the truth?

Sowell argues that "[the vision] become[s] inextricably intertwined with the egos of those who believe ... ." Certainly, the vision is part of one's identity, part of how one sees and understands the world. It is hard to relinquish or revise it. But, with respect to progressives, he adds an additional factor: "a special state of grace for those who believe in it." Not just the "feel good" factor, but the "feel superior" factor. The "I am a better person, a more moral person" factor. The "political correctness" factor, in today's terminology.

> "[T]hose who disagree with the prevailing vision are seen as being not merely in error, but in sin. ...[T]he anointed and the benighted do not argue on the same moral plane or play by the same cold rules of logic and evidence. ...Nor are such attitudes inherent in polemics, as such. Some very strong polemicists have argued that their opponents were well-meaning and even intelligent—but dangerously mistaken on the issue at hand. ...It is a vision of differential rectitude. It is not a vision of the tragedy of the human condition: Problems exist because others are not as wise or as virtuous as the anointed."

Id., pp.4-5.

What are the results? Lack of dialogue and foolish policies.

"Nor are such attitudes inherent in polemics, as such. Some very strong polemicists have argued that their opponents were well-meaning and even intelligent—but dangerously mistaken on the issue at hand." *Id.*

Sowell focuses on public policy and what happens when the outcome does not match the goal. First, he says, supporters claim external factors skewed the results. Second, they criticize the data or claim experimental error. These are common responses, frequently encountered in the natural sciences. But, he claims twentieth century progressives also resort to restating or altering the original goals in light of the results or, even, renouncing them as pretense. These are not legitimate responses. The proper methodology is to establish an experiment and specify the expected outcome in advance. Then, run the test. Clearly so. Sowell gets particularly agitated about issues that he claims are subject to empirical testing. "Today, despite free speech and the mass media, the prevailing social vision is dangerously close to sealing itself off from any discordant feedback from reality." *Id.*, p.2.

Sowell fills his book with examples—the War on Poverty, sex education, criminal justice reform, race and gender discrimination, and so on. I had reached many of the same conclusions about the evidence in examining particular topics, but it is startling to confront a seemingly endless list of examples.

Yet another illustration appears in Steven Pinker's *The Blank Slate,* examining the twentieth century's denial of "human nature" determined by genetics resulting from, Pinker suggests, its implications with respect to race, gender and social engineering issues. A case of political, moral considerations trumping "the science."

> "Throughout the twentieth century, many intellectuals
> tried to rest principles of decency on fragile factual claims
> such as that human beings are biologically indistinguishable,
> harbor no ignoble motives, and are utterly free in their
> ability to make choices....I will refer to those convictions as
> the Blank Slate: the idea that the human mind has no
> inherent structure and can be inscribed at will by society or
> ourselves.

...

"[T]he Blank Slate has become the secular religion of modern intellectual life. ... [and has] led others to mount the kinds of bitter attacks ordinarily aimed ...at heretics and infidels.... According to the doctrine, any differences we see among races, ethnic groups, sexes, and individuals come not from differences in their innate constitution but from differences in their experiences."

Pinker, *The Blank Slate*, pp.xi, 2, 4.

Pinker addresses academic views rather than political policies. He demonstrates how liberal orthodoxy on a very wide range of topics— racism, gender discrimination, violence, crime, punishment, rape, child-rearing and education, among others—are in conflict with the evidence (the facts), oblivious to common sense and reason and generally driven by personal agendas. And, he chronicles how non-conforming views are generally met with serious, blatant mischaracterizations and vicious, often personal, attacks.

Between these two books, the program of the left is left in tatters: a record consistent only in its series of utter failures interpreted as reasons for more of the same, but on a grander scale.

In his 2016 Afterword, Pinker observes:

"[C]ould the hostility to genetics and evolution just be rooted in a defensible scholarly skepticism? ... I argued that much of the opposition is in fact political rather than scientific.

...

"[D]isfiguring science and intellectual life: denying the possibility of objectivity and truth, dumbing down issues into dichotomies, replacing facts and logic with political posturing."

Pinker, p.434, 421.

What is going on? The banishment of common sense and observation? The abandonment of logic and reasoning? All done in favor of casting blame and wallowing in one's perceived victimhood?

"I find it hard to credit that anyone with an acquaintance with biology, a pair of eyes, and a dose of common sense could really believe that men and women are indistinguishable, that children's personalities are sculpted by their parents, that all individuals have the same native intelligence, that people can be trained to find anything as aesthetically pleasing as anything else, or that all aggression is a cultural fad."

Pinker, *The Blank Slate*, p.434.

Many of Sowell's points have broader application: the political exploitation, the failure to recognize tradeoffs, the unthinking extrapolation, the misuse and misinterpretation of data. These errors are found across the political spectrum.

Today

We now seem to have a new political phenomenon—the complete disregard of facts: an indifference to truth and to "truth." Thrust upon us by Donald Trump, and enthusiastically seized upon by his opponents in their frenetic efforts to destroy him.

It now is pretty clear that many of the attacks on Trump have been partisan in a peculiar way, intended to keep the focus on him and off current government policies and performance. Indeed, rather than trying to keep him out of politics, the critics hope to help him become the GOP nominee in 2024. Why? Because the Democrats are apparently saddled with Joe Biden and Trump is likely the only opponent that Biden can beat. Talk about cynical politics. You accept a weak candidate, then work to get the other party to select an even weaker one. The good of the country be dammed. Of course, the Republicans put themselves in this position.

The irony is that I doubt that much of anyone was misled by Donald Trump—he was quite upfront about his bluster, his abusiveness and his buffoonery.

But, Biden, the man who promised a return to normalcy, has misled almost everyone beyond his most progressive supporters. He has "misled" (I hesitate to say "has lied to" only because there is a serious question whether he had the requisite *mens rea*, whether he understood what he was doing. But, his staff certainly did) the people of the United States, various of our allies, his political opponents and, even some members of his own party. *See, e. g.,* Joe Manchin, "Biden's Inflation Reduction Act Betrayal: Instead of implementing the law as intended, his administration subverts it for ideological ends," *WSJ.com,* March 29, 2023; The Editorial Board, "Janet Yellen Blames Everybody Else for the Financial Panic," *WSJ.com,* April 2, 2023.

He has misled us about his political agenda, the withdrawal from Afghanistan, immigration, the COVID emergency, inflation, the deficit, the banking crisis, his clean energy programs, the debt ceiling and taxation. If he has understood his words and actions, then he has headed one of the most deceitful administrations in our history. Perhaps, he has just been our most manipulated President, while constantly a congenial puppet.

"In 2020 Americans didn't choose Joe Biden for his executive experience —he didn't have any. Nor was there much of a record of legislative accomplishment ... . [C]andidate Biden presented himself to voters as a bipartisan healer who would restore the customs and the culture of our politics." James Freeman, "Biden's Dangerous Debt Ploy," *WSJ.com*, April 3, 2023.

"The routine violation of political norms worsened under the Trump and Biden administrations but began under President Obama. He personally upbraided the Supreme Court in his 2010 State of the Union address... . His administration weaponized the Internal Revenue Service against grass-roots conservative groups and initiated the Federal Bureau of Investigation's interference in the 2016 election." Mark Penn and Andrew Stein, "Trump Indictment Accelerates America's Race to the Bottom," *WSJ.com,* April 5, 2023.

Of course, Biden is not alone. He was anticipated by, for example, Adam Schiff and Stacey Abrams and is now being mimicked by many others.

For example, "Randi Weingarten, the American Federation of Teachers president, ... attempted to erase two years of Covid history in testimony ... to the House of Representatives that was, literally, unbelievable. 'We spent every day from February on trying to get schools open. We knew that remote education was not a substitute for opening schools,' she told the House." The Editorial Board, "Randi Weingarten's Incredible Covid Memory Loss," *WSJ.com*, April 30, 2023.

Can we expect politicians ever to resist temptation and put country ahead of party? Apparently, that is a rhetorical question today. Many politicians say outrageous things; but, it is the deceitfulness that is most troubling. Much more than hypocrisy. More like fraud. Is it all really necessary? Will we be able ever to resume reasoned, rational discourse? Just another rhetorical question.

> "Opposition to the vision of the anointed is due not to a different reading of complex and inconclusive evidence, but exists because opponents are lacking, either intellectually or morally, or both."

Id., p.241.

So it seems. Still, after 28 years.

ONE "PRAGMATIST'S" WORLDVIEW

As I have been doing more solitary observing and thinking, I am realizing the extent to which certain beliefs (which one could call prejudices) influence my reactions. So, I have tried to sort out and organize these beliefs.

I consider the following propositions to be true:

I.

- All people act in pursuit of their own self-interest, as they perceive it.
- Most people are inherently lazy; they will take the path of least resistance. Their default position is idle.

- Yet, many people are capable of great ingenuity, commitment and hard work when there are rewards available for successful endeavors, whether such rewards are wealth or fame or power or self-realization.
- As a result, the structure of incentives people face—the combination of the rewards and punishments, the opportunities and obstacles—is an important determinant of people's behavior and of the resulting oucomes for them and their communities.

"With the explosion of means-tested transfer payments, the portion of prime work-age persons in the bottom quintile who actually work has fallen to 36% from 68%. In the second quintile, households with a work-age adult who actually works have declined to 85% from 90%. ...[T]he percentage of middle-income households with a prime work-age person who works has risen to 92% from 86%. ...For about the same income, 2.4 times as many work-age persons in the second quintile actually work and on average work 85% more hours than those in the bottom quintile. And 2.5 times as many work-age middle-income persons actually work and work on average 108% more hours."

Phil Gramm and Jodey Arrington, "Welfare Is What's Eating the Budget: Means-tested programs, not Medicare and Social Security, are behind today's massive debt," *WSJ.com*, September 11, 2024.

"These different institutions create very disparate incentives for the inhabitants of the two Nogaleses and for the entrepreneurs and businesses willing to invest there. These incentives created by the different institutions of the Nogaleses and the countries in which they are situated are the main reason for the differences in economic prosperity on the two sides of the border."

...

"The United States is also far richer today than either Mexico or Peru because of the way its institutions, both economic and political, shape the incentives of businesses, individuals, and politicians."

Daron Acemoglu and James A. Robinson, *Why Nations Fail: The Origins of Power, Prosperity, and Poverty* (2012), pp.9, 42.

- However, people vary greatly in aptitude, drive, abilities and effectiveness as a result of genetic inheritance and upbringing. There are only relatively few who will be at the top performance level in almost every type of endeavor.
- Working more (more hours) with greater commitment will generally result in the acquisition of additional skills and enhanced abilities, leading to greater lifetime earnings.

"Higher lifetime hours contribute to lifetime earnings via two channels: a direct channel (more hours spent in production at given productivity) and a human capital channel (more hours spent investing in human capital, which increases future productivity). Between a third and a half of the effect of lifetime hours on lifetime earnings is due to the human capital channel." Alexander Bick, Adam Blandin and Richard Rogerson, "Hours Worked and Lifetime Earnings Inequality," Working Paper 32997, *NBER*, September 2024.

II.

- Human happiness and well-being benefit from traditions (even dumb ones): a sense of a history and of continuity, as well as a sense of community, of belonging and of being part of something bigger than one's self. These are the things that give direction to life and provide the constraints and boundaries that inevitably shape a life, whether one "goes with the flow" or strives to burst the banks.

"The customs of the institution structure the soul, making it easier to be good. They guide behavior gently along certain time-tested lines. By practicing the customs of an institution, we are not alone; we are admitted into a community that transcends time." David Brooks, *The Road to Character* (2015), p.116.

"People who look backward to see the heroism and the struggle that came before see themselves as debtors who owe something, who have some obligation to pay it forward." David Brooks, *The Second Mountain* (2019), p.283.

- There is wisdom (that of the ages) captured in traditions. And, common sense.

"The real comparison ... is not between the knowledge possessed by the average member of the educated elite versus the average member of the general public, but rather the total direct knowledge brought to bear through social processes (the competition of the marketplace, social sorting, *etc.*), involving millions of people, versus the secondhand knowledge of generalities possessed by a smaller elite group. Moreover, the existing generation's traditions and values distill the experiences of other millions in times past."

Sowell, p.114.

- Work is good for a person. It reduces idle time—and its temptations—and provides a sense of independence and an identity.
- Charitable acts are beneficial to the doer. The acts themselves foster empathy and help create the sense of belonging. Of course, they also enhance the community.

"[L]ife is defined by commitments and obligations. The life well lived is a journey from open options to sweet compulsions." Brooks, *The Second Mountain*, p.56.

III.

- Bureaucracies are like people—their top priority is self-preservation and they tend to get fatter over time.
- In most organizations, 20% of the people do 80% of the work. Less than 10% of the people generate most of the value.
- The world is exceedingly complex. Most plans will go wrong. Intended consequences will often not be realized; unexpected consequences will almost always intrude and will often overwhelm the best laid plans. The broader the scope, the greater the change and/or the longer the time horizon of the plan, the greater the likely error.
- Decentralized decision-making minimizes the impact of errors and bad judgment, while allowing successes to be copied and, thereby, to multiply. It brings decision making closer to the matters at issue. Decentralization also allows diversity, promotes innovation and experimentation and encourages the taking of responsibility.
- Some systems consist of processes that appear generally to generate desirable results from voluminous inputs.

"[A]n order which arises as a consequence of individual interactions directed toward various and conflicting ends, not toward the creation of this order itself. ...Legal traditions, family ties, social customs, and price fluctuations in an economy are all systemic ways in which the experiences and preferences of millions of people powerfully influence the decisions of millions of other people." *Id.*, pp.124-5. Sowell frequently uses the phrase "systemic causation" to refer to this phenomenon. He has used the phrase in his writings on economics, but it does not appear to have been otherwise adopted. The phrase does not seem very helpful to me. Not all systems so function. (Perhaps, most long-lived ones—the ones that survive— do.) The key is decentralization of decision-making. What characteristics of a decision-making system are beneficial to achieving desirable outcomes? I suggest the following:

> 1. The decision-makers are numerous and independent, not controlled by others, so the consequences of the inevitable mistakes are localized.
> 2. The decision-makers have a stake in the outcome—they will benefit from good decisions and suffer the consequences of bad ones.
> 3. The decision-makers are located close to and have direct access to the relevant information.
> 4. Information is transmitted rapidly and accurately, and things happen promptly.
> 5. The outcome is visible to most everyone.

(Characteristics of a free market.)

- Effective exercise of responsibility requires personal accountability. If a position has room (or a need) for excellence or improvement and is one in which mediocrity is not sufficient, then there needs to be personal rewards and consequences, incentives and discipline, selection and selectivity, in order to realize the potential that is there.

- The biggest disadvantages of bureaucracies, of unions and of the civil service are that they all diminish accountability, protect incompetence and stifle initiative. Such organizations are adequate only for positions as to which people are fungible, where the job requirements and opportunities are within the reach of almost everyone—among whom some will struggle, some will be comfortable and some will lean back and contentedly vegetate.
- The possession of power over people or things or events is both addictive and corrupting.
  Government invites corruption. It comes with the power to grant benefits, which power corrupts.

"America's rugged individualism makes it most compatible with real capitalism. Sure, the U.S. always has had some patronage and cronyism. ... But now we've entered an era of kickback capitalism, which has created a mangy mob of meritless mooches. ...The thing [big government] does best is throw your tax money at favored constituents. Since Covid hit, the U.S. has deployed $11 trillion in spending, loans, disbursements and asset purchases. You thought markets allocated capital?"

Andy Kessler, "The Rise of Kickback Capitalism," *WSJ.com*, March 5, 2023.

- Government largesse, conversely, seems always to be accompanied by fraud. Temptations are just too great, probably because stealing from bureaucrats with no personal accountability is so easy, possibly because there seem to be no real victims.

Look at Social Security fraud, whether stealing one's neighbor's benefit checks or collecting checks for your deceased relatives. Or, Medicare fraud

---

by doctors and other health care providers. The pandemic relief programs have been fraught with fraudulent claims for unemployment benefits, PPP loans, and small business relief.

"The IG [Inspector General] ... "found more than 70,000 suspicious loans, totaling $4.6 billion. The report calls the level of fraud 'unprecedented'... . ...The IG has also flagged about $80 billion in suspicious transactions via another SBA pandemic program, Economic Injury Disaster Loans. The fraud in Covid unemployment benefits was possibly worse... ..'" The Editorial Board, "Covid Fraudsters Are Still At Large," *WSJ.com*, June 7, 2022.

"Many who participated in what prosecutors are calling the largest fraud in U.S. history — the theft of hundreds of billions of dollars in taxpayer money intended to help those harmed by the coronavirus pandemic — couldn't resist purchasing luxury automobiles. Also mansions, private jet flights and swanky vacations. ...[W]hat experts say is the theft of as much as $80 billion ... of the $800 billion handed out in a Covid relief plan known as the Paycheck Protection Program, or PPP. That's on top of the $90 billion to $400 billion believed to have been stolen from the $900 billion Covid unemployment relief program — at least half taken by international fraudsters... . And another $80 billion potentially pilfered from a separate Covid disaster relief program."

Ken Dilanian and Laura Strickler, "'Biggest fraud in a generation," *NBC News*, March 28, 2022.

"States have long known that they paid billions in fraudulent unemployment claims during the pandemic. But this week the federal government more than doubled its estimate in stolen payments to as much as $135 billion. The new figure comes from a report released Tuesday by the Government Accountability Office (GAO)."

The Editorial Board, "Pandemic Fraud Hits a New Height:: Up to $135 billion was stolen, and Washington still shrugs," *WSJ.com*, September 15, 2023.

The magazine Rolling Stone provided perhaps the most shocking report of the events. Sean Woods reports that Haywood Talcove, CEO of LexisNexis Risk Solutions, apparently tried repeatedly to warn the government about the lack of security and likelihood of fraud, starting in 2020. He was unsuccessful. The result:

> "The list of various CARES Act schemes is endless and astounding: the couple who scammed some $20 million off unemployment insurance while living as high rollers in Los Angeles; the Chicago man under indictment for selling bunk Covid tests and allegedly raking in $83 million (he has declared his innocence); the Florida minister who the feds allege faked the signature of his aging accountant, suffering from dementia, to steal $8 million in PPP loans... . One particularly loathsome and effective plot: offering fake meals to underprivileged children in Minnesota to reel in a whopping sum of $250 million."
>
> ...
>
> "Inspector General Michael Horowitz told congress that more than a $100 billion in Covid aid money may have ended up misappropriated, but many experts and members of law enforcement think the number is much higher. The AP estimates $280 billion went to fraudsters and another $123 billion was misappropriated, some 10 percent of the relief money.For his part, Talcove estimates the actual losses blow past the tallies being thrown around. 'The real number is much higher. **I think the government lost a trillion dollars due to fraud in the pandemic**,' he says. 'One trillion.'"

Sean Woods, "The Trillion-Dollar Grift: Inside the Greatest Scam of All Time," Rolling Stone. July 9, 2023 (emphasis added).

IV.

- Private gifts to relieve hardships or to enable opportunities have the advantages of being targeted, discriminating, responsive to changing circumstances, personal and voluntary. Such philanthropy is rewarding for the provider and likely to be appreciated by many beneficiaries. It is also beneficial to the community.
- The drawback to reliance on private philanthropy is that there will be deserving persons who are overlooked, missed or left out. An arguable negative is that some recipients will feel demeaned.
- Government programs to relieve hardships or enable opportunities have the disadvantages of being overbroad by encompassing persons not in need; being mechanical and susceptible to fraud and manipulation because they are rule-based; fostering a sense of entitlement among actual and potential beneficiaries and creating continual demands for more. As a result, they are always wasteful and, at least, somewhat counterproductive.
- Government programs are also susceptible to being co-opted by those in positions of control.

"Of the promised money, 20 percent of it was taken as UN head office costs in Geneva. The remainder was subcontracted to an NGO, which took another 20 percent for its own head office costs in Brussels, and so on, for another three layers, with each party taking approximately another 20 percent of what was remaining. The little money that reached Afghanistan was used to buy wood from western Iran, and much of it was paid to Ismail Khan's trucking cartel to cover the inflated transport prices. ...Many studies estimate that only about 10 or at most 20 percent of aid ever reaches its target. ...Throughout the last five decades, hundreds of billions of dollars have been paid to governments around the world as 'development' aid. Much of it has been wasted in overhead and corruption... ."

Acemoglu and Robinson, p.452.

- The supposed "advantages" of government programs are that they give people the ability to use other people's money to pursue their own goals and allow the electorate, rather than the philanthropists, to decide where and how much help is to be provided.

V.

- The application of science to issues of public policy in the messy world in which we live is particularly challenging, involving many potential pitfalls, and is ripe for misunderstandings. Science will rarely have the answer to policy questions.
- A policy question will generally involve (i) a concept or vision of the resulting state of affairs that one would like to achieve through the actions to be taken; (ii) an accurate assessment of the current state of affairs; and (iii) a correct prediction of the likely outcomes of the various potential actions under consideration.
- Errors in the assessment of the initial conditions will lead to significant "mistakes" in policy. Even if the choices would have been correct if the initial conditions were as they were perceived to be, they often have unexpected consequences because the initial conditions were actually different. Even small differences in the initial conditions can lead to large differences in the outcomes.
- Most, if not all, of the assessments of past events or of existing facts will be subject to uncertainty. And, we then need to predict both future events and the consequences of proposed policies, both of which predictions are inherently difficult, if not impossible.
- All policy choices will have redistributive and re-allocative consequences. They will result in the transfer of wealth and disposable income among persons and groups. They will affect the use of

resources as prices adjust to the impact of the policy. They will alter incentives and stimulate some behavior while discouraging other.

- Science is never certain, humankind is inherently fallible, and the real world is very complex.

"As the twentieth century drew to a close, the connection between hard scientific fact and public policy became increasingly elastic. In part this was possible because of the complacency of the scientific profession; in part because of the lack of good science education among the public; in part, because of the rise of specialized advocacy groups which have been enormously effective in getting publicity and shaping policy; and in great part because of the decline of the media as an independent assessor of fact."

Michael Crichton, "Aliens Cause Global Warming", *Caltech Michelin Lecture*, January 17, 2003.

VI.

- One should be scared of majority rule, if not buffeted and moderated by lobbyists, influential people and groups with their own agendas and an independent media.
- But, one should be even more frightened of government by experts and unaccountable bureaucrats or of an unfettered President.

"The democratic political sphere can turn into one in which the logic is not cooperation and growth but rather confiscation and redistribution—with 'deserving' and 'undeserving' standing in, respectively, for the friends and enemies of the powerful." J. Bradford DeLong, *Slouching Towards Utopia: An Economic History of the Twentieth Century* (2022), p.93.

So ...

These beliefs color my opinions on most matters, in combination with a strong commitment to tolerance and individual liberty. And, I can see how these propositions provide a basis for a conservative political view.

I have criticized social policies and the positions of various politicians on the bases of logic, empirical evidence and common sense. But, I now see that I have a more fundamental and profound bias coloring my views. To get it in focus, I examined why I have such a deep affinity for the England. It is that I share its love of tradition, of ceremony. Its reverence of the classics, whether literature, art, music or science. Its understanding of quality, whether intellectual or material. The continuation of prayer, religious music and Latin at the Cambridge Colleges, independent of religious beliefs. The love of gardens and gardening, of Nature, of hiking and of walking. I could go on and on. But, I see that it is all essentially conservative, basd on a respect of history and for our incredible heritage. And, I have been deeply disappointed by events in the U.K. The Tories should be better than this. They should at least be competent at governing, whatever one thinks about the particular policies. What has happened to tradition, continuity, stability? We would previously have said, insensitively: "It's not like the U.K. is some 'banana republic'."

I value personal security, law and order. Relative safety of your person, your family, your home and your possessions. I also realize that I fear "revolution"—like the French and Russian Revolutions or Pol Pot's Cambodia and Mao's China—and, other forms of mob action and the random violence driven by sadism or psychopathology. The disrespect of tradition, the rejection of humanity, anonymity, the absence of individual responsibility and the lack of the need to make one's own decisions all enable the emergence of evil.

Presumably, my perspective is a result of upbringing and, perhaps, genetics. It is deeply ingrained and highly personal. It is fundamental, really, to who I am.

"Some people seem **to have been born into this world with a sense of indebtedness for the blessing of being alive.** They are aware of the transmission of generations, what has been left to them by those who came before, their indebtedness to their ancestors, **their obligations to a set of moral responsibilities that stretch across time.**"

Brooks, *The Road to Character,* p.126 (emphasis added).

CHAPTER II

Some Stubborn "Facts"

A vision is well and good, but from time to time, it will run into aspects of reality. Here are some things about us and our world that must be accomodated.

I.

HUMAN NATURE

"Our theory of human nature is the wellspring
of much in our lives. We consult it when we want
to persuade or threaten, inform or deceive.
It delineates what people can achieve easily,
what they can achieve only with sacrifice or pain,
and what they cannot achieve at all.
It affects our values: what we believe we can
reasonably strive for as individuals and as a society."

Steven Pinker
The Blank Slate
(2002), p.1.

Steven Pinker in *The Blank Slate: The Modern Denial of Human Nature* (2002, 2016) exposes the denial of science (and sense) by the twentieth-century left orthodoxy in its insistent embrace of "the blank slate" view of human nature.

"The Blank Slate"

"Throughout the twentieth century, many intellectuals tried to rest principles of decency on fragile factual claims such as that human beings are biologically indistinguishable, harbor no ignoble motives, and are utterly free in their ability to make choices. ... ... refer to those convictions as the Blank Slate: the idea that the human mind has no inherent structure and can be inscribed at will by society or ourselves."

Id., p.xi.

With a little science and a lot of logic, he demostrates that the commitment to that view was mistaken, foolish and imposed by fervent biases. He goes on similarly to discredit (demolish) relativism, deconstructionism, social constructionism, critical theory, postmodernism and identity politics, as well as the then yet to be propounded status of the "woke."

Pinker makes the effort to appear balanced by criticizing the Christian right for "also" resisting contemporary neuroscience because it supposedly calls into question the existence of the human soul and of free will. But, the issues and evidence are very different. The existence and reality of human nature is beyond reasonable dispute as a matter of science and logic; although, its precise parameters are still unknown. The existence of free will may be put at issue by future scientific discoveries but is favored by logic (as Pinker demonstrates). The existence (or non-existence) of the soul seems well beyond both science and logic today and, perhaps, forever.

Actually, Pinker himself equivocates about free will: "We have every reason to believe that consciousness and decision making arise from the electrochemical activity of neural networks in the brain [, but] how moving molecules should throw off subjective feelings (as opposed to mere intelligent computations) and how they bring about choices that we freely make (as opposed to behavior that is caused) remain deep enigmas to our Pleistocene psyches." *Id.*, p.240.

Human nature must be genetic, or it would not be "human," but still specific to a particular time or location, a particular culture. Why do we conclude that the brain contains particular things genetically determined rather than being just a blank "learning machine?" Well, even a learning machine needs instructions to be built. In addition, the act of learning requires a set of at least initial assumptions about relationships and processes. Then, there is the abundant evidence of what appear to be universal characteristics of *homo sapiens*. For example: "Humans speak some six thousand mutually unintelligible languages. Nonetheless, the grammatical programs in their minds differ far less than the actual speech coming out of their mouths. We have known for a long time that all human languages can convey the same kinds of ideas." *Id.*, p.37.

"The effects of differences in genes on differences in minds can be measured, and the same rough estimate—substantially greater than zero, but substantially less than 100 percent—pops out of the data no matter what measuring stick is used." *Id.*, p.47. "A conventional summary is that **about half of the variation in intelligence, personality, and life outcomes is heritable**—a correlate or an indirect product of the genes. It's hard to be much more precise than that, because heritability values vary within this range for a number of reasons." *Id.*, p.374 (emphasis added).

So:

> "I think we have reason to believe that the mind is equipped with a battery of emotions, drives, and faculties for reasoning and communicating, and that they have a common logic across cultures, are difficult to erase or redesign from scratch, were shaped by natural selection acting over the course of human evolution, and owe some of their basic design (and some of their variation) to information in the genome."

Id., p.73.

These characteristics may, indeed, be the result of biological evolution, as Pinker believes. I have explored at length the theories of evolution and their abilities to explain cooperation, altruism, cultural developments, beauty and so on in my first book, *Important Things We Don't Know About Nearly Everything* (initially published as *Limits of Science?*). I will not try to add to what I have already said, but I will remind the reader that I found considerable inadequacies in the various theories' abilities to explain either life itself or human consciousness.

The Nature of Human

What is included in human nature?

Surely, the inclinations toward selfishness and the fear of injury or loss, acquisitiveness, jealousy, and so on. Also, protectiveness towards one's family and, to some extent, one's community. And, an inclination towards violence? Probably. Clearly, we find "good" qualities like empathy, generosity, courage, altruism and reason. Then, ambiguous qualities, like the desire for the respect of and recognition by others, the need for self-respect, pride.

These conflicting inclinations reach some type of resolution or compromise each time a decision or an action is precipitated. "The mind is a complex system composed of many interacting parts. The upshot is that an urge or habit coming out of one module can be translated into behavior in different ways—or suppressed altogether—by some other module." *Id.*, p.40.

Only a few people fall at the extremes. Pinker cites evidence that only 3 to 4% of men are sociopaths, devoid of empathy, and even fewer woman. However, "[s]tatistical analyses show that a psychopath, rather than merely falling at the end of a continuum for one or two traits, has a distinct cluster of traits (superficial charm, impulsivity, irresponsibility, callousness, guiltlessness, mendacity, and exploitiveness) that sets him off from the rest of the population." *Id.*, p.261. Perhaps, a similarly small percentage of people are all altruism, with a defining cluster of traits. That leaves more than 90% with a mixture of competing characteristics from a mixture of traits.

> "Most people, of course, are in the middle of the range, displaying mixtures of reciprocity, pure generosity, and greed. Why do people range across such a wide spectrum? Perhaps all of us are capable of being saints or sinners, depending on the temptations and threats at hand. Perhaps we are predisposed to being nastier or nicer by our genes. "

Id., p.260.

And, "liberal and conservative political attitudes are largely, though far from completely, heritable ... because they come naturally to people with different temperaments." *Id.*, p.283 (citing Gilbert and Sullivan).

"In the economic or social contract tradition, society is an arrangement negotiated by rational, self-interested individuals. The modern theory of evolution falls smack into the social contract tradition. It maintains that complex adaptations, including behavioral strategies, evolved to benefit the individual (indeed, the genes for those traits within an individual), not the community, species, or ecosystem. [Yet, b]ands, clans, tribes, and other social groups are central to human existence and have been so for as long as we have been a species."

Id., pp.285-6.

Some Consequences

If various characteristics are to a non-trivial extent determined by genetics (say, height, body type or athletic ability, or, more relevant here, intelligence, temperament, self-discipline or ambition), then not only will individuals differ to varying degrees, but groups of people with genetic similarities greater than average (families, stable communities, isolated populations, races, tight knit religious groups) will vary statistically from one another. For example, the average heights, IQs, motivation, dedication, focus, discipline (if they could be quantified and averaged) will vary from group to group. Importantly, however, nothing much can be said about any particular individual. He or she may have had a greater or lesser probability *ex ante* of being smarter or taller than someone else, but after-the-fact, they either are or are not.

Environmental factors are also non-trivial determinants of human nature, but peoples who are genetically close are more likely to grow up together and share environments. So, the genetic predispositions will tend to be reinforced.

What does this mean for social science and for public policy?

1. Well, for example, it means that profiling can be a rational and socially desirable law-enforcement strategy under certain factual circumstances. One can estimate the aggregate adverse effects on innocent victims of the profiling and the danger or injury averted by the identification of the perpetrator. The availability and efficacy, as well as the burdens, of alternative methods is an important consideration.

2. Another example is the use of aggregate data to infer causation, such as discrimination causing a difference in average income or wealth or in representation in particular groups or positions. One needs to control for every factor that materially affects the phenomenon being assessed. So, not just gender, educational status and age distribution, but also genetic and environmental inheritance. That makes statistical investigations very difficult. The creative design of experiments is necessary for the attainment of meaningful results.

3. "The partial heritability of intelligence, conscientiousness, and antisocial tendencies, implying that some degree of inequality will arise even in perfectly fair economic systems, and that we therefore face an inherent tradeoff between equality and freedom." *Id.*, p.294. And, tradeoffs between equality (of outcomes) and fairness (equality of opportunities) and, if one accepts neoclassical economic theory, between equality and efficiency and equality and growth.

4. The innate demand for justice looks for "just desserts" and rebels against cheats and free-loaders. It disapproves of disincentives to honesty and hard work. "This psychology makes people oppose indiscriminate welfare and expansive social programs not because they are callous or greedy but because they think such programs reward the indolent and punish the industrious." *Id.*, p.304.

5. "The moderate success of democracies, like the failures of radical revolutions and of Marxist governments, is now widely enough agreed upon that it may serve as another empirical test for rival theories of human nature." *Id.*, p.296. (For some reason, Pinker here displays uncharacteristic understatement.)

History provides an approximation of social science experimentation. The last 300 years starkly establish which world view conforms with reality. Utopian visions have consistently resulted in disasters, some just sad, others, catastrophic. Similarly, parliamentary democracy with checks and balances has had "moderate success," and the systems based on relatively free markets and private property have far outstripped, and are gradually replacing, all other types of economic organization.

I have just finished two new books about Richard II, Henry IV and Henry V, covering about 50 years at the end of the Fourteenth and the beginning of the Fifteenth Centuries in England (1367-1422). Helen Castor, *The Eagle and the Hart: The Tragedy of Richard II and Henry IV* (2024); Dan Jones, *Henry V: the astonishing triumph of England's greatest warrior king* (2024).

Several things struck me as relevant to this discussion, given England's importance to the emergence of liberal society:

1. The power and influence of Parliament, tied to but extending well beyond the control of taxation.

2. The amount of the kingdom's wealth was held by others than the king— by merchants, other nobles and the Church—as evidenced by the extensive reliance of the kings on loans in addition to taxation to finance their exploits.

3.The frequency of attempts by other nobles to overthrow the king and the related plotting and conspiring and the frequency of uprisings by the common folks.

4. The independence of the subjects from the king and the related need of the king and the nobles to buy loyalty and military assistance with the grant of annuities and the payment of wages.

5. The resulting pluralistic nature of English society, power and governance, despite being a monarchy.

The successful development of English society, like the success of its economy, was dependent upon decentralization and pluralism that emerged with the Magna Carta in 1215.

One might respond that it depends on what goals one has for society. Perhaps, but unattainable goals are useless for establishing policy. If we live in a Hobbesian world (the world reflected in modern game theory models, like the "Prisoner's Dilemma"), then it is far better to face facts. In such a world, a reasonable "goal of a peaceful and prosperous society is to minimize the use of dominance, which leads to violence and waste, and to maximize the use of reciprocity, which leads to gains in trade that make everyone better off." *Id.*, p.297.

"Hobbe's analysis of the causes of violence, borne out by modern data on crime and war, shows that violence is not a primitive, irrational urge, nor is it a 'pathology' ... . Instead, it is a near-inevitable outcome of the dynamics of self-interested, rational social organisms. But Hobbes is famous for presenting not just the causes of violence but a means of preventing it: 'a common power to keep them all in awe.' A governing body that has been granted a monopoly on the legitimate use of violence can neutralize each of Hobbes's reasons for quarreling. By inflicting penalties on aggressors, the governing body eliminates the profitability of invading for gain. That in turn defuses the Hobbesian trap in which mutually distrustful peoples are each tempted to inflict a preemptive strike to avoid being invaded for gain. And a system of laws that defines infractions and penalties and metes them out disinterestedly can obviate the need for a hair trigger for retaliation and the accompanying culture of honor. People can rest assured that someone else will impose disincentives on their enemies, And having a third party measure the infractions and the punishments circumvents the hazard of self-deception, which ordinarily convinces those on each side that they have suffered the greater number of offenses. Adjudication by an armed authority appears to be the most effective general violence-reduction technique ever invented."

Id., pp.329-30.

The Founding Fathers had a peculiar view of the dangers the new country faced, and they adopted an almost unprecedented objective for members of a ruling elite: The creation of a governing structure that prevents the consolidation, extension and perpetuation of power. The historical norm is the precise opposite: The use of vigorous, even extreme, measures to keep power. The Founders had to have recognized that the leaders to be constrained would come from among themselves. But, they still refused to trust human nature.

Why?

"The feature of human nature that most impressed the framers was the drive for dominance and esteem, which, they feared, imperils all forms of government. Someone must be empowered to make decisions and enforce laws, and that someone is inherently vulnerable to corruption."

...

"Checks and balances were instituted to stalemate any faction that grew too powerful. They included the division of authority between federal and state governments, the separation of powers among the executive, legislative, and judiciary branches, and the splitting of the legislative branch into two houses."

Id., pp.296, 297. *See also, id*, p.128.

"Where Hobbes fell short [and the Founders did not] was in dealing with the problem of policing the police. He did not seem to appreciate that in practice a leviathan would not be an otherworldly sea monster but a human being or group of them, complete with the deadly sins of greed, mistrust, and honor." *Id.*, p.331.

So, for some 250 years, we have enjoyed the benefits of a government designed by people who recognized, not denied, human nature.

II.

THE PETER PRINCIPLE

We are surrounded by mediocrity and incompetence. Why? Are my current expectations and standards just too unrealistic? Has my memory been warped? Perhaps, the child just did not notice the mistakes, the blundering, the waste.

Over the years, I have been the direct supervisor for more than 200 people, at least half of whom were lawyers. I also interviewed several hundred applicants for jobs. The strongest lesson from these experiences was that people vary dramatically in their abilities. There are, of course, the differences in personal physical and behavioral characteristics, which have an effect on performance; but, more importantly, there is something else that makes certain individuals stand out, far above the others. While the bulk of the people fall along a continuum from useless to useful, a handful are qualitatively different, with an unbridgeable gap in between.

The rare few bring initiative, insight, instinct and creativity to every task. They "own" the work. They feel deeply responsible for the results —for their own assigned tasks and for the tasks of others that affect the outcome. They are perfectionists; they care. Intelligence certainly matters, but it seems supplementary to this other something.

The other takeaway is that the critical extra something is very difficult to ascertain during an interview (I was never able to master the skill), but its presence or absence would generally become obvious very quickly on the job. For the quiet or shy, it can take a little longer, but the presence or absence is unmistakable. The fact is that some people are markedly better than others at almost everything. Fortunately, the most able and effective do not all have the same interests or aspirations. The result is that they are scattered among vocations.

I was convinced in 1970 by the relevance of the Peter Principle: that within hierarchies, people get promoted until they reach jobs that they cannot adequately do, to their position of incompetence. I think, however, it is not a universal truth but a phenomenon of the second half of the twentieth century. Of course, for it, we need employment structures with hierarchical positions that can be filled from below. We need the practice of actually filling positions from within. And, ironically, we need a relative meritocracy.

If employment is based on family, or connections or political correctness (in the traditional sense); then there will be different outcomes. So, the crafts and trades operate differently, as will family businesses and entrepreneurial start-ups and small business. Even large organizations with more entrepreneurial and innovating mindsets can avoid the Peter Principle. The most susceptible will be administrative offices, retail banks, insurance companies, government departments and bureaucracies generally.

Of course, people earned their livelihoods quite differently in the nineteenth century. And, people in the nineteenth century took a very different view of employment.

"[The garden's] preservation was owing merely to the fact that their gardener was blessed with **a wholesome stupidity** rendering him incapable of unlearning what his father, who had been gardener there before him, had had marvellous difficulty in teaching him. We do not half appreciate **the benefits to the race that spring from honest dulness.** The CLEVER people are the ruin of everything."

George McDonald, *Thomas Wingfold, Curate.*(1880), Vol. I, Ch. VII (emphasis added).

Large numbers were self employed, many as farmers, skilled tradesmen and shopkeepers. Few worked in bureaucracies. For many workers, there was a quite direct and unmistakable link between how well they performed and the survival of their families. Mistakes had visible consequences. You knew if you screwed up. And, your family and neighbors knew. It was a more fragile, more vulnerable and more transparent existence. In addition, many children learned trades or useful skills from their parents. Occupations were passed from one generation to the next. People learned how to do things. They achieved proficiency. All one needed was common sense coupled with a strong sense of responsibility. Industrialization resulted in more and more working in factories and on assembly lines. Much has been written about the resulting alienation of these workers, but, at least, they knew when they made a mistake, and they could see and feel the output of their collective labors.

Compare that to today's typical office workers. In the twenty-first century, for a variety of reasons, including the explosion of employment litigation and of sensitivity training programs, many office workers and bureaucrats are largely sheltered from consequences of poor performance. The injuries from their mistakes are borne by others—customers, employers, coworkers. They are also still separated from the output of the enterprise. Not surprisingly, many feel little commitment, loyalty or, even, responsibility toward their work. They do the minimum, focused on their rights and benefits. Pay is now an entitlement, not something earned. However, not for all:

"Mr. Moller had performed the morning's repetitive tasks multiple times a day for more than four decades, yet still he did them with the purposefulness and lightheartedness of an applicant looking to land the job. ...The admirable marriage of consistency and mirth got me thinking about this bus driver's job, and the one to which I was returning. All things being equal, work done joylessly is work done less effectively, for nothing ever happens in a vacuum."

...

"Someone is always watching, whether it's an office colleague or a bus passenger, and influenced accordingly. This means that **whatever a man's vocation in life happens to be, what he does is scarcely more important than how he does it**."

Mike Kerrigan, "St. Bernard on the Hertz Shuttle: What we do isn't nearly as important as how we do it," *WSJ.com*, September 11, 2024 (emphasis added).

III.

"MAKERS AND TAKERS"

I want to try clearly to express a few thoughts about an uncomfortable line of thought.

Aptitudes and Abilities

I have written about differences in abilities among people, but I failed to grasp how dramatic they are or, then, to consider the implications. The differences in physical abilities are well known, but they extend way beyond athletics. They include manual dexterity, balance and coordination in everyday movement; eyesight, hearing; visual and auditory perceptions; reaction times; *etc.* Of course, there are the many intellectual skills or capabilities and, even, personality traits that affect performance.

Take an example: Two people watch the performance of a relatively simple, multi-step task. After three times, the first observer, when asked, performs the task perfectly and suggests an improvement in the process. After 100 times (or 1,000), the second observer, when asked to try it, has no idea even where to start. Unrealistic? If you think so, then you have been sheltered (or, are like our second observer). People who show initiative, pay attention and try are few.

What is the problem? A lack of curiosity, certainly; a lack of interest, probably; an inability to understand the purpose of the task, possibly; an inability to visualize how the steps relate, perhaps.

And, I think that the performance difference will persist across a broad range of activities. There may be some job at which the second can outperform the first, but not many. Of course, that is neither here nor there. The real question is whether there are things that the second person can do that will generate a net positive, that is, the costs of supervision and of the correction of mistakes is less than the person's output. Unfortunately, my experience indicates that there is a sizable, and growing portion, of the population for which the answer is no.

It is obvious that many of the people with the lesser abilities could not survive in the so-called State of Nature. They need the support of the community or, today, of the government to live.

I suppose that in small groups (family, clan, close communities), the group finds some way for each member to be useful and assigns that task as a condition of membership and receipt of group support. Likely, some members will be supported by the group even with no ability to contribute, but how many will depend on available resources and the productivity of the rest. Presumably, it would be rare for the group to continue to support individuals who refuse to cooperate and to participate.

We know that most characteristics related to performance are to a significant extent (probably around 50%) determined by genetics (including height, body type, athletic ability, intelligence, temperament, self-discipline and ambition). Thus, not only will individuals differ to varying degrees, but groups of people with genetic similarities greater than average (families, stable communities, isolated populations, races, tight-knit religious groups) will vary statistically from one another (but less than the variation amongng individuals). For example, the average heights, IQs, motivation and self-discipline (to the extent any such characteristics can be quantified and averaged) will vary from group to group.

Importantly, at the same time, nothing can be said about any particular individual. He or she may have had a greater or lesser probability, *ex ante,* of being smarter or taller than someone else, but after-the-fact, he or she either is or is not.

Also, since genetically influenced, the prevalence of particular levels of ability in the population will depend on rates of survival and reproduction. Over time bearers of various traits will come to represent larger or smaller percentages of the population. It is entirely possible in a modern, industrialized nation for the less able to out-reproduce the more able, especially if the survival rates are not too disparate—a reversal of the model of Darwinian evolution.

Not that I am concerned about the genetic future of the species from this phenomenon (unlike things like increasing pollution or toxins causing more frequent mutations). The more able will not be outcompeted by the less able for resources and, thus, disappear. They will survive, even if increasingly outnumbered. These stronger genetic makeups will still be here, ready to resurge following the next apocalypse, just as in *The Walking Dead*. And, as in that TV series, some of the capable will be good and some will be evil.

Survival rates of different groups may continue to diverge as a result of violent crime, obesity, diabetes, substance abuse, depression and mental illness. That certainly seems to be the trend for twenty-first century America. How the contrasting rates will balance out remains to be seen.

Work

This discussion reminds me of alarmist warnings 50 years ago about the impending dangers of automation. The fear was that the result would be the loss of maybe 90% of all jobs, with 10% of workers producing enough for everyone. (I think that the experts underestimated the expandability of "enough.")

"The human-machine frontier has shifted, with businesses introducing automation into their operations at a slower pace than previously anticipated. ...But while expectations of the displacement of physical and manual work by machines has decreased, reasoning, communicating and coordinating—all traits with a comparative advantage for humans—are expected to be more automatable in the future. Artificial intelligence, a key driver of potential algorithmic displacement, is expected to be adopted by nearly 75% of surveyed companies and is expected to lead to high churn—with 50% of organizations expecting it to create job growth and 25% expecting it to create job losses."

World Economic Forum, *The Future of Jobs Report 2023*, 30 April 2023.

Today, many people probably wonder why the prospect of such a development was not a cause for celebration. It may seem strange now; but, in those days, work was thought to be essential to human happiness. I recall the emphasis was on the importance of work to a person's, and family's, sense of identity, of belonging, of participation, of contributing. Of course, the feeling of economic security was important, but so too was the sense of independence gained from earning one's support.

The prophesies were of increases in alcoholism, drug abuse, crime, "broken" homes, depression and suicides. Well, those prophesies came true, even if the promises of automation did not. Although, there is probably more than automation at work.

In 2017, the World Economic Forum printed on article on boredom (in the context of automation), observing that boredom itself can cause most of these deadly problems for individuals. The author noted that in current times, fewer people recognized the benefits of effort, of doing. James Hewitt, "This is the hidden risk of automation that no one is talking about," *World Economic Forum*, Nov 30, 2017. He wrote:

"Prevailing models in cognitive psychology, neuroscience, and economics suggest that mental or physical effort is costly. Given a choice, we prefer to avoid it. In this light, assistive technology which reduces effort may be welcomed. Perhaps it will make us less stressed, less tired and offer us more free time. A utopian angle might herald a future of automated abundance and mass leisure."

Yet, leisure and underemployment can cause boredom. And,

"[B]oredom has been implicated in significant health problems:

- Premature death due to cardiovascular disease
- Increasing risk of anxiety and depression
- A reason for recreational drug use in some populations."

Id.

"There are many definitions of boredom, but recent descriptions characterise it as a subjective state of low arousal and dissatisfaction, likely caused by a lack of interest, coupled with an inadequately stimulating environment." *Id.*

"Real trouble doesnt begin in a society until boredom has become its most general feature. Boredom will drive even quietminded people down paths they'd never imagined." Cormac McCarthy, *The Passenger* (2022), p.142.

So, one can predict that less work will result in more boredom which will result in poorer health. And, in lower life expectancies.

Indeed:

> "[L]ife expectancy at birth fell in 2021 to its lowest level
> since 1996, a decline of nearly a year on average from 2020.
> That was after a decline by 1.8 years from 2019 to 2020,
> producing the worst two-year decline since 1921-23.
> ...COVID is far from the only explanation for America's
> dismal trend line. The pandemic accounted for about half
> the decline in life expectancy, according to the CDC. **'Un-
> intentional injuries,' a category that includes drug over-
> doses, contributed an additional 16%, followed by heart
> disease (4.1%), chronic liver disease and cirrhosis (3%)
> and suicide (2.1%)."**

Michael Hiltzilk, "Column: America's decline in life expectancy
speaks volumes about our problems," *Los Angeles Times*, April 5, 2023
(emphasis added).

Is there, by the way, actually a causal connection between increasing
inequality and declining life expectancy?

Hiltzlik says that there is.

The facts Hiltzlik cites are: There is a strong statistical correlation
between income and life expectancy and the "Red" states have lower
life expectancies than the "Blue" states. Of course, more of the" Blue"
are among the wealthiest states. And, is the correlation between income
and life expectancy one of causation or are they both the results of
something else (or some combination of things) that is the cause?

How might we address that question?

Well, would giving money to people increase the lengths of their lives? Not necessarily. It certainly depends on how they use the money and on many other things.

The source Hiltzilk relies on is Jeremy Ney, who he describes as "an expert in graphically displaying social and economic disparities." (Oh my!) However, Ney was addressing a different question (with which I will not bother now). The question posed here is about changes over time, so little of what Hiltzilk goes on to say is even relevant. Are incomes in real terms or constant dollars less in 2023 than they were in 1998 or 1970? If not, then falling life expectancies cannot be the result of falling income. Does a smaller percentage of the population have health/medical insurance now than in those earlier years? Are government benefits per person less now? Is unemployment higher now. All, "no." So, we know what potential causes can be ruled out, as a matter of the evidence and logic.

At the same time, as a matter of logic (and math), increasing life expectancies will result in more inequality, because the older population is the wealthiest and will become more so the longer they live.

In his 2017 article, James Hewitt noted:

> "As we focus on ways to reduce human effort, we may be overlooking its benefits....Outcomes can be more rewarding if we apply more, rather than less, effort to achieve them.
>
> ...
>
> "Effort can also be valuable and rewarding in its own right. Many individuals enjoy cognitive effort for its own sake. Effort is associated with improved wellbeing, demonstrating positive associations with enhanced goal-directed behaviour: we get better at doing what we aim to do, rather than be side-tracked by distraction or temptation."

Effort is certainly suspect today. Many people chose not to work. Many more want to "work" from home or remotely from anywhere. They want flexible hours, paid time off, more vacation. During the beginning of the pandemic, such flexible arrangements seemed to work, perhaps because people had few other things to do. After three years, it is obvious that the result of increased freedom is decreased work and reduced output.

We encounter people who want paychecks and benefits but do not want "jobs." No inconveniences, no stress, no coping with demanding bosses or unreasonable customers, no physically or emotionally demanding tasks. The problem is the loss of the principle of reciprocity. The lack of the realization that with rights and entitlements, come obligations. (I have elsewhere discussed how reciprocity is fundamental to society, community, civilization.)

Let me give an example. I had an employee who, after we had agreed on hours and pay rate, wanted to negotiate paid days off. I thought that that would at least eliminate future disputes. She took the agreed number of days off during the first three months (as we had discussed and I expected). Thereafter, however, she continued to request paid days off. I was sure that she understood that I was allowing the additional days off on the condition that she made them up, but there was never the right opportunity. I realized that she could not accept working without being paid, but was happy to be paid without working. No sense whatsoever of reciprocity; it was all about getting as much as you could. In the end, she had almost twice as many paid days off as we had agreed. She did not makeup a single day. I had believed that the guarantee established a maximum; she viewed it as an entitlement to a minimum, with no reciprocal limitation.

In my prior life, I had encountered a few employees who clearly viewed a job as an adversarial relationship. Their goal was get as much as possible while giving as little. Any employer latitude was viewed not as employer kindness, but as an employee success. They spend hours of work time, for example, pursuing their medical reimbursements, but at 15 minutes to quitting time, are putting their coats on. Most of the employees, in contrast, thought of themselves as part of a team, as a result of which they were.

"...I will not—no never, never—get behind a trend that urges people to take nonjobs so they can be 'amazing humans.' As any truly amazing person will tell you, to become amazing, you have to get knocked around by life and even fall down and get up again. Those hard and decidedly unlazy experiences can be uncomfortable, and maybe make you feel anxious. But in the long run, and perhaps sooner, that's better than feeling bored."

Suzy Welch, "'Lazy Girl Jobs' Won't Make Gen Z Less Anxious," *WSJ.com*, July 23, 2023.

A Possible Future

So, where might we be heading?

The percentage of the adult population who are genetically unproductive may be increasing; a growing number of the potentially productive will be less productive because of attitude; it appears that a growing percentage of the highly productive are choosing part-time work or early retirement for "lifestyle" reasons (and may, in fact, make good use of their extra leisure). The second category is very influenced by government welfare policies which currently reduce the incentives to work. For many, not working may provide more opportunities for consumption than does working. (That fact leads some to assert that the solution is to raise the minimum wage, ignoring that the effects will be a higher standard of performance for employment, further increasing the number of non-productive—unemployable—adults.)

Thus, we may find relatively fewer and fewer people producing the goods and services, the means of production and the innovations that drive growth, in other words, the nation's wealth, to support relatively more consumers. And, that minority will not just do all the work, but will also pay (in taxes) to support the rest. How sustainable is that situation?

There are several things that will affect the dynamics. For example, artificial intelligence ("AI") may dramatically improve the productivity of those who work but is likely also to reduce total employment. And, it will matter how the increasing extra time is used. If it is devoted to social media, television, reality shows, following celebrities (as seems to be so now), then we can expect more isolation and alienation. Physical, emotional and mental health problems will to continue to grow, and probably also crime and substance abuse, while life expectancy may continue to fall. Pretty grim. Under this scenario, inequality would almost certainly increase, especially between the middle and the top. The bottom and the middle are likely to be squeezed closer together, as a result of economics and government social policies.

In these circumstances, will it be possible to maintain economic growth? Or, at least, stagnation, avoiding a collapse? Can we answer that question?

Well, first, what will the demands of the unproductive be? Presumably, the demands will continue to increase every year. And, second, what incentives will the productive face? Higher taxes for sure. Perhaps, less personal security, greater social stigma. Will they choose different vocations? Devote their energies somewhere else? How many will simply flee? Will other places offer a more hospitable environment? Maybe. (Perhaps, in outer space?)

A thinking person could become rather pessimistic. Maybe, it is good that these subjects are now taboo. Maybe, since solutions are politically out of reach, we will be happier with our heads "in the sand" or, in a more modern metaphor, "glued to our phones."

The future be damned.

P.S.: Some day, I suspect, humankind will get a fresh start. Maybe, we will do better next time.

IV.

EVIL

"A lot of people see doubt as
a legitimate philosophical posture.
They think of themselves in the middle,
whereas, of course, really they're nowhere.
**No battle was ever won by spectators,
was it?**"

John le Carré
The Honourable Schoolboy, p.115.
(Emphasis added.)

A few months ago, I was asking myself this question: Have we out-grown evil? Then, in April 2022, I received this question from a friend from middle school in Northville, Michigan, who was reading the essays in *Wanderings of a Captive Mind*:

"A final thought or perhaps a question for you.
Do you see Evil as part of your *Wanderings*?"

Of course.

But, what to say about it?

We have all seen evil. Recently, the Hamas slaughter of Israeli civilians, the 90 minute long school shooting sprey in Ulvalde, Texas and mass shootings around the country, some "hate crimes", some inexplicable. Before that, there was 9/11, Rwanda, ISIS, Sarajevo, the Khmer Rouge, on and on. Not just killings, but atrocities. The intentional infliction of terrible pain, of suffering, of terror. Premeditated and intentional. Poisonings, decapitations, violent rapes. Genocide.

> "'We continue to receive unrelenting and appalling reports of sexual and gender-based violence and forced disappearance, arbitrary detentions and grave violations of human and children's rights,' Clementine Nkweta-Salami, the UN humanitarian coordinator for Sudan, told a news conference on Friday. 'What is happening is **verging on pure evil**.'"

Al Jazeera, November 11, 2023 (emphasis added).

"Verging on"? Really?

I suppose that these evil acts are only almost evil because they occur in the context of motivations that, broadly speaking, are arguably legitimate. Contrast that with the Hamas "attack" of October 7, 2023. That bloody incursion into Israel could not have been intended for any legitimate purpose. Strategically, it presumably was intended to provoke a massive retaliation by Israel, demonstrating an eager willingness by Hamas to sacrice Palestinian lives in order to attract international criticism of Israel. Former President Obama says that the situation is "complex." The Hamas attack is not. All that is complicated is the establishment of parameters for the appropriate Israeli response. The difficulty arises primarily because Palestinian civilians are effectively human shields for Hamas.

We knew evil could still be perpetrated by rogue groups or by governments in secret. Indeed, sometimes evil seems to be just an inevitable part of the environment, like bad weather. But, now, in the Russian invasion of the Ukraine, we see a civilized nation violating international law and norms out in the open, arrogantly, in a cloud of transparent lies. The assault on Ukraine is what should no longer happen.

We had convinced ourselves that such acts were unthinkable in our new world. The events we are witnessing in the spring of 2022 must give rise to doubts in even the staunchest pacifist, the most dedicated advocate of nonviolence. Moral suasion did not stop the invasion of Ukraine; it is not deterring continuing widespread criminal behavior. Perhaps, sometimes it becomes necessary for us to stand up to and oppose evil with our bodies, not just our words.

Graeber and Wengrow assert that: "'Good' and 'evil' are purely human concepts ... made up in order to compare ourselves with one another." *The Dawn of Everything: A New History of Humanity* (2022), pp. 1-2. Do we see either elsewhere in nature? As I wrote in *Important Things We Don't Know*, p.591:

> "[W]e all know that evil exists, even if the idea offends our materialistic inclinations. Of course, it is a unique hallmark of Homo sapiens, if not of the genus Homo, at least on this world. It is curious that the concept exists in our minds; it is more curious that so much evil (violence, cruelty, greed, dishonesty, anger, vengefulness) appears among humans. How 'adaptive' is evil?"

Systemic or Individual?

There has also been a tendency to see evil as the result of institutions, social structures, philosophies or beliefs. But, sometimes we must realize that the evil is in the person.

> "All my life I had battled against an institutionalised evil. It had had a name and most often a country as well. ...But the evil that stood before me now was a wrecking infant in our own midst, and I became an infant in return, disarmed, speechless and betrayed. For a moment, it was as if my whole life had been fought against the wrong enemy. ...[T]he evil **was not in the system, but in the man.**"

John le Carré, *The Secret Pilgrim* (1990), p. 377 (emphasis added).

As the sole Western survivor of the Cambodian terror camps says: "Human beings: The optimal being, the supreme creature, the natural aristocrat of the living world? Man who—when, exceptionally, he becomes his true self—can bring about excellence, but also bring about the worst. **A slayer of monsters**, and forever **a monster himself** . . ." Francois Bizot, *The Gate* (2002), p.6 (emphasis added).

A recent science fiction book is based, in part, on the premise that in the entire Universe, only humans engaged in deceIt: "deception was an important defensive weapon they had to consider, but to wield it, the Trisolarans first had to understand the only species known to possess such a capability—humans." Baoshu, *The Redemption of Time*, p.36.

We all probably remember knowing children who seemed possessed, driven to misbehave, to act up or act out. Such children tend to grow up and find ways to manage their demons. Adults, of course, regularly commit bad acts, but in most of these people, there exists a core of vulnerability, of humanity, with some capacity for empathy. The worst people are self-centered, calculating, manipulating and greedy. But, even most of these people still have a human core. Most, not all. There are some sociopaths. These people never ask forgiveness, never apologize. They embrace their actions. They do not blame their behavior on temptation or on others, except in order to manipulate someone. They are certainly cynical, they certainly do harm, but are they "evil"?

I have no answer.

Moral Judgments

Yet, the point of this essay is closer to home. It is about the desirability of reincorporating moral judgment into our society, our relationships and our lives.

In our relativistic modern world, good and evil were seeming increasingly anachronistic. We could make no quality distinctions among cultures, religions, traditions or personal proclivities. Everything was relative. A continuum, colored by our prejudices, of course, but still a continuum. For example, as an adult, I have struggled to consider the behavior resulting from mental illness as just symptoms of disease, despite the hurt being done to others, often to innocent people. Indeed, with respect to many aspects of personality or traits, we do all fall somewhere along a continuum. (Yet, those people who oppose—or favor—abortion, who are homophobic, who are racist or sexist, or who are libertarians are ... what? Misguided—just lost?)

So, do we still value character? Is it even relevant any more? Perhaps, we have "outgrown" the need for responsible adults. We have government, schools, universities and other institutions to protect us and take care of us, to shelter us and to comfort us when the sheltering is insufficient. A little whining can go a long way. And, medication: Pharmaceutical solutions to our problems. And, drugs for distraction. A mandatory instruction for late twentieth century parents was "it is always the act that is bad, never the child." Well, okay. But, that approach can be misunderstood by children. It can separate acts from responsibility. We may continue to wonder, by the way, are there bad people or only bad acts?

Responsibility

The problem today is that "[w]e ... are morally inarticulate. We're not more selfish or venal than people in other times, but we've lost the understanding of how character is built." David Brooks, *The Road to Character* (2015), p.5. Where we draw a line between normal and abnormal (illness) is pretty arbitrary. "[W]e have obscured the inescapable moral core of life with shallow language ... and thus become increasingly blind to the moral stakes of everyday life." *Id.*, p.54.

In my precollege days, I did not recognize mental "illness." Harmful aberrant behavior was simply bad. Lying, manipulating or using others, abusiveness, all were wrong, inside a family or out. We all have our own personal demons (for me, a violent temper, a tendency toward self-righteousness and reoccurring bouts of self-centeredness). But, I was taught that these were the things against which I was expected to fight, to struggle—a bit like a Whac-A-Mole game. The objective was to overcome them, recognizing that that goal can never be fully achieved. Small steps. Progress today. Success. Then, ...

The successes and failures experienced during our daily challenges to be better are what develop character. Despite the contrary advice of modern psychiatrists, psychologists, child rearing experts and life coaches, I think we need to try to own our weaknesses and faults, to struggle with ourselves, to confront our demons and to recognize that life is not just about "me." The development of character is part of the transformation of a child into a responsible, contributing adult, into someone who can and will protect his or her family and community.

There is something quite compelling about Catholic confession. "Father, forgive me for I have sinned." An admission that one has done wrong. Powerful. And, made with confidence in a forthcoming forgiveness. Yes. So much more to the point than the long-winded and mushy Presbyterian statements of confession that I hear on Sundays. "I have sinned" acknowledges that I did something. Not that it just happened or just happened to me, but that it was a volitional act, one for which I ask forgiveness.

That is owning one's own actions.

Why Bother?

Yet, one might ask, why? Why grow up? Why not all aspire to live like Peter Pan? Well, I guess the answer is "for ourselves". The meaningful, satisfying experiences in life involve struggle, sacrifice and loss. They involve confronting ourselves. They are moral events. Things are not, or should not be, just different shades of gray. We need especially to judge ourselves. To expect and to demand personal responsibility and personal accountability, from ourselves as well as from others.

As John Steinbeck wrote in *East of Eden*:

> "Humans are caught—in their lives, in their thoughts, in their hungers and ambitions, in their avarice and cruelty, and in their kindness and generosity too—in a net of good and evil. I think this is the only story we have and that it occurs on all levels of feeling and intelligence. Virtue and vice were warp and woof of our first consciousness, and they will be the fabric of our last... .

...

"A man, after he has brushed off the dust and chips of his life, will have left only the hard clean questions: **Was it good or was it evil? Have I done well—or ill?**"

Id. (1952), p.582 (emphasis added).

And, Sin

David Brooks put the matter as follows:

"Sin is a necessary piece of our mental furniture because it reminds us that life is a moral affair. No matter how hard we try to reduce everything to deterministic brain chemistry, ... no matter how hard we strive to replace sin with nonmoral words, like 'mistake' or 'error' or 'weakness,' **the most essential parts of life are matters of individual responsibility and moral choice:** whether to be brave or cowardly, honest or deceitful, compassionate or callous, faithful or disloyal."

The Road to Character, p.54 (emphasis added).

So, we need more sin, but less evil?

Actually, I have trouble with Brooks' use of sin. A prominent theme in his book is that mankind is fundamentally flawed (original sin), which he refers to as the "crooked timber" viewport (after Immanuel Kant: "Out of the crooked timber of humanity, no straight thing was ever made") and the essential role of grace or unconditional love. I may not fully understand his argument, but I think most of what Brooks says can stand powerfully without this biblical overlay. Brooks also contrasts "moral realism" with "moral relativism," using philosophical schools of thought to explain his position, but I think that this context is as unnecessary as the religious one.

I perceive mankind as born with a moral capacity—maybe even a moral compass, but certainly a moral craving. At the same time, we are physically mammals, with the drives and needs of all mammals— for food, shelter and reproduction. We also seem to have some rather unique inclinations like greed, envy and pride. And, we clearly have weaknesses. Our mammalian instincts push us to take the safe road, the easy path. We are inclined to sit rather than stand, to duck rather than stand up, to evade rather than embrace responsibility. This is where upbringing, life examples and expectations come in.

Yet, as suggested, I have trouble with "original sin". I am more comfortable with the view of the new born as an innocent with the potential for sin and also for rising above. It is the things that happen as the child grows that have moral dimensions. The decisions and the choices and the actions. Those can be morally good or bad.

As Brooks says, the key questions one faces in life are: "[W]hether to be brave or cowardly, honest or deceitful, compassionate or callous, faithful or disloyal ...Whether one strives to be better, to do the right thing. Whether one sees the moral fabric of life, of living, of the inevitable forks in the road." *Id.,* p.263.

"Once the necessities for survival are satisfied, **the struggle against sin and for virtue is the central drama of life.**"

...

"You become more disciplined, considerate, and loving through a thousand small acts of self-control, sharing, service, friendship, and refined enjoyment."

...

"Each struggle leaves a residue. A person who has gone through these struggles seems more substantial and deep."

...

"There's joy in a life filled with interdependence with others, in a life filled with gratitude, reverence, and admiration. There's joy in freely chosen obedience to people, ideas, and commitments **greater than oneself.**"

Id., pp.264, 268, 269 (emphasis added).

For a less traditional perspective on original sin, I turn to a twentieth-century Jesuit priest and scientist:

"As far as the mind can reach, looking backwards, we find the world **dominated by physical evil, impregnated with moral evil** ...—we find it in a state of original sin.

...

"[Perhaps] ... original sin expresses, translates, personifies, in an instantaneous and localized act, **the perennial and universal law of imperfection** which operates in mankind in virtue of its being 'in fieri' [in the process of becoming]. ... [T]he drama of Eden would be the very drama of the whole of human history concentrated in a symbol profoundly expressive of reality."

Pierre Teilhard de Chardin, *Christianity and Evolution: Reflections on Science and Religion* (1969), pp.47, 51-2 (emphasis added).

So?

I agree that we need to reintroduce "sin" into our vocabulary and into our view of the world. We need to recognize, acknowledge and name the bad, the disappointing, the demeaning and dehumanizing. If we learn to make moral judgments and distinctions again, to acknowledge sin; we might regain the strength, and fashion new tools, to confront evil.

Maybe, then...

More sin,

Less evil.

A NOTE ON FREE WILL

I want to comment on a new book by Robert M. Sapolsky, *Determined: A Science of Life without Free Will* (2023). His main argument is that free will does not exist because all actions are necessarily and inevitably the result of everything that proceeded them. I discuss that elsewhere. Here, I want to examine his much repeated sub-theme that, assuming the correctness of his thesis as a matter of science, it is not right to condemn the villains or to admire the heroes.

"That there can be no such thing as blame, and that punishment as retribution is indefensible—sure, keep dangerous people from damaging others, but do so as straightforwardly and nonjudgmentally as keeping a car with faulty brakes off the road ... but never because they deserve it."

Id., p.5.

Does this mean that evil does not exist? Well, it suggests that the hypothesis that the devil tempts persons to do bad things is not a very good scientific explanation for evil. The world, in reality, is much more complicated. Surprised?

But, what about blame? The bad acts still hurt people, threaten communities and undermine societies. The good acts still help people and strengthen communities. Perhaps, it is matter of evil actions, not evil people. But, what does that actually mean, especially if those people are simply destined to commit evil acts? Are not those people, from the standpoint of society, "evil"? Sapolsky constantly castigates aspects of our criminal jurisprudence, all of which evolved long before the science on which he relies. Greater knowledge can contribute to better policy, but sarcasm is neither appropriate nor helpful.

Is it fair or just for people to be judged and rewarded based upon performance? That is the wrong question. The question is "why" are people so judged? The "why" is because it works and only it works.

> "[P]erformance cannot be due solely to individual merit where the influence of other individuals and circumstances is at work. The case for rewarding performance is that we can do it, not that it is the same as rewarding merit. Likewise, holding individuals personally responsible for the consequences of their own actions is a social expedient for prospective control, not a cosmic retrospective moral judgment. Moreover, applying the impossible standard of merit forfeits benefits attainable under the feasible standard of performance in satisfying consumer desires more fully."

Thomas Sowell, *The Vision Of The Annointed: Self-congratulation As A Basis For Social Policy* (1995), p.202.

So, do we conclude that humans are not moral beings? Do we also, then, conclude that deterrence cannot work, that rehabilitation is impossible and that, as a result, the only solution is the separation of the miscreants from the rest of society? I discuss Sapolsky's main argument in my writings on science. It is sufficient here simply to note that if free will does not exist, then this book is pretty irrelevant. It is premised on the contrary belief—that mankind can and does choose—and the hope that we could do so better.

A final note. Sapolsky describes a situation in which he agreed to be an expert witness for a man accused of a particularly vile series of hate crimes. He took the unusual step of requesting to meet personally the defendant. Did he do so better to understand what factors may made the defendant the way he was?

His answer:

**"No.
I wanted to see close up
what the face of evil looked like."**

Id., p.384 (emphasis added).

So, he does not believe in evil?

Really?

CHAPTER III

Morality, Identity and Leadership

GOOD CITIZENS

In the very early days of this country, George Washington wrote:

"[T]he Government of the United States gives to bigotry no sanction, to persecution no assistance, requires only that they who live under its protection should demean themselves as good citizens, in giving it on all occasions their effectual support."

"Letter to the Jews of Newport," 18 August 1790, *Washington Papers*, 6:284-85.

The emphasis was upon commitment to a type of government and civil order, backed with a willingness to provide "effectual support" as required, that is, to make sacrifices for the good of the country—to be "good citizens." It is obviously beneficial in a political order to have the vast majority of the members be good citizens. But, what is a good citizen and what circumstances lead to the sufficient presence of them? Those are the questions addressed below.

Neighborliness

I grew up in southern Michigan. My parents and, as far as I could tell, most of their friends were the epitome of "good citizens". They willingly paid their taxes, were generous and supportive neighbors, participated in community activities, voted, engaged in various public displays of patriotism and made meaningful sacrifices for the country. During World War II, my father served in the U.S. Army in Italy, while his father was a Seabee in the South Pacific.

When I moved to New York City, I was surprised to find myself surrounded by people who regularly "gamed" the system, aggressively avoiding and sometimes evading taxes, finding ways to circumvent the rules and regulations (like rent control, sales taxes and parking restrictions) and, in general, constantly seeking to promote their own interests at the expense of the community (although, not necessarily at the expense of identifiable individuals).

Over 40 years ago, when I was at the University of Cambridge, I was told by some Nigerian friends that the appointment as head of the port of Lagos was worth $1 billion. That was a lot of money back in 1970s. While, as a naïve American, I was shocked at that assertion; I was more surprised that these young aristocrats viewed the rumored fact not as a scandal, but as evidence of the opportunities for them for the future. (I was also shocked to hear my Greek friends talk about the CIA activities in their country and to read the rampant speculation in Europe of a likely military coup in the United States in response to Watergate and the Richard Nixon scandal. Remember Alexander Haig?)

Importantly, and fortunately, the relevant virtues for good citizens have never been limited to the elite, to the nation's leaders, nor to WASPs, and certainly not to any particular political party, religion, race or gender. Evidence of this assertion can be found in the millions of immigrants who arrived with nothing, yet who considered themselves blessed to be here and were eager to "live under [the United States'] protection ... demean themselves as good citizens [and give the United States] on all occasions their effectual support." These virtues have had a presence in the nation that cuts across all distinctions, including social class. (Although, it seems that it was always less so in New York City and more recently in several of the coastal metropolises.) The virtues are also closely allied with nationalism and a sense of national identity.

Also, importantly, and unfortunately, egregious conduct that is clearly not the behavior of a good citizen is pretty common, whether criminal—such as stealing the neighbors' social security checks, filing fake income tax returns claiming refunds or engaging in Medicare fraud (whether by performing unnecessary procedures, at the risk of the patients, or simply submitting claims for procedures or services never performed)—or that simply seeks to avoid one's communal responsibilities, such as declining to work (at all or for more hours) in order to obtain governmental benefits. I have also become increasingly aware of how government contracts, programs and entitlements always tend to attract corrupt and fraudulent behavior.

So, even if most of the population is essentially law-abiding, an underlying question is how many free riders society can tolerate before it begins to breakdown. There will always be those who prefer to take the advantages provided by the sacrifices of others without making corresponding contributions, and society can tolerate a certain amount of such selfishness. Various societies make it more or less difficult to be a free rider. But, a point can be reached where the prevalence of free riders both strains the capabilities of the system and undermines the willingness of others to make the necessary sacrifices.

One of the biggest challenges for the United States today is how to create and maintain a sufficient number of good citizens. This issue is relevant to our social welfare policies, our tax policies and, of course, our immigration policies. (The first two categories seem more or less under control at this time, but the last is a national disgrace. Unfortunately, both parties have incentives to maintain the *status quo* on immigration. A fair and rational solution would deprive each of a powerful issue with some significant part of its constituencies.)

Leadership

On the day of the funeral ceremony for George H.W. Bush at National Cathedral, the *New York Times* printed a column by one of its regulars, Ross Douthat, entitled: "Why We Miss the WASPs," December 5, 2018. There were three points made that have stayed with me. First, despite what we now see as serious shortcomings, the WASP elite governed pretty wisely and pretty well. Second, the WASP elite voluntarily surrendered its position of leadership and moral authority, despite alternative options. And, third, its successors have not done as good a job.

As to the first point, the perceived shortcomings of WASPs were racism, certain moral intolerances or prejudices, relative emotional detachment and sexism. The strengths, in contrast, lay in the WASP commitment to the virtues of service, sacrifice, discipline, duty, honor, courage, self-restraint, civility and stoicism. These virtues were perceived to set a standard, one to be lived up to by the elite (and their children) and emulated or aspired to by others. They placed demands upon the members of the governing establishment, but they also set a standard by which people might judge themselves and others. And, the standard was broadly accepted, even if not regularly met.

These virtues have obvious benefits when it comes to governing. All one needs to do is to consider the result of the opposites: selfishness, greed, self-indulgence, self-dealing, whining and incivility. Where the governing elite embraces these opposites, you have a Nigeria, Congo, Venezuela, Malaysia, or Philippines (or the many other nations with governments known for corruption and exploitation). In addition to the benefits of being governed by a group that adheres to the WASP virtues (*e.g.*, less corruption, fraud, exploitation and deceit), the elite group's moral standing or authority and its ability to assert moral leadership are enhanced by such virtues. That is a clear win for the society and nation involved.

The second point is that sometime in the late '60s onward, the WASPs began to abandon voluntarily their position of moral authority. Curiously, when confronted with accusations of racism, sexism and political incorrectness, this elite, rather than fighting back, became increasingly introspective. Apparently, the WASPs' ability to empathize with those who had been discriminated against led first to embarrassment and then to a crisis of confidence. (At least, that is what I perceived in my family. I assume that the response of the "elite" was similar to that of the upper-middle class WASPs.)

The gradual withdrawal from moral leadership emboldened the critics to increase their attacks and their demands. Their positions became, in my mind, more extreme and went from credible, and often persuasive, to ludicrous; but, one could not reason with these critics, and attempts to do so invited being attacked as racist.

WASPs could have acknowledged the validity of some of the criticisms and undertaken steps to reform their behavior, while continuing to assert their moral authority. For example, there is nothing in the list of virtues that precludes more inclusiveness. Catholics and Jews and others had emulated the WASP values and enter the elite, families like the Kennedys and the Buckleys.

Douthat continued: "[A]n aristocratic spirit was transferable to a more diverse elite, that there could be Catholic and African-American and Jewish aristocrats ... who could adopt the WASP establishment's upperclass virtues without the ethnic and religious chauvinism." Of course, to have done so would have invited accusations of paternalism, elitism and prejudice. But, sometimes the right thing is to stand up and assert one's values.

The third point is that the new leadership has been less effective than the old. As to that, we have neither the length of experience nor the historical perspective to pass judgment. But, the early signs are not good.

Some commentators have recently been attracted to comparisons between today's leaders and Winston Churchill. For example, Bret Stephens writes: "'[Churchill] mobilized the English language and sent it into battle,' John F. Kennedy said (stealing a line from Edward Murrow) in awarding Churchill honorary United States citizenship in 1963. Of how many leaders now in office could that be said today—in any language?" "An Antidote to Idiocy in 'Churchill,'" *NYTimes.com*, December 14, 2018.

Churchill, like Washington and Lincoln, showed authentic leadership and asserted moral authority—to inspire, to call forth from others strength, courage and determination. To repeat Stephens' question: Of how many leaders now in office could this be said today? There is certainly a lack moral authority among the political leaders at all levels of government today. But, is that really a change? Were not the exceptional leaders of the past, just that—exceptions?

Douthat further wrote:

> "[T]he meritocratic ideal ends up being just as undemocratic as the old emphasis on inheritance and tradition, and it forges an elite that has an aristocracy's vices (privilege, insularity, ar- rogance) without the sense of duty, self-restraint and *noblesse oblige* that WASPs at their best displayed. ...This spirit discourages inherited responsibility and cultural stewardship; it brushes away the disciplines of duty... ."

I have my doubts that meritocracy needs to be this way; but, even if Douthat is right, the appearance of a vacuum in today's political sphere is not surprising. The increasing emphasis has been on diversity, political correctness, multiculturalism and "correct" views on social issues like abortion and gay marriage. These concepts are insufficient bases for effective governing and certainly insufficient for the exercise of moral leadership.

It may be observed that the WASP elite was born into and lived lives of privilege, including material wellbeing. Thus, one might say, they did not need to view political positions as a way to make their fortunes (because they already had fortunes). If so, one might say there is a benefit of having a government run by individuals of privilege and property. Certainly, people who consider themselves as victims of the system, who are resentful or who seek reparations, compensation or revenge, are not very attractive prospects for leadership positions. The same is true of those who whine or complain, who are driven by envy or who are weak, timid and insecure.

So, should we limit government positions to persons of property and privilege? No. Being born to privilege is neither a guarantee of nor a requirement for having the virtues enumerated above. But, a love of country and community may be.

Consider two groups of potential leaders, one with the virtues of service, sacrifice, duty and courage, and the other with the characteristics of selfishness, self-dealing, political correctness, and personal cowardice (or a group of envious, resentful complainers seeking to get their "just deserts"). Which group would you want with you on the Titanic, on the battlefield of Gettysburg, in dark days of 1944 or on the morning after 9/11? Do these virtues matter to us only during times of great danger, or are they still relevant to the little challenges and crises of everyday existence.

Community

Leadership is essential, but only part of it can come from the political arena. In fact, it may be that national political leadership does not make much difference, at least, not directly. What we need is persons in all areas to be leaders and decision-makers, setting standards and serving as examples. Is it not possible, or even likely, that it is family, community, church and other associations that make the real difference? The layers between family and national government can be most important, what Timothy Carney calls the "middle."

Carney argues that the sense of community comes from participation in associations, particularly churches but also sports teams, social clubs, volunteer organizations, the PTA, *etc.* It is these associations of people that, he claims, foster civil society. *Alienated America* (2019). When they wither, the (physical) communities themselves die, as does the sense of community. So, maybe what we need to do is promote communities and try to increase the sense of community.

A recent opinion column noted, in a specific context, the potential effectiveness of local leadership and local sources of moral authority:

> "Hillary Clinton pointed the way in her book 'It Takes a Village.' Of course, ... Mrs. Clinton's village turns out to depend on federal bureaucrats. But the principle [of the title] is worth rescuing. ...[Yet,] far from empowering ... local leaders to act when they spot trouble—teachers, scoutmasters, pastors, police chiefs, shopkeepers, coaches—we have spent the past half century undermining their authority."

William McGurn, "Guns and the Do-Something Fallacy," *WSJ.com*, August 12, 2019.

Certainly, good citizens are mainly found in communities, acting as good neighbors, as volunteers in a wide range of community activities, as the bulwark of protection against the hostile world beyond. The heart of good citizenship is participation in the life of the community and, by extension, the country. The hallmark of such good citizenship is the sense of individual responsibility both for the well-being of that community and for the well-being of the country.

THE SITUATION TODAY

The Decline of Moral Authority

Effective moral authority presumably plays a role in the creation and maintenance of a successful percentage of good citizens. From where does such authority come and how is it promoted or created? Originally, moral authority was presumably based upon and enforced by a common religion and the civil characteristics promoted by that religion. In more modern times, moral authority must necessarily become more secular and more dependent on the setting of examples.

I do think that we have clearly experienced a deterioration in the level of moral authority and moral leadership in this country and around the world.

The key to the problem may be the word "authority". It bespeaks hierarchy. The recognition of virtue implies that some people are more virtuous than others, that there are distinctions of value among people, that some people are better people than others. Such views are contrary to the current emphasis on equality. We insist that all people are of equal worth; even though, they are obviously of widely differing abilities, skills and effectiveness, just as they are of different heights, weights, races and genders.

I perceived the shift as arising out of the civil rights movement and the challenges to racism in the 1960s. There followed the ideas of cultural and moral relativism. These concepts were not compelled by the rejection of racism; that moral worth is not a matter of race does not mean that varying degrees of moral worth do not exist. The concepts were more a matter of the growing emphasis on tolerance and inclusiveness and, of course, equality. There was also a trend increasingly to reject nationalism, carrying with it diminishing willingness to sacrifice for one's country.

There is evidence that this "problem" with authority (moral, cultural, religious, academic, *etc.*) is now pervasive and fundamental, representing a major cultural shift. As a result, for example, the elite American educational institutions are in danger of failing to fulfill their fundamental responsibilities to preserve and promote the striving for knowledge, conservation of the past and the training of future leaders. The indispensable vigor of discourse and self-examination is being eroded by the demise of the "core curriculum" and distribution requirements, by grade inflation and "pass/fail" courses, by the emphasis on inclusiveness and comfort (rather than independence and effort), by the increasingly expensive student amenities, limitations on speech, the creation of safe spaces and the erasure of memorials to the past that have unpleasant connotations.

Higher education should be hard and challenging, disruptive and provocative. It should require strenuous efforts and intense self-examination. Anthony Kronman, in *The Assault on American Excellence* (2019), argues that the goal of elite education "is to preserve, transmit and honor an **aristocratic tradition of respect for human greatness.**" (Emphasis added.) The premise, once taken as a given, is "that there is such a thing as character; that a person's character can be better or worse; that character is shaped by education; and that one of the goals of higher education is to instill in the student a love of those things for which a person of fine character should care." *Id.*

While I largely agree with what Korrman says about the symptoms of the disease, I largely disagree with him about the causes. I do not think that an emphasis on vocational training is part of the problem. There is a need and a valid place for vocational education. And, the eroding culture at a Harvard, Yale or Amherst is not a result of a growing emphasis on job training. I also disagree that the humanities hold any exclusive claims with respect to the study of the deeper questions about existence and meaning. Those issues arise in the serious study of any subject. Finally, I disagree that careers and ambition are inconsistent with an acute awareness of the issues of meaning and morals. Indeed, I think that grappling with action in the face of the realities of our messy, complex and ambiguous world gives a special poignancy to such issues.

The problem in the academy, in my view, is the lack of courage and commitment on the part of the academic leadership. In part, this is a result, like with the WASP elite, of empathy (and embarrassment) leading to deference and then to the undermining of the strength of conviction in the core values of the academy. In part, it is a result of pandering to students to succeed in the highly competitive process of attracting the "best" applicant and in securing the highest rating from the media. The institutions have become increasingly businesses catering to their "customers" rather than beacons of excellence attracting those willing to accept the challenge and make the commitment.

So, there has been a decline of political, academic and religious leadership, bringing a general decline in moral authority. One result is the failure to perceive anyone as setting an example for the rest of us to follow. Who do we now admire or look up to? Is there anybody?

Our cultural heroes? I was raised on *The Lone Ranger*, *Bonanza* and *Gunsmoke*—with Ben, Adam, Hoss, Little Joe and Matt Dillon. It was a time of innocence, of self-restraint (or self-denial, in today's terminology), the era of the "strong silent type", as reflected in Toby Keith's 1993 song, "Should've been a cowboy": "I bet you've never heard ol'

Marshal Dillon say Miss Kitty, have you ever thought of runnin' away? ...They never tied the knot, his heart wasn't in it He just stole a kiss as he rode away He never hung his hat up at Kitty's place"

But, today?

Our heroes appear to be reality show stars, YouTube and Twitter sensations, professional celebrities and anyone who can "earn" at least $10 million a year without actually producing anything. If these personalities represent our new societal standards and aspirations, what are the likely consequences for the country?

The Decline of Virtue

Winston Churchill wrote:

> "...[T]he behavior of the male passengers [on the Titanic] reflects nothing but honour upon our civilization. . . . I cannot help feeling proud of our race and its traditions as proved by this event. Boatloads of women and children tossing on the sea safe and sound—and the rest—silence. Honour to their memory. ...How differently imperial Rome or Ancient Greece would have settled the problem. The swells, the potentates would have gone off with their concubines and pet slaves and soldier guards. . . . whoever could bribe the crew would have had the preference and the rest could go to hell. But such ethics could neither build Titanics with science nor lose them with honour."

Quoted by Lance Morrow, "Did Chivalry Go Down With the Titanic?", *WSJ.com*, December 14, 2018.

Churchill spoke of "our race" and "our civilization," of course; but, his focus was upon the acts, not the color or religion, of the men on board the Titanic. The acts of a person are not determined by race, religion, gender or sexual orientation, but by what we have called "character."

Higher standards could have been expected of much of the community, despite the failings of our political leadership. Remember the words of George Washington, the United States "requires only that they who live under its protection should demean themselves as good citizens, in giving it on all occasions their effectual support." All that is required is commitment, loyalty and sacrifice. Or, as John F. Kennedy famously said in his inaugural address in 1961: "Ask not what your country can do for you—ask what you can do for your country." But, that has not happened. Instead, these virtues have rapidly crumbled as the aspirational norm for American education and society. Many have lamented the decline in service, duty, honor, courage and civility. Unfortunately, the loss of these individual virtues seems to be most marked among the highly educated, multicultural urban elite, who seem to have more in common with their similarly situated colleagues around the globe than with their fellow citizens at home.

How would today's political values look to

"... a 1960s Democrat. Those liberals were patriots who loved America and would have had no use for people who see only its misdeeds. They stood up for what was right and had an exhilarating confidence in American justice and greatness. They knew the country had problems, but also knew we could solve them."

F.H. Buckley, "Trump May Be the True Liberal," *WSJ.com*, January 1, 2019.

To what is this change attributable?

Morrow goes on to ask:

> "Would the social evolutions of the past century, includ-
> ing recent politics of gender, have any bearing on the behav-
> ior of men and women and on the life-or-death choices they
> made on the deck of a sinking ship? . . . In the absence of the
> old gentility—under which men were expected to hold the
> door for women, to rise when they entered the room, and to
> give up their seats in lifeboats—would the simpler principle
> of dog-eat-dog assert itself? ...Is it possible that the doctrine
> of equality has, among other things, relieved the male of his
> duty to behave like a gentleman and left him free to be a cad?"

"Did Chivalry Go Down With the Titanic?", *WSJ.com*, December 14, 2018.

From my standpoint, the initial inflection point came in the late 1960s with the slogan "better Red than dead," a sentiment that deeply shocked my parent's generation. A slightly later but similar slogan, "make love, not war," seemed like a modern (and more decadent) version of the Greek comedy *Lysistrata*, using the carrot rather than the stick to end war—offering more fun and less sacrifice for everyone. (Sometimes, the more appropriate "make peace, not war" was used.) Despite strong desires for a more just and peaceful world, there was the emergence of a strong "me" philosophy, particularly among the better educated and more cosmopolitan. That is not to say that my generation did not do many good deeds, especially in the spirit of humanitarianism. But, the changes in the national values accelerated in this new century, leading to today's "identity politics" and, with it, the dismissal of personal responsibility.

Probably the most significant societal changes underlying all of this have been the increasing rejection of religion and religious teaching and the increasing reliance on the State as the potential solution to all problems. This phenomenon was described in a recent speech by Attorney General William P. Barr:

> "... [T]his idea of the State as the alleviator of bad consequences has given rise to a new moral system that goes hand-in-hand with the secularization of society. ...Christianity teaches a micromorality. We transform the world by focusing on our own personal morality and transformation. The new secular religion teaches macromorality. One's morality is not gauged by their private conduct, but rather on their commitment to political causes and collective action... ."

"Remarks to the Law School and the de Nicola Center for Ethics and Culture at the University of Notre Dame," *U.S. Department of Justice,* October 11, 2019.

Although the speech has been much maligned by the media, I think that it is hard not to accept that Barr's observation captures something important about what has happened. It represents the decline of individual virtue as a guiding principle and an emphasis, instead, upon collective responses to perceived inequities and injustices. One may think that good, but not that it did not happen. I find it also hard to dispute the conclusion that while Government programs have ameliorated some of the consequences of bad decisions, destructive life styles and unequal opportunities; they have done little to address the underlying causes and may have actually exacerbated some of the problems. (This argument is continued in other chapters.)

Where there is ample room for fair debate is on the question of what to do now. Will more Government involvement finally eliminate the problems? Would reduced Government involvement improve the situation? Are there other alternatives?

The Decline of Heroes

And now, the vigorous efforts to denigrate and erase major historical figures because they had flaws currently deemed unacceptable. All humans have flaws and imperfections. We are bundles of strengths and weaknesses. Different cultures appear to rank flaws (and strengths) differently. Some defects (and strengths) are prioritized over others. Today, shockingly to me, cowardice, greed and self-centeredness are forgivable; while racism and sexism are not, even when having existed at a time when those attitudes were the "norm." At the same time, the courage to act, the ability to achieve and independence from the crowd are overlooked.

Is there not much that is admirable in Stonewall Jackson and Robert E. Lee, despite the side on which they fought? Indeed, should we not be impressed by the courage shown by Lee in facing his terrible choice between the Union and his home state of Virginia, by the fact that he made a decision based on his sense of honor (whether right or wrong) and that he bore the consequences of his choice fully and with dignity?

"Acting through an intermediary—Francis Blair, father of Postmaster General Montgomery Blair—Lincoln offered Lee command of all Union land forces. That same day Lee learned that Virginia had seceded. For Lee this was a wrenching moment. He considered slavery 'a moral and political evil' and looked upon secession 'as anarchy.' Writing to Blair, he said, 'If I owned the four million slaves in the South I would sacrifice them all to the Union; but how can I draw my sword upon Virginia, my native state?' He needed time. He spent two days in personal torment considering the offer before formally notifying General Scott in a letter on April 20 that he had decided to resign from the Army. He would have done it 'at once,' he told Scott, 'but for the struggle it has cost me to separate myself from a service to which I have devoted all the best years of my life and all the ability I possessed.' To which Scott replied, 'You have made the greatest mistake of your life, but I feared it would be so.' Lee felt he had no choice. '...I cannot raise my hand against my birthplace, my home, my children.'"

Erik Larson, *The Demon of Unrest: A Saga of Hubris, Heartbreak, and Heroism at the Dawn of the Civil War* (2024), pp.469-470.

The "renaming movement" not only removes the heroes from our worldview; it suggests that the monuments were erected for the flaws, not the men. A good reason for removal where the facts and history supports it.

Some, perhaps even many, were erected for such reasons.

"[New Orleans] Mayor Landrieu's eloquent and heartfelt address hours before the last monument was taken down ... drew an instructive contrast between then and now: The historic record is clear: the Robert E. Lee, Jefferson Davis, and P. G. T. Beauregard statues were not erected just to honor these men, but as part of the movement which became known as The Cult of the Lost Cause. This 'cult' had one goal—through monuments and through other means—to rewrite history to hide the truth, which is that the Confederacy was on the wrong side of humanity ... ."

Adolph L Reed, *The South: Jim Crow and Its Afterlives* (2022), pp.131-132.

But, the movement aims and strikes far more broadly. And, it threatens to diminish our recognition of the fundamental fact of moral ambiguity (and complexity), to cheapen (and disguise) the important history of civilization's faltering efforts to be better and more just. Is that what we want?

> "Are we really so faint of heart that we can no longer bear to allow the honoring of great men of the past who fail in some respects to meet our current specifications? It's true that all three men held either slaves or racist beliefs. Does that exhaust everything we need to know about them?"

Wilfred M. McClay, "The Weaponization of History," *WSJ.com*, August 25, 2019.

So, there is no one to admire; only those to whom we do not object.

Ultimately, what do we need in political leaders? Is bland inoffensiveness preferable to vigor, with all its flaws? But, how could it ever really be sufficient? Where would we be without those who act and do so bravely, accepting the consequences? Those who actually grapple with the grubby, messy world in which we live, rather than just complain about it.

Teddy Roosevelt famously asserted:

> "It is not the critic who counts; not the man who points out how the strong man stumbles, or where the doer of deeds could have done them better. The credit belongs to the man who is actually in the arena, whose face is marred by dust and sweat and blood; who strives valiantly; who errs, who comes short again and again, ... but who does actually strive to do the deeds... ."

Do we still believe these words are relevant or have they been relegated to the historical trashcan as an example of patronizing elitism? Is the critic or the complainer now king? Do we no longer admire and salute those who "actually strive to do the deeds"? Have we lost all common sense? Let me repeat a question I asked above about leaders: Consider two groups, one with the virtues of service, sacrifice, duty and courage, and the other with the characteristics of selfishness, self-dealing, political correctness, and personal cowardice (or a group of envious, resentful complainers seeking to get their 'just deserts'). Which group would you want in your community or as your neighbor?

NATIONALISM

Three new books address the recent apparent rise in nationalism around the world: *The Virtue of Nationalism* (2018), by Yoram Hazony; *The Nationalist Revival* (2018), by John B. Judis; and *Identity* (2018), by Francis Fukuyama. Hazony's book is primarily political theory, with incidental references to current events. In contrast, Judis largely just describes what is currently happening in various countries. Fukuyama presents a combination of theory and description.

Nationalism and Identity

All three authors agree that nationalism traditionally depends upon the existence of a common language, a common religion and very similar customs and traditions. It is also associated with a specific geographical area. Often, there was or had been a common adversary or enemy. In general, the members of a nation would have a common ethnicity, but Fukuyama considers a common religion to be the most crucial element in the emergence of nations. Fukuyama, *The Origins of Political Order* (2011), pp. 59-63.

It seems to me that some form of racism is a natural and inevitable stage in the evolution of the nation-state, the result of defining one's community in contrast to others. Indeed, it may also be a necessary part of mankind's evolution as a social animal. But, it need not be the final stage. Of course, nations were (and are) not congruent with "peoples" having these common characteristics. They will always be both over-inclusive and underinclusive at the sametime.

> "[In the second half of the nineteenth century,] when Europeans used labels like 'German' and 'Italian,' they were not usually thinking about political citizenship. They were thinking... about individuals with a language, culture, and traditions in common."

> ...

> "Starting in the nineteenth century and continuing in the twentieth, many peoples who had never controlled a state were engulfed by political movements that sought an alignment of their peoplehood with political arrangements: they wanted nation-states to express their sense that they already had something important in common."

Kwame Anthony Appiah, *The Lies that Bind: Rethinking Identity* (2016), p.72.

"As a rule, people do not live in monocultural, monoreligious, monolingual nation-states, and they never have." Id., p.88. Appiah elaborated on these assumptions based upon historical examples of the formation of nation states. *Id.*, pp.69-104.

"[O]nce we reject the notion that some natural unity gives countries their shape, we're left with a puzzle. What does hold countries together?" *Id.*, p.99.

"[A] nation is a group of people who think of themselves as sharing ancestry and also care about the fact that they have that supposed ancestry in common. To be a nation, it is not enough to meet an objective condition of common descent; you have to meet a subjective condition, a condition that lies in the hearts and minds of its members." *Id.*, p.76.

"[I]f you want to build states around nations, you're going to have to do more than simply summon an existing people and make a constitution. You're going to have to make a nation: you will take a population most of whom wish, for some reason, to live under a shared government, and then, after wresting them from whatever states they currently live in, you will need to build in them the shared sentiments that will make it possible for them to live productively together." *Id.*, p.77.

Fukuyama presents the United States as a successful example of a "creedal" nation, a nation based upon a commitment to a recognized creed, reflected in a set of foundational documents and principles. The idea is that people of different ethnicities, religions, family traditions and, perhaps, even languages can bond together to form a successful nation based upon common commitment to shared civic and political values. Certainly, in America today, ethnicity is not a defining factor of membership. Nor is religion.

The strength of the nation as a unit of political order is that membership would typically be perceived as a matter of identity, shared interests and shared destiny. This is especially true for the liberal democratic nations and for other nations with a reasonable degree of individual rights and freedom. In such cases, membership can almost be viewed as consensual, as if arising from a social contract. Of course, members to do not "choose" to join, but are born into the nation. (Of course, their parents or grandparents may actually have chosen to join.) However, it is assumed that the perception of the members is that their participation is not coerced, even though there is necessarily some sacrifice of individual choice and freedom. The benefits of participation are believed easily to exceed the costs.

The entire concept seems to depend upon a recognition of the nation of which they are citizens as being worthy of their loyalties and sacrifices. "[T]he truth of every modern nation is that political unity is never underwritten by some preexisting national commonality. What binds citizens together is a commitment... to sharing the life of a modern state, united by its institutions, procedures, and precepts." Appiah, p.103.

This perception is especially important for liberal democratic nations and other nations with a reasonable degree of individual rights and freedom. Yet, it is assumed that the perception of the members is that their participation is not coerced but freely given. Even though there is necessarily some sacrifice of individual choice and freedom, the benefits of participation are believed easily to exceed the costs.

Over 100 years ago, in the early twentieth century, Teddy Roosevelt made a statement about immigration that would cause public outrage today:

"[W]e should insist that if the immigrant who comes here in good faith becomes an American and assimilates himself to us, he shall be treated on an exact equality with everyone else, for it is an outrage to discriminate against any such man because of creed, or birthplace, or origin. But this is predicated upon the person's becoming in every facet an American, and nothing but an American... We have room for but one flag, the American flag... We have room for but one language here, and that is the English language... and we have room for but one sole loyalty and that is a loyalty to the American people."

This position is contrary to what has been accepted as "politically correct" since the 1970s, but I think that it actually reflects the view of most of our good citizens today. And, it is not racism. Why should we not expect Americans to speak English? To respect our political values and institutions? Such conduct does not require the renunciation of one's own cultural heritage.

In addition, the significance of membership as part of one's identity and as a source of meaning to one's life should not be underestimated. As recently stated by columnist David Brooks: "If you stop the love songs to America, take the celebration of America out of public life, you leave people spiritually bereft, robbed of a great devotion." "Yes, I'm an American Nationalist," *NYTimes.com*, October 25, 2018.

Nationalism and Social Order

All three of the authors cited above also agree that nationalism as a basis of political order, compared to globalism or empire, has the typical benefits that one would expect from decentralization of authority: the promotion of diversity, creativity and innovation and the prospect of positive evolution arising from competition (among various nations). (These are the benefits thought to arise from the Federal system with states' rights in the United States.) They agree that such a system of organization also tends to promote greater individual autonomy and freedom or, at least, the perception of such among the members (because they would not perceive the necessary coercion by the collective as being imposed on them by strangers or foreigners). The three authors also observed that a liberal political order based on nationalism makes possible social welfare programs, because of the belief of most that there is a common shared interest in the well-being of all members of the nation.

Such benefits are the result of the perception of legitimacy. The basis of legitimacy is the perception of consent:

> "Democracy functions on the basis of consent by the governed. Or, more accurately, it rests on the consent of the minority to be governed by the majority. Labour voters in regions that always return Conservative members of Parliament don't challenge the legitimacy of those who govern them—because they respect the political integrity of the U.K. as a whole."

Gerard Baker, "The Great Brexit Breakdown," *WSJ.com*, Dec. 7, 2018.

In short, national identification promotes good citizenship. But, there is more. "An important virtue of the nation-state is that it is a constraint. The contemporary peaceable nation takes what it is given— its borders and territory and resources, its citizens and tribes, its affinities and antag- onisms, its history and traditions and ways of getting along—and makes the most of them." Christopher DeMuth, "America's Nationalist Awakening," WSJ.com, July 20, 2019. The strength of nationalism is in being a product of history:

"Nations evolved organically over centuries of struggle, trial and error and acquired staying power. Man is naturally social and fraternal, and successful nations have learned how to transmute group loyalties into broader allegiance. Citizens understand that their security and freedoms depend on their nation and its imperfect institutions—that their fortunes are linked for better or worse to those of their disparate compatriots."

DeMuth, "Why America Needs National Conservatism," WSJ.com, November 12, 2021.

The nation-state faces its problem within the confines of its history and its established institutions. Globalism's approaches to the world's problems lack such context and grounding. The freedom from constraints and the perception of limitless options are not, in the end, good things for policy-making. Policy decisions should be made within a context and with a full recognition of the relevant history, traditions and culture.

The fact is that "[t]he nation-state remains, despite 70 years of global integration, the political unit that commands the greatest legitimacy among people. It isn't just Britain. The potential tragedy of the EU is that the continuing urge to integrate is not only ignoring this legitimacy; it is stoking the problem by further alienating voters." DeMuth, "America's Nationalist Awakening," *WSJ.com*, July 20, 2019.

Nationalism, Imperialism and Globalism

The "creedal" nation is historically unusual. Most multi-cultural political orders have been empires, based upon overt coercion. Hazony asserts that nationalism is concerned with matters (more or less) within the national borders (there may be disputes about the exact location of such borders), whereas globalism is by definition empire-building or imperialism, that is, focused on extending and imposing its influence and reach to other groups or nations. Thus, Hazony adds an additional element to the definitions both of nationalism and globalism.

Leaving aside for the moment the matter of definitions, I think it is useful to distinguish between a government and people concerned with their own affairs and a government and people intent on expanding their control over others and creating an empire. If nationalism is characterized by the former, then it would be improper, for example, to call Nazi Germany or Imperial Japan examples of nationalism. (Judis would not agree, because he uses a different definition of "nationalism.")

The contemporary political movements in Hungary and Poland, however, would seem to qualify as nationalism under Hazony's definition, as would Brazil (with the recent election) and, at least until 2022, arguably, Russia. But, not Putin's Russia. And, not Xi Jinping's China.

"...America is preserving more than its role in the international system. It is trying to preserve the system itself—which Mr. Xi is working to overthrow by promoting imperial-era Chinese concepts. The idea that underpinned the imperial tributary system was that states near and far were obligated to acknowledge Chinese rule. Chinese emperors claimed they had the Mandate of Heaven over tianxia, or 'All Under Heaven.'" Gordon G. Chang, "Xi Changed My Mind About Trump: The president defends not only U.S. sovereignty but the entire world order," *WSJ.com*, July 24, 2019.

Hazony's dichotomy seems useful, but his unequivocal characterizations of nationalism and globalism do not, to me. He deems any political organization broader than the nation to be necessarily imperialist. For example, he is unstinting in his criticism of the European Union.

The interesting question to me is whether and under what circumstances entities that would be considered nations can voluntarily join together to form a union that has the characteristics of a nation state, that is, a broad perception of common interest, of common civic values and of the relative lack of coercion. Hazony asserts that such a union is impossible.

The difficulties of the European Union are well known. Fukuyama attempts to address this question. As to the EU, he concludes that a successful union is not impossible, only not (yet) achieved. (He blames the failure on improper or inadequate implementation, and suggests various possible "fixes", such as a strengthening of the European Parliament and a curtailment of the powers of the European Commission, as well as advertising. Pretty weak stuff for such a serious challenge.)

But, the challenge for the EU is more profound than Fukuyama acknowledges:

> "The 19th-century French philosopher Ernest Renan argued that 'a nation is a soul, a spiritual principle': 'These are the essential conditions of being a people: having common glories in the past and a will to continue them in the present; having made great things together and wishing to make them again. One loves in proportion to the sacrifices that one has committed and the troubles that one has suffered.'"

David Brooks, *NYTimes.com*, October 25, 2018.

So, how do we achieve "soul" at a multi-national or a global level if "soul" requires a history of shared sacrifice, service and commitment?

Realistically, in all events, Hazony's image of a world organized around traditional nation states is not an adequate prescription for today or the future. Cosmopolitism is a fact for the educated and well-off people around the world. Multi-culturalism is only going to increase. But, imperialism is not acceptable. So, we ask how we can retain the benefits of nationalism in a world of increasing globalization. More specifically, can a multi-national and multi-cultural form of political and community organization command from its citizens sufficient loyalty and the willingness to make sacrifices. Could the proper spirit be generated by new leaders with charisma and a vision of a reformed and broadened community? And, can such an organization stop the empire-builders?

CHAPTER IV

Inequality

"UNEQUAL-ITY"

"Unequal" is the norm in our world. We find "not equal" things every where—not equal in size, in ability, in attractiveness, in resources, in living and in dying. As they say, it is only in death that we are all equal.

Yet, we find ourselves surrounded by protests about "inequality," identifying it as a matter of significant societal concern. "Inequality" suggests unfairness or impropriety. The same seems not so true yet for "unequal." Curious, since they are simply a noun and an adjective for the same concept. The spelling difference appears because the prefix "un" comes from old English, while the noun comes from the French (which came from the Latin). There are similar examples, like unable and inability or ungrateful and ingratitude. Even in those examples, the adjective seems only to state a plain fact, while the noun invokes the image of a state of affairs, with some overtones of moral judgment (or, is it just me).

So, I will use the word "unequality" for this discussion. The mean-ing is the same (and, I am assured by *Merriam-Webster*, it is proper

English), but I do so in the hope of making the discussion somewhat more neutral.

Unequal Wealth (and Income)

As I previously wrote: "[t]he branch of human 'knowledge' known as economics has ancient roots, reflecting man's long-standing interest in trade and money (media of exchange). But, then, we see in the eighteenth century a new focus on two rather distinct questions: Why are certain nations richer than others, even when one controls for natural resources? Why are diamonds—intrinsically useless—worth more than water—an essential of life?" *Important Things We Don't Know About Nearly Everything* (2022), p.122. [For convenience, I quote myself below, rather than rewrite these points.]

Those were new questions at the time, arising from rather recent events in human history.

"Most people of a few centuries ago led lives comparable to those of their remote ancestors—and most other individuals around the globe—millennia ago, ...[For] the entirety of human history up until the recent dramatic leap forward [,] the fruits of technological advancements were channelled primarily towards larger and denser populations and had only a glacial impact on their long-term prosperity."

Oded Galor, *The Journey of Humanity: The Origins of Wealth and Inequality* (2022), pp.3-4.

Then, came the Age of Industrialization. As I have previously written: "some striking insights were achieved into causes of increased productivity and growth. Adam Smith [in his *Wealth of Nations* (1776)] identified the importance of the division of labor and specialization, attributing much of the progress and promise of industrialized economies to the **benefits that were derived from the increasing division of labor that greater scale and free trade would enable**. The benefits of the specialization ... include improved skill at the task at hand resulting from repetition, improved techniques that may be discovered as a result of the greater experience gained..., new technology made feasible as a result of the increases scale of the process at issue, reduced time and resources spent in frequently changing tasks, efficiencies in training for specialized jobs and, even, the opportunities to capture differences in relative differential abilities in performing particular tasks through trade; although, the full theory of 'comparative advantage' awaited David Ricardo, 50 years later." *Important Things*, pp.122-3 (emphasis added).

Following the Industrial Revolution of the nineteenth century, economic progress exploded. As J. Bradford DeLong writes:

> "[T]he watershed-crossing events of around 1870—**the triple emergence of globalization, the industrial research lab, and the modern corporation** ushered in changes that began **to pull the world out of the dire poverty that had been humanity's lot for the previous ten thousand years,** since the discovery of agriculture. ...Today, the luckier economies of the world have achieved levels of per capita prosperity at least twenty times those of 1870, and at least twenty-five times those of 1770... ."

Slouching Towards Utopia: An Economic History of the Twentieth Century (2022), pp.1, 11 (emphasis added).

And, the wealth accumulation among nations was very unequal and has continued so. For example, today, with about 5% of the world's population, the United States holds some 30% of the world's wealth.

(In the United States today, the top 1% of households hold about 30% of the wealth.)

In his recent book, Oded Galor has summarized what he found in his research as the causes of the differences in wealth and economic growth among nations. There are many. Several clearly apply to countries—geography (absence of *tse-tse* flies and malaria carrying mosquitoes, fertile soil, East/West orientation, suitable climate, abundant and diverse local plant life, access to navigable waters), political structure (decentralized, public participation), legal structure (stable and robust property rights, enforceability of contracts, relative security for people and property). But, several others describe characteristics of societies and people—future-oriented, competitive, risk tolerant, committed to investment in human capital (care of children, good nutrition, education, training), trusting of others (promoting trade and the exchange of knowledge), relative gender equality (women in the workforce), genetic and cultural diversity (conducive to the generation of new ideas). (We might find here some insight into why certain communities, like certain nations, are notably less prosperous than others.)

In contrast, Thomas Piketty endorses:

> "Ken Pomeranz's study, published in 2000, on the 'great divergence' between Europe and China in the eighteenth and nineteenth centuries, [that] ... the development of Western industrial capitalism is closely linked to systems of **the international division of labor, the frenetic exploitation of natural resources, and the European powers' military and colonial domination over the rest of the planet.**"

Thomas Piketty, *A Brief History of Equality* (2022), p.3 (emphasis added).*

This theory addresses part of the rise of the Western colonial powers, like Britain, France and Spain, but not the more general phenomenon of economic growth that proceeded and followed that rise and occurred elsewhere. Indeed, DeLong explains that even during the nineteenth century, "[p]opulation growth ate the benefits of invention and innovation in technology and organization, leaving only the exploitative upper class noticeably better off." *Slouching Towards Utopia*, p.30.

Yet,

> "[a]fter 1870, sending a family member across the ocean to work became a possibility open to all save the very poorest of European households. And humans responded by the millions. ...[M]igration did not raise wages much in the ... economies of China and India. Both had such substantial populations that emigration was a drop in the bucket. **Through misfortune and bad government, India and China had failed to escape the shackles of the Malthusian Devil** [population growth consuming increases in productivity]."

Id., pp.40, 44.**

Adam Smith's answer to the second question (supply and demand) led to the development of Neo-classical economic theory purporting to explain how markets work. Consistent with that theory, was what happened next. "The growth of trade meant that the logic of comparative advantage could be deployed to its limit. ...And so the surge in real wages was worldwide, not confined to where industrial technologies were then being deployed. This was the consequence of finance and trade following labor." DeLong, *Slouching Towards Utopia,,* pp.49, 50. "The market economy enables the astonishing coordination and cooperation of by now nearly eight billion humans in a highly productive division of labor." *Id.*, p.13. Moreover, "[t]he unique American advantage was greatly reinforced by the fact that in the United States, the period of explosive prosperity set in motion around 1870 ... lasted without interruption longer than elsewhere in the world. China collapsed into revolution in 1911. Europe descended into the hell of World War I in 1914." *Id.*, pp.78-9.

Now, 250 years later, attention has focused on the differences in the wealth of individuals, a subject on which Neo-classical economics had indirectly offered an explanation not now considered acceptable. *See,* Joseph E. Stiglitz, *The Price of Inequality: How Today's Divided Society Endangers Our Future* (2013), p.30 ("The theory that came to dominate, beginning in the second half of the nineteenth century—and still does—was called 'marginal productivity theory'; those with higher productivities earned higher incomes that reflected their greater contribution to society").

The Noble Prize winning economist argues that:

> "**Technology and scarcity, working through the ordinary laws of supply and demand, play a role in shaping today's inequality**, but something else is at work, and **that something else is government.** Inequality is the result of political forces as much as of economic ones. ...[A]nother way to get rich. You can simply **arrange for the government to hand you cash.** ...A little-noticed change in legislation ... can reap billions of dollars. ...[A]lmost every law has distributive consequences,** with some groups benefiting, typically at the expense of others."

Id., pp.30, 48, 58 (emphasis added).

With his conclusion applied to today. I whole heartedly agree. The difference is that Stiglitz views it as a compelling reason for more government, while I view it as a compelling reason for less.

Stiglitz goes on:

> "[W]e have a political system that gives inordinate power to those at the top, and they have used that power not only to limit the extent of redistribution but also to shape the rules of the game in their favor, and to **extract from the public what can only be called large 'gifts.'** Economists ... call them **rent seeking, getting income not as a reward to creating wealth but by grabbing a larger share of the wealth** that would otherwise have been produced without their effort."

Id., pp.31 (emphasis added).

He concludes "..Those at the top have learned how **to suck out money** from the rest in ways that the rest are hardly aware of—**that is their true innovation**." *Id.*, p.32 (emphasis added).

"[T]heir true innovation"?

Really?

Ignoring the hyperbole, I agree that much of the wealth in this country is attributable to "economic rents," but I think Stiglitz unfairly characterizes and stigmatizes that phenomenon. Economic rent arises from scarcity. When there are few of something that many people (or a few wealthy people) want, the price will be bid up until it is determined who wins the prize. The cost of production (whether average or marginal or total) of the desired product is irrelevant, because the supply of the product cannot be increased, at least in the short run (if can be increased in the long run, we may have "quasi-rents" in the short run). Such rent plays an indispensable role in the allocation of scarce resources.

Stiglitz is misleading in his repeated assertion that the receipt of rent takes money away from others. It does so only in the rather trivial sense that the persons paying the rents might have spent that money on something else if they had not paid the rent and someone else may have benefitted.

Take some examples. A football player may have little value to society, but differential pay is a way to allocate the players among teams and will reflect the players' relative values to the owners. The result is stupendous income for some, in the form of "rent." The same market mechanism works for CEOs, babysitters, caregivers and skilled tradesmen. Celebrities receive rent for their performances. Many, many others would eagerly take their roles for far less (even for no pay), but the producer chooses to pay millions for the star. Economists call that rent, but that does not mean the star does not deserve it or that the star has taken (or to use Stiglitz' preferred verbs in this context, "grabbed" or "sucked out") money from your pocket or mine. We pay willingly. (Some even pay eagerly.)

Consequences of Unequality

What are the consequences today of past disparities in the distribution of wealth among nations but, more importantly, among individuals within nations? Significant concentrations of wealth have given us art, music and grand architecture: cathedrals, castles, palaces and stately homes and gardens. Some monumental architecture was the result of collaborative community effort, but much of our rich cultural heritage is a result of the ambitions, egotism and patronage of the very wealthy. Of course, another consequence is some part of the unequality of wealth that exists today (but, probably only a modest part, as I discuss in the following essay on mobility).

So, what are the consequences today of today's wealth unequality? For one thing, the world is more diverse, colorful and interesting because of unequality. Although I will never own one, I am glad that exotic cars exit. The same for luxury yachts, private planes, *haut couture*, handmade watches and fine jewelry. I am glad that skilled artisans still exist. And, even fashion designers. Not to forget expensive wines and glamorous hotels and palatial houses.

In addition, and very importantly, the possibility of wealth unequality provides the incentives for saving and investment, as well as for entrepreneurship and innovation. Another consequence is huge amounts of private philanthropy: creative, experimental and idiosyncratic. Such private undertakings have a far different impact than government programs. Admittedly, there is also obscene waste and tasteless excess. But, that still seems better than bland, stifling uniformity to me.

What about unequality of income? The possibility of such unequality creates incentives for innovation, hard work and risk taking. Income unequality also rewards skill and ability, as well as blind luck. And, as noted above, unequality of income through economic rent is a means of allocating unique or scarce resources. In addition, such unequality spurs capital formation, since the higher income recipients save much more of their income than the lower income recipients do.

There is a close relationship between unequality of wealth and unequality of income, obviously. The consequences of both are similar. One consequence I have not mentioned is influence, of all kinds. But, we may be especially concerned about the political. The remedy for that problem are rules concerning campaign finance and diligence to prevent corruption.

In a 2012 speech cited by Stigliz, then Chairman of the Council of Ecnomic Advisers Alan Krueger identified "potential [adverse] consequences of rising inequality for the economy."

They are:

- "...as inequality rises, the prospects for intergenerational mobility fall [an alleged phenomenon that he dubs "The Great Gatsby Curve"].
- ...rising inequaity and slow income growth encourag[e] many families to borrow beyond their means to try to maintain their consumption.
- .. [rising inequality and slow income growth] reduc[e] aggregate consumption....if another $1.1 trillion had been earned by the bottom 99% instead of the top 1%, annual consumption would be about $440 billion higher.
- ...in a society where income inequality is greater, political decisions are likely to result in policies that lead to less growth.
- ...wage discrepancies can be bad for employee morale and productivity. ... a more fair distribution of wages ... would raise morale and productivity."

"The Rise and Consequences of Inequality in the United States," *Council of Economic Advisers*, January 12, 2012.

Well, pretty thin stuff. The evidence for the first assertion is based on relative, not absolute, mobility and does not establish the direction of any causation anyway. Not much to say about the second, except there is no proof that it is true. In any event, it is a poor reason to promote equality. The third consequence is more likely a benefit of unequality, not a harm, if one favors growth. The fourth contradicts the third and is unsupported. The fifth is simply not relevant to the issue here concerning the gap between the top and the bottom.

Of course, one may recognize the desirability (and inevitability) of unequality, but still ask how much is enough or can there be too much? Unfortunately, there is no answer to either question, and the evidence from historical and international comparisons is only suggestive, at best.

Unequality in the United States

So, let's look at some of the facts about unequality in the U.S.

Although, it is hard to find a good measure, it is generally agreed that unequality in the United States dramatically decreased from 1928 through 1945, then leveled off until the late 1970s. Some 50 years. The next 15 years saw some upward movement; then, it appears to have increased sporadically again after 1986.*** In 2010, by one measure, the United States was less unequal than France, Germany and Italy and similar to Sweden, Poland, Spain, Japan and the United Kingdom in income before taxes and government transfers. When taxes and transfers are taken into account, it becomes more unequal. *See* Alan B. Krueger, "The Rise and Consequences of Inequality in the United States," Council of Economic Advisers, January 12, 2012, Fig.11.

"In 2017, federal, state and local governments redistributed $2.8 trillion, or 22% of the nation's earned household income. More than two-thirds of those transfer payments went to households in the bottom two income quintiles." Phil Gramm and John Early, "Incredible Shrinking Income Inequality," *WSJ.com*, March 23, 2021.

Indeed, "the U.S. today redistributes a larger share of its gross domestic product, 29.4%, through transfers and taxes than any developed country in the world except France with 30.1%." Phil Gramm and Jodey Arrington, "Welfare Is What's Eating the Budget: Means-tested programs, not Medicare and Social Security, are behind today's massive debt," *WSJ.com*, September 11, 04.

There are disagreements about which such "transfers" to include as "income."

> "Remarkably the Census Bureau chooses to count only $900 billion of that $2.8 trillion as income for the recipients. Excluded from **the measurement of household income is some $1.9 trillion of government transfers.** These include the earned-income tax credit, whose beneficiaries get a check from the Treasury; food stamps, which let beneficiaries buy food with government issued debit cards; and numerous other programs... ."

Id. (emphasis added).

When corrected to reflect total government benefits, the measurement shows a continuing decline in unequality after 1986. *Id.* Moreover,

> "[I]n the bottom quintile, there are on average only 1.92 people living in a household. The second and middle quintiles have 2.41 and 2.62 people respectively. After adjusting income for the number of people living in the household, ...[t]he blockbuster finding is that **on a per capita basis the average bottom quintile household received 14% more income than the average second-quintile household and 3.3% more than the average middle-income household."**

Phil Gramm and John Early, "Income Equality, Not Inequality, Is the Problem," *WSJ.com*, August 29, 2022 (emphasis added).

"Gerald Auten of the U.S. Treasury and David Splinter of Congress's Joint Committee on Taxation ... find that the income share of the top 1% climbed to 13.7% in 2019 from 9.2% in 1970—or an increase in pre-tax income inequality that is only 37% as large as the Saez and Zucman work suggests. ...Incorporating the increase in redistributive government policy that occurred over this time, the income share of the top 1% only increased to 8.8% in 2019 from 6.8% in 1970."

Joshua Rauh and Gregory Kearney, "The Economists Who'd Rather Be Influencers," *WSJ.com*, July 17, 2023.

"Using individual tax returns, Piketty and Saez (2003) concluded that the top one percent income share at least doubled since 1960. But these estimates are biased by tax base changes, missing income sources, and major social changes. ...Our results suggest that recent top income shares are significantly lower and that there has been relatively little change since 1960, though a modest increase since 1980. The most important reason our results differ from Piketty, Saez, and Zucman (2018) is our allocation of underreported income according to detailed IRS audit studies rather than proportional to income reported on tax returns.

...

"Our estimates show that despite a decrease in the top federal individual income tax rate from 91 to 39.6 percent between 1960 and 2015, base-broadening reforms and the decreased use of tax shelters caused effective tax rates of the top one percent to increase from 14 to 24 percent. Considering all taxes, effective tax rates of the top one percent increased while those of the bottom 90 percent fell... ."

Gerald Auten and David Splinter, "Income Inequality in the United States: Using Tax Data to Measure Long-term Trends," August 23, 2018.

There is a lot of talk about the top 1%, some about the top 0.1%, but the real action is with the top 0.01%—a mere 16,000 households. That is where the enormous increases are occurring and is the principal source of the growing unequality. Most other measures of inequality are actually rather misleading, because of the impact of this tiny group. Much of the wealth of this group is attributable to the rapid appreciation of equities and other assets in general, but a lot of it reflects the staggering successes of businesses that members started or supported with an investment early.

And, most of that wealth consists of unrecognized gains, so it would not yet have been considered income. (There are some pretty significant disconnects between wealth and income.) This wealth is also rather transitory, in reality. The market value may drop. If the stock is sold, income taxes will be paid; if (when) the holder dies, either the stock will go to charity or some 40% will go to the government in estate taxes.

For perspective, about half of U.S. households have negative or nominal net worths (less than $10,000, excluding home ownership), the top 1% have net worths in excess of $11 million, the top 0.1% have net worths over $40 million and the top 0.01%, from over $100 million to $260 billion. The top 0.01% hold roughly half the wealth of the top 0.1%, which in turn hold roughly half of the wealth of the top 1.0% (the top 10 % actually hold about 40% of the total wealth of all households).

As for income, households in the top 1% have incomes in excess of $500,000, while the top 0.1% have incomes in excess of $3 million and the top 0.01% have incomes ranging from $8 million well into the hundreds of millions. This top income category generally includes a number of professional athletes, a lot of entertainers and CEOs, some lawyers, a bunch of investment bankers and fund managers and a couple of lottery winners. Many of these will be in the top net worth category as well, but not all. There is much greater disparity in net worth than in income.

Now, all of these numbers are estimates, but they indicate the nature and magnitude of the relationships. So, what does this all mean?

Some Hypotheticals

The average U.S. household income is now about $98,000 a year. The median (the midpoint) is about $68,000 a year.

- If one imagines that half the income of the top 10% were received instead by the bottom 10%, both the average and the median would stay the same.
- If one imagines that income were allocated equally, the average would still not change, but the median would equal the average, since that would be the income of every household. In addition, if the income of the top 10% were simply cut in half, then average income would go down about 10%, the median income would stay the same. In comparison, if the income of the bottom 20% were to double, then average income would go up, median income would still be unchanged. In these examples, of course, unequality would be reduced.
- If all of the wealth of the top 1% were distributed equally among the 99%, everyone would get a one time payment of about $14,000. Would that permanently change the world?
- Finally, suppose the net worth of all households were equalized and income of all households were to be made the same for three years, but all of our institutions were to remain the same, what would happen after the three years? I suggest that unequality would start to increase and would do so rapidly and exponentially. Moreover, I suspect that before long, many, maybe most, households would again be in the same quintile they were in just before this experiment began, both by income and by net worth.

Indeed, even Thomas Piketty seems to agree that redistribution will not accomplish much. *See A Brief History of Equality,* p.164.*** If our institutions were changed to prevent this result, I think that total national income would fall dramatically, bringing down both the averages and the medians.

Yet, Stiglitz says:

> "[T]hose at the top are **grabbing** an increasing fraction of the nation's income—so much of a larger share that what's left over for the rest is diminished.... . There's been **redistribution away from the bottom and middle, and almost all of what's been redistributed has gone to the very top, the top 1 percent.** This is **a direct corollary** of the fact that incomes at the bottom and in the middle have been falling, while those at the very top have been rising."

Id., pp.25, 298 (emphasis added).

Apparently taking a cue from Paul Krugman (who became a leading *New York Times* columnist through arrogant sarcasm, exaggeration and the hurling of insults), Stiglitz abandons any pretense of objectivity in his choice of words to express this conclusion. But, he also abandons logic. The fact that the wealth or income of the top 1% goes up at the same time that the wealth or income of the bottom 20% goes down simply does not mean that money was taken by one group from the other or even moved from one to the other. It is not a corollary.

For example, your raise is likely not the cause of or even related to the decline in my income (I retired). Suppose the stock market soars, as it has during the last five years. People who own stock become wealthier. People who do not own stock become relatively less wealthy, but their actual wealth does not go down. Nothing was "grabbed" from them.

Now, suppose that government blunders result in rapid inflation, as has happened in the last year. The bottom half's real income goes down, not because the income of the top 1% has gone up. The wealth of the debtors goes up; that of the savers goes down. Over the first six months of 2022, stock prices fell, decreasing the wealth at the top. Are the poor better off?

Another example. Suppose that housing prices go up, with the prices for luxury properties rising much faster than prices for the average homes, as has happened over the last three years. All homeowners are wealthier. The family that can now sell their mansion for $11 million, having bought it for $5 million five years ago, is certainly now wealthier, but not at the expense of the owners of average homes (unless you believe that there is a fixed amount of money that will spent on housing, which was "sucked up" by the sellers of mansions).

Conclusions

It seems to me that all of this suggests rather strongly that much of today's political rhetoric is seriously misdirected. The matter for concern and for action is not the 1% or the more important top 0.01%; it is the behavior of the bottom 50%. Why do they not save, why do they not invest? Increases in income will not change the picture materially without changes in spending habits. People need to work "on the books" so they accrue Social Security benefits. They need to contribute to retirement plans. They need to use credit cards carefully. And, they need to believe in a future.

Curiously, during the pandemic, savings by the bottom half went up. Why? For many, the relief payments and loan suspensions were a complete windfall. The money may have been saved because of fear and uncertainty, because of lockdowns and because future payments were an unknown. It appears that spending is now increasing in 2022 and savings are decreasing. An increase in income will make little lasting difference absent a corresponding increase in net worth. An increase in net worth will make little difference if it is transitory, that is, if it is just spent. I do not mean to suggest that emergency relief is not helpful or not necessary. It is both. But, it should be deemed to be temporary and transitional, even if the transition may take a long time. Financial aid programs should either be explicitly of limited term or contain a plan for a transition to its termination for each included individual or family.

And, I am not arguing in favor of any particular level of inequality. Perhaps, it is too great today. But, as I previously wrote, I have seen no good evidence or even arguments to that effect. However, I have elsewhere set out my proposals for the rationalization of the U.S. Federal tax system. Implementation of those proposals would reduce inequality. However, I propose them not as a redistribution scheme, but as a commonsense, rational approach to taxation, one that is in the interests of the country.

There are government actions that could promote the changes that would help make a difference and reduce unequality. For example, instead of the current Earned Income Credit, we could pay $5 per hour for all hours worked that are reflected in a W-2 to each person with an income below $40,000 a year. We could match contributions made to a traditional IRA, taxable only upon withdrawal. We could offer subsidies for the teaching of "home economics" and financial management. There are many possibilities for programs that encourage constructive behavior and that do not reward those who do not try.

Unequality is pervasive and inevitable. It is also beneficial, providing much of the "spice" in life. This is especially true for unequality in wealth. Thus, we should not obsess about the top 16,000 households making up the top .01% (or even the the 1,600,000 making up the top 1%). We should not focus on the actions of the tail but on the health of the dog. Public policy should strive to create the opportunities for everyone to achieve healthy, constructive lives. And, of course, everyone should pay their taxes and abide by the law.

But, for context, remember:

"[A]t least since the end of the eighteenth century there has been a historical movement toward equality. The world of the early 2020s, no matter how unjust it may seem, is more egalitarian than that of 1950 or that of 1900, which were themselves in many respects more egalitarian than those of 1850 or 1780."

Piketty, *A Brief History of Equality*, pp. 1-2.

Endnotes

* Thomas Piketty insists that the significant global trend toward wealth equality from 1915 to 1980 was due to the emergence of the welfare state and progressive taxation ("progressive taxation, as it functioned in the course of the twentieth century, enabled us not only to more fairly distribute taxes on wealth and income but also to impose narrow limits on inequalities before taxes"). *A Brief History of Equality*, p.157. Yet, he describes the tremendous amounts of private wealth that were lost as a result of WWI, the Great Depression, the collapse of the colonial empires, WWII and the cancelation of massive public debt in Western Europe. In the U.S., the welfare state improved the standard of living of the recipients, but did little for their wealth or their futures; progressive taxation reduced the after-tax incomes of some of the top 10%, but it also caused alterations in how people were compensated or received earnings and resulted in the diversion of resources to tax avoidance, reducing reported taxable income.

** DeLong describes his conclusions about the impact on wages of the migration of some 1 out of every 7 people in the world following 1870. The immigrants generally found the higher wages for which they had immigrated; the laborers staying behind saw their real wages rise as the local labor supply shrank, except in China and India. In the Northern, industrialized countries, wages in general went up, despite the increase in the supply of labor. In the Southern, agricultural countries, where most of the Chinese and Indian immigrants went, the wages were suppressed by the influx of workers willing to work for very little. Overall, the dramatic increase in the mobility of goods and of resources, including labor, enabled by the plummeting costs of transportation delivered large improvements in the living standards of the working classes around the world. *Slouching Towards Utopia,* pp.44-50.

*** "Redistribution of property alone does not suffice to transcend capitalism [,]... simply to replace large property owners with small and middle-sized property owners who are just as greedy and careless of the social and environmental consequences of their actions... ." So, Piketty advocates for much more dramatic changes in the existing economic/political systems. He rejects authoritarian alternatives (like Stalinism and contemporary China), favoring "a new form of democratic socialism: self-managing, decentralized, and based on the continual circulation of power and property [regularly imposed redistributions of wealth]." *A Brief History of Equality,* pp.166-167. Yet, he acknowledges that: "[t[he internal organization of these quasi-state, hypercentralized authorities is not at all clear, ... how they might function in a truly democratic and emancipatory way. It would be premature, **to say the least**, to assume ... that any **risk of bureaucratic and authoritarian excess** can be ruled out." *Id.,* p.169 (emphasis added).

ORIGINS OF INEQUALITY

"Changing climates did not create
the need for political systems,
pave the way for the rise of towns, cities or states
or lead to the development of writing systems.
All were the product of rising population numbers,
greater demands on water and food resources
in particular and the need for social organization."

Peter Frankopan
The Earth Transformed, p.78.

Inequality: From where or what and why did it emerge?

I start with the recent work of two U.K. anthropologists, David
Graeber and David Wengrowth (*The Dawn of Everything: A New History of Humanity* (2021)), with the main conclusions of which I largely
disagree, then consider the views of some other recent contributors.
Graeber and Wengrow observe (pp.1, 3-4, 15) that:

"Our species, *Homo sapiens*, has existed for at least 200,000
years, but for most of that time we have next to no idea what
was happening. ...[But,] evidence that has accumulated in
archaeology, anthropology and kindred disciplines ... points
towards a completely new account of how human societies
developed over roughly the last 30,000 years. ...[W]e always
find that the realities of early human social life were far more
complex, and a good deal more interesting, than any modern-
day State of Nature theorist would ever be likely to guess."

They assert:

> "For Diamond and Fukuyama, as for Rousseau some centuries earlier, what put an end to that equality—everywhere and forever—was **the invention of agriculture**, and the higher population levels it sustained. Agriculture brought about a transition from 'bands' to 'tribes.' Accumulation of food surplus fed population growth, **leading some 'tribes' to develop into ranked societies known as 'chiefdoms.'"**

Id., p.10 (emphasis added).

Thomas Hobbes (1651) and Jean-Jacques Rousseau (1754) set forth depictions of the supposed "state of nature" (sharply contrasting ones, reflecting opposing views of the inherent nature of man). But, neither purported to be presenting an historically accurate account of stone-age human existence. They were using their respective characterizations as analytical tools in the construction of political theories. The writings of modern "State of Nature theorists" are, specifically, Francis Fukuyama (*The Origins of Political Order: From Prehuman Times to the French Revolution,* 2011), Jared Diamond (*The World Until Yesterday: What Can We Learn from Traditional Societies?,* 2012) and Steven Pinker (*The Better Angels of Our Nature: Why Violence Has Declined,* 2011). The point Graeber and Wengrow seem to be making is that these subsequent theorists have tended to treat one or the other as an authoritative source about early mankind's social circumstances. This charge seems unfair and incorrect (certainly, as to Fukuyama, whose book I have read.) Their real complaint is with the conclusions expressed about the evolution of human societies. (They also challenge these writers' qualifications to opine on such subjects.)

They claim that the available evidence, much of it discovered in the last 50 years, presents something very different:

> "...[H]uman societies before the advent of farming were not confined to small, egalitarian bands. ...Agriculture, in turn, did not mean the inception of private property, nor did it mark an irreversible step towards inequality. In fact, many of the first farming communities were relatively free of ranks and hierarchies. ...[A] surprising number of the world's earliest cities were organized on robustly egalitarian lines... ."

Id., p.4.

Indeed, there is also evidence that agriculture may have followed and been encouraged by a heirarchical poltical order, not *vice versa.*

"It was not that the Natufians lived in an area uniquely endowed with wild species that made them special. It was that they were sedentary before they started domesticating plants or animals. ...In order for sedentary life to emerge, it therefore seems plausible that hunter-gatherers would have had to be forced to settle down, and this would have to have been preceded by an institutional innovation concentrating power in the hands of a group that would become the political elite, enforce property rights, maintain order, and also benefit from their status by extracting resources from the rest of society. ...The archaeological evidence indeed suggests that the Natufians developed a complex society characterized by hierarchy, order, and inequality... . The emergence of political elites most likely created the transition first to sedentary life and then to farming."

Daron Acemoglu and James A. Robinson, *Why Nations Fail: The Origins of Power, Prosperity, and Poverty* (2012), pp.138, 139, 140.

In the body of their book, Graeber and Wengrow present evidence that in the Paleolithic world there were much more diversity of social arrangements, a substantial amount of travel and regular social interactions among disparate groups, communal projects and "investment" in the future without centralized coercion and numerous centers of signifiant population. It also seems likely that most hunter-gather families consumed greater caloric intake with far, far fewer hours of labor than an English 19th century factory worker's family (while enjoying, perhaps, as short a work week as a modem Frenchman).

"[H]uman remains from early agricultural societies do not attest to improved health or wealth but rather to deteriorating living standards as compared to those of hunter-gatherers living millennia before. Hunter-gatherers evidently lived longer, consumed a richer diet, worked less intensively and suffered fewer infectious diseases." Oded Galor, *The Journey of Humanity: The Origins of Wealth and Inequality* (2022), p.30.

They also present examples of insightful critiques of Western "civilization" by indigenous inhabitants of the Americas, evidence of pre-civilization deliberations over political issues concerning the type of society in which people want to live and stories of how people exposed both to indigenous and Western living almost always opted for the former when they had the opportunity (*Dancing with Wolves* was not pure fantasy).

The rise of agriculture, then, may have been the result of climate change—compelled, not chosen.

"Many scholars have sought to associate behavioural change with environmental factors during the Younger Dryas ... [16,000 to 10,000 years ago], arguing ... that the earliest experimentations with plant cultivation were responses to the need to increase food production during periods of declining resource abundance. ...These were translated into more systematic and successful efforts to grow food once climate conditions became more favourable. These in turn prompted innovations in tool manufacture as well as the generation of surpluses which enabled human groups to select and establish themselves in ... ever larger communities to live together."

Peter Frankopan, *The Earth Transformed: An Untold History* (2023), pp.58-9.

Private Property and Kingdoms

The two U.K. anthropologists find early forms of private property and of social/political hierarchy occurring in connection with sacred objects and religious practices. They assert that neither was the inevitable or necessary consequence of agriculture.

However, they offer no explanation for the broad emergence of both. Few generalization arises from their many anecdotes. They fail to explain the origins of private property, of capitalism (or feudalism), or of kingdoms, hierarchies or, even, of social stratification. In the end, their examination of the archeological and anthropological evidence fails to answer their fundamental question: Why is it that we have come to live in societies dominated by self-centeredness, greed, stress, insecurity and dramatic inequality, leaving so many isolated and lonely?

Oxford historian Peter Frankopan offers some thoughts on these questions consistent with my own speculations, including the assertions:

- Private property arises out of scarcity and community; yet, inequality requires a surplus.
- The incidents of claims of personal possession would arise out of relative scarcity. Things found in abundance are not likely to attract such claims. (For example, the law of water rights developed quickly in the American West as the demand for water began to exceed the supply.) So, "...the start of the Holocene saw the emergence and expansion of new ways of dealing with food and with animals, and of seeking to optimise their benefits." Frankopan, *The Earth Transformed*, p.57.

"...Staying put may ... have been an effective way of protecting land that yielded wild cereals and of ensuring that the best sites were not taken over opportunistically by others[,] ... with goods that were not easily transportable like grindstones becoming more common as people stayed in or close to fixed locations." *Id.*, p.67.

- Possessed things must be durable. Thus, a certain level of technology would seem necessary. It seems quite possible to me that people began to create useful objects that required work or skill to make and asserted ownership of those objects and that that practice spread.

"[T]he motors that drove the rise of cities—and therefore of 'civilisation'—were powered by pressures that forced populations into narrow bands of environmentally hospitable and productive land, where the ability to expand ecological footprints were limited. ...[C]o-operation was essential to prospects of survival. ...The establishment of permanent settlements required that ideas take shape about personal possessions, including movable and non-movable goods, and about access to and control over land and the resources it could yield.

...

"[T]he communities living in the alluvial plains of the Indus and its tributaries were more egalitarian... . [T]he fact that a ruling class does not seem to have emerged in the same way in the Indus and the Andes as it did elsewhere may reflect a culture of plenty of production: greater quantities and qualities of land, and the absence of anxieties about food shortage, in turn meant that the need to protect assets and demonstrate status was simply not so acute."

Id., pp.84, 92.

- The right to exclude was the hallmark of European private property. Over time, the concept of property expanded to include a variety of rights. In American Constitutional law, both the due process clause and eminent domain reference "property." Do they protect contract rights, market value, the enjoyment of common goods? In modern jurisprudence, property is conceived as a bundle of rights (and some responsibilities).
- These rights require the existence of a legal system and some central authority. Indeed, the concept of private property requires community. (Of course, the same is true of most legal concepts, like contracts and torts and criminal law.) For a solitary person or small family in isolation, the concept is quite meaningless. The same for isolated small groups with sporadic interactions—the

stronger take what they want. Only in stable communities does private property became relevant and feasible.

- The community recognition of ownership is key. Similarly, traditional economics presumes communal relationships because it is based on exchange. For a solitary individual, an object might have utility, but it will not have "value."

"Property consists of public recognition. ... community recognition can, over time, endow a claim with legal force. In property law, prescription doctrine means that a trespass can 'ripen' into legal title—that, under certain circumstances, courts will legalize theft.

...

""Notice is one of the things that makes property property. In seventeenth-century England, buying and selling land required not only writing a deed 'executing' (literally doing) the conveyance, but also a stylized public performance called 'livery of seisin,' where the seller stood in front of witnesses, recited certain words, and actually handed a twig or clod of dirt to the new owner. In the thirteen colonies, white landowners walked their boundaries with crowds of neighbors, establishing their ownership claims in public memory and creating witnesses who could testify about creeks and notched trees and other markers if there were ever a dispute."

...

"When I say I own my car, I am not describing my legal relationship to the car; I'm saying something about my legal relations with other people about the car—the dealer who sold it to me, my neighbors who see me park it, the police who stop me on the highway, the strangers who see me driving it. In other words, property is fundamentally social ....As the legal theorist Carol Rose puts it, you 'cannot have property all alone.'

Dylan C. Penningroth, *Before the Movement: The Hidden History of Black Civil Rights* (2023), pp.10, 11, 81.

- By definition, surpluses were necessary to enable at least some people to live above subsistence level. (*E.g.*, "the construction and ownership of ploughs and carts produced rewards and surpluses for those who owned them." Frankopan, p.70.) Surpluses came with agriculture, as did concentrations of people.

"The availability of reliable wild and domesticated food supplies not only facilitated the rise of sedentary life and of villages, but also enabled the concentrations of people that they could support. ...linked with changes in cultural and socio-economic practices that were driven by climatic shifts around 8,000 years ago. ...[P]erhaps the most important result of the improving climate conditions that marked the onset of the Holocene was a sharp rise in human population."

...

"The establishment of permanent settlements required that ideas take shape about personal possessions, including movable and non-movable goods, and about access to and control over land and the resources it could yield. property ownership—whether of fields, crops, animals or goods —whose relevance is enhanced by higher population densities... Wealth disparities became a signature of the populations that urbanised earliest and most intensively."

Frankopan, pp.67, 84.

- The presence of rulers seems tied to religious practices or warfare. It is not difficult to imagine how such a hierarchy would persist once established; but, why would a community submit to it in the first place? One reason would be a crisis or external threat.

One could assume that the emerging leader was perceived to offer something of value and then delivered.

"The ruling class who dominated land ownership, owned herds and controlled production were able to provide incentives as well as to use coercion to accumulate more for themselves, producing ambitions and efficiencies that shaped the physical setting of cities and determined socio-political structures ... [D]ual principles of secular and priestly authority evolved and likewise built up monopolies of power by a ruling class that dominated land ownership and affirmed their status through the erection of temples, stone buildings and elaborate burial monuments... .

...

"[T]he scale and positioning of public buildings testify not only to central planning but to the effective mobilisation of mass labour. Elite control of the infrastructure of new cities was such that workers neither owned nor had rights over agricultural lands that supported the populations. Instead, ... they depended on institutions, temples and the wealthy for compensation in the form of rations, or by way of a share of the produce they were responsible for.

...

"[H]igher population densities are also closely connected with the emergence of social stratification."

Id., pp.85, 87, 88.

Our Choice?

Actually, our U.K. anthropologists' central thesis, or argument, is that we today could and should choose to live a different sort of life—a different lifestyle, motivated by different values and goals. All in, however, I do not think they have made that case.

First, and, most importantly, their analysis fails to demonstrate that meaningful different alternative societies would be feasible in a world with billions of people. They do not address the impact of the inevitable appearance of scarcity in early societies. Certain things that are possible in a world of abundance become much more difficult and unlikely when resources become scarce. So, "[t]he inability to sustain the growing population, as well as climatic changes, eventually induced humanity to explore an alternative mode of subsistence—agriculture." Galor, *The Journey of Humanity,*, p.20.

"There were then in 1870 1.3 billion people alive, 2.6 times as many as there had been in 1500. Farm sizes were only two-fifths as large, on average, as they had been in 1500, canceling out the overwhelming bulk of technological improvement, as far as typical human living standards were concerned."

J. Bradford DeLong, *Slouching Towards Utopia: An Economic History of the Twentieth Century* (2022), p.16.[1]

"[T]he population size of agricultural societies stabilised at a new and higher level, but this time, in reverting to subsistence level, their living conditions actually became significantly lower than those of hunter-gatherers who had lived millennia before them, when existing ecological niches were not yet densely populated. Compared to the living standards of the hunter-gatherers who were their more immediate ancestors, however, the transition to agriculture was entirely rational, perhaps even inevitable; in fact, it did not reflect a deterioration."

Galor, *The Journey of Humanity,* p.3.

The fact is that if everyone concluded that they wanted to live like the American Plains Indians, it would simply be impossible. Some very few of us, yes; but, only if all the rest of us disappeared.

Second, inequality of wealth requires wealth, which means there must be both a surplus over subsistence and the existence of things that can store value.

"It is apparent ... that neither surpluses nor shortages prevailed indefinitely during the Malthusian epoch. The introduction of novel crops or technologies magnified the rate of population growth, mitigating their impact on economic prosperity, while the long-term economic devastation of ecological disasters was ultimately averted by their adverse effects on population *via* famine, disease and wars." Galor, p.39.

But, "back in the preindustrial Agrarian Age, technological progress led to little visible change over one or even several lifetimes, and little growth in typical living standards even over centuries or millennia." DeLong, *Slouching Towards Utopia*, p.14.

So, what we need to know is what forms of society have the capability to escape the Malthusian trap of population growth denying anything beyond mere subsistence level poverty in the long run. There is only one we can condiently identify—the capitalist market economy that "banished" Malthus after 1870.

"Things changed starting around 1870. Then we got the institutions for organization and research and the technologies—we got full globalization, the industrial research laboratory, and the modern corporation. These were the keys. These unlocked the gate that had previously kept humanity in dire poverty." *Id.*, p.2.

Third, they fail to establish that people today would choose their proffered alternative even if it were practical or feasible. There have been a multitude of popular demands for reform and change, and many of them have been successful. But, only for modifications in the system, not radical transformation.

For example, in 1896, the U. S. middle rejected the radical Democrats and elected McKinley as President. In 1848, the French peasantry rejected reforms that would have assisted the urban poor. *See* DeLong, pp.100-03 ("It was not so much that crucial swing voters ... swung to the Republican side. It was, rather, a huge countermobilization against William Jennings Bryan and a turnout increase that determined the outcome of the election"), 106-09 ("the farmers of Tocqueville's France sided against the socialists").

Even today, the protesters do not generally advocate a change in the underlying system, but rather a reallocation of the sysem's abundant output. The key differences in political views are about what it is that will kill the "goose that lays the golden eggs." The dispute is over whether the wealthy are "the gift that can keep on giving" regardless of government policies.

Why, then, was the capitalist market economy so dramatically successful?

"[Friederich August von] Hayek observed, the market economy crowd-sources—incentivizes and coordinates at the grassroots—solutions to the problems it sets.... All societies ... face profound difficulties in getting reliable information to the deciders and then incentivizing the deciders to act for the public good. The market order of property, contract, and exchange can—if property rights are handled properly—push decision-making out to the decentralized periphery where the reliable information already exists, solving the information problem. And by rewarding those who bring resources to valuable uses, it automatically solves the incentivization problem."

Id., pp.2, 93.

How many of today's societal "ills" are inherent in or crucial to that economic success? Market-based capitalism clearly implies inequality, because it depends on there being winners and losers. It is facilitated by arbitrage, so "windfalls" are an integral part of the system. The prospect of gain and the threat of loss power the system, providing the incentives to do things better. Trade itself involves inequality as the result and depends on covetousness as the impetus. The benefits of division of labor, specialization, economies of scale, comparative advantage, decentralized decision-making and rapid transmission of relevant information result in economic growth. Private ownership of the means of production and of natural resources brings the discipline of the marketplace to the allocation and utilization of assets and capital.

"In a market economy, the good cause that justifies inequality is that we need to incentivize economic growth by rewarding skill, industry, and foresight, even if doing so inevitably involves rewarding good luck as well." *Id.*, p.415.

The fact is that most people are not much bothered by inequality as such. They are much more focused on their own standard of living and how it compares to that of their neighbors. Most people will continue to assess the size of their slice of the pie and not be pleased with a larger percentage of a smaller pie if it means a smaller piece.

"Perhaps there was, at bottom, a near-innate human aversion to even semicentralized redistributive arrangements that take from some and give to others. **We do not always want to be the receiver: it makes us feel small and inadequate. We do not always want to be the giver: that makes us feel exploited and grifted.** And as a matter of principle and practice, we tend to disapprove whenever we spy a situation in which somebody else seems to be following a life strategy of always being the receiver.

...

"[The] rights that society will attempt to validate do not—or might not—be rights to anything like an equal distribution of the fruits of industry and agriculture. And it is **probably wrong to describe them as fair: they are what people expect,** given a certain social order. **Equals should be treated equally, yes; but unequals should be treated unequally.** And societies do not have to and almost never do presume that people are of equal significance."

Id., p.96 (emphasis added).

This is not like the feudal world where the land holdings of a few nobles deprived the masses of plots of their own. Land reform had the potential to increase the size of the total pie, while also altering its allocation. I see no current proposals for redistribution that have that potential. Instead, many well-off individuals highlight the apparently growing inequality as a means of achieving political power, an historic reason for the fomenting of class warfare.

Wealth of Nations

Why were the benefits of capitalism so unevenly shared among countries?

"[T]he immense disparities in the wealth of nations are rooted in a chain of causal factors: at the surface are proximate factors, such as the techno-logical and educational differences between countries; at the core are the deeper and ultimate factors—institutions, culture, geography and population diversity—that lie at the root of it all." Galor, *The Journey of Humanity*, p.142.

"While in industrial nations the gains from trade were directed primarily towards investment in education and led to growth in income per capita, a greater portion of the gains from trade in non-industrial nations were channelled towards increased fertility and population growth." *Id.*, p.137.

The economic historians identify a few important differences among nations that contributed to the different economic results.

Education/Human capital

- "[I]n the centuries leading up to industrialisation, as Europe started to make strides in technology and trade, the importance of education began to intensify. During the subsequent phases of the Industrial Revolution, the demand for skilled labour in the growing industrial sector markedly increased. From here on, and for the first time in history, human capital formation—factors that influence worker productivity, such as education, training, skills and health—was designed and undertaken with the primary purpose of satisfying the increasing requirements of industrialisation for literacy and numeracy as well as mechanical skills among the workforce."

- "[O]ther civilisations that had previously outpaced Europe in technological development, including the Chinese and the Ottoman, had started to lag behind... . This technological divergence was reflected in a widening literacy gap between Europe and the rest of the world. ... In non-European societies, however, literacy rates started to rise only in the twentieth century."

- "[I]nvesting in the education and the skills of the workforce became increasingly more important to the capitalist class, not less so, as they came to realise that of all the capital at their disposal, it was human capital that held the key to preventing a decline in their profit margins."

Galor, pp. 64, 67, 64, 65, 74.

- "The United States made the creation of a literate, numerate citizenry a high priority. And that encouraged those with richer backgrounds, better preparations, and quicker or better-trained minds to go on to ever-higher education."

DeLong, p.77.

Government

- "One short and too-simple answer is that the fault lies with governments—specifically, with governmental institutions that were 'extractive' rather than 'developmental,' ... . We are talking here about kleptocracy: rule by thieves."
- "Most governments at most times in most places have followed policies that show little interest in nurturing sustained increases in productivity. ...Only after the government's seat is secure will debates about development policy take place. But the pursuit of a secure hold on power almost always takes up all the rulers' time, energy, and resources."
- "Through misfortune and bad government, India and China had failed to escape the shackles of the Malthusian Devil [until the second half of the twentieth century]."[2]
- "Reza Shah Pahlavi's answer was to try to turn Iranians into Europeans—that is, to follow an authoritarian state-led development road reminiscent of pre–World War I Imperial Germany. But this left scant place for Islam. And the state that resulted was highly corrupt. ...In January 1979 Reza Shah Pahlavi fled into exile. Thereafter, Iran's economy stagnated."

- "Those countries where the armies of Stalin or Mao or Kim Il-Sung or Ho Chi Minh or (shudder) Pol Pot had marched were, on average, only one-fifth as well-off when 1990 came and the curtains were raised as those that had been just beyond those armies' reach."[3]
- "Successful economic development depends on a strong but limited government. Strong in the sense that its judgments of property rights are obeyed, that its functionaries obey instructions from the center, and that the infrastructure it pays for is built. And limited in the sense that it can do relatively little to help or hurt individual enterprises, and that political power does not become the only effective road to wealth and status. ...Only a state that is limited in the amount of damage it can do to the economy, or a state that is secure enough, independent enough, and committed enough to rapid economic growth, can avoid these political survival traps."

DeLong, pp.349, 350, 44, 352.

- "To Egyptians, the things that have held them back include an ineffective and corrupt state and a society where they cannot use their talent, ambition, ingenuity, and what education they can get. But they also recognize that the roots of these problems are political. All the economic impediments they face stem from the way political power in Egypt is exercised and monopolized by a narrow elite."
- "Countries such as Great Britain and the United States became rich because their citizens overthrew the elites who controlled power and created a society where political rights were much more broadly distributed, where the government was accountable and responsive to citizens, and where the great mass of people could take advantage of economic opportunities."

Daron Acemoglu and James A. Robinson, *Why Nations Fail: The Origins of Power, Prosperity, and Poverty* (2012), pp.2, 3-4.

Redistribution (*vs.* Consumption)

- "One can imagine an alternative scenario in which European governments maintained and expanded wartime controls in order to guard against substantial shifts in income distribution. In such a case, the late 1940s and early 1950s might have seen the creation in Western Europe of allocative bureaucracies to ration scarce foreign exchange ...[or take other steps] to protect the living standards of the urban working classes—as happened in various countries of Latin America, which nearly stagnated in the two decades after World War II."
- "Yet Europe avoided these traps. ...Western Europe's mixed economies built substantial systems for redistribution. But they built these systems on top of—and not as replacements for—market allocations of consumer ((producer goods and the factors of production."
- "Argentina's leaders responded to the social and economic upheavals by adopting new policies aimed at stimulating demand and redistributing wealth. At the same time, Argentina's leaders became ... more inclined to use controls instead of prices as mechanisms to allocate goods. ...Post–World War II Argentina saw foreign exchange allocated by the central government in order to, first, keep existing factories running and, second, keep home consumption high."
- "In Latin America, an overvalued exchange rate would see a lot of society's wealth spent on the purchase of foreign luxuries, as the upper class preferred to live well... ."

DeLong, pp.317, 352, 354, 366-7.

The balance between things that promote growth and those that retard it seems to be rather delicate. It is hard to know what changes would make a difference. And, experimentation is difficult because it can take years to see the consequences, by which time corrective action may be difficult. Indeed, much depends upon the attitudes/expectations of the people. It is psychological, which can be very difficult to alter. Take inflation. Once everyone believes that inflation is inevitable, it is inevitable. The discipline of the market breaks down.

Winners of the Nobel Prize in Economics in 2024, Daron Acemoglu and James A. Robinson, were recognized for their work in explaining how and why certain nations are, and have long been, prosperous while others have been poor. The importance of secure property rights, a predictable and reliable legal system and a "culture" of entrepreneurship have long been recognized as fundamental. These economists focused on how societies came to have, or not to have, these characteristics. They assrt that the answer is "politics." Acemoglu and Robinson, p.83.

Their analysis of the history of the colonization of the Americas suggests some interesting conclusions. Where the colonized territories had substantial riches and high population densities, the likely result was the establishment of extractive political and economic institutions in which the few in power exploited the territories and their inhabitants to enrich those few. In contrast, where the territories contained limited available wealth, or too many colonizers relative to the wealth, and low population density; the likely result was the establishment of economic and political structures that provided incentives to utilize the territories's resources in a manner that generated wealth. In other words, the motivations or moral standards of the colonizers were not the real determinants of the outcome.

I note that the different types of economies identified appear to have existed prior to colonization, suggesting that the relative availability of wealth, like gold and silver, and higer population densities tended to determine the type of economic structures that arose initially and that they just continued under a new set of rulers following colonization.

Moreover, the authors point out that relative wealth also affected the political structures within the colonizing nations themselves. For example,

> "[I]t is clear now that human societies before the advent of farming were not confined to small, egalitarian bands. ...Agriculture, in turn, did not mean the inception of private property, nor did it mark an irreversible step towards inequality. In fact, many of the first farming communities were relatively free of ranks and hierarchies. ...[A] surprising number of the world's earliest cities were organized on robustly egalitarian lines... ."

Id., p.105.

However, they also emphasize the role of contingency (or chance) and elaborate on how small initial instituuinal differences can lead to major societal divergences, such as the dramatic reduction in the supply of labor following the plague led to higher wages and greater workers' rights in England but to greater worker exploitation in Eastern Europe.

"[T]he differences between these areas initially seemed very small: in the East, lords were a little better organized; they had slightly more rights and more consolidated landholdings. Towns were weaker and smaller, peasants less organized. In the grand scheme of history, these were small differences.

Yet these small differences between the East and the West became very consequential for the lives of their populations and for the future path of institutional development when the feudal order was shaken up by the Black Death."

Id., p.101.

"The exact path of institutional development during these periods depends on which one of the opposing forces will succeed, which groups will be able to form effective coalitions, and which leaders will be able to structure events to their advantage. The role of contingency can be illustrated by the origins of inclusive political institutions in England." *Id.*, p.110.

"[T]he differences between these areas initially seemed very small: in the East, lords were a little better organized; they had slightly more rights and more consolidated landholdings. Towns were weaker and smaller, peasants less organized. In the grand scheme of history, these were small differences. Yet these small differences between the East and the West became very consequential for the lives of their populations and for the future path of institutional development when the feudal order was shaken up by the Black Death."
Id., p.101.

"The exact path of institutional development during these periods depends on which one of the opposing forces will succeed, which groups will be able to form effective coalitions, and which leaders will be able to structure events to their advantage. The role of contingency can be illustrated by the origins of inclusive political institutions in England." *Id.*, p.110.

"The consequences of this economic expansion for institutions were very different for England than for Spain and France because of small initial differences. Elizabeth I and her successors could not monopolize the trade with the Americas. Other European monarchs could. ...There were small but consequential differences between England and the rest, which is why the Industrial Revolution happened in England and not France." Id., pp.106, 114.

"Edward's government ... snapped into action to protect the economic structures on which the powerful depended, imposing a statutory maximum wage at the low rates to which landowners had been accustomed before death claimed half their workforce. ...[But,] with half the population dead, labor was no longer a cheap and endlessly renewable resource. Together they had tried to enforce Edward III's hastily enacted law fixing wages at pre-plague levels, and to impose landlords' rights over their tenants to the full. But in the end they had to break ranks to secure the services of laborers, servants, and artisans who suddenly found themselves able to demand higher wages, better conditions, shorter hours."

Helen Castor, *The Eagle and the Hart: The Tragedy of Richard II and Henry IV* (2024), pp.6-7, 47-48.

These economists use the term "inclusive" to refer to the characteristics of the political and economic structures associated with prosperity. Prosperity is facilitated by inclusive institutions through innovation and creative destruction, necessary elements of technological progress. Innovation is likely to be more abundant when the abilities of much of the population, not just of a small elite, are enabled to participate with incentives providing rewards to successful innovation. Creative destruction represents the continual displacement and replacement of established methods, processes and businesses by and with new ones and of the existing wealthy with the new wealthy. Thus, prosperity requires political and economic institutions that do not permit the protection of the privileges of the few through the suppression of change.

The other type of institutions they call "extractive," where a small elite seizes the surpluses arising in the country. The populus of an extractive state will be poor both because the controlling few seize most of the wealth and because the institutions create disincentives and prohibitions that prevent sustained economic growth.

(I was astonished by the scope and depth of exploitation and corruption reflected in the parade of examples presented, especially by those occurring during my adulthood. Perhaps, the last 50 years have seen a decline in violence and warfare, but corrupt exploitation of the defenseless apparently rages on.)

The conclusions of the authors seem largely obvious. The interesting question to me is whether the absence of extractive institutions that enrich those in power will tend to give rise to inclusive institutions and economic prosperity. That seems to be the assumption underlying the authors' prescription. ("The solution to the economic and political failure of nations today is to transform their extractive institutions toward inclusive ones." Acemoglu and Robinson,, p.402.)

They persuaively argue that readily accessible riches inevitably attract ruthless, greedy exploiters and that extractive structures, once established, are very tenacious as long as the wealth to be stolen lasts. But, while poor communities may not attract the exploiters, will they generally tend to become inclusive and then prosperous if left alone? Kind of a Rousseau *vs.* Hobbes question again.

"Most important perhaps, in most of these cases there were enormous benefits from holding power. These benefits both attracted the most unscrupulous men... who wished to monopolize this power, and brought the worst out of them once they were in power. There was nothing to break the vicious circle. ...[U]nder inclusive economic institutions there are more limited gains from holding political power, thus weaker incentives for every group and every ambitious, upstart individual to try to take control of the state."

Id., p.364.

"Nations fail economically because of extractive institutions. These institutions keep poor countries poor and prevent them from embarking on a path to economic growth. ...There are notable differences among these countries. Some are tropical, some are in temperate latitudes. Some were colonies of Britain; others, of Japan, Spain, and Russia. They have very different histories, languages, and cultures. What they all share is extractive institutions. In all these cases the basis of these institutions is an elite who design economic institutions in order to enrich themselves and perpetuate their power at the expense of the vast majority of people in society."

Id., pp.398-399.

Generally, "good" (supportive of development) government cannot be created overnight. Indeed, it can take hundreds of years of tradition. The same with a pro-development culture.[4] The exceptions seem to be South Korea and several Southeast Asian Pacific Rim countries that embraced the model of Japan—export led growth stimulated by currency and trade policies that made imports expensive and exports very competitive. That strategy could not work for everyone, since it required other countries that were avid consumers willing to bear trade deficits. (Not every country can have a positive balance of payment at one time.) For these successful countries, the United States was their savior.[5]

As to the matter of what will kill the "goose that lays the golden eggs," we might ask whether extractive instutions require a privileged few receiving the benefits. Could a majority be the exploiters seizing the surplus produced by others?

An Obvious Caveat

Of course, the market deals largely with property and money, so it best serves those who have both. "A market economy can only produce "good" results if it defines the general welfare appropriately— if it weights the material well-being and utility of each individual in an appropriate manner as it adds up and makes tradeoffs. And the problem is that the value that a market economy gives an individual depends on his or her wealth." *Id.*, p.332.

The market has been less successful with labor, since labor is harder to unitize than capital or natural resources. Labor is not easily standardized or measured and is quite "lumpy." What is the unit? So, we have persons receiving stupendous economic rents and others not being paid enough to live independently. DeLong observes, "Depending on which aspect of income distribution was highlighted, either industrial capitalism produced an income distribution that was too unequal (rich get richer, the rest stay poor) or not unequal enough (respected lower middle classes slip into joining the unskilled proletariat)." DeLong, p.265.

And, no one has figured out how to create a functioning market solution for other human needs.

Endnotes

1. I was quite impressed with this book, despite its length. DeLong actually presents quite fairly what are conflicting ideas. Writing primarily as an historian, he provides insight after insight. I am not knowledgeable enough to recognize which are original and which are borrowed, but I learned a lot. Although, he pays lip service to the liberal talking points (excess inequality, too much priority given to money and property, too little promotion of other rights), his analytical skills keep pushing his prejudices to the periphery, a problem his intellectual hero Paul Krugman certainly does not have.

2. "The failure of the British Raj to transform India poses an enormous problem for all of us economists. Under the British Raj in the late nineteenth and early twentieth centuries India had a remarkable degree of internal and external peace, a tolerable administration of justice, and easy taxes." DeLong, *Slouching Towards Utopia*, p.120.

3. "[With the] government by Park Chung-Hee in 1961, everything changed. Park was brutal ... but remarkably effective. The shift of Korea's development strategy from one of import substitution to one of export-led industrialization was very rapid. The consequences were astounding." *Id.*, p.369.

4. "[In Japan,] [t]here followed the rapid adoption of Western organization: prefects, bureaucratic jobs, newspapers, language standardization on Tokyo samurai dialect, an education ministry, compulsory school attendance, military conscription, railways built by the government, the abolition of internal customs barriers to a national market, fixed-length hours of the working day to improve coordination, and the Gregorian calendar, all in place by 1873. Representative local government was in place by 1879." *Id.*, p.133.

5. "East Asia started with the assumption that it would have to export ... if only because its resources were thin and scarce. ...Japan then provided a model for how its ex-colonies, South Korea and Taiwan, should attempt to play catch-up ..., which then provided models for Malaysia, Thailand, and others. ...[T]rade, but managed trade. Undervalue the exchange rate... . Very patient cheap capital ... .Add a high rate of savings... . Tilt the economy's price structure so that machines that embodied modern technological knowledge were cheap and foreign-made and luxurious consumption goods were expensive. ...Taking these steps ... mean[t] ... heavy, hidden taxes on labor... ." *Id.*, pp.365, 366, 367.

MOBLIITY

I have had a special interest in "mobility" for the last eight years, but my attention was drawn to a different type of mobility when, in 2022, I read the 2010 book *The Price of Inequality* by Joseph E. Stiglitz. (Stiglitz is a Noble Prize winning economist who majored in Economics at Amherst College a decade before me. He was a legend in the Department.) The issue is economic mobility in the United States. My interest was peaked because Stiglitz' assertions were so inconsistent with my own experience and my observations. He claims: "Belief in **America's essential fairness,** that we live in a land of equal opportunity, helps bind us together. That, at least, is **the American myth**, powerful and enduring. Increasingly, it **is just that—a myth.**" *Id.*, p.17 (emphasis added). I was surprised, so I looked at his sources. It turns out that the story is far more nuanced, more interesting and more informative than Stiglitz implies.

Stiglitz borrows this analogy from one of his sources: "The relationship between parents' income and that of their children is, in fact, **very similar to that between parents' height and that of their children.**" *Id.*, p.307 (emphasis added).

"Alan Krueger... has pointed out, 'The chance of a person who was born to a family in the bottom 10 percent of the income distribution rising to the top 10 percent as an adult is about the same as the chance that a dad who is 5' 6" tall having a son who grows up to be over 6' 1" tall. It happens, but not often.'" *Id.*

Think about it.

Height is determined by some combination of nature and nurture, of heredity, nutrition and life style. Over time, people have become significantly taller. The same is true of economic well-being. Family background matters because certain talents and abilities are genetically inherited, because certain skills are taught and because certain values and attitudes are transmitted by example. To isolate the impact of family income, we would need to control for genetic and family cultural inheritance. On average, tall offspring have tall parents. Is it not likely that, on average, people in the top quintile similarly will have more favorable genetic inheritances and more supportive families than those in the bottom quintile?

There are also several types of problems embedded in his analysis.

Brandishes a misleading yardstick, he asserts that,

> "if America were really a land of opportunity, the life chances of success—of, say, winding up in the top 10 percent —of someone born to a poor or less-educated family would be the same as those of someone born to a rich, well-educated, and well-connected family. ...With full equality of opportunity, **20 percent of those in the bottom fifth would see their children in the bottom fifth."**

Id., p.18 (emphasis added).

First, that conception of "equal opportunity" would be satisfied only by the completely random assignment of outcomes. Does anyone believe that everyone has (or should have) equal odds of achieving any particular outcome? That ability and effort play no role? Do we really think that family and background are (or should be) irrelevant? That would be quite shocking to people who take parenting seriously.

Second, his analogy suggests the next problem. What do we consider to be significant mobility? Does the offspring of the 5' 6" parents need to be 6' 1" to count as as evidence of height mobility or would 5' 10" be meaningful? Look at some of the examples of statistical mobility that Stiglitz considers insignificant :

- "...58 percent of children born to the bottom group make it out" *Id*. pp.18-19.
- "...8 percent of American men at the bottom rose to the top fifth." Jason DeParle, "Harder for Americans to Rise From Lower Rungs" *NYT.com*, January 4, 2012.
- "[A]bout 62 percent of Americans (male and female) raised in the top fifth of incomes stay in the top two-fifths..." *Id*.
- "...22 percent of Americans [raised in the bottom tenth of incomes stayed there as adults]." *Id*.
- "...26 percent of American men raised at the top tenth stayed there... ." *Id*.
- "About 36 percent of Americans raised in the middle fifth move up as adults, while 23 percent stay on the same rung and 41 percent move down... ." *Id*.

Do these numbers suggest lack of mobility to you? Did you, in believing the "myth," expect more?

Third, Stiglitz notes that there are studies indicating that the United States falls behind other developed countries in economic mobility. But, look at the studies. They expressly acknowledge that the methodology used may prejudice the United States. The other countries have more compressed income scales, so a much smaller absolute income gain will move children into a higher income category. (This factor could partly explain why some analyses find less mobility where there is more un-equality.) And, the analyses are intergenerational, requiring income data for both fathers and sons, thereby excluding many immigrants, who are particularly mobile in the United States. Also, the studies are based on fathers and sons, because that is the data available. Yet, women working is a very significant source of household mobility. *See, e.g.,* DeParle, "Harder for Americans to Rise From Lower Rungs"; Julia B. Isaacs, Isabel V. Sawhill, Ron Haskins, "Getting Ahead or Losing Ground: Economic Mobility in America", *The Brookings Institution*, February 2008. pp.37-45. Finally, these other countries tend to have more homogenous populations than the United States, making differences in family, upbringing and social environment less important determinants of outcome than here.

Fourth, Stigitz central argument is founded on a misrepresentation of the "American dream." The promise is not that every person will succeed; it is that ability, hard work and determination will pay off. That you can be anything you want, not that you will. That dreams followed by appropriate actions can be realized, not just dreams standing alone. As Isaacs, Sawhill, Haskins explain (emphasis added): "Since our nation's founding, the promise of economic opportunity has been a central component of the American Dream. An economy that ... held out **the promise that hard work, vision, and risk**—regardless of family background—**would be rewarded.**"

"Perhaps the most remarkable byproduct of the growth of the American economy over the past century has been steady growth in the share of Americans who have been able to achieve a comfortable life and have every hope of seeing their children do even better. ...Americans strongly believe that hard work and talent lead to economic success. This underlying belief in the fluidity of class and economic status has differentiated Americans from citizens in the majority of other developed nations." *Id.*

Finally, even Stiglitz' own sources conclude that there is significant mobility.

DeParle: "Even by measures of relative mobility, Middle America remains fluid. ...The 'stickiness' appears at the top and bottom, as affluent families transmit their advantages and poor families stay trapped."

Isaacs, Sawhill, Haskins: "We find considerable fluidity in American society. One's family background as a child, measured in terms of either income or wealth, has a relatively modest effect on one's subsequent success as an adult, especially if one grew up in middle-class circumstances. Those at the top or bottom of the ladder are somewhat less mobile."

Both statements contain probably the most important message for policy-makers. The poorest Americans are persistently the least mobile, at least on average. Of course, many of the most dramatic success stories came from the lowest economic rungs, but a large percentage of the poor stay poor. They seem trapped in a prison consisting of a toxic social environment, often coupled with neglectful or, even, abusive family circumstances. The children lack constructive examples and encouragement. The community in which they live cripples rather than empowers them.

The trap of the poorest is the real problem the country faces concerning economic opportunities. It will not be solved by redistribution of wealth or income. Or, helped by talk about inequality. So, where are the insightful discussions of possible solutions?

Stiglitz predicts: "...[A]s the reality sinks in, as most Americans finally grasp that the economic game is stacked against them, all of this is at risk. Alienation has begun to replace motivation. Instead of social cohesion we have a new divisiveness." *Id.*, p.20. Is that assertion really helpful? And, in fact, is it really right?

It appears that there are substantial numbers of Americans who still believe that hard work pays off. Recent survey data from *Echelon*

Insights says: "Strong progressives don't evidence much faith in upper mobility, endorsing the ... statement on the questionable efficacy of hard work by 88-12. Hispanic voters, on the other hand, embrace the view that hard-working people are likely to get ahead by 55-39, as do working class voters by 55-40." Ruy Teixeira, "Working Class and Hispanic Voters Are Losing Interest ... : White College-Educated Voters ... Are On Board," *The Liberal Patriot*, July 14, 2022.

And, it may be that Stiglitz has the causation reversed.

Those who believe will make greater efforts, are more likely to notice even small successes and are much more likely to attribute their successes to their efforts. The disillusioned are likely not to try, not to recognize progress and to put good things down to chance. Of course, the believers are more likely to succeed and the disillusioned are much more likely to fail, those of both groups thereby proving to themselves that they were right.

Is there evidence that effort makes a difference?

> "[In 2017,] [t]he average second-quintile household earned almost five times as much as the average household in the bottom quintile, because it **had 2.4 times as many working-age members working** and on average **each worker worked 80% more hours**. The average middle-quintile household earned almost 10 times as much and had 2.6 times the percentage of its working-age people working, **each working twice as many hours**. Yet the bottom 60% of American households received **essentially the same income** after accounting for taxes, transfer payments and household size."

Phil Gramm and John Early, "Income Equality, Not Inequality, Is the Problem," *WSJ.com*, August 29, 2022 (emphasis added).

There is the challenge to.the American Dream.

AN INEQUITABLE "LEG UP"?

Suddenly, legacy admissions have become a hot topic. Presumably, this obsession was caused by the Supreme Court's decision about affirmative action: if a college cannot give admission preference based on race, why should it be allowed to give preference based on one's ancestor having graduated from there? Of course, the relevant question really is: why not?

I address this question by asking and answering two other questions.

- First, what, if any, objectives may be served by legacy admissions?
- Second, does admission to a"prestige"college give one a "leg up" in life?

I submit that "legacy" admissions are legitimate, can serve useful purposes and should be permitted.

Note: I am assuming that the legacy admissions meet the academic standards of the institution (are not mediocre).

The Why of Legacy Admissions

Legacy admissions, like early decision, provide useful predictability and stability in class selection. Some control is needed. I cannot help but notice that collecting acceptances has become something of a "thing." The current record, I believe, is 127 acceptances and $8 million of financial aid offers. This behavior benefits no one (apart from the applicant's "jollies" from the 15 minutes of fame).

Legacy admissions can improve balance. The inclusion of students with family connections to the institution who are more likely to recognize the institution's personality and values can strengthen a class. Also, I think it good to have a significant number of regular "guys" (in those days). Not all "stars" in some field (athletics, music, art, science, *etc.*) Legacies are not the only source of that kind of balance. I think that was why I (not a legacy) was admitted. I knew some legacies and I think that they made my class better, stronger and more interesting. Of course, I cannot know what the alternative class would have been like, so let's just say that the legacies made a positive contribution. Balance or mix. I would question the wisdom of a class of all first generation college students.

Legacy admissions strengthens family bounds (as experienced by many in my class whose children attended Amherst) and adds something meaningful to the various communities. Of course, it also promotes giving and giving back.

If the purpose is to teach a small number of qualified kids critical thinking, open mindedness, tolerance and an awareness of and respect for the grandeur of the Western tradition, legacies have as much need for that teaching as anyone else.

A Note on Supposed Origins

Look at this: Erin Blakemore, "Why do colleges have legacy admissions? It started as a way to keep out Jews: Standardized tests. Interviews. Extracurricular activities. In the early 20th century, universities used these tactics to ensure their students were predominantly Protestant,"

National Geographic, July 28, 2023.

Note that that headline refers only to legacy admissions. But, the listed ways to keep out Jews are "Standardized tests. Interviews. Extracurricular activities." Not legacy admissions. The body of the article provides support for the claim that the intention to limit Jewish acceptances motivated the adoption of new application requirements, especially requirements that facilitated the identification of applicants who were Jewish, so that the schools could better discriminate. "Robert Nelson Corwin, Yale's admissions chairman, in 1922[,] ... recommended that Yale implement 'non-intellectual requirements,' including letters of recommendation, in-person interviews, and psychological testing, to limit its number of Jews."

But, as for legacy admissions, the only thing the author cites is the following:

"'All properly qualified sons of Dartmouth alumni and Dartmouth College officers will be accepted,' wrote Dartmouth College in its alumni magazine in 1922..., promising that it would prioritize 'men who plainly possess the qualities of leadership or qualities of outstanding promise' over those 'qualified by high scholarship ranks but with no evidence of positive qualities otherwise.'"

It is clear that many colleges in the 1920s discriminated against Jews and did so directly. Legacy preferences, however, would be an unlikely tool for doing so, since most of the established universities had Jewish graduates. Yet, the article singles out legacy admissions. Why?

My research suggests that this characterization of the origins of legacy admissions arose in 2011 in an "academic" journal article. Deborah L. Coe, James D. Davidson, "The Origins of Legacy Admissions: A Sociological Explanation," *Review of Religious Research*, Vol. 52, No. 3

(March 2011), pp. 233-247. It was picked up by the *New York Times* years later (September 7, 2019, editorial). The assertion is now treated as fact and as common knowledge.

I have read the article.

The authors purported to use an established sociological methodology ("a conflict approach") to investigate the issue. First, they cite evidence that certain prestigious Northeastern universities engaged in acknowledged efforts to restrict the number of Jewish students admitted, including through the use of quotas. Then, they opine: "it is reasonable to believe that legacy admissions were yet another way members of elite Protestant denominations prevented their church-affiliated schools from being overrun by Jews... ." Reasonable to believe?

To "test" their hypothesis, they asked four questions:

1. Were legacy admissions first introduced at Protestant institutions?
2. Were they introduced in the late 19th or early 20th centuries?
3. Were they first introduced in the Northeast where more minorities lived?
4. Did they appear at schools where applications from Jews and Catholics were increasing?

Allegedly, if the answers are all "yes", then "we can conclude that the data support our theoretical argument." Seriously?

The authors report that the first appearance of legacy admissions was in the Ivy League, 62% of which had Protestant historical ties (5 of 8). (Rather ambiguous to me, but enough to satisfy the authors.) Lacking information on the origins of the practice (except for Dartmouth, 1922, and Yale, 1925), the authors noted that the percentages of legacies among students were higher in the 1930s than in the 1920s, concluding that their second test was met. The third test was whether the practice arose in regions where there were significant minorities. They observed that the Ivy League schools were all in the Northeast and Middle Atlantic regions where more minorities (and more Protestants) lived (which areas were also the first settled). As for the fourth test, the authors found that the percentages of Jewish and Catholic students was increasing at the 4 Ivy institutions located in major metropolitan areas (4 of 8).

> "Thus, we argue that legacy admissions have been an important element in the persistence of stratification in general and religious stratification in particular."

The authors even expressed surprise that, following the 1920s, legacy admissions preferences spread across the country to colleges that do not meet the authors' criteria, including to public universities and Catholic universities (but, without even acknowledging that that fact undercut their conclusion). They noted that the institutions' proffered reasons for the practice were improved fundraising, the promotion of tradition and loyalty and the maintenance of student diversity (not based just on test scores). But, indicating their skepticism, they invited further research to test empirically those claims.

However:

- The original colleges in the U.S. were established by Protestant denominations in order to educate future clergy;
- Until the 20th century, these schools had to hunt for students—there was little competition for admission;
- Very late in the 19th century, the demand for higher education, especially at prestige institutions, started growing rapidly;
- The prestige institutions were the oldest (*i.e.*, Protestant);
- Those schools became increasingly selective as applicants outnumbered places;

- The number of legacy applicants grew rapidly in the 1920s, as the children of alumni reached the age to apply.

Given the facts, is it possible, even probable, that legacy admissions were introduced by institutions that were experiencing competition for admissions and that had a substantial alumni body? And, further, that that happened when those conditions existed—thus, spreading across the country—and for the reasons colleges claim?

The article is a disgrace for the social sciences, yet its conclusion has been cited, with and without attribution, by the *New York Times*, *National Geographic* and, most recently, *The Guardian* (11 August 2023). So much for a competent press.

The Consequences?

Certain facts have been statistically well-established and known:

- "The average or mean income of people who attended prestige colleges is no higher than the mean income of people with comparable academic credentials from secondary school who did not attend a prestige college but went to a state college."
- A disproportionate number of children of high income parents (top 3-5%) attend prestige colleges.

So, the big news?

"New research published this morning from three economists ... confirms that these kids do indeed become elites. Compared with attending one of the best public colleges, attending an Ivy or another super-selective private school **increases a student's chance of reaching the top of the earnings distribution by 60 percent...** . These schools 'amplify the persistence of privilege across generations'... ."

Annie Lowrey, "Why You Have To Care About These 12 Colleges: Change them, and you change America," *The Atlantic,* July 24, 2023 (emphasis added).

The study is: Raj Chetty, David J. Deming, John N. Friedman, "Diversifying Society's Leaders? The Causal Effects of Admision to Highly Selective Private Colleges," *National Bureau of Economic Research,* July 2023.

NPR and *Planet Money* find the conclusions of the study significant (no, exhilarating: "We at Planet Money have already dubbed Raj Chetty the Beyoncé of Economics because of his long list of popular hits in empirical economics. And, let me tell you, this is another Flawless classic in his catalog"), because the conclusions are thought to confirm their preconceptions.

The study posed some challenging questions, especially for a statistical analysis.

"First, how much of the disproportionate representation of students from high-income families at highly selective private colleges is **driven by preferential admissions** practices vs. student choices about where to apply and matriculate?

"Second, do such colleges **have a causal effect on students' post-college outcomes,** or would the students they admit have done equally well if they had attended other colleges?"

(Emphasis added.)

Althoughr, the authors collected a frightening amount of information (social security numbers, income, parental income, test scores); the resulting analysis is very complicated, requiring a host of assumptions and many extrapolations.

But, before examining the methodology, let's look at the conclusions, taking them at face value.

- "Two-thirds of the difference in enrollment rates at Ivy-Plus colleges by parental income can be explained by **higher admissions rates for students from high-income families.**"
- "[T]he higher admissions rates at the schools attended by children from high-income families arise entirely from differences in non-academic rather than academic factors."
- "Students' credentials at the point of college application depend on many factors that are associated with parental income, such as the quality of K-12 schools, the neighborhoods in which they grow up, and family inputs. Since highly selective colleges typically seek to admit students with the strongest credentials, these disparities in childhood environment contribute to differences in children's chances of attending highly selective colleges."

- "SAT/ACT scores differ sharply by parental income, with children from high-income families having much greater chances of scoring at the top of the distribution than those from lower-income families. Even holding fixed test scores, there are still large differences in students' chances of attending Ivy-Plus colleges by parental income."
- "Children from families in the top 1% have a substantially higher chance of reaching the top 1% of the income distribution after college than those from lower-income families even among Ivy-Plus attendees." *See* Figure A.27: Share of Ivy-Plus Attendees in Top 1% of Income Distribution at Age 33 by Parental Income.

(Emphasis added.)

Yet,

- There is no observable relationship between an Ivy-Plus education and mean income or reaching the top quintile ("we find very small impacts of attending an Ivy-Plus on average earnings").
- "[W]e find [only] a **small and statistically insignificant impact** of admission from the waitlist on mean earning ranks and the probability of reaching the top quartile of the income distribution... ."
- An impact on outcomes is found in only a very narrow slice—the likelihood of being in the top 1% by income. "Relative to those rejected from the waitlist, applicants admitted from the waitlist are significantly more likely to reach the top 1% of the income distribution... ." That is the result Lowrey reports. Ivy-Plus attendance supposedly boosts one's odds of reaching the top 1% from about 10% to some 15%, an almost 60% improvement.
- "[T]he causal impacts of Ivy-Plus colleges are concentrated entirely in reaching the upper tail of the distribution... ." *See* Figure 12, "Treatment Effects of Ivy-Plus Admissions, by Age" (a) Share in Top 1% "Waitlist Rejects Waitlist Admits." "[S]tudents

admitted from the waitlist are 5 percentage points more likely to reach the top 1% at age 33 than those who are rejected."

- "Although we reject the null hypothesis that admission to any Ivy-Plus college has no effect on the share of students reaching the top 1% at age 33, **the confidence interval for the point estimate ... is quite wide**. The reason the estimate is imprecise is that we observe outcomes at age 33 for relatively few cohorts in our sample."

(Emphasis added.)

Moreover,

- "Attending an Ivy-Plus college instead of a state flagship university has a similar and positive effect along the entire parental income distribution."
- "These estimates imply that about 60% of difference in the share who reach the top 1% ... between individuals who attended Ivy-Plus colleges *vs*. highly selective state flagships is due to the causal effect of Ivy-Plus colleges, with the remaining 40% driven by the fact that Ivy-Plus colleges select stronger students."

So,

- There is no positive relationship between being a legacy and success. "[L]egacy status and the other factors that lead to higher admissions rates for students from high-income families are uncorrelated with post-college outcomes... . Ivy-Plus applicants' chances of reaching the top 1% after college are essentially unrelated to legacy status or their non-academic ratings." *See* Figure A.23 (a) Association Between Predicted Top 1% and Admissions Criteria.

Think of that. Legacy preferences result in more wealthy students in Ivy-Plus schools. And, Ivy-Plus students are more likely to be "successes." Yet, legacies are **not** more likely to be "successes".

Curious. Why an effect only in the very tail? We find some hints in the methodology employed.

Methodology

The first problem was how to identify groups to compare where the only difference is Ivy-Plus attendance. The solution adopted was to use only wait-listed applicants, presuming that they all have similar credentials. "We first focus on the subset of applicants who are waitlisted at a given college and are thus on the margin for admission;" then, to compare the futures of those from the waitlist who were admitted (and who attended) with the futures of those from the waitlist who were rejected. A rather narrow portion of the students in the study. The authors just assumed that the dynamics of waitlist decisions are the same as those of the initial admissions decision. (But. "[a] practical complication in implementing this test is that some colleges make strategic decisions to admit students from their waitlists to manage yield.")

In addition, the analysis was based on student matriculation, not graduation.

The next problem was how to measure outcomes. The authors adopted a three-part standard: income (the top 1% for the age group), attendance at an elite graduate school or employment at an elite or prestige firm. The elite and prestige firms were defined as firms that had a demonstrated preference for Ivy-Plus graduates. Not surprisingly, such firms were found to have hired Ivy-Plus attendees more often (attendance being a prerequisite for graduation). Attendance at the identified graduate schools was also higher among Ivy-Plus attendees, which I suggest is a result heavily reflecting self selection by the students and graduate schools.

For income (and the other standards), the authors only had data through age 25. They concluded that one's situation at age 25 was too early for judging life success. So, they projected income at age 33. (Obviously, still way too early.) Interestingly, of the wait-listed group, the accepted students had slightly higher incomes at 25 and 26, very similar incomes at 27 and 28, then increasingly higher incomes until 33. "The difference is near 0 at age 25 and grows steadily with age, indicating that those admitted to Ivy-Plus colleges are placed on a different wage trajectory relative to those who are rejected."

But, the differential at 33 is due to the different **assumed** income trajectories for the two groups. If the trajectories were exchanged, then the results would be reversed. And, the trajectories appear to be based upon an assumed faster income growth for those employed at "elite" and "prestige" firms.

"**We estimate** that attending an Ivy-Plus college instead of a highly selective state flagship increases a student's predicted chance of reaching the top 1% [at age 33] **based on their age 25 employer** from 10.4% to 15.0%."

...

"Because the samples defined above focus on relatively recent cohorts, **they do not allow us to examine earnings and other outcomes after age 25.** We address this limitation by **building prediction models for long-term outcomes based on the shorter-term proxies (*e.g.*, initial employer)** that we observe at age 25 in our main analysis samples."

...

"Because income ranks do not stabilize until graduates are in their early thirties, we use data on individuals' employers and graduate schools **to predict incomes at age 33.**"

(Emphasis added.)

Another important point concerns the conclusion that about 2/3s of the acceptance advantage for students of well off parents is due to legacy admissions. The difficulty with that conclusion is that we do not know how many of the legacies would have been admitted without legacy preferences. Surely, some; perhaps, many. In addition, the study shows that the most significant differences in acceptance rates for legacies occurs among those whose parents are wealthy or poor (being a legacy seems to be a disadvantage if your parents are middle income).

"[T]he legacy advantage is particularly large among high-income families."

"[A]ttendance conditional on application ris[es] sharply in the upper tail of the income distribution at Ivy-Plus colleges and other highly selective private colleges, but virtually flat or even slightly downward sloping at flagship public colleges. This pattern again holds systematically across colleges within each of the three groups... ."

Is it just possible that some Ivy-Plus colleges give acceptance preference to children of very wealthy parents, whether legacies or not? **Just, maybe.**

As to outcomes, we see not very robust results based upon pretty questionable assumptions. Not something an objective observer would celebrate.

In fact, the study finds that the only predictor of success, as defined, is one's academic qualifications, not legacy or athletic status! Therefore, the policy suggestion is to base acceptances on standardized test scores to maximize the number of graduates in the top 1%.

> "Both objective and subjective measures of academic qualifications are highly predictive of students' post-college success, with **predictive power comparable in magnitude to the causal effects of attending an Ivy-Plus college** instead of a state flagship college. However, **the other (non-academic) factors that are responsible for the higher admissions rates of students from high-income families do not predict** (or, if anything, negatively predict) the measures of post-college success we consider."

> "[O]ur results raise questions about the **equity implications of holistic evaluation policies**. Highly selective public colleges that follow more standardized processes to evaluate applications exhibit smaller disparities in admissions rates by parental income than private colleges that use more holistic evaluations."

(Emphasis added.)

Let's keep our priorities straight!

Moreover, the authors point out: "[B]ecause Ivy-Plus colleges account for less than 1% of total college enrollment and have little impact on average incomes, creating more social mobility through higher education requires changes at the colleges that serve most students (*e.g.*, community colleges)."

Maybe Harvard and Yale are stepping stones to wealth and power, but most other "prestige" colleges are not. Ending legacy admissions at Harvard and Yale may provide some others access (other wealthy students?), but I think that long-term it will primarily reduce the role of those institutions in feeding the power structure. Many undoubtedly would think that a good thing. I am not so sure. But, it would reduce inequality: equality of opportunity, not of results. Some different students will get into Harvard and Yale and some students will not. Their admission will be less significant, because Harvard and Yale will be less significant. But, inequality of results is not likely to change much. Just somewhat different people will be the rich and powerful.

Will that be an improvement?

I don't know, but I doubt it.

CHAPTER V

Taxation

A PROPOSAL FOR REFORM

There are many social and policy problems that present true dilemmas, sometimes because of deep, irreconcilable differences in values, sometimes because of a genuine lack of understanding (of the facts and/or of the relevant causal relationships) and sometimes because of both. Tax does not seem to me to be one of those subjects. Take out personal interest and any non-tax political agenda and identify the legitimate goals of tax policy, the answers suggest themselves.

Setting the Stage

PROPER GOALS OF A TAX SYSTEM

We want our tax system to reflect certain objectives in addition to suf- ficient revenue collection. First, the system should be generally fair (an income tax should tax actual income and do so on a reasonable basis reflecting some combination of benefits received, ability to pay and consumption of society's resources). Second, the system should minimize the distortion of the allocation of resources and the incentives to engage in wasteful and nonproductive activities. Third, the system should be designed and implemented so that compliance is high (with opportunities to cheat or evade tax as limited as reasonably possible). Finally, the system should give most of the population a stake in the costs of the operation of government. An additional objective advocated by many is that the system be progressive (for the explicit purpose of redistributing income).

The first three of these objectives would probably be pretty widely accepted. Most people would likely agree that it would be better if a significant portion of our national human resources (and our individual time) were not spent in tax planning or "gaming" the tax system and that there be a high degree of compliance with the rules that are in place. The reductions of wasted resources, gaming and cheating could all be promoted by a system that is simple, with a minimum of special provisions and "loopholes". They will also be promoted by lower marginal rates, making the gaming and cheating less profitable.

A smaller, but probably still a large, number of people would agree that tax incentives that redirect investment and efforts into less productive activities are undesirable, at least in theory. Obviously, there is support for tax incentives designed to encourage socially useful activity. The problem is that, in my opinion, such social planning often has consequences other than what was intended. Moreover, programs that offer money or benefits from the government clearly encourage gaming and manipulation, as well as fraud and corruption.

The other two objectives—a broad base and a progressive structure —may be subject to more debate. I do not intend to engage in such debate here. My interest is simply in outlining the implications for tax policy if one accepts these objectives. My proposals below would result in a very progressive tax system with a broad base.

I do not consider an analysis of who benefits most or least from tax pro- visions to be a legitimate tax policy consideration. It certainly should not be the only or primary criterion by which a tax bill is judged, as it was for critics of the 2017 Act. If the structure is right, the allocation of burdens can be adjusted through the tax rates.

DIFFICULTIES WITH DATA

Before undertaking that analysis, however, I want to comment briefly on some issues concerning data and facts. We can discuss certain of the "rules," like the marginal tax rates for various groups or particular deductions or special rates (*e.g.*, capital gains) in the abstract; but, it can also be interesting to see what is happening in practice. For that investigation, however, we need to know what people actually pay on what they actually receive.

Such information would seem to be especially important for discussions of the consequences of different tax rates in different countries, since the relationship between the rates on the books and the amounts actually paid varies significantly from country to country. The reasons involve attitudes toward and practices concerning compliance and enforcement, as well as differences in the treatment of different geographical sources of income and the rules concerning tax residency. For example, the United States taxes its citizens on worldwide income; many other countries do not.

For many reasons, we would also want to know the amounts of income received but not captured by the system, such as the income arising in the cash or black-market economy, the unreported income of non-employees and the non-taxed "perks" provided to employees (cars, lunches, childcare, *etc.*).

Much of this information is simply not available. The gaps in knowledge of the facts become particularly great in efforts to compare the situations in different nations, but they are still very serious within the U.S. Thus, much of the more inflamed rhetoric about taxes can and should be dismissed simply on the basis of its reliance on unreliable data.

Revisions the The Current System

There are, of course, several proposals for the radical restructuring of our tax system. Those proposals could be analyzed using the same criteria discussed above. At this time, however, I shall be addressing our current structure and suggesting "modest" revisions that, in my opinion, would dramatically improve the functioning of the system.

PAYROLL AND INCOME TAXES

I am assuming as a primary objective that everyone, within reason, should pay income tax and, thereby, have some financial "skin" in the choices among government policies and programs.

To that end, I would eliminate payroll taxes on employees. They are premised, I think most agree, on a seriously misleading characterization of Social Security as a personal savings plan, and they are simply a compli- cation that confuses the analysis of tax burdens. The "contributions" are not deductible and the subsequent payments are fully taxed. The tax also burdens earned income specifically. Moreover, the payroll tax, including the charge for Medicare, invites avoidance. *See, e.g.,* Christy Bieber, "Biden's Tax Returns Show Why His Payroll Tax Plan May Not Save Social Security," *The Motley Fool,* September 13, 2020 ("To understand the problem with Biden's plan to raise payroll taxes, you just need to take a look at his tax returns from 2017 and 2018. They show how the Bidens were able to avoid paying hundreds of thousands of dollars in payroll taxes that fund Medicare.") These taxes are also frequently evaded in the cash ("off-the-books") economy by small businesses and individuals.

Then, I would impose a minimum 10% income tax on all income above a relatively modest personal exemption (say $10,000 per person, capped at $40,000 for a family). Further, as a matter of fairness, I would have progressive rates above the 10% minimum Personally, I think it is oppressive to be taxed more than one-third of one's income, but I recognize that we probably need higher rates to generate sufficient revenue. So, I would propose a top rate of 35%, with a special 50% rate imposed on in- come above $10 million a year. I justify this special rate on the debatable ground that certain income levels are just outside of the norms by which we should determine policy. Where the steps between 10% and 35% occur should be a matter of meeting legitimate revenue needs.

I would prefer, thereafter, that increases in the Federal budget that require more tax revenue be met by proportional increases in all marginal rates (say 10%, bringing the bottom rate to 11% and the top rate to 38.5%). In that way, we would all share the burden of more spending.

DEDUCTIONS

Deductions are obviously controversial, because many individual interests are at stake.

As one of the many supposed beneficiaries of the 2017 Tax Act who pay significantly more income tax as a result of the Act, I understand the appeal of deductions for state and local income taxes (if such taxes are essentially based upon total adjusted gross income), on the grounds that income taxes imposed by any source reduce income and the ability to consume (unlike sales taxes or a VAT-type tax, both of which effectively tax consumption). However, to address the question rationally, one must decide which is the first or primary tax. It is the secondary income tax where the deduction for taxes paid belongs. Thus, if the state or locality taxed Federal net after-tax income only (allowing a deduction for Federal income taxes paid), then a Federal deduction would not be appropriate.

One should view a 10% state income tax on AGI as really a 16.2% tax on net income, assuming a 38% Federal rate. And, the higher the Federal rate, the higher the effective state net rate will be. Perhaps this way of looking at the issue would be useful. I think that most would view the Federal tax as primary. This approach also identifies the real burdens of state and local taxes.

There is no reason to allow an income tax deduction for local property taxes. Like the mortgage interest deduction, it is just a subsidy for home ownership.

(House Democrats seek to restore larger deductions for state and local income and property taxes, eliminating the Trump tax increase on high earners in high-tax states, like me.)

I would allow deductions for charitable contributions, but I would eliminate the benefits from contributing appreciated assets. The deduction should be limited to the basis in the asset (or the appreciation should be recognized at the time of the contribution). Not only would such a rule be fair, it would reduce controversies over valuation. But, I would phase out the mortgage deduction or, at least, limit it to principle residences (with only one per family) and impose a lower cap (say $250,000 of debt). Similarly, I would eliminate the deduction for property taxes.

CAPITAL GAINS

With respect to capital gains (and dividend income, next), I look to what I consider to be the stronger fairness arguments that have been made.

A capital asset held for a long period will generally have suffered a serious impact from inflation. Thus, the apparent gain is often largely not gain at all. The relevant test is what would the sale price realized enable the seller to buy in terms of some representative basket of goods. If the basket has not increased in size, then how can one say that the seller had income?

This consideration may not be of particular relevance with respect to certain types of capital gain, however. Someone who invests $10,000 in a startup business and ends up with stock worth $10,000,000 after a few years has clearly enjoyed significant gain. There may be policy reasons for preferential tax rates on such gain, but the inflation factor is not one of them. In contrast, the person who buys a house for $200,000 and sells it for $350,000 some 30 years later may have actually lost money on the investment.

Indexing the cost basis for inflation and taxing the resulting gain at normal ordinary income rates would be the fairest solution. It would also happen to eliminate the current issues about "carried interests" and stock options, since there would be little or no cost basis to index. (For the purist, gain should be recognized on long-term debt as reduced by inflation.)

Absent indexing, I would suggest a capital gain tax rate of half the other- wise applicable income tax rate for assets held for at least 3 years and 25% of the otherwise applicable rate for assets held for at least 10 years. Gains on sales of assets held less than 3 years should be ordinary income. Thus, much of the speculative trading would be treated as ordinary-income-generating activity. In addition, I would treat "carried interests" as ordinary income, taxed when realized. None of the fairness arguments for capital gains applies to such compensation, which is received for services rendered and is not based on a capital asset subject to inflation risk. The same approach would apply to all stock options and other incentive compensation schemes.

DIVIDENDS

The argument against taxing dividends is that the income has already been taxed once at the corporate level. The solution I propose is to provide the corporation with a deduction from current income for dividends paid during the tax year. To the recipient, the dividend would be ordinary income. If the corporation elects to hold or invest the income (or use the funds for stock buybacks), then it would be taxed on that income as a result of that decision. In such a case, the corporation would retain the benefit of the income generated. If the income is subsequently distributed as a dividend, it would be taxed again to the recipient, but I would argue that there would have been two taxable events in that case, justifying two taxes.

BUSINESS TAXES

Publicly-traded corporations should be taxed at a low rate (say 20%), with a deduction for dividends paid, as discussed above.

These corporations should also be taxed on the same accounting basis that they use to report results. I suggest that their fiscal year should also be their tax year. Eliminating the two sets of books would result in cost savings, the incentives for managers would be better aligned (currently, there are strong incentives to have low income for tax purposes and high income for stock market purposes) and resources devoted to tax "planning" would be reduced.

"Corporations are required to report income to investors according to generally accepted accounting principles, which are set by the private standards-setting Financial Accounting Standards Board (FASB). But Congress writes the tax code. Most differences between financial and taxable income were created by Congress to encourage certain business spending. These include tax credits for research and development, green energy and low-income housing. ..[Also,] accelerated depreciation, which lets companies immediately expense investment in equipment. This contrasts with financial accounting, which requires companies to depreciate assets roughly tracking their decline in productivity."

The Editorial Board, "Kyrsten Sinema Reads the Book Tax," *WSJ.com*, August 4, 2022.

For all privately-held corporations or limited-liability entities (as well as all unincorporated businesses), I would tax the owners on the income as if they were in a partnership, with no tax on the entity itself. Thus, the earnings would all be taxed at the individual earned income rates applied to the percentage ownerships. To the extent that earnings are retained in the entity, the cost bases of the owners would be increased. The deduction for pass-through entities (currently 20%) should be eliminated. It has no justification. Under this approach, I think that certain abuses could be more clearly isolated and discouraged (including the payroll tax issue mentioned above).

Finally, much stricter rules should be imposed concerning the allocation of income among countries of operation. I would simply require that for multinational corporate groups (companies with, say, more than 50% common ultimate ownership) operating in the United States (regardless of domicile), the income allocated to the US be no less as a percentage of total income than the revenues derived in the US represents as a percentage of total revenues of the group. Thus, the repatriation of earnings from abroad to the United States would not be a taxable event. Also, the choice of location for the "headquarters" or the incorporation of the entity would not be influenced by US income tax.

ESTATE TAXES

My preference, based on reasons like those set forth concerning the income tax, would be either to eliminate the estate tax or to have an exemption of $20 million, with a rate applied to the next $30 million of 25% and a rate of 40% for amounts above $50 million. If the amount of the exemption were to be raised and the rate lowered as suggested, I would eliminate the marital deduction.

For appreciated assets subject to the estate tax (40%), a stepped-up basis for the beneficiaries makes sense. It is excessive to tax the gain again when the asset is sold. However, elimination of the stepped-up basis would reduce some of the perceived need for the estate tax. So, I suggest that for estates not subject to the estate tax, appreciated assets, like individually-owned businesses (including farms) and family homes, be included in the estate at their cost bases (not at their fair market value). The gain would be taxed (at applicable capital gains rates, based upon combined ownership periods) only when the asset is sold and the gain realized by the beneficiaries. (Note, this approach is very different from President Biden's current proposal.)

VARIOUS OTHER MATTERS

I would liberalize the rules concerning retirement plans. As long as there are requirements restricting the access to the funds or penalizing early withdrawals, I would continue to allow the gains to accrue tax-free. The limits on the annual contributions should be raised (say to $500,000), with only a much lower amount to be deductible (say $10,000). When distributions are allowed, they should be treated as return of capital (for the after-tax contributions) and as ordinary income (for the gain and the deductible portions). I also favor more regulations to discourage the cash or black market economy. To some extent, at the same time, lower, fairer tax rates would promote compliance and make avoidance and evasion less appealing.

I would also favor an alternative minimum 20% tax on all AGIs in excess of $500,000 and the elimination of the current Alternative Minimum Tax.

Lastly, I would support the elimination of all tax subsidies and incentives. (I have no issue with the taxing of undesirable activities or of activities with externalities that the market cannot capture, but such taxes should not be characterized as income taxes.) If it is decided that an activity should be subsidized, it should be done so directly rather than through the income tax system. The allocative distortions will be less, the cost more clearly revealed and the decision to subsidize more transparent.

Concluding Comments

The main benefits that I see from my proposals are:

- the favorable realignment of incentives affecting behavior and the allocation of society's resources;
- increased simplicity, reducing compliance costs and uncertainty;
- more and better compliance, because of clarity and lower costs;
- greater fairness and
- the presentation to voters of a more rational choice as to the impact of increased government spending—it will be harder to push the costs on to others and increased spending would have an impact on a greater percentage of the electorate.

Of course, the current Biden plan is quite different in detail and philosophy. Its focus is primarily on who pays, presuming that 'fairness" is only a matter of relative tax burden—with the more skewed or progressive, the "fairer," with certain exceptions for Democratic strongholds. This proposed plan achieves none of the objectives with which I started, not even the generation of sufficient revenue. It offers none of the benefits of my proposals. As a matter public policy, it is myopic—a monument to political expediency.

THE CURRENT POLITICAL CLIMATE

There is now near hysteria among parts of the media and various politicians over income and wealth inequality, which has led to a focus on taxes. The rich do not pay their "fair share."

Tax Avoidance

In 2021, *ProPublica* combed through a "trove" of illegally disclosed IRS information about wealthy Americans to expose how the rich "avoid" paying taxes. The result makes no claim of finding tax evasion, nor even shady tax avoidance. Instead, it "discovers," for example, that of the rare entrepreneurs (out of millions) who are extraordinarily success-ful, a handful choose not to "cash in" but maintain ownership of the companies they founded and built. Not surprisingly, these individuals now are many of the ultra-wealthy. Also, not surprisingly, those few paid little income tax relative to their enormous wealth. Of course, had these individuals sold much of their interests early, they would be much less wealthy today and would have paid much more in tax. And, other people would be wealthier today if they had sold their investments and paid tax, rather than holding on while the values dropped.

As for the policy implications, would we all really be better off if the successful individuals had "cashed out"? If these ultra-wealthy continue to hold these assets until death, a 40% estate tax will be due on the fair market value, unless they utilize the "loophole" of giving the assets to charity (which many ultra-wealthy today are pledging to do). Would we all really be better off if that money goes to the government instead?

All that was news for me was the assertion that in the 1920s, the Congressional decision not to tax as income unrealized capital gains was highly controversial because it created a major "loophole": Build a successful company, borrow against it, then die, leaving it to charity. Wow. You might wonder why not everyone does it. *ProPublica* also "found" a technique to avoid tax that does not require dying. Before you are wealthy, create a Roth IRA, buy some very, very cheap assets that will subsequently soar in value, watch your investment grow tax free, then withdraw the money tax free after you turn 59 1/2. We should all have done so.

These examples reflect totally legal behavior. The fact that tax was (legally) avoided is almost coincidental. These remarkable situations did not arise through astute tax planning. They arose because a few people were extraordinarily lucky or extraordinarily astute or both. Of course, the rules can be changed, but one should not base tax policy on or for the flukes or the exceptional cases.

Tax "Evasion"

The media in mid-2021 has also been full of stories proclaiming that the rich evade taxes more than others. The assertion is based on a working paper published earlier in the year: John Guyton, Patrick Langetieg, Daniel Reck, Max Risch, Gabriel Zucman, "Tax Evasion at the Top of the Income Distribution: Theory and Evidence," *equitablegrowth.org*, March 2021. That paper hardly establishes the proposition.

The authors conclude that two methods of evasion most difficult for auditors to find are off-shore bank accounts (significantly reduced today by new reporting requirements) and abuse of pass-through business entities, which the authors say are most used by the rich. The support is that the reported income by pass-through entities is heavily weighted in favor of those with the highest reported income.

What we are interested in, instead, is the unreported income. Small business owners use pass-through entities, and they are numerous. Do they underreport income? Of course. There are also other sources of unreported income that are difficult to detect on audit, like the "cash economy" and illegal activities (crime). These sources logically are more likely to be enjoyed by the less rich in terms of reported income. The "cash economy" is estimated at 10-13% of GDP. Criminal proceeds, including fraud, is probably as much. So, 20-26% of additional GDP. The top quintile in reported income represents about 60% of the total. Assuming the other 4 quintiles report 40% of the income and these types of unreported income goes mainly to them, the actual in- come of the 4 lower quintiles goes up by some 40-50%.

The authors correctly observe that the current income categories are based on reported income only. The members of each category would change if unreported income were included. That is, the identities of many of the "rich" would be different.

Indeed, the failure to report income is probably much more common among those who are not rich by reported income than among those who are. The authors seem to realize that, but do not explore what it means. So, in short, the media consensus view of tax evasion by those who the media thinks are the rich is false. In September 2021, the Treasury Department stated: "Today, the 'tax gap'—the difference be- tween taxes that are owed and collected—totals around $600 annually... . The tax gap can be a major source of inequity. ... [E]stimates from academic researchers suggest that more than $160 billion lost annually is from taxes that top 1 percent choose not to pay." Natasha Sarin, "The Case for a Robust Attack on the Tax Gap," September 7, 2021. The Commissioner of the IRS recently testified before Congress that the tax gap may be as high as $1 trillion.

So, the top 1% may account for 16% to 27% of the total tax gap. But, the top 1% receives over 20% of the reported income and pays 40% of the total income taxes. Thus, the alleged $160 billion is neither "excessive" nor "unequal" on its face! The claims about tax evasion increasing inequality are simply unsupported. Moreover, much more could be gained by closing the gap for the 99%. Ironically, the Treasury proclaims: "The Administration has been clear that audit rates will not rise relative to recent years for those with under $400,000 in actual income." *Id*. But, absent the audits, the IRS will not know the actual incomes, only the reported. The message is clear: a straight forward invitation to evade tax! We can agree that among those with similar actual incomes, those who do not report much of it will be richer than those who do report.

We may conclude that the "rich" evade more taxes than the non-rich; but the rich are just not who we think they are. And, so-called "tax cuts for the rich" are really tax cuts for those who pay taxes. You cannot cut taxes for those who pay none already.

"Fair Share"

Now for "fair shares". The top 1% pays 40% of total collected individual income taxes, the top 20% pays 80%, the bottom 40-60% pays effectively 0%. Are those shares fair?

Is it "fair" for more than 40% of the population to pay nothing for the protections and services of the Federal government? (It is certainly not good for representative government.) The top 1% receives over 20% (and the top 20% receives some 60%) of the reported income. Does that tell you what is "fair"? What might be informative would be the percentages of income paid in taxes by the big-time lawyers making $3-5 million a year, the CEOs making $10-20 million and the fund managers making $50-100 million. Or, even all the members of the 1%, excluding the top 0.01%. The answer is probably between 30% and 40% of total income. That might make for a more relevant comparison with the average worker.

What is clearly not fair is the amount of taxes paid by those who do not report their income. On that, most of us can agree. So, we should try to reduce tax evasion. But, increased marginal tax rates will not help that problem. It would probably aggravate it. And, more audits focused on the persons with high reported income, as is being advocated, is not the answer. The important types of evasion, we have discussed, are not easily found through audits. Moreover, persons with high reported income are probably not the serious tax evaders.

CHAPTER VI

"Indigenous" Americans

THE FIRST AMERICANS

I have been reading some popular books describing new discoveries about the early days of the Americas. This revised history rings true, and it is a different story than the one I learned.

In this and the next chapter, I rely heavily on Pekka Hämäläinen, *Indigenous Continent: The Epic Contest for North America* (2022)—a most comprehensive study. Its reviews were somewhat mixed, partly reflecting competitive rivalry and significantly reflecting political agendas (facts again unnecessarily intruding upon "correct" orthodoxy). None challenge his facts, however—only his choices of adjectives and verbs and his decision to end this history in the 1880s, covering only 400 years. The review that I found most balanced and insightful is by Daniel Immerwahr, from which I quote at the end of this section.

---

1. The Americas were settled by people migrating from Asia, over land and by water across the Bering Straits and down the western coastline of the continent, perhaps the first some 30,000 years

ago. These First Americans were largely everywhere in the Western Hemisphere by 12,000 years ago.

- "Indians were here far longer than previously thought, these researchers believe, and in much greater numbers." Charles C. Mann, *1491 (Second Edition): New Revelations of the Americas Before Columbus* (2011), p.23.
- "[Across] the Bering Strait, ... about seventy thousand years ago, a six-hundred-mile-wide landmass emerged to connect Asia and America. That swath of new land—Beringia—was scored by rivers, speckled with small lakes, and covered with grasses and shrubs that supported thriving animal communities, drawing people into America from the west. ...By 10,000 BCE, there were people in nearly every part of the Western Hemisphere," Pekka Hämäläinen, *Indigenous Continent: The Epic Contest for North America* (2022), pp.3, 9.
- "Over the past three decades, ... archaeological research has made it increasingly clear that the hunters were preceded by much earlier cultures that colonized the Americas between 24,500 and 16,000 years ago. This week a new academic study upended even those migration timelines by proposing that what is now central-west Brazil was settled as early as 27,000 years ago... ." Franz Lidz, "When Did Humans First Occupy the Americas? Ask the Sloth Bones," *NYTimes,* July 14, 2023.
- "The earliest traces of people in North America have been found in the Southwest, where human presence dates back twenty-three thousand years." Hämäläinen, *Indigenous Continent*, p.5.
- "As the second millennium approached its midpoint, nearly every corner of North America was inhabited or used by humans. People had studied, selected, and perfected seeds, and they had harnessed rivers and streams to carve gardens out of the desert. Their communities were prosperous and growing in numbers, and they were spreading beyond their core territories, filling in

the vacant spaces between them. The continent was home to approximately five million people." *Id.*, p.24.

2. **These First Americans adopted agricultural not long after Mesopotamia did, developing maize (corn) from an inedible plant. They cultivated it with beans and squash, providing an abundant, highly nutritious food supply. Planting the three crops together generated substantial growing synergies. Most First Americans were farmers or fishermen, as well as hunters and gathers.**

- "[A] second, independent Neolithic Revolution occurred in Mesoamerica. The exact timing is uncertain—archaeologists keep pushing back the date—but it is now thought to have occurred about ten thousand years ago, not long after the Middle East's Neolithic Revolution. ... Most important were the village orchards that marched back from the bluffs for miles. Amazonians practiced a kind of agro-forestry, farming with trees, unlike any kind of agriculture in Europe, Africa, or Asia." Mann, *1491*, pp.45, 56.
- "Experts now identify between fifteen and twenty independent centres of domestication, many of which followed very different paths of development... ." David Graeber and David Wengrow, *The Dawn of Everything: A New History of Humanity* (2021), p.252.
- "Highland peoples domesticated corn between nine and six thousand years ago. With skilled human help, this highly adaptive species was poised to take over the world. When farmers began growing beans and squash along with maiz de ocho some fifteen hundred years ago, they created an ecologically compatible triad of crops—the 'three sisters'—that revolutionized food production and diets in North America." Hämäläinen, *Indigenous Continent*, pp.12-3.
- "The majority of North American Indians became generalists who farmed, hunted, and gathered to sustain themselves." *Id.*, p.22.

3. The First Americans lived in a wide variety of social structures, from centralized, hierarchical societies to egalitarian clusters of loose alliances. And, many lived in large cities, some among the largest in the world.

Central America

- "[A]t the time of Columbus the great majority of Native Americans could be found south of the Río Grande. They were not nomadic, but built up and lived in some of the world's biggest and most opulent cities." Mann, *1491*, p.42.
- "[T]he Olmec, the first technologically complex culture in the hemisphere. Appearing in the narrow 'waist'"of Mexico about 1800 B.C., they lived in cities and towns centered on temple mounds." *Id.*, p.46.
- "Whatever the Olmec were, they seemed to represent the 'mother culture', as it came to be known, of all later Mesoamerican civilizations, having invented the region's characteristic calendar systems, glyphic writing and even ball games." Graeber, *The Dawn of Everything*, p.383.
- "[A]ll the way from Alaska south to the area of Washington State[,] [t]hey ... shared the same basic social structure, with hereditary ranks of nobles, commoners and slaves. Throughout this entire region, a 1,500-mile strip of land from the Copper River delta to Cape Mendocino, inter-group raiding for slaves was endemic ... ." *Id.*, p.182.
- "Sometime in the late twelfth century, a new city, Paquimé, rose south of the Rio Grande in the foothills of the Sierra Madre Occidental range. Surrounded by several wide rivers, Paquimé quickly emerged as a major commercial and political center commanding a hinterland of some ten thousand people living in hundreds of settlements. ...[They] sought stability, security, and solidarity. Instead of priestly rulers, they preferred leaders whose principal obligation was to maintain consensus and support participatory

political systems. Power flowed through the leaders, not from them. This sweeping retreat from hierarchies, elite dominance, and large-scale urbanization may have turned North America— along with Australia—into the world's most egalitarian continent at the time." Hämäläinen, *Indigenous Continent*, pp20, 23.

- "By the fourteenth century AD the city of Tlaxcala was ... already organized on an entirely different basis ... . There is no sign of a palace or central temple, and no major ball-court (an important setting, recall, for royal ritual in other Mesoamerican cities). Instead, archaeological survey reveals a cityscape given over almost entirely to the well-appointed residences of its citizens ... ." Graeber, *The Dawn of Everything*, pp.357–8.

- "Elsewhere, the historical momentum was toward greater concentrations of power, monumental ceremonial centers, and cities, and nations of many thousands persisted, reaching apogees in the major Mayan city-state of Chichén Itzá in northern Yucatán, the Inca Empire that extended more than two thousand miles north–south along western South America, and in the fifteenth-century city of Teotihuacán in the Valley of Mexico, home to 150,000 people and ruled by an Aztec emperor and high priests." Hämäläinen, *Indigenous Continent*, p.21.

- "Sometime around AD 1150, a people called the Mexica migrated south from a place called Aztlán—its location is now unknown —to take up a new home in the heart of the Valley of Mexico, which now bears their name. There they were eventually to carve out an empire, the Aztec Triple Alliance, and build its capital at Tenochtitlan, an island-city in Lake Texcoco... . ...[I]t was the Aztec rulers of Tenochtitlan who finally broke with tradition, creating a predatory empire ... ." Graeber, *The Dawn of Everything*, pp.328, 358.

- "[T]the Aztec Empire was really a confederation of noble families. The Inca, in contrast, insisted their sovereign was himself the incarnate Sun." *Id.*, p.373.

North America

- "North American Indians had experimented with ranked societies and all-powerful spiritual leaders and had found them deficient and dangerous. They had opted for more horizontal, participatory, and egalitarian ways of being in the world—a communal ethos available to everyone who was capable of proper thoughts and deeds and willing to share their possessions." Hämäläinen, *Indigenous Continent*, p.24.

- "The Yurok were what we've called 'possessive individualists'. They took it for granted that we are all born equal, and that it is up to each of us to make something of ourselves through self-discipline, self-denial and hard work. ...[T]the indigenous peoples of the Northwest Coast were just as industrious as those of California, and in both cases those who accumulated wealth were expected to give much of it away by sponsoring collective festivals." Graeber, *The Dawn of Everything*, p. 179.

- "[P]erhaps a quarter of the indigenous Northwest Coast population lived in bondage—which is about equivalent to proportions found in the Roman Empire, or classical Athens, or indeed the cotton plantations of the American South. What's more, slavery on the Northwest Coast was a hereditary status: if you were a slave, your children were also fated to be so." *Id.*, pp.185,199.

- "The junction of the Hudson and Mohawk Rivers was one of the most coveted places in early-seventeenth-century North America, and it belonged to the formidable Iroquois, the peoples of the longhouse, who had lived in the region for centuries. Because the Dutch sought profits, not dominance, and were generous with their wares, the Iroquois allowed them to stay. Roughly twenty thousand strong, the Iroquois lived in thirteen heavily fortified and nearly impregnable towns that the Europeans appropriately called 'castles.'" Hämäläinen, *Indigenous Continent*, pp.81-2.

- "[S]ometime after 1700 BCE, people started moving earth to a narrow and slightly elevated landform near the lower Mississippi

Valley. ...[T]heir experiment lasted for six centuries, until about 700 BCE. ...Theirs was a society that depended on connections among peoples. Those linkages disintegrated rapidly when corn and beans became staples in the fifth century; the life-giving plants made kinship networks self-sufficient. Populations expanded, people moved into walled towns, and face-to-face connections gave way to more formal relations." *Id.*, p.15.

- "Cahokia, near modern St. Louis, ... was once the greatest population center north of the Río Grande." Mann, *1491*, p.55.
- Cahokia's "elites—the chiefs and priests—desired luxuries for their own aesthetic pleasure and as status symbols. The city was encircled by satellite townships whose chiefs owed loyalty to Cahokia's paramount chief and made their allegiances tangible through gifts. ...From the city's position near the confluence of the Mississippi, Missouri, and Illinois Rivers, its commercial hinterland extended from the Great Lakes to the Gulf coast and the Appalachians. Cahokia may have begun as a collective effort of people who understood themselves as a single kin community, but over time it transformed into an elite-run state. The triggering factor was the colossal building projects... . Hämäläinen, *Indigenous Continent*, pp.17-8.
- "Numbering more than twenty thousand, ... the Creeks claimed a vast region. When the first British colonists landed in North America, the Creek domain stretched west from coastal Georgia's Savannah River to the Tombigbee River of eastern Mississippi and south from the Tennessee River to northern Florida... . ... [The] women owned the homes, family property, and probably the agricultural plots, giving them far greater security and economic independence than northern women. The Creeks cherished the freedoms that accompanied their lack of a strong central authority. They also prized the security that came from belonging to one of fifty matrilineal clans... ." Peter Cozzens, *A Brutal Reckoning: Andrew Jackson, the Creek Indians, and the Epic War for the American South* (2023) (Kindle), loc.394-486.

South Ameica

- "Flush with wealth, Tiwanaku city swelled into a marvel of terraced pyramids and grand monuments. Stone breakwaters extended far out into Lake Titicaca, ...With its running water, closed sewers, and gaudily painted walls, Tiwanaku was among the world's most impressive cities." Mann, *1491*, p.50.
- North and west of Tiwanaku, in what is now southern Peru, was the rival state of Wari, which then ran for almost a thousand miles along the spine of the Andes. More tightly organized and military minded than Tiwanaku, the rulers of Wari stamped out cookie-cutter fortresses and stationed them all along their borders." *Id.*, p.50.
- "[S]cientists used light-based remote sensing technology ... to ... identify the ancient ruins of a vast urban settlement around Llanos de Mojos in the Bolivian Amazon that was abandoned some 600 years ago. ...[A] stronghold of the socially complex Casarabe Culture (500-1400 C.E.) with urban centers boasting monumental platform and pyramid architecture. Raised causeways connected a constellation of suburban-like settlements, which stretched for miles across a landscape that was shaped by a massive water control and distribution system with reservoirs and canals." Brian Handwerk, "Lost Cities of the Amazon Discovered From the Air: Mapping technology cut through the canopy to detect sprawling urban structures in Bolivia that suggest sophisticated cultures once existed," *Smithsonian Magazine,* May 25, 2022.
- "Archaeologists have uncovered a cluster of lost cities in the Amazon rainforest that was home to at least 10,000 farmers about 2,000 years ago. ...Recent mapping by laser-sensor technology revealed those sites to be part of a dense network of settlements and connecting roadways, tucked into the forested foothills of the Andes, that lasted about 1,000 years. The settlements were occupied by the Upano people between about 500BC and AD300 to 600... . Residential and ceremonial buildings erected

on more than 6,000 earthen mounds were surrounded by agricultural fields with drainage canals. The largest roads were 33 feet (10 meters) wide and stretched for 6-12 miles (10-20km). ...[T]he site was home to at least 10,000 inhabitants--and perhaps as many as 15,000 or 30,000 at its peak... ." "Valley of lost cities that flourished 2,000 years ago found in Amazon: Laser-sensor technology reveals network of earthen mounds and buried roads in rainforest area of Ecuador," *The Guardian*, 11 January 2024.

4. Before the arrival of the Europeans, there were a succession of large, culturally complex civilizations, some lasting many centuries, longer than the Roman Empire. Like Rome, they too fell. And, not because of the Spanish or other Europeans, but from issues of their own. The Olmecs, the Toltecs, the Mayan, the Puebloans, the Cahokians, *etc.*

- "Nestled in the jungle of northern Guatemala, a vast network of interconnected Maya settlements built millennia ago has been mapped in unprecedented detail. The civilization featured towering pyramids, palaces, terraces, ball courts and reservoirs connected by a sprawling web of causeways, ... [A] 'level of infrastructure that is just mind-boggling,' said Dr. Timothy Beach ....The archaeologists identified nearly 1,000 Maya settlements, which they said were mostly built between 1,000 B.C. and 150 A.D. ... Richard Hansen ... [t]he findings ... 'tell a story of the rise and precocious development of an incredibly organized, sophisticated society'." Aylin Woodward, "Vast Maya Kingdom Is Revealed in Guatemalan Jungle," *WSJ.com*, January 31, 2023.
- "By the middle of the eleventh century (around 1050 CE) the ten-mile-long Chaco Canyon in the Colorado Plateau had become a dominant urban center that nearly monopolized the highly lucrative trade in turquoise stones, a luxury item. There, over three centuries, the Ancestral Puebloans built a monumental communal stone building—later known as Pueblo Bonito—that served

as the political, commercial, and religious center of the Chacoan world." Hämäläinen, *Indigenous Continent*, p.14.

- "[There was] a veritable urban explosion with its epicentre at the site of Cahokia, which was soon to become the greatest city in the Americas north of Mexico. ...Cahokia lies in an extensive floodplain along the Mississippi known as the American Bottom. [A]round AD 1050 Cahokia exploded in size, growing from a fairly modest community to a city of over six square miles, including more than 100 earthen mounds built around spacious plazas. Its original population of a few thousand was augmented by perhaps 10,000 more, coming from outside to settle in Cahokia and its satellite towns, totalling something in the order of 40,000 in the American Bottom as a whole... ." Graeber, *The Dawn of Everything*, p.468.

- "Cahokia was the zenith of ... a widespread Mississippian culture that encompassed much of the Eastern Woodlands for more than eight centuries in an ever-shifting constellation of regional variations." Hämäläinen, *Indigenous Continent*, p.19.

- "After AD 1400 the entire fertile expanse of the American Bottom ... along with the territory from Cahokia up to the Ohio River, became what's referred to in the literature as the Vacant or Empty Quarter: a haunted wilderness of overgrown pyramids and housing blocks crumbling back into swamp, occasionally traversed by hunters but devoid of permanent human settlement." Graeber, *The Dawn of Everything*, p.468.

- "By the time the Spaniards arrived, six centuries after the collapse of cities in Petén, Mayan societies were thoroughly decentralized, parsed into a bewildering variety of townships and principalities, many without kings." *Id.*, p.378.

5. The First Americans shaped and altered their environment. They did not live passively with nature, but controlled and designed it. And, their lives, societies and relationships were, in turn, shaped by the physical environment and changes in in it.

- "[T]hey were so successful at imposing their will on the landscape that in 1492 Columbus set foot in a hemisphere thoroughly marked by humankind." Mann, *1491*, p.23.
- "The forests were bridged by raised berms, as straight as a rifle shot and up to three miles long. ...[T]his entire landscape— thirty thousand square miles or more of forest islands and mounds linked by causeways—was constructed by a technologically advanced, populous society more than a thousand years ago. ...Beginning as much as three thousand years ago, this long-ago society—... probably founded by the ancestors of an Arawak-speaking people now called the Mojo and the Bauré—created one of the largest, strangest, and most ecologically rich artificial environments on the planet. ...These people built up the mounds for homes and farms, constructed the causeways and canals for transportation and communication, created the fish weirs to feed themselves, and burned the savannas to keep them clear of invading trees. A thousand years ago their society was at its height." Hämäläinen, *Indigenous Continent*, pp.23, 37-8.
- "Tiwanaku, one of many settlements around the lake, began after about 800 B.C. to drain the wetlands around the rivers that flowed into the lake from the south. A thousand years later the village had grown to become the center of a large polity ... ." *Id.*, p.50.
- "Spread across more than ninety acres was a variety of earthworks in direct lines, in squares and elevated mounds, including one dominant, conical burial mound thirty feet high. Rufus Putnam ... found 'those works so perfect as to put it beyond all doubt that they are the remains of a work erected at an amazing expense perhaps some thousand years since, by a people who had very considerable knowledge of fortifications.' ...[T]he whole complex was the work of what was known as the Ohio Hopewell culture and that the Great Mound was built between 100 BC, when the Hopewell began to occupy southern Ohio, and AD 500, making it more than 2,000 years old." David McCullough, *The Pioneers:*

The Heroic Story of the Settlers Who Brought the American Ideal West (2019), pp.48, 50.

- "[O]ver the centuries the Indian inhabitants had repeatedly burned off large portions of the forest to create grazing lands that stimulated growth of the deer population." Cozzens, *A Brutal Reckoning*, loc.614.

- "American forests, too, were shaped by flame. Indians' 'frequent fiering of the woods, 'made the forests east of the Mississippi so open and 'thin of Timber'... . Indigenous pyromania had long pumped carbon dioxide into the air." Charles C. Mann, *1493: Uncovering the New World Columbus Created* (2011), p.70.

* * *

- "Groups of people began moving southward through the passage around 11,000 BCE, eventually arriving in the great continental grasslands that were swarming with huge mammals: imperial mammoths, six-ton mastodons, eight-foot-tall bison, giant ground sloths, short-faced bears, camels, horses, and several species of antelope. ...[G]roups of hunters began using flint, chert, obsidian, and other malleable stone to craft sharp-edged, fluted spear points that could penetrate a beast's thick skin with lethal efficiency. ...The profusion of game persisted for two millennia, but then the continental ice sheets began melting rapidly, and the giant mammals began dying out, debilitated by a warming and increasingly erratic climate. By 8000 BCE, some three dozen species of giant animals had become extinct." Hämäläinen, *Indigenous Continent*, pp.8-10.

- "Nutrient-rich kelp beds supported colonies of fish, shellfish, seabirds, seaweed, and sea otters, enabling people to enjoy rich and balanced diets. For these amphibian people, the quest for food was safer and most likely more efficient than that of the big-game hunters in the interior. Shifting from one bounteous habitat to another, splintering when necessary, highly mobile maritime hunter-gatherers may have reached Monte Verde in modern-day southern Chile—ten thousand miles south of the Bering Strait—as early as 16,500 BCE." *Id.*, pp.4-5.

- "Acorns ... are rich in iron, calcium, potassium, fiber, carbohydrates, monounsaturated fats, and vitamins A, B, and E. They also stabilize the human metabolism and blood sugar levels. Nomadic peoples built settlements near acorn groves, anchoring themselves to the land, and before long they were practicing small-scale agriculture under local leaders who coordinated fire-fallow cultivation and the allocation of land and crops." *Id.* p.10.

***

- "[I]in the late 1500s and early 1600s ... a global drop in surface air temperatures occurred—part of the 'Little Ice Age' ... . Quite likely, European expansion in the Americas played a role. With perhaps 90 per cent of the indigenous population eliminated by the effects of conquest and infectious disease, forests reclaimed regions in which terraced agriculture and irrigation had been practised for centuries. In Mesoamerica, Amazonia and the Andes, some 50 million hectares of cultivated land may have reverted to wilderness. Carbon uptake from vegetation increased on a scale sufficient to change the Earth System and bring about a human-driven phase of global cooling." Graeber, *The Dawn of Everything*, p.258.

- "[T]he Little Ice Age ... [e]nduring from about 1550 to about 1750 in the Northern Hemisphere... . Formerly open grasslands fill with forest—a frenzy of photosynthesis. [William F.] Ruddiman's idea was simple: the destruction of Indian societies by European epidemics both decreased native burning and increased tree growth. It was today's climate change in reverse, with human action removing greenhouse gases from the atmosphere rather than adding them—a stunning meteorological overture to the Homogenocene." *Id.*, pp.68, 69, 72-3.

- "The Little Ice Age ushered in a world where almost everything had to be smaller: harvests, markets, settlements, mounds, alliances, and ambitions." Hämäläinen, *Indigenous Continent*, p.19.

6. **During the seventeenth century, the indigenous tribes were focused on their own struggles for dominance and power. They even viewed the colonists as potential allies, pawns in their political and physical battles, and only a sometime nuisance. They entered into treaties, sold land and engaged in substantial trade. And, they fought among themselves. All the while, they effectively contained the European colonists to small pockets along the Eastern Seaboard. "After generations of colonial expansion, many Native nations still considered other Indians to be their main rivals." Hämäläinen, *Indigenous Continent*, p.79.**

- "The ... Wampanoags were desperate to secure new allies.... . Squanto, a Patuxet Indian, helped mediate a mutual defense pact between Ousamequin ... and the colonists. Ousamequin believed that the pact entitled him to collect tribute from the newcomers, and he soon recruited them into a fight against a rival sachem. He allowed the English to build a colony—Plymouth... ." Hämäläinen, *Indigenous Continent*, p.73.
- "Over time, the Wampanoag ... had learned how to manage the European presence. They encouraged the exchange of goods, but would only allow their visitors to stay ashore for brief, carefully controlled excursions. ...He would permit the newcomers to stay for an unlimited time—provided they formally allied with the Wampanoag against the Narragansett. ...In the next decade tens of thousands of Europeans came to Massachusetts. Massasoit shepherded his people through the wave of settlement, and the pact he signed with Plymouth lasted for more than fifty years." Mann, *1491*, p.61.
- "[T]he Wabanakis began to carefully consider the extent to which they should engage with the Indians in the interior. For them the

interior was a terrifying place where the contest over territory un-
balanced the world. The amphibious Mi'kmaqs, not the English,
were their most dangerous neighbors." Hämäläinen, *Indigenous
Continent*, p.75.

* * *

- "[T]he Powhatans were ruled by a paramount leader, Wahunse-
nacawh, ... [who] had subjugated several rival nations and elevated his sons, brothers, and sisters to lead some of them, ...[He]
expanded his empire by absorbing the English... ." Hämäläinen,
Indigenous Continent, pp.60-1.
- "Opechancanough nurtured outwardly friendly relations with
the English while planning a massive assault. On March 21, 1622,
large numbers of unarmed Powhatans visited the English in various settlements along the James River and stayed overnight. Some
shared breakfast with their English hosts the next morning. Then
they made their move, snatching weapons from their hosts and
joining other Powhatans in a coordinated attack." *Id.*, p.66.

* * *

- "The Narragansetts would weaken their rivals by having the English do their bidding: kill and diminish the Pequots. More than
three hundred Narragansett, Mohegan, and Wangunk soldiers
fought alongside the English. Like the colonists, these Native
peoples wanted to redefine their relationship with the Pequots,
who dominated trade with the English." Hämäläinen, *Indigenous
Continent*, p.79.
- "When the English moved against the Pequots, Uncas supported
the colonists ... . When the Pequots were crushed, he adopted
several survivors as newly born Mohegans. He was one of the crucial signers of the 1638 Treaty of Hartford, which dispossessed
all the Indians who were not party to it. With the Pequots utterly

defeated, the Mohegans emerged as a major regional power." *Id.*, pp.86-7.

* * *

- "The Iroquoian nations had fought one another for generations, but in the late fifteenth century the Great League of Peace and Power, a ritual and spiritual compact, put an end to the bloodshed. ...[A] layered alliance of five nations, or council fires, that clustered along the Finger Lakes south and east of Lake Ontario. ... The Mohawks ...served as the Keepers of the Eastern Door, ... the Senecas ... served as the Keepers of the Western Door ... the Oneidas, ... the Onondagas ... and the Cayugas in the middle." Hämäläinen, *Indigenous Continent*, p.98.
- "By 1660, the Iroquois had fought every nation in the Great Lakes, creating a vast shatter zone of destruction. ...Overwhelming Iroquois military dominance quickly translated into economic, political, and cultural power. Their place in the world secure, the Iroquois made a concerted effort to stabilize their borderlands through trade, diplomacy, and alliances." *Id.*, p.107.
- "[T]he Iroquois launched a new campaign that took their armies west, south, and north. They banished the Shawnees from the fertile Ohio River valley to the south, and launched a devastating attack on a Mahican village in the east, finally putting an end to the decades-long war with the Mahican people. They pushed the Atikamekws far to the north ... ." *Id.*, p.117.
- "[T]he great Sioux Confederacy, the Očhéthi Šakówiŋ, the 'Seven Council Fires,' which controlled the lands west of the Great Lakes, commanding a roughly sixty-thousand-square-mile core territory that stretched out on both sides of the upper Mississippi Valley... ." *Id.*, p.131.
- "There is no record of these two powerful Indigenous confederacies ever clashing. The Sioux and the Iroquois were compatible. ...[T]he Iroquois sought pelts and captives; the Sioux sought

bison and, increasingly, horses. Expanding simultaneously to the west, the two powers always had space between them." *Id.*, p.142.

* * *

• The Creeks "struck a Faustian bargain with the merchants of Charles Towne.... [T]hey would extirpate the Westos in exchange for arms and ammunition and the same marvelous array of trade goods that had enticed their enemies and that soon replaced traditional tools, clothing, and adornments in Creek society. The Cussetas and Uchees made short work of the Westos, after which the Cussetas turned on the Uchees, killing scores and enslaving the remainder. To acquire an ongoing supply of guns and goods from the Carolinians, however, the Creeks needed something to offer them besides a temporary alliance of convenience. And so they sold other Indians into bondage. ...Between 1670 and 1715 the Creeks funneled at least twenty thousand Indian captives to Carolina... ." Cozzens, *A Brutal Reckoning*, at loc.642-52.

THE CONTEST FOR NORTH AMERICA

"By 1776, various European colonial powers together claimed nearly all of the continent for themselves, but Indigenous peoples and powers controlled
it....Time and again, and across centuries, Indians
blocked and destroyed colonial projects, forcing Euro-
Americans to accept Native ways, Native sovereignty,
and Native dominance. ...From the beginning of
colonialism in North America to the Lakotas' final
military triumphs [Red Cloud's War and Custer's Last
Stand], a multitude of Native nations fought fiercely
to keep their territories intact and their cultures
untainted, frustrating the imperial pretensions of
France, Spain, Britain, the Netherlands, and eventually
the United States."

Pekka Hämäläinen
Indigenous Continent, pp.ix-x, xi.

The Intruders

1. The first 200 years of the European "conquest" of the Americas was significantly ecological—bacteria, viruses, domesticated
animals, earthworms, honey bees, *etc.*

- "[The] critical advantage was biological, not technological. The
ships that sailed across the Atlantic carried not only human
beings, but plants and animals—sometimes intentionally, sometimes accidentally. After Columbus, ecosystems that had been
separate for eons suddenly met and mixed.... The exchange took
corn (maize) to Africa and sweet potatoes to East Asia, horses and
apples to the Americas, and rhubarb and eucalyptus to Europe
—and also swapped about a host of less-familiar organisms like

insects, grasses, bacteria, and viruses. This ecological imperialism ... provided the British, French, Dutch, Portuguese, and Spanish with the consistent edge needed to win their empires." Mann, *1493*, p.20.

- "Before Colón none of the epidemic diseases common in Europe and Asia existed in the Americas. The viruses that cause smallpox, influenza, hepatitis, measles, encephalitis, and viral pneumonia; the bacteria that cause tuberculosis, diphtheria, cholera, typhus, scarlet fever, and bacterial meningitis—by a quirk of evolutionary history, all were unknown in the Western Hemisphere. Shipped across the ocean from Europe these maladies consumed Hispaniola's native population with stunning rapacity. ...Throughout the sixteenth and seventeenth centuries novel microorganisms spread across the Americas, ricocheting from victim to victim, killing three-quarters or more of the people in the hemisphere." *Id.*, p.42.

- "The 1600s-1700s was a period of change and uncertainty in North America. Few factors threatened survival as much as the microbial pathogens that infiltrated the continent. Unfortunately, ignorance of the diseases they were bringing did not prevent the devastation these pathogens wreaked as they spread throughout the pilgrim's colonies and the indigenous population of North America." Ashley Hagen, "The Toxin-Based Diseases Common in North America during the 1600-1700s," *American Society for Microbiology*, July 5, 2019.

- "Based on accounts of the symptoms, the epidemic was probably of viral hepatitis, ...the sick, carrying the disease with them to neighboring communities. Beginning in 1616, the pestilence took at least three years to exhaust itself and killed as much as 90 percent of the people in coastal New England." Mann, *1491*, pp.93--4. Or: "The malady may have been leptospirosis, which had been spread by the urine of European rats." Hämäläinen, *Indigenous Continent*, p.71.

- "[I]n 1633, ... an unusually virulent smallpox epidemic devastated the immunologically defenseless Indians around New England. More than eighty percent of the Native Americans in the region died." *Id.*, p.77.
- "Falciparum [malaria] thrives in most of Africa but gained a foothold only in the warmest precincts of Europe: Greece, Italy, southern Spain, and Portugal. Vivax [malaria], by contrast, became endemic in much of Europe, including cooler places like the Netherlands, lower Scandinavia, and England. From the American point of view, falciparum came from Africa, and was spread by Africans, whereas vivax came from Europe, and was spread by Europeans." Mann, *1493*, p.145.
- "Humankind ha[d] lived here for many thousands of years, erecting some of the world's first urban complexes in the valleys north of Lima. [In the late 1520s], smallpox swept in. After it came other European diseases, and then Europeans themselves. Millions died, fearful and suffering, in shattered mountain villages. Now [the 1640s], slopes terraced and irrigated for centuries remain[ed] empty." *Id.*, p..63.
- The outbreak of a virulent smallpox epidemic in 1781—the same epidemic that devastated Cornwallis's army in Yorktown—was key to Lakota expansion in the upper Missouri Valley. The epidemic shocked the Lakotas ..., but it nearly destroyed the more sedentary agricultural nations in the region. More than seventy-five percent of the Arikaras may have perished, reducing the ancient Missourian civilization to a mere shadow of its former self... ." Hämäläinen, *Indigenous Continent*, p.353.
- "In early 1622 a ship arrived in Jamestown that was loaded with exotic entities: grapevines, silkworms, and bees. The grapes and silkworms never amounted to much, but the bees thrived. Most bees pollinate only a few plant species and tend to be fussy about where they live. But European honeybees, promiscuous little beasts, pollinate almost anything in sight and reside almost

anywhere. Quickly they set up shop throughout the Americas. Indians called them 'English flies.'" Mann, *1493*, p.129.

- "[B]efore the arrival of Europeans, New England and the upper Midwest had no earthworms—they were wiped out in the last Ice Age. They arrived with Europeans, probably in Virginia, and spread with them. Like the colonists, the worms were conquering a new place." *Id.,* p.83.
- Domesticated livestock meant fences. "Cows and hogs could destroy a carefully cultivated field in a matter of hours, invalidating weeks of Native women's work." Hämäläinen, *Indigenous Continent,* p.152. Fences were a European intrusion.
- "Removing forest cover, blocking regrowth on fallow land, exhausting the soil, shutting down annual burning, unleashing big grazing and rooting animals, introducing earthworms, honeybees, and other alien invertebrates—the colonists so profoundly changed Tsenacomoco [Virginia] that it became harder and harder for its [original] inhabitants to prosper there." Mann, *1493*, p.130.

2. **Following the defeat of the Spanish Armada, England was in a position to participate in the colonization of the New World. Queen Elizabeth I authorized charters for the acquisition of lands 'unclaimed by Christians" in the Americas. However, such territories were limited to North America. Unlike the territories conquered by the Spanish, the eastern seaboard of North America was lacking in gold, was sparsely populated and the indigenous peoples lacked strong centralized, hierarchical political organization. So, the opportunities for profitable conquest did not exist.**

- "[I]n 1588, the lucky rout of the Spanish Armada ... was ... a sign of growing English assertiveness on the seas that would enable them to finally take part in the quest for colonial empire. ...[T]he English began their colonization of North America... . But they were already latecomers. They chose North America not because it was attractive, but because it was all that was available. The 'desirable' parts of the Americas, where the indigenous population to exploit was plentiful and where the gold and silver mines were located, had already been occupied. The English got the leftovers." Daron Acemoglu and James A. Robinson, *Why Nations Fail: The Origins of Power, Prosperity, and Poverty* (2012), p.19.

- "...Queen Elizabeth I granted charters to colonize the North American territories 'unclaimed by Christians... .' Michael Harriot, *Black AF History: The Un-Whitewashed Story of America* (2023), p.15.

- "The {indigenous] population density of the United States, outside of a few pockets, was at most three-quarters of a person per square mile. In central Mexico or Andean Peru, the population density was as high as four hundred people per square mile... ." Acemoglu and Robinson, *Why Nations Fail*, p.25.

3. Unlike the Spanish, the English efforts to colonize the New World were undertaken, not by the Crown, but by private enterprises operating pursuant to Royal charters, that is, by businessmen. The explorers sent were not battle hardened soldiers (nor farmers), but aristocratic Protestants. Some survived, barely.

- "Elizabeth I and her successors could not monopolize the trade with the Americas. Other European monarchs could. So while in England, Atlantic trade and colonization started creating a large group of wealthy traders with few links to the Crown, this was not the case in Spain or France. The English traders resented royal control and demanded changes in political institutions and the restriction of royal prerogatives." Acemoglu and Robinson, *Why Nations Fail*, p.106.

- "[T]he first four attempts failed. ...[The] reason they failed was because of disease, lack of food, lack of navigation skills, and the inability to convince the natives of English superiority. No one knows what happened to the fourth attempt, aptly named the Lost Colony of Roanoke." Harriot, *Black AF History*, p.15.

- "Perhaps the Virginia Company's biggest mistake was who they sent to conquer the new land. Unlike Portugal and Spain, who had a head start in the white-people-discovering-things trend, England was relatively new to the colonizing game. ...Portugal and Spain had a class of explorers and soldiers whose full-time job was conquering. Instead of sending uncouth conquistadors, the British sent wealthy Protestant aristocrats to stake out the area... ." *Id.*, p.17.

- "As the winter of 1607 closed in, the settlers in Jamestown began to run low on food, and the appointed leader of the colony's ruling council, Edward Marie Wingfield, dithered indecisively. The situation was rescued by Captain John Smith. ...With [Captain Christopher] Newport sailing back to England for supplies and more colonists, and Wingfield uncertain about what to do, it was Smith who saved the colony. He initiated a series of trading missions that secured vital food supplies." Acemoglu and Robinson, *Why Nations Fail*, p.21.

- "Once more Jamestown survived only because of his resourcefulness. He managed to cajole and bully local indigenous groups to trade with him, and when they wouldn't, he took what he could. Back in the settlement, Smith was completely in charge and imposed the rule that 'he that will not worke shall not eat.' Jamestown survived a second winter." *Id.*, p.23.

- "An early colonizing attempt at Sagadahoc River in the Gulf of Saint Lawrence by English Puritans and West Country promoters failed miserably under the leadership of the headstrong Raleigh Gilbert. Algonquian vessels commanded the coast, leaving the uninvited strangers isolated and starving. The dejected colonists sailed home at the first opportunity." Hämäläinen, *Indigenous Continent*, p.71.

- "...Jamestown was so well-known in England for the horrors its unprepared settlers suffered that by the time the Puritans sailed their main goal was to avoid Jamestown's very well-publicized failures. Among the many reasons the Puritans did not want to settle in Virginia was to avoid contamination with Jamestown's perpetual bad luck (which the Puritans put down in large part to the colony's lack of a commission from God). Even Plimoth Plantation, founded by Separatists just 10 years earlier, wasn't exactly thriving." R. Sós, *thehistoricpresent.com.*

4. **By 1618,the Virginia Company, presumably influenced by the strong views of Captain John Smith, had adopted a new strategy for recovering its investment and making the New World venture profitable. It was centered on agriculture and trade. But, labor was essential. The enslavement of the indigenous peoples was inadequate, and efforts to compel indentured English workers to provide what was needed were faltering. The poor performance led to the decision to provide meaningful inducements skilled Englishmen to immigrate to Virginia and to work hard to produce marketable crops. The most important inducement was the grant of land ownership, something not achievable in England, but the settlors motivation once here was enhanced by the unprecedented opportunity for significant self-government. During the subsequent 150 years, this business model proved to be the key to prosperity and was adopted in all of the original 13 Colonies.**

- "It was Smith who was the first to realize that the model of colonization that had worked so well for Cortés and Pizarro simply would not work in North America." Acemoglu and Robinson, *Why Nations Fail*, p.22.
- [Captain Christopher] Newport set sail ... for England, in December 1608. He took with him a letter written by Smith pleading with the directors of the Virginia Company to change the way they thought about the colony. There was no possibility of a get-rich-quick exploitation of Virginia along the lines of Mexico and Peru. There were no gold or precious metals, and the indigenous

people could not be forced to work or provide food. ...[I]f there were going to be a viable colony, it was the colonists who would have to work. He therefore pleaded with the directors to send the right sort of people: 'When you send againe I entreat you rather to send some thirty carpenters, husbandmen, gardeners, fishermen, blacksmiths, masons, and diggers up of trees, roots, well provided, then a thousand of such as we have.'" *Id.*, p.23.

- "Starting in 1618, a dramatically new strategy was adopted. Since it was possible to coerce neither the locals nor the settlers, the only alternative was to give the settlers incentives. In 1618 the company began the 'headright system,' which gave each male settler fifty acres of land and fifty more acres for each member of his family and for all servants that a family could bring to Virginia. Settlers were given their houses and freed from their contracts, and in 1619 a General Assembly was introduced that effectively gave all adult men a say in the laws and institutions governing the colony. It was the start of democracy in the United States. ...[T]he only option for an economically viable colony was to create institutions that gave the colonists incentives to invest and to work hard." *Id.*, p.26.

- "[I]n 1618, the Virginia Company gave land, and freedom from their draconian contracts, to the colonists it had previously tried to coerce, the General Assembly in the following year allowed the colonists to begin governing themselves. Economic rights without political rights would not have been trusted by the colonists, who had seen the persistent efforts of the Virginia Company to coerce them. Neither would these economies have been stable and durable." *Id.*, p.82.

- "By the 1720s, all the thirteen colonies of what was to become the United States had similar structures of government. In all cases there was a governor, and an assembly based on a franchise of male property holders. They were not democracies; women, slaves, and the propertyless could not vote. But political rights were very broad compared with contemporary societies elsewhere. It was these assemblies and their leaders that coalesced to form the First Continental Congress in 1774... ." *Id.*, p.28.

5. Native assistance and forbearance enabled both the Plymouth and the Jamestown colonies to survive.

- "Paradoxically, the [Jamestown] colony's desperation was its salvation; Powhatan apparently couldn't bring himself to regard the starving [colonists] as a threat. Certain that he could oust the English at any time, he allowed them to occupy their not-so-valuable real estate as long as they provided valuable trade goods: guns, axes, knives, mirrors, glass beads, and copper sheets, the last of which the Indians prized much as Europeans prized gold ingots." Mann, *1493*, p.108.

- "After abducting John Smith, [Powhatan] learned enough from his captive to conclude that the profit from trade ... tomorrow was worth giving them grain today. He sent [Smith] back to Jamestown in January 1608 with enough maize to keep his few remaining companions alive for a while. ...[B]oth natives and newcomers could treat Pocahontas's wedding to Rolfe as a *de facto* cease-fire ... Opechancanough used the suspension of hostilities to take the levers of power... . Opechancanough manipulated Jamestown into attacking his native rivals, augmenting his empire even as the English domain expanded. The cease-fire with Powhatan let colonists expand [tobacco] production explosively." *Id.*, pp.108, 120.

- "A new effort in 1620, consisting of a single ship, the Mayflower, brought 102 colonists who landed on a widowed coast; a recent disease outbreak had killed almost ninety percent of the Wampanoags. The colonists swiftly occupied a vacant Native village. The horribly reduced Wampanoags were desperate to secure new allies, and they took in the serious and zealous newcomers. Squanto, a Patuxet Indian, helped mediate a mutual defense pact between Ousamequin—...[the] 'great sachem'... of the Wampanoag Confederacy—and the colonists. Ousamequin believed that the pact entitled him to collect tribute from the newcomers, and he soon recruited them into a fight against a rival sachem. He allowed the English to build a colony—Plymouth." Hämäläinen, *Indigenous Continent*, p.73.

The Seventeenth Century

6. At the end of the seventeenth century, the First Americans went to war against the encroaching colonists, almost eliminating all European settlements north and west of Spanish Florida.

- "[B]etween 1675 and 1690, every colonial project on the Indigenous continent seemed to either wobble or expire altogether. Suddenly, the New World seemed to have become a graveyard for Old World empires as Native Americans mounted a concentrated counterattack against generations of colonial aggression." Hämäläinen, *Indigenous Continent*, pp.145-6.
- "By early 1675, Metacom and the Wampanoags had seen enough. The colonists refused to recognize the Wampanoags and their allies as sovereign nations, and they allowed their beasts to graze on Indigenous lands. ...The Narragansetts took the initiative. Canonchet, their sachem, organized an army of nearly two thousand soldiers and practically emptied central Massachusetts of colonists. Experts in mobile battle, the Narragansetts burned villages and destroyed almost all the farms west of the Narragansett Bay. Their path could be traced by dead farm animals, torn books, strewn church bells, bodies, and body parts." Hämäläinen, *Indigenous Continent* pp.151, 158.
- "[In 1675,] Indians attacked fifty-two colonial settlements and ruined twelve of them in an exercise of total war, targeting women, children, men, cows, hogs, horses, houses, and Bibles. The colonists had anticipated a war, but when it came, its

intensity was shocking. The English realized how very little they knew about the surrounding Indians and their plans and ambitions." *Id.,* p..145.

- "But then the tide turned. The New England Confederation launched a joint campaign against the Indigenous armies, mobilizing their citizens, their god,and, most important, their Indian allies ... .The colonists convinced loyal mission Indians and Mohawks to join them with lavish gift-giving.... . When the Mohawks organized a winter campaign in 1676–77 against Metacom's coalition, they were fighting for themselves. The New England Confederation was the most formidable colonial project in the East, and the Mohawks wanted it on their side. [T]he Mohegans, Pequots, and their Connecticut auxiliaries located a group of Narragansetts at Nipsagchuck Swamp. The Mohegans and Pequots advanced in the middle, while the English launched a mounted charge on the flanks." *Id.,* pp.161-2.

- "The conflict, brutal and sad, tore through New England. The Europeans won. Indeed, after the war Massachusetts sold more than a thousand Indians into slavery—perhaps one out of every ten native adults in the region. Most went to the Caribbean, but a few ended up as far away as North Africa." Mann, *1491,* p.103.

- "Metacom's War, or King Philip's War to the English, w[as] a shocking calamity to the colonists, even in apparent victory. Hämäläinen, *Indigenous Continent,* p163.

- "In the winter of 1704, a multiethnic party of two hundred French, Mohawk, Wyandot, and Wabanaki soldiers attacked the town of Deerfield in Massachusetts." *Id.,* p.214.

* * *

- "The Susquehannocks went to war, just weeks after Metacom's War erupted. ...The war against the Susquehannocks expanded into a civil war among Virginians. ...Having failed to locate the elusive Occaneechis and Susquehannocks, Bacon and his soldiers

began killing the peaceful Pamunkeys, Nanzaticos, Rappahan-
nocks, Portobaccos, Wicocomocos, and Appomattucks. Emboldened, Bacon's followers pushed through laws that legalized the
enslaving of all Virginia Native Americans, whether tributary Indians or foreign ones, and they systematically banishesd friendly
Indians from their homelands to make room for tobacco."
Hämäläinen, *Indigenous Continent,* p.173.

- "In the end, it was the Iroquois who restored order in the
region. ...By this point, the Iroquois League had become the
central power in the Northeast, monitoring behaviors, enforcing
policies, and conducting wide-ranging 'forest diplomacy.' ...The
Virginians pledged to abolish the trade in Indian slaves... ." *Id.,*
p.174.

* * *

- "In the spring of 1715, South Carolina dispatched agents to conduct a census of the Native towns surrounding the colony, which
the Indians saw as a preamble to more slave raids. The Yamasees,
Muscogees, Choctaws, and Apalachees went to war. ...They then
joined with the Muscogees, Choctaws, and Apalachees in killing traders and destroying English settlements, plantations, and
garrisons. ...South Carolina had become a fiasco. Almost all its
citizens were hiding in Charles Town, and it lost its status as a
proprietary colony." Hämäläinen, *Indigenous Continent,* p.200.

* * *

- "On August 10, 1680, knotted cords of yucca fiber began to
appear among the Pueblo Indians across New Mexico, officially
a kingdom of the Spanish Empire. The cords were carried by
trained runners, each of whom covered hundreds of miles. In
every town the runners delivered the same message from Po'pay:
untie one knot each day, and on the morning of the last knot, kill

the Spanish in your town. ...The Pueblos had already launched a war against New Mexico. ...It was a carefully orchestrated war launched by the sovereign Pueblo people against Spain's imperial pretensions. ...When the time came, in each location Pueblos brought overwhelming numbers against the Spanish and forced them to fight for survival in many separate battles, thus preventing any attempts at a colony-wide military response." Hämäläinen, *Indigenous Continent*, p.177.

- "The Pueblo uprising had proved contagious, triggering a series of rebellions against Spanish rule from Coahuila to Sonora and Nueva Vizcaya. Janos, Sumas, Conchos, Tobosos, Julimes, and Pimas attacked colonists and destroyed missions, towns, and farms, rolling back Spanish colonialism across a vast area." *Id.*, p.186.

The Eighteenth Century

7. The eighteenth century brought the beginning of European expansion into the interior, and it met stiff resistance. But, the colonists keep coming, and coming and coming. No longer did most of new arrivals promptly die, and the settlers successfuly established families.

- "[I]n the early eighteenth century, colonial pressure brought by land-hungry colonists was becoming uncontainable along the Eastern Seaboard; by the 1730s, due to immigration and improved farming methods, the number of English colonists reached nearly six hundred thousand." Hämäläinen, *Indigenous Continent*, p.207.
- "Colonists now lived longer, had larger families, and became more mobile. They also became more aggressive, clamoring for Indigenous lands and Native slaves, but they lacked the necessary military muscle to seize them." *Id.*, p.198.

- "[In 1790,] [a] makeshift frontier army of almost 1,500 men, regulars and militia, under the command of General Josiah Harmar, had set out to punish the Miami and Shawnees. Harmar and his men were soundly defeated by a much smaller force led by the Miami war chief, Little Turtle. Of the regulars and militia 183 were dead or missing. The Indian loss had been fewer than a dozen. Even more ominous ... was the vanished presence of the numerous Delawares and Wyandots who for so long had been part of the everyday life." McCullough, *The Pioneers,* pp.87-8.

- "[1791] In total, the native force numbered some 1,000 warriors, representing eight more tribes other than the Miami and Shawnee—Delawares and Wyandots, Ottawas, Kickapoos, Chippewas, Pottawatomies, Mohawks from Canada, and Creeks from the south A retreat had to be called. The battle had become a one-sided slaughter. ... Many more of the wounded left behind—men, women, and children—were massacred, their bodies desecrated. St. Clair's Defeat, as the battle came to be known, had been a total disaster, worse than any suffered by the American army during the entire Revolution... ." *Id.,* pp.99-108.

- "President George Washington had no desire for war with the Creeks over what he knew to be a dubious Georgia claim. With the tribes north of the Ohio River already hostile, and the newly raised Regular army small and poorly trained, the president could ill afford a two-front conflict....[T]he public treaty, signed on August 7, 1790, granted the Creeks considerable concessions. It prohibited states from negotiating for Creek land, effectively disarming Georgia. The Treaty of New York also guaranteed to the Creek confederacy 'all their lands within the limits of the United States' and permitted the Creeks to deal as they pleased with any non-Indian who 'shall attempt to settle on any of the Creek lands.'"Cozzens, *A Brutal Reckoning,* loc.913.

- "George Washington and his one-term successor, John Adams, had refrained from demanding major land cessions. Jefferson, however, assumed office in 1801 keen to acquire every inch of

Indian country between the Appalachians and the Mississippi River he could without provoking war. The Atlantic Seaboard groaned beneath the weight of a burgeoning citizenry. In Georgia alone, the population doubled during the last decade of the eighteenth century. By 1800, there were 101,066 whites and 59,699 slaves residing between coastal Georgia and the Oconee River." *Id.*, loc.1103-16.

The Nineteenth Century

8. The Cherokee were quite successful as neighbors to the Georgians, many owning land, large houses, farm animals and, even Black slaves. But, the Georgians were determined to drive the Indians out apparently largely for racist reasons, not economic ones. The State legislature passed a law purporting to deny them the right to stay. President John Quincy Adams refused to assist in its enforcement. Then the Supreme Court declared the law void. But, by then, Andrew Jackson had become President. Determined to remove the Cherokee Nation. Jackson ignored the Court and secured Congressional action dispossing the Cherokee. His successor, Martin Van Buren effected the removal. It was badly managed, resulting in thousands of deaths on "the Trail of Tears." Numerous Cherokee escaped and remained behind. The United States similarly sent the Army to attempt to eliminate the Seminoles in Florida.

- "The Cherokee Constitution, modeled after the U.S. Constitution and ratified in July 1827, declared the Cherokees to be a sovereign people on a par with the United States. ...These and other reforms created a sovereign nation as White Americans understood it, but it did not bring the Cherokees acceptance." Hämäläinen, *Indigenous Continent*, p.392.
- Instead, the Georgians "aimed to purge the Cotton Kingdom of Indigenous southerners, especially the Cherokees, Chickasaws, Choctaws, and Muscogees, who owned the most fertile lands on

the continent. ...[T]hey would be deported to a designated area in the West that became known as the Indian Territory. ...The Indians resisted the removal schemes fiercely, and they had a compelling case: Congress was concerned that the supply of public land far exceeded the demand. ...It was clear that the underlying motives driving Indigenous dispossession were not economic but racial." *Id.*, p.391.

- "The Georgia assembly demanded that John Quincy Adams remove the Cherokees, and when he refused, the assembly denied Cherokee sovereignty." *Id.*, p.393.
- "General Andrew Jackson became president in 1829 and announced 'Indian removal'—a euphemistic term if there ever was one—as his main ambition. The Cherokees sent envoys to Washington, D.C., in March 1830. ... The House of Representatives debated the expulsion of Indians from the South for two weeks before passing the Indian Removal Act by a paper-thin margin of 102–97. The Senate vote was 28–19 in favor of the act. Jackson declared that the new Indigenous domain in the West would be called the 'Indian Territory.'" *Id.*, p.394.
- "Congress reaffirmed federal supremacy over Indian affairs in the two Cherokee cases, *Cherokee Nation* and *Worcester*. There, the State of Georgia tried to assert the authority to legislate the Cherokee Nation's government out of existence, and then to confiscate Indian lands and resources. In the first case, a deeply split Court held that the Cherokee Nation was a domestic nation, but neither a state nor a foreign nation. In the second case, the Court held that the state laws had 'no force' in Indian country, barred under the Supremacy Clause by federal statutes and the Cherokee Nation's treaties with the United States." Matthew L.M. Fletcher, "A Short History of Indian Law in the Supreme Court," *ABA*, October 01, 2014.
- "They won their case in the Supreme Court, only to witness Jackson refusing to enforce the ruling." Hämäläinen, *Indigenous Continent*, p.398.

- "Guwisguwi signed the Treaty of New Echota on December 29 [1835], ceding all Cherokee lands east of the Mississippi to the United States for $5 million. He hoped at least to be able to shape the conditions of his people's dispossession. Most Cherokees denounced the Treaty Party as traitors, and they categorically refused to leave their homelands." *Id.*, p.398.

- "When Martin Van Buren, Jackson's successor as president, ordered the army to march fifteen thousand resisting Cherokees to the Indian Territory in 1838 at gunpoint, the Cherokees were too fractured to resist. As many as four thousand may have died of diseases, exposure, and polluted drinking water on their Trail of Tears." *Id.*, p.399.

- "[T]housands of Indians avoided being forced to the west through evasion, making themselves inconspicuous and unreachable by leaving their homelands of their own volition and retreating into hard terrain... . They effectively neutralized U.S. military and administrative might, preserving their sovereignty. [A]pproximately twenty percent of the Native Americans targeted for removal remained in the South, humiliating the growing U.S. bureaucratic machine." *Id.*, p.398.

* * *

- "In 1836, General Winfield Scott, one of the United States' most accomplished generals, was sent to Florida to subdue the Seminoles and force an unconditional surrender. ...By 1841, after years of jungle war on unstable terrain where soil and water often swapped places, nearly half of the four thousand U.S. troops in Florida were ill... . The American government announced the end of hostilities. Some four thousand Seminoles and former Black slaves had been removed to the Indian Territory. Roughly a thousand remaining Seminoles kept fighting, but by 1842, only a few hundred remained. Seminole leader Coacoochee resisted removal by leading his people to Mexico. The United States declared victory in a war that had no winners." Hämäläinen, *Indigenous Continent*, p.399.

* * *

- "Harboring no illusions about the trustworthiness of the American state, the Chickasaws sold their land—ten thousand square miles in all, some of it the richest on the continent—before it could be taken from them. They placed the resulting money in trust with the U.S. government... ." Hämäläinen, *Indigenous Continent*, p.393.

9. **Largely unnoticed by Americans, the Comanches established a large empire in the Southwest of North America and the northern half of what became Mexico, trading extensively with the Spanish occupiers and driving out other tribes, in particular, the the Lipan Apaches. The Comanches were accomplished horse men, and their resulting mobility gave them great advantages. After Mexico gained independence in 1821, the Comanches effectively drove the Mexican army south to Mexico City and controlled most of what was to beocme Texas. After Texas declared its independence, they negotiated a treaty with Sam Houston claiming most of the interior of the territory.**

- "With horses, Comanches, Kiowas, Cheyennes, and Lakotas could kill large numbers of buffalo and trade their hides east to America or south to Mexico. Horses also made them dangerous warriors. Aside from the Confederacy, they were the most powerful fighting force the U.S. Army would encounter until World War I." Heather Cox Richardson: *How the South Won the Civil War: Oligarchy, Democracy, and the Continuing Fight for the Soul of America* (2020), p.98.
- "[In the Southwest, there was a] domineering Indigenous power, the nearly forty-thousand-strong Comanches. ..The first [phase],

in the early eighteenth century, had relied heavily on violence. ...The second phase, in the early nineteenth century, had relied on a mix of diplomacy and coercion." Hämäläinen, *Indigenous Continent*, p.409.

- "Boosted by horses, the Comanches set out to control the southern plains and the region's animal bounty through war. ...[T]he Comanche thrust set off a long and bitter war with their old foes, the Lipan Apaches, In mid-March 1758, an army of two thousand Norteños gathered at the gates of the mission. The sacking of the San Saba Mission was a major turning point in the history of the North American West, and its shock waves reached all the way to Mexico City. The Comanches absorbed some Lipans into their ranks and banished scores to the desert lands to the west. ...The Comanches were an instant territorial superpower." *Id.*, p.412.

- "Covering approximately a quarter million miles of grassland, it was the most expansive Indigenous territory in North America by a large margin." *Id.*, p.413.

- "The Comanches relied on a fluid mix of diplomacy, commerce, coercion, and co-optation to secure essential resources, and Comanche and Spanish soldiers joined forces to expel the Apaches from New Mexico's borderlands. Whereas the Comanches built a more centralized nation and, eventually, an empire, the Apaches preserved the fluid and seasonally dynamic political system that had served them well before the Comanche ascendancy. Boosted by new trade outlets, the Comanches reached their apogee in the 1840s." *Id.*, p.420.

- "The Comanches faced very little resistance from Mexican soldiers. The Comanche tide had splintered the Mexican Republic into numerous small entities that were each preoccupied with their own survival." *Id.*, p.428.

- "[They] demanded a boundary line that gave the Comanches all of Texas except for a 125-mile belt along the Gulf coast. Houston signed away half of Texas's claimed territory to the Comanches. Texas was utterly exposed." *Id.*, p.425.

- "They ranged widely but ruled lightly, seeking resources and loyalty, not unconditional submission or sameness. ...The Comanches turned mobility into an imperial strategy, using horses to compress time and distance, bringing remote resources near while keeping violence at bay... ." *Id.*, p.428.

- "[T]he Comanches represented the pinnacle of Indigenous power in North America." *Id.*, p.429.

- "The United States managed to weaken the Comanches only after 1872, when the Kansas Pacific Railway enabled professional hunters—generously sponsored by the U.S. Army—to kill buffalo on an industrial scale and ship the robes to the East. The hunts were spectacularly wasteful... ." *Id.*, p.445.

10. The Central Plains Tribes, the Kiowas, Cheyennes, Appache and Lakotas, adopted horses brought by the Spanish, becoming much more mobile and formidable warriors. They essentially preserved their territories until the 1860s, despite increasing incursions by the "white man." By the mid-nineteenth century, the Latokas had established a large empire in the northern plains, displacing the Crows, Kiowas, and Shoshones, and then the Pawnees, Omahas, and Otoes. They commenced wars while the Union was struggling against the armies of the Confederacy, and they were largely successful. Even when President Grant sent General Sherman to defeat the Indians, they held on. The negotiated treaties that followed, however, were violated repeatedly by the U.S.

- "Plains nations were one-time farmers who had largely abandoned cereal agriculture, after re-domesticating escaped Spanish horses and adopting a largely nomadic mode of life. In late summer and early autumn, small and highly mobile bands of Cheyenne and Lakota would congregate in large settlements to make logistical preparations for the buffalo hunt. ...Once the hunting season [and rituals] ... were complete, such authoritarianism gave way to ... 'anarchic' forms of organization, society splitting once again into small, mobile bands." Graeber, *The Dawn of Everything*, pp. 108-109.

- "The Kiowas, Crows, and Shoshones, whose territories stretched around the Black Hills, had become full-fledged horse people decades earlier and were determined to keep intruders out. ...When the Lakotas expanded west along the Missouri's tributaries, they clashed with several nations. They forged an alliance with the Cheyennes and Arapahos, who had already become horse people, and pushed out the Crows, Kiowas, and Shoshones, making the Black Hills theirs. ...[T]he Lakotas could now extend their reach in all directions." Hämäläinen, *Indigenous Continent*, p.401.

- "In 1837, smallpox returned to the Missouri Valley, devastating the Pawnees once more, but the Lakotas were largely untouched. They destroyed a grand Pawnee village, the last of its kind, with a swift mounted attack. The Lakotas now held sway over the central Great Plains and its animal wealth. The Lakotas had become the dominant power in the vast continental grasslands. Exploiting their strategic advantages, the Lakotas moved to expel the agricultural nations—Pawnees, Omahas, and Otoes—from the river valleys of the central plains." *Id.*, p.403.

- "If the Lakotas started a war, the United States would lose it. The U.S. Army and government read the situation correctly, and in the spring of 1851 they sent runners to invite the Plains Indians to a peace conference at Fort Laramie. The Lakotas made it clear that they expected a two-hundred-mile southward extension of their domain. In the northern Great Plains, colonial borders would bend around Lakota borders; Americans would have to remove the Pawnees to the south to make space for the Lakotas. The United States had sided with power." *Id.*, p.407.

- "The Native reservations were a sign of American weakness, not strength. The United States simply lacked the capacity to defeat and domesticate the Indians or, as its experience with the predominant Lakotas had shown, even the power to keep them at bay." *Id.*, p.408.

• "The Lakotas went to war, attacking immigrant trains and U.S. Army patrols in the Platte Valley. Simultaneously to the south, the Cheyennes, Arapahos, Utes, and three Apache divisions—Jicarillas, Mescaleros, and Chiricahuas—ambushed settlers along the Oregon Trail, which skirted their territories." *Id.*, p.434.

• "The federal government's design for a subjugated Indigenous America was in tatters after only five years." *Id.*, p.434.

• "When the U.S. Army stopped fighting in the South in 1865, it simply turned its attention to the wars on the Great Plains against the Apaches, Kiowas, Comanches, Cheyennes, and Lakotas. ...There was *special* urgency to the Indian Wars in 1865, for postwar Americans were eager to push their way into the West and Indians were stopping them." Richardson, *How the South Won the Civil War*, p.132.

• "U.S. Army set out to end the raiding once and for all. Skirmishes culminated in the Battle of Cieneguilla near Pilar, New Mexico, when about 250 Apaches and Utes routed 60 soldiers, killing 22 and wounding another 36, while losing about 20 of their own warriors. ...This marked the start of an all-out war between the Apaches and the American settlers. Within a year, Cochise had allied with legendary Apache leader Mangas Coloradas and the much younger Geronimo to drive Americans out of their land." *Id.*, p.99.

• "In 1851, Dakotas in Minnesota Territory had given up 24 million acres of their land in exchange for a narrow strip of land along the Minnesota River and promises of food, supplies, and cash payments forever. In 1862, the cash-starved U.S. government reneged on its treaty obligations and refused to provide Dakotas with food. Starving Indians fought to retake their lands. In late summer, just as Union prospects on the battlefields of the South were at a low ebb, Dakotas killed between four hundred and eight hundred Minnesota settlers." *Id.*, p.109.

- "...For the next two years, the conflId.ict, dubbed Red Cloud's War, raged, with the Lakotas quickly gaining the upper hand. In August 1867 they attacked men haying near Fort C. F. Smith, then attacked again near Fort Phil Kearny, where the men threw together wagon boxes for defense. A few days after the 'Wagon Box Fight,' Lakota warriors attacked a Union Pacific freight train in Nebraska." *Id.*, p.134.

- "Congress rejected Sherman's plan for extermination of the native peoples, and instead sent a peace commission to push the Indians onto two giant reservations, one on the southern plains and one to the north." *Id.*, p.134.

- "In October 1867, the commissioners met with tribal leaders near Medicine Lodge Creek in Kansas, where they persuaded a critical mass of Apaches, Comanches, Kiowas, Cheyennes, and Arapahos to sign a series of treaties known collectively as the Treaty of Medicine Lodge. The Indians agreed to stop attacking railroad crews and settlers, and to exchange claims to about 90 million acres of land for firm titles to about 3 million acres in what is now Oklahoma." *Id.*, p.134.

- "Having demonstrated that he held the upper hand over the U.S. Army, Red Cloud signed a peace treaty primarily to gain trading rights at the fort in exchange for promises to stop killing settlers. The 1868 Treaty of Fort Laramie was a mirror of the Treaty of Medicine Lodge. It established a 22-million-acre tract of land in the western half of what is now South Dakota, along with a piece of Nebraska." *Id.*, p.135.

- "With the Civil War still raging, the War Department, at long last, accepted that there was no military solution to the crisis." *Id.*, p.439.

- "The Lakotas and their allies had won what became known as Red Cloud's War. The United States proposed peace talks, now as a defeated party. In April 1867, U.S. envoys approached the Lakotas."The Americans were negotiating from a position of weakness, and the 1868 Treaty of Fort Laramie reflected that. It

recognized Lakota hegemony in the northern Great Plains, transferred tens of thousands of square miles that had belonged to
other Native nations, and granted the Lakotas generous hunting
privileges outside the Great Sioux Reservation, which covered
roughly forty-eight thousand square miles." *Id.* p.440.

- "By the early 1870s, the Lakotas were raiding horses in Crow
  country... . There, they kept the U.S. Army away from the
  Powder River Country, extending their empire all the way to the
  Little Bighorn River. Soon the Lakotas dominated 'the larger part
  of' the Crow reservation—a stinging embarrassment to the U.S.
  authorities. The Utes and Apaches ignored their treaties with the
  United States and kept raiding New Mexico, now a U.S. territory.
  In 1868, a high-powered Indian Peace Commission was assigned
  to pacify the American West by negotiating treaties with the
  Native nations." *Id.,* p.440.

* * *

- "In 1857, the Dog Soldiers, members of a new militant Cheyenne division in the central plains, confronted Colonel Edwin
  Sumner, who was leading the First Cavalry to attack them. The
  Dog Soldiers claimed the western half of the central plains between the Arkansas and Platte Rivers as their sovereign domain,
  a safe haven that had been secured by truces, treaties, and kinship politics. Whereas the Cheyenne government, the Council of
  Forty-Four, focused on preserving peace, the Dog Soldiers went
  to war to keep their world inviolate." Hämäläinen, *Indigenous
  Continent*, p.435.

* * *

- "The Navajos, too, fought back against American incursions. In
  the fall of 1858, in a misguided campaign, U.S. soldiers invaded
  Canyon de Chelly, 'the seat of the supreme power of the Navajo

tribe.' The Navajos retaliated in April 1860 by sending nearly a thousand soldiers to attack Fort Defiance, the westernmost U.S. Army post in the New Mexico Territory. The battle ended in a draw, which was symptomatic: the U.S. Army was reacting to events rather than driving them, and the results were disastrous." Hämäläinen, *Indigenous Continent*, p.436.

- "[T]he Navajos thrived almost immediately. They revived their pastoral economy of sheep-, goat-, and horse-herding, and by 1870 their population had reached fifteen thousand. Between 1878 and 1886, five additions quadrupled the Navajo territory, and the Navajo Nation was never targeted for allotment, the forced subdivision of communal landholdings. At more than twenty-seven thousand square miles, the Navajo Nation reservation remains North America's largest Indigenous domain by a wide margin." *Id.*, p.442.

* * *

- "Once more, gold came between the Lakotas and the Americans. A U.S. Army expedition led by George Armstrong Custer found traces of gold in the Black Hills in 1874. ...The Lakotas may have lacked the United States' military-technological might—railroads, steamboats, machine guns—but they had accumulated a vast amount of knowledge of the U.S. Army's tactics and weaknesses." Hämäläinen, *Indigenous Continent*, p.448.
- "Crazy Horse led a band of soldiers nearly a mile downstream along the Little Bighorn, outflanking the Americans. Soon there were fewer than one hundred American soldiers alive, Custer among them. The Lakotas had won an overwhelming and galvanizing victory, but they would lose the war." *Id.*, p.449.
- "A vengeful Congress seized Pahá Sápa, willfully violating the Treaty of Fort Laramie, and the army launched attacks to force the horse nations into reservations, eliminating their most important asset, mobility." *Id.*, p.450.

* * *

- "The Nez Perces, led by Chief Joseph, or Thunder Rolling Down the Mountain, went to war. The first clash with U.S. troops, along Clearwater Creek in June 1877, was an exception: the only prolonged battle in a war that featured large-scale maneuvers, sustained volleys, and repeated charges. The fight was inconclusive, and soon after, the Nez Perces decided to leave their homelands.The U.S. Army apprehended the Nez Perces and handed them over to the Indian Office, which would see to their removal to the Indian Territory." Hämäläinen, *Indigenous Continent*, p.451.
- "The last official military engagement between the United States and North America's Indigenous peoples was over." *Id.*, p.452.

11. Of course, like all other peoples, not all of their decisions ended favorably and the consequences were not always as intended. Examples include the Tlaxcalteca's decision to join Cortez in attacking the Aztecs, Metacom's decision to launch the late war in Massachusetts, many supporting the British in 1775 and again in 1812, the nations choosing war in the Northwest Territories and some supporting the Confederacy.

- "The Tlaxcalteca were out to settle old scores. From their perspective, an alliance with Cortés might bring to a favourable end their struggles against the Aztec Triple Alliance, and the so-called 'Flowery Wars' between the Valleys of Puebla and Mexico." Graeber, *The Dawn of Everything*, p.348.
- "Opechancanough had defeated the Virginia Company. But victory over the company did not mean victory for the Indians. Opechancanough did not launch a final, killing assault, pushing the foreigners into the sea. Indeed, a second coordinated attack didn't take place for twenty-two years, when it was far too late." Mann, *1493*, p.126.

- "When the colonists resisted the British and mounted an armed defense that evolved into full-scale war, Native people, squeezed by both sides, had to choose alliances. As the conflict intensified, many large and influential Native nations leaned toward Great Britain." Nikole Hannah-Jones, *The 1619 Project: A New Origin Story* (2021), p.136.

- In July 1784, ... General George Washington awarded [an officer] 573 acres on the Keowee River. This fertile land had previously belonged to the Cherokees, who had generally sided with the British in he conflict and had been badly beaten by Washington's army." Hannah-Jones, *The 1619 Project,* p.136.

- "On November 28, 1785, ... American and Cherokee negotiators agreed to the terms of the first Treaty of Hopewell. The Cherokees would accept the 'protection of the United States of America, and of no other sovereign.' This first Treaty of Hopewell wasan followed by two others that winter, with the Choctaws and the Chickasaws, with nearly identical stipulations." *Id.,* pp.138-9.

- "[W]ithin the nations that had signed treaties at Hopewell Plantation, slavery gradually took root. Among the Indigenous nations, Cherokees enslaved the largest number of people, but Creeks, Choctaws, and Chickasaws also developed entrenched systems of Black enslavement tethered to racial prejudice." *Id.,* p.127.

- "In mid-December [1788,] some 200 members of different native tribes marched down the western shore of the Muskingum to Fort Harmar [Ohio] ... . Thus commenced the procedures of a new treaty. The Delawares, Wyandots, and Ottawas had formed a loose confederacy. But the most important members of the confederacy, the Shawnees and the Miamis, had refused to attend. ...The treaty that was finally signed on January 9, 1789, would bring little change for the better. ...With the advance of spring more scouts were ambushed on duty. ... On May 3 [1791], Congress, having decided something had to be done, authorized Governor St. Clair to raise a force of 2,000 to put down the native confederacy and to do so without delay." McCullough, *The Pioneers*, pp.63, 95.

- "[T]he great Shawnee chief, Tecumseh, with some of his followers had joined the British Army [during the War of 1812], in the belief that an English triumph would allow him to establish the Indian state he envisioned. In October [1813], Harrison won another decisive victory over British forces and Tecumseh and followers in a battle in which Tecumseh was killed and his following dispersed." *Id.*, pp.186, 189.

- "A dispute that began as a Creek civil war became a ruthless struggle against American expansion, erupting in the midst of the War of 1812. Not only was the Creek War the most pitiless clash between American Indians and whites in U.S. history, but the defeat of the Red Sticks—as those opposed to American encroachment were known because of the red war clubs they carried—also cost the entire Creek people as well as the neighboring Chickasaw, Choctaw, and Cherokee nations their homelands." Cozzens, *A Brutal Reckoning*, loc.181-6.

- "The Creek War began as a civil war within the Creek community and gave rise to the Red Stick militants who precipitated conflict with the United States. It was the most devastating internecine struggle that any Native people suffered as a consequence of contact with white Americans." *Id.,*, loc.221.

- "When the Civil War erupted in South Carolina, it had an impact far beyond the American Southeast. Native leaders to the West in Indian Territory faced a dire decision. Their governments and towns stood within a unique territory on the margins of the United States and the Confederate states. Like the slave states in the South, they might choose to secede and ally with the Confederacy, which would include political representation in the Confederate Congress, or they could elect to remain 'loyal' to the Union. ...[I]n many of these nations significant factions chose to support the Confederate states." Hannah-Jones, *The 1619 Project*, p.152.

12. The First Americans confronted and controlled their circumstances, protecting their lands and comunities through warfare, diplomacy and stratagems. Unlike the Southern, highly centralized and hierarchical Aztec and Inca empires, the occupants of North America successfully resisted the Spanish for 150 years, even controlling the Caribbean islands until reduced by Spanish-borne illnesses. And, the Eastern North Americans contained the English to a few precarious costal villages for 100 years and to the Eastern seaboard for an additional 150 years. The colonists were strikingly brutal and unprincipled, consistent with practices of punishment and warfare in Europe; but, the First Americans were better fighters.

- "So overwhelming was Indigenous sea power that it kept much of the Atlantic coast free of colonial bases for decades." Hämäläinen, *Indigenous Continent*, p.71.
- "A loose alliance of four Taino groups faced off against the Spaniards and one Taino group that had thrown its lot in with the foreigners. The Taino, who had no metal, could not withstand assaults with steel weapons. But they made the fight costly for the Spaniards. In an early form of chemical warfare, the Indians threw gourds stuffed with ashes and ground hot peppers at their attackers, unleashing clouds of choking, blinding smoke. Protective bandannas over their faces, they charged through the tear gas, killing Spaniards. When the Spaniards counterattacked, the Taino retreated scorched-earth style, destroying their own homes and gardens... ." Mann, *1493*, pp.37-8.
- "...The Wabanakis on the sea and the powerful Pequots on land surrounded the New Englanders. Like the Powhatans, the Pequot Confederacy had expanded rapidly in the early seventeenth century, drawing several neighboring groups into their orbit." Hämäläinen, *Indigenous Continent*, p.76.
- "[O]n March 22, 1622, ... Opechancanough [of the Powhatans] attacked. ...The assault was brutal, widespread, and well planned.

So swift were the blows that many colonists died without knowing they were under attack. ...[T]he attackers killed at least 325 people. The aftermath claimed as many as seven hundred more. ...His forces now more numerous and better supplied than the enemy, they raided English settlements at will." Mann, *1493*, pp.123-5.

- "Powhatan soldiers killed more than four hundred English. ...By 1646, both sides were reeling, and the Virginia General Assembly opened peace talks with Necotowance, Opechancanough's successor. ...The Powhatans' decades-long resistance to English expansion confined colonial settlements to the tidewater and the eastern shore of the Chesapeake for a long time, inadvertently providing a protective shield for many Indigenous nations in the interior. ...Virginia survived, but it was curbed, cramped, and unhealthy. Tens of thousands of Indians and powerful Native confederacies hemmed it in on three sides, reducing it to a mere foothold at the edge of an Indigenous continent... ." Hämäläinen, *Indigenous Continent*, pp.67-8.

- "Uncas's opportunistic diplomatic maneuvering and his ability to create and break alliances placed the colonists at a significant disadvantage in the contest for position and power. Uncas and his Mohegans endured endless colonial challenges, large and small— not just surviving as a people but controlling the world around them." *Id.*, pp.86-7.

- "Despite European guns, the Indians' greater numbers, entrenched positions, knowledge of the terrain, and superb archery made them formidable adversaries. ...Contemporary research suggests that indigenous peoples in New England were not technologically inferior to the British... .Even for a crack shot, an unrifled, early seventeenth-century gun had fewer advantages over a longbow than may be supposed." Mann, *1491*, p.98.

- "Native men were superior soldiers, having trained and prepared for war from a young age, internalizing an exacting warrior code that was drilled in by military societies." Hämäläinen, *Indigenous Continent*, p.85.

- "Only the wealthy tobacco colonies—Virginia and Maryland— managed to dispossess Native Americans on a large scale; everywhere else the Indians held the line." *Id.*, p.88.

So,

We must conclude that the myth of the "Noble Savage" (solitary or communal, peaceful and one with nature)—hypothesized by Rousseau, embellished by Margaret Mead and embraced by the progressive orthodoxy in the twentieth century—is just that: a myth. And, a very poor guide for public policy. The variety and complexity of those evolving civilizations appear quite surprising today. And, the European "conquest" of the New World was a precarious, costly (especially, in human lives) undertaking, with an uncertain outcome. The First Americans fought among themselves over territory, even after the arrival of European settlors. Some fought with the settlors against other Native Americans. Some fought with settlors against other Europeans. And, many fought against the intruders. They negotiated over boundaries and bargained over the sale of lands. They negotiated treaties. They schemed and plotted, engaged in comples strategem.

"The most powerful nations and confederacies—the Six Nations of the Iroquois Confederacy, the Indian Confederacy, the Wyandots, Lakotas, Comanches, Muscogees, Cherokees, and Seminoles—defeated the colonists in battle repeatedly and controlled the diplomatic proceedings that followed. ...They possessed the authority, savvy, and will to dictate terms to the Spanish, French, British, and U.S. empires."

Hämäläinen, *Indigenous Continent*, p.459.

We now say that the intruders "stole" the land from the Indians, probably because, knowing the end, we believe that the success of the newcomers was always assured due to a clear military superiority. But, the actual history was much more ambiguous and complicated. And, the military superiority did not exist until after the Civil War. Who has the strongest moral claim to the lands of the Northeast, the area of Lake Superior or the Central Plains? The first to settle there? The penultimate occupants (immediately preceding the Europeans? The longest residents? The most numerous? Obviously, there is no compellingly correct answer.

(So much for "settlor colonialism," in my view.)

And,

"...[W]hat does explain eventual European dominance?"

"... [O]ne source of the colonizers' strength jumps out: there were **just more settlers** than Native people. **A lot more.** While French and Spanish populations in the Americas grew at normal rates, the Anglo populations— enjoying congenial climates and the backing of energetic British markets—exploded. By the middle of the eighteenth century, Benjamin Franklin observed that, astonishingly, the number of British colonists was **doubling every twenty-five years**. This was a 'rapidity of increase probably without parallel in history,' wrote the economist Thomas Malthus. Immigration played a part but so did birth rates... ."

Daniel Immerwahr, "Contest or Conquest? A provocative history of Indigenous America," *Harper's Magazine,* November 2022 (emphasis added).

CHAPTER VII

Slavery: A History

The Beginnings

1. The treatment of humans as property or chattel slavery has been an ancient and almost universal practice. It was generally based not on race but on kinship or identity and mainly arose out of military conquest. Slavery was particulaly prevelant and long lasting in Africa. Slave trading and slave traders are also of long and disparate lineages. To some extent, supply created demand; and the existence of slavery in a society had economic consequences that promoted its continuation.

- "Slavery and the slave trade had been global phenomena for centuries by the early 17th century, involving Europeans and non-Europeans as slave traders and the enslaved." Bret Stephens, "1619 Chronicles," *The New York Times*, October 9, 2020.
- "The slave trade was complex and evolved out of existing networks of exchange indigenous to Africa. Before European slavers arrived, African chiefs and merchants were already trading among themselves, along well-established routes from West to East, from the Saharan north to the sub-Saharan south, and all points in between. ...African elites did not typically sell their own kin.

Captives tended to be 'culturally and ethnically alien to those who enslaved them... .'" Nikole Hannah-Jones, The New York Times Magazine, Caitlin Roper, Ilena Silverman, and Jake Silverstein, *The 1619 Project: A New Origin Story* (2021), p.77.

- "Slavery existed in parts of Africa before the fifteenth century, but with the advent of the transatlantic trade in enslaved Africans, abductions and inter-ethnic conflicts greatly increased in West Africa as local chiefs responded to the immense demand from European slave traders." Oded Galor, *The Journey of Humanity: The Origins of Wealth and Inequality* (2022), pp.173-4.

- "It rarely makes economic sense to breed slaves—which is why, globally, slaves have so often been the product of military aggression... ." David Graeber and David Wengrow, *The Dawn of Everything* (2021), p.188.

- "[However, in Seventeenth Century Morocco, an army of Black slaves was] constantly replenished by the great breeding farms and nurseries that Moulay Ismail had established outside Meknes. He visited these nurseries each year and would take back all the ten-year-olds to Meknes. The girls were taught cooking, washing and housekeeping in the imperial household, while the boys were prepared for military training." Giles Milton, *White Gold: The Extraordinary Story of Thomas Pellow and Islam's One Million White Slaves* (2004), p.150.

- "[D]uring the reduction of the rural population to the status of serfs, slavery disappeared from Europe. ...Feudalism also created a power vacuum in which independent cities specializing in production and trade could flourish. But when the balance of power changed after the Black Death, and serfdom began to crumble in Western Europe, the stage was set for a much more pluralistic society without the presence of any slaves." Daron Acemoglu and James A Robinson, *Why Nations Fail: The Origins of Power, Prosperity, and Poverty* (2012), p.176.

- "[S]lavery ... appears to have expanded in Africa throughout the nineteenth century. ...[A] number of existing accounts written by travelers and merchants during this time suggest that in the West African kingdoms of Asante and Dahomey and in the Yoruba city-states well over half of the population were slaves. More accurate data exist from early French colonial records for the western Sudan, a large swath of western Africa, stretching from Senegal, via Mali and Burkina Faso, to Niger and Chad. In this region 30 percent of the population was enslaved in 1900. ...In most parts of colonial Africa, slavery continued well into the twentieth century." *Id.*, p.257.

2. Almost all Africans sold into slavery were sold by other Africans. The extent of the slave trade within Africa caused seious damage to the local social organizations and adversely affected subsequent economic development, but it provided wealth to the African elites. Of the estimated 25 million Africans so sold, more than half went to the Middle East. The largest number of slaves from the trans-Atlantic trade went to Brazil, the second largest number went to the Caribbean. Only some 300,000 out of 10.5 million successfully transported to the New World came directly to North America. Most of the slaves brought into the United States were brought from the Caribbean, already having been slaves there.

- *See, e.g.,* Hakim Adi, "Africa and the Transatlantic Slave Trade," *BBC*, updated 5 October 2012.
- "In much of Africa the substantial profits to be had from slaving led not only to its intensification and even more insecure property rights for the people but also to intense warfare and the destruction of many existing institutions; within a few centuries, any process of state centralization was totally reversed, and many of the African states had largely collapsed." Acemoglu and Robinson, *Why Nations Fail*, pp.115-116.
- "Kingdom of Kongo was governed by the king in Mbanza, subsequently São Salvador. Areas away from the capital were ruled by an elite who played the roles of governors of different parts of the

kingdom. The wealth of this elite was based on slave plantations around São Salvador and the extraction of taxes from the rest of the country. Slavery was central to the economy, used by the elite to supply their own plantations and by Europeans on the coast." *Id.*, p.88.

- "East Africa became a major supplier of slaves to the Arab world, and West and Central Africa would be drawn into the world economy during the European expansion associated with the Atlantic trade as suppliers of slaves. ...While in England the profits of the slave trade helped to enrich those who opposed absolutism, in Africa they helped to create and strengthen absolutism." *Id.*, p.178.

- The first sub-Saharan African taken to Europe as a slave was a woman seized by Portuguese slave traders in 1441. By the early 1500s, the Portuguese were transporting 3,000 enslaved Africans a year to Central and South America. The British participation began in 1563, with the capture and sale of 300 people from Sierra Leone to planters in the Dominican Republic. *See* William Yoo, *What Kind of Christianity: A History of Slavery and Anti-Black Racism in the Presbyterian Church* (2022), pp.51-4.

- The demand for slave labor increased dramatically in the Caribbean as a result of the success of the plantations and the deaths of the indigenous slaves from imported diseases. *Id.*

- "By 1775, slave ships had carried 160,000 Africans to the Chesapeake colonies, 140,000 to new slave colonies that opened up in the Carolinas and Georgia, and 30,000 to the northern colonies. These numbers were small compared to the myriads being carried to sugar colonies, however. Slave ships landed more than 1.5 million African captives on British Caribbean islands (primarily Jamaica and Barbados) by the late 1700s and had brought more than 2 million to Brazil. In North America, however, the numbers of the enslaved grew, except in the most malarial lowlands of the Carolina rice country." Edward E. Baptist, *The Half Has Never*

Been Told: slavery and the making of American capitalism (2014, 2016), p.3.

3. The first slaves in the Americas were captives of indigenous peoples in Central and South America. In North America, the indigenous peoples of the Pacific Northwest had slaves. The former Mississippian societies (throughout the Southeast, from the Mississippi to the Atlantic) had substantial involvement in slavery.

- "[P]erhaps a quarter of the indigenous Northwest Coast population lived in bondage—which is about equivalent to proportions found in the Roman Empire, or classical Athens, or indeed the cotton plantations of the American South. ...[S]lavery on the Northwest Coast was a hereditary status: if you were a slave, your children were also fated to be so." Graeber and Wengrow, *The Dawn of Everything*, p.185.
- "Slavery ... became commonplace on the Northwest Coast [of North America] largely because an ambitious aristocracy found itself unable to reduce its free subjects to a dependable workforce." *Id.*, p.207.
- "The result, from the nobles' point of view, was a perennial shortage, not of labour as such but of controllable labour at key times of year. This was the problem to which slavery addressed itself. And such were the immediate causes, which made 'harvesting people' from neighbouring clans no less essential to the aboriginal economy of the Northwest Coast than constructing weirs, clam gardens or terraced root plots." *Id.*, p.198.
- "[S]outhern colonies coexisted with former Mississippian societies with many slaves and considerable experience in trading them." Charles C. Mann, *1493: Uncovering the New World Columbus Created* (2011), p.167.
- "Carolina's leaders came up with an elegant scheme; they asked nearby native groups to provide them with slaves by raiding the Indians who were allied with Spain and France, destabilizing

their enemies and reducing their labor shortage at the same time. Economically speaking, indigenous slavery was a good deal for both natives and newcomers. Indian captives cost £5–10, as little as half the price of indentured servants... . Unsurprisingly, the colonists chose Indian slaves over European servants." *Id.*, p.166.

- "[F]or its first four decades the [Carolina] colony was mainly a slave exporter—the place from where captive Indians were sent to the Caribbean, Virginia, New York, and Massachusetts. Data estimated that Carolina merchants bought between thirty and fifty thousand captive Indians between 1670 and 1720. In the same period, ships in Charleston unloaded only 2,450 Africans (some came overland from Virginia, though)." *Id.*, p.167.

4. Europeans enslaved by North Africans, "a trade that had ensnared at least one million Europeans and Americans," suffered experiences remarkably similar to the worst experiences of Africans enslaved in North America—families torn apart, captives publicly humiliated and abused, enslaved tortured and confined in dungeons.

- "[F]or more than a century [as of 1700], the trade in white slaves from across Europe and colonial North America had been destroying families and wrecking innocent lives." Milton, *White Gold*, p.4.
- "Crowds of townspeople had gathered at the palace gates to abuse them, 'offering us the most vile insults ... and giving us many severe boxes.'" *Id.*, p.5.
- "Flogged by black slave-drivers and held in filthy slave pens, these abject captives were forced to work on what the sultan intended to be the largest construction project in the known world. ...Algiers, Tunis and Tripoli also had thriving slave auctions, in which thousands of captives were put through their paces before being sold to the highest bidder. These wretched men, women and children came from right across Europe—from as far afield

as Iceland and Greece, Sweden and Spain. Many had been seized at sea by the infamous Barbary corsairs. Many more had been snatched from their homes in surprise raids [on seaside villages, particularly in Southern England and Spain]." *Id.*, p. 8.

- "The captives were also ceremoniously marched through the town on their first arrival, so that the locals could curse them and offer degrading and hostile treatment. ...The matamores were underground cells, which each accommodated some fifteen or twenty slaves. The only light and ventilation came from a small iron grate in the roof; in winter, rain poured through this opening and flooded the floor. The grate provided the only access to the outside world." *Id.*, pp.67, 68.

- "[T]hey were stripped and put through their paces. They were made to jump and skip to test their agility; they had foreign fingers poked into mouths and ears. The experience of being auctioned was both terrifying and humiliating, and every individual had his own tale of suffering." *Id.*, p.70.

- "This punishment, used widely throughout Barbary, inflicted terrible pain. Almost every surviving slave account mentions it, and there were very few captives who avoided a bastinading." *Id.*, pp.82-83.

5. The capture and enslavement of white Europeans and North Americans by North African pirates in the sixteenth, seventeenth and eighteenth centuries came to an end in 1816 as a result of military action by the English and American governments. Thereafter, the prevailing incidences of slavery were of Africans. The European governments so opposed to the slavery of white Christians were willing to accept the slavery of Black "heathens," and African rulers were often complicit or active participants in the sales of Africans to the slave traders.

- "Morocco was not the only place in North Africa where white captives were held as slaves. Algiers, Tunis and Tripoli also had thriving slave auctions, in which thousands of captives were put through their paces before being sold to the highest bidder." Milton, *White Gold,* p.8.

- "The call to arms against Barbary was led by the eccentric British admiral Sir Sidney Smith. He was passionate about the issue of white slavery and had established a movement devoted to ending the trade forever. It was called the Society of Knights Liberators of the White Slaves of Africa and it rapidly drew influential members from across Europe. When at the end of the Napoleonic Wars crowned heads and ministers gathered to discuss peace at the Congress of Vienna, which began in 1814, Smith and his knights elected to join them."*Id.*, p.270.

The Trans-Atlantic Trade

6. It is likely that the "plantation style" production of sugar from sugarcane emerged on the west coast of Africa in the sixteenth century, developed by the Portuguese, who subsequently transported it to Brazil and then to the Caribbean. The Portuguese's slaves were primarily Africans.

- "São Tomé ..., an island 150 miles (240 kilometers) west of Gabon in the Gulf of Guinea, was first settled by the Portuguese in the late 15th century. ...By 1495, to supply labor for the sugar trade, the Portuguese rulers forced convicts, Jewish children and enslaved Africans to move to the island. ...[I]n the São Tomé sugar plantation system, enslaved people — largely from what are now Benin, the Republic of the Congo, Angola and the Democratic Republic of the Congo — performed nearly all the tasks, from the harvesting and processing of sugarcane to the carpentry and stone masonry needed to build and run the mills. ...[T]he Portuguese moved many of their operations to Brazil in the early 17th century, taking the plantation operating model with them." Kristina Killgrove, "Plantation slavery was invented on this tiny African island, according to archaeologists," *LiveScience*, August 17, 2023.

7. African slaves were brought to the New World in the first two decades of the 16th century, specifically to South America and the Caribbean.

- "In 1441, Henry sent two knights—Nuno Tristão and Antão Gonçalves—... to explore Africa.... While filling his boat with seal pelts, Gonçalves ran across a naked African and his Berber female servant, the first native Africans Gonçalves had encountered in his twenty years of exploration. ...[H]e kidnapped them. ...Most of the duo's profits came from the human cargo. ...In 1444, the Portuguese discovered it was easier to barter for their human cargo than capture them. ...Nuno Tristão and Antão Gonçalves can go down in history as the first Europeans to purchase Africans from Black slave traders and resell them in Europe." Michael Harriot, *Black AF History: The Un-Whitewashed Story of America* (2023,. pp.30-1.
- "[T]he first Africans in the Spanish colonies were actually bought from Portuguese traders, enslaved on the Iberian Peninsula, and then hauled as cargo to the New World. The Spanish believed that these Africans would be immune to European diseases and 'sturdier.'" *Id.*, p.38.
- "[U]p to the end of the eighteenth century, the heart of the plantation economy was French and British. ... In the 1780s, the French slaveholding islands held the largest concentration of slaves in the Euro-American world—about 700,000—compared with 600,000 in the British possessions, and 500,000 on the plantations in the southern United States. ...[T]hese were truly slave islands, in the sense that the proportion of slaves rose as high as 90 percent of the total population ...in the 1780s (or even 95 percent if we include free Blacks and métis, those of mixed-race descent).

...In comparison, during the same period slaves represented ... [30-35] percent of the population of the southern United States and [50% in] Brazil, and the available sources suggest comparable proportions in Athens and in Rome in antiquity." Thomas Piketty, *A Brief History of Equality* (2022), pp.68-69.

- The first African slaves arrived in North America in 1619, only because the ship on which they were being transported to Mexico was seized by British privateers. Unfortunately, buyers were found. They were brought to Jamestown, Virginia, established as a fort in 1607, briefly abandoned in 1610, and becoming a town in 1619 (subsequently, the colonial capital).
- The demand for slave labor in the Caribbean had grown with the cultivation of sugar cane. The demand in the United States exploded in the early 1800s with the cultivation of cotton, replacing tobacco on much acreage. *The Lowcountry Digital History Initiative.*
- "Different climatic conditions might ... have contributed to the long-term effects of colonisation on local institutions. The climate and soil in Central America and the Caribbean were best suited for growing coffee, cotton, sugar cane and tobacco—crops for which efficient cultivation requires large plantations. The agricultural sector that emerged in these regions during the colonial era was therefore characterised by centralised land ownership, which led to unequal wealth distribution, coerced labour and even slavery—the most extractive of all institutions... ." Galor, *The Journey of Humanity*, p. 155.

8. The New World and the slave trade both proved to be quite dangerous for Europeans, in part because of diseases brought from Africa.

- "Hidden on the slave ships was a hitchhiker from Africa: the mosquito *Aedes aegypti*. In its gut *A. aegypti* carried its own hitchhiker: the virus that causes yellow fever, itself also of African origin. "The first yellow fever onslaught began in 1647 and lasted five years. Six thousand died on Barbados alone in those five years, according to one contemporary estimate. Almost all of the victims were European... ." Mann, *1493*, p.180.

- African diseases slew so many Europeans ... that slave ships often lost proportionately more white crewmen than black slaves... . [I]n the American falciparum and yellow fever zone the English were, compared to Africans, somewhere between three and ten times more likely to die in the first year." *Id.*, p.173.

- There was "the so-called 'white man's grave' when Europeans involved in the slave trade died in droves." Peter Frankopan, *The Earth Transformed: An Untold History* (2023), p.120.

- "As in Virginia, malaria came to Carolina. Unfortunately, Indians were just as prone to malaria as English indentured servants—and more vulnerable to other diseases." Mann, *1493*, p.168.

9. In total, about 400,000 of some 12 million enslaved Sub-Saharan Africans transported in the Atlantic trade were delivered to North America—between 3% and 4%. Given that the Atlantic trade itself accounted for less than half of the total African peoples enslaved from 1500 through 1800 (the majority being sold in Mediterranean/Middle East), the colonies received probably less than 1.5% of the total of enslaved Africans.

The Southern Colonies

10. Between 1520 and 1630, England's population had more than doubled, and labor shortages which had kept wages up at the beginning of that period turned to a surplus. The founding of Virginia was facilitated by helping to deal with the high numbers of poor and unemployed in England. The primary source of labor in Virginia was indentured servants, who contracted to work for a specified number of years in exchange for transportation to the

New World and room and board for the duration, generally with little or no other compensation.

- "Virginia Company leaders enslaved local Indians and then imported English workers, mostly young men. They had a vast pool from which to draw. England had undergone a population boom in the years after the Great Plague had ripped through the country from 1346 to 1353 in an epidemic that killed 60 percent of Europe's population. As the population rebounded over the centuries, inflation soared, and in the late 1500s, English planters pushed tenant farmers off their land in order to enclose fields for sheep and make their own plantations more efficient. ...Some, desperate or hopeful or crazy—or all three—raised the money for passage by promising to work for an employer in the colony for a period of time, usually from four to seven years, to work off the debt. Planters snapped up their contracts." Heather Cox Richardson, *How the South Won the Civil War: Oligarchy, Democracy, and the Continuing Fight for the Soul of America* (2020), pp.45-7.
- "Year after year, the company spent outsize sums to send colonists to Virginia—more than a hundred shiploads all told. Year after year, most of the would-be settlers perished within weeks or months—men and women, rich and poor, child and convict. ...England shipped about seven thousand people to Virginia between 1607 and 1624. Eight out of ten died." Mann, *1493*, p.114.
- "Before the onset of the 18th century, the terms 'slave' and 'servant' were sometimes used interchangeably, and the differences in the conditions of white indentured servants and black servants were not well-defined." Slavery Law & Power, *Codifying Enslavement*, The Virginia Slave Code of 1705.
- "The... newcomers, more often than not, were indentured servants, allowing successful planters simultaneous access to land and labor, with no upfront cost to the company. Merchants and mariners reaped a benefit, too, for they recruited prospective servants, bargained their indenture terms with them, and then sold

the contracts to planters in Virginia. ... Approximately 50,000 servants—or three-quarters of all new arrivals—immigrated to the Chesapeake Bay colonies between 1630 and 1680." Brendan Wolfe, "Indentured Servants in Colonial Virginia," *Encyclopedia Virginia*, October 2022.

- "In the early days of colonial America, the vast majority of people compelled to work for landowners were vagrant children, convicts, and indentured laborers imported from Europe. The wealthy settlers who benefited from their unfree labor did not at first distinguish between the status of European, African, and Indigenous servants." Hannah-Jones, *The 1619 Project*, p.49.

- "[T]he English colonies initially turned to indentured servants and largely avoided slaves. Indentured servants comprised between a third and a half of the Europeans who arrived in English all of Virginia in 1650. Slaves were rare—only three hundred lived in North America in the first century of colonization." Mann, *1493*, p.158.

- "The two primary systems of labor in the North American colonies were wage labor, in which employers and employees agreed upon monetary compensation for specific tasks or hours of labor, and indentured servitude, a contractual system in which one person agreed to labor for another person for a specific amount of time, such as four to seven years, to repay a loan, which was often the cost of the person's transatlantic passage, housing, and food. ...Colonial policies were careful to note that the indenture gave the holder rights to a servant's labor contract and not the personhood of the servant." Yoo, *What Kind of Christianity*, pp.66-7.

- "Black enslavement in the immediate years following 1619 sometimes resembled indentured servitude, and some seventeenth-century Africans labored as indentured servants, with a specified length of contract, and not as uncompensated enslaved laborers in perpetuity." *Id.*, p.67.

11. The situation of Blacks in the Chesapeake during the eighteenth century was quite complicated and fluid. Numerous families were made up of both free persons and enslaved persons. There were individuals who had come to the colonies clearly as indentured servants, others who were so treated and others who were treated as slaves in violation of their employment contracts. In any event, the number of free Blacks grew substantially, and many Blacks owned property and used the court system.

- "Black people accounted for a tiny fraction of the population at the time—less than 1 percent in the 1660s and 1670s—and most of them ... had been born in the Caribbean or had spent time there or elsewhere in the Americas. ...Many spoke English, practiced Christianity, knew how to navigate life in the European colonies, and worked side by side with white laborers." Rachel L. Swarns, *The 272: The Families Who Were Enslaved and Sold to Build the American Catholic Church* (2023), p.5.
- "Black people ... were not always assumed to be slaves. And in the early decades following the Jesuits' arrival, Maryland had become a place where they could wrest some autonomy from employers and enslavers and savor a measure of independence and freedom. ...Some Black people—likely a small and rapidly shrinking number—continued to work as indentured servants, and some even took their employers to court to defend their rights." *Id.*, pp.5, 7.
- "All across the state, freedom fever was spreading. ...[S]ome Black people had begun to arm themselves, not with weapons but with lawsuits. Emboldened by the egalitarian ideology of the Revolutionary War, hundreds of enslaved Black men and women had begun to fight for their freedom in Maryland's courts." *Id.*, p.27.
- "Many enslaved people in Maryland had free people in their families... .The courts had provided a pathway to freedom for some, while others had purchased their freedom or been manumitted by their owners.enslaved and free blacks often shared common

aspirations and worked hand in hand to press for better treatment. Free in name but restricted by the laws and practices of the white people around them, they had learned how to navigate white-dominated society. "*Id.*, pp.64, 65.

- "[T][he number of free Blacks in the state had swelled dramatically. In the decade between 1790 and 1800, the number of free Blacks in Maryland more than doubled, jumping from 8,043 to 19,587." *Id.*, p.29.

- "As the flurry of manumissions inspired by the fervor of the Revolutionary War faded and unfavorable legal decisions made it harder for the enslaved to win their freedom through the courts, fear began to replace hope among the enslaved people on the Catholic plantations." *Id.*, p.31.

12. In English North America, slavery was an economic institution. It's reason for being was economic—the New World had an amazing abundance of land and other natural resources and a scarcity of labor and farming skills.

- "The strengths of African workers became their undoing. British colonists in the West Indies, for example, saw Africans as 'a civilized and relatively docile population,' who were 'accustomed to discipline,' and who cooperated well on a given task. Africans demonstrated an immunity to European diseases, making them more viable to the colonists than were the indigenous people the Europeans had originally tried to enslave." Swarns, *The 272*, p.42.

- "The southern political institutions, both before the Civil War and after, had a clear economic logic, not too different from the South African Apartheid regime: to secure cheap labor for the plantations. But by the 1950s, this logic became less compelling." Acemoglu and Robinson, *Why Nations Fail*, p.415.

13. Plantation slavery developed according to a logic inherent in the institution. Slaves were to be property, so a legal structure was

needed to define and protect the rights in that property. Slavery depended on coercion, so rules concerning and providing coercion were needed. The circumstances in English North America, unlike in some other regions allowed slaves generally to live through their reproductive years, so the status of children had to be specified. The issue was different from that of primogeniture. The children had economic value. Looking to the mother made economic sense. Maternity was unambiguous; if the mother "belonged" to someone who provided room and board for her, the child would be expected to follow.

14. In the earliest days, slavery was reconciled with Catholicism on the premise that the people enslaved were not Christian. Thus, in many colonies, slaves who converted were freed under the law. (White slaves in northern Africa who converted to Islam, even under severe duress, were abandoned by their European governments.) However, as the colonies became increasingly dependent on slave labor, economics won out over the religious rationale. By the beginning of the eighteenth century, most colonies had enacted laws providing that baptism or conversion were not grounds for manumission.

- "The exact number of renegades forced to serve under Moulay Ismail [of Morocco] remains unknown. They rarely figure in the tallies of captives that were compiled by ambassadors and padres. Nor were they considered worthy of being included in negotiations conducted by their home governments. Despised for having forsaken their Christian faith, they were abandoned to their fate." Milton, *White Gold*, p.146.
- "This was a foolish mistake on the part of Europe's ministers, for the sultan's renegades vastly outnumbered the captives being held in the slave pens and played a crucial, if unwilling, role in keeping Moulay Ismail in power. Without the services of these apostates—many of whom were desperate to escape—the sultan

would been hard pressed to contain the country's frequent rebellions." *Id.*

- "Fear of Islam was a subject of equally heated debate in the crown colonies of North America—especially New England, which had lost a number of merchants and mariners to the Barbary corsairs. One of Boston's Puritan ministers, Cotton Mather, was particularly taxed by the issue of apostasy. He conceded that the slaves were suffering terrible deprivations in Morocco, yet believed that physical hardship was no excuse for spiritual weakness... ." *Id.*, p. 166.

15. The popularity of the milder Virginia tobacco grown from Spanish seeds made tobacco the most profitable crop in the Southern colonies in the seventeen century. The demand for labor soared. African slave labor began replacing the European indentured servants largely in the Virginia tobacco fields by the early eighteenth century, largely because of their relative resistance to malaria.

- "Virginia Company's 'Great Charter of privileges, orders, and laws' offered free land grants to anyone who provided funds for poor people to move to the colonies. An affluent landowner would receive the rights to fifty acres for each 'head' they brought over, garnering as much as two hundred acres for a family of four. ...In 1638, George Menefie..., a merchant, farmer, and member of the governor's council, was able to receive a patent for 3,000 acres, 1,150 of which he claimed for 'the Negroes I brought out of England with me.'" Harriot, *Black AF History*, p.57.
- "[B]etween 1680 and 1700, the number of slaves suddenly exploded. Virginia's slave population rose in those years from three thousand to sixteen thousand—and kept soaring thereafter. In the same period the tally of indentured servants shrank dramatically." Mann, *1493*, p.158.

- "The increasing demand for enslaved Africans was closely tied to labor shortages in the Americas." Yoo, *What Kind of Christianity*, p.52.
- "Virginia and points south ha[d] already proven so unhealthy for Europeans [because of mosquito borne diseases like malaria] that plantation overseers [we]re finding it difficult to persuade laborers to come from overseas to work in the tobacco fields. Some landowners ... resolved this problem by purchasing workers from Africa." Mann, *1493*, p.74. "European servants had become increasingly scarce, and the colony soon shifted from an indentured to an enslaved workforce." Swarns, The 272, p.11.
- "Mounting hostility toward Catholics in Maryland helped propel the shift to a reliance on slave labor, particularly among the wealthy Catholics—gentry and priests—who dominated the rural economy. ...[T]he colony's Protestant English leaders passed a series of discriminatory laws that targeted the Catholic minority, including a tax on the importation of 'all Irish Papist Servants imported into the Province.' Indentured servants could no longer be counted on as a reliable labor source." *Id.*, p.13.
- "Socially speaking, malaria—along with another mosquito-borne disease, yellow fever—turned the Americas upside down. Before these maladies arrived, the most thickly inhabited terrain north of Mexico was what is now the southeastern United States, and the wet forests of Mesoamerica and Amazonia held millions of people. After malaria and yellow fever, these previously salubrious areas became inhospitable." Mann, *1493*, p.140.
- "[A]dult West and Central Africans were and are less susceptible to malaria than anyone else on earth. In vivax-ridden Virginia and Carolina, they were more likely to survive and produce children than English colonists." *Id.*, p.173.
- "By the early 1700s, enslaved Black people accounted for between two-thirds and three-quarters of Maryland's workforce." Swarns, *The 272*, p.

- "The Mason-Dixon Line roughly split the East Coast into two zones, one in which falciparum malaria was an endemic threat, and one in which it was not. It also marked the border between areas in which African slavery was a dominant institution and areas in which it was not... ." Mann, *1493*, p.173.
- Similarly, "Bantu peoples spread out into much of west and central West Africa around 3,000 years ago, when built-up resistance to malaria was a key factor in the expansion of culture, language, identity and genetics." Frankopan, *The Earth Transformed,*, p.71.

16. By the beginning of the eighteenth century, African slaves in South Carolina had begun to grow rice for their own consumption. When their owners discovered that rice could be grown there, they made it one of the principle crops. By 1776, South Carolina was a major supplier of rice, and rice was a source of considerable wealth. The South Carolinian owners were organizing their slaves's tasks based on individual skills.

- "In 1672, Morris Matthews was granted several hundred acres ... a few miles outside of ... Charles Towne at Albemarle Point. Four years later, Matthews gave up and sold the property to Thomas and Ann Drayton... . However, the brackish water made growing tobacco, vegetables, or most food staples nearly impossible on a large scale, and the phosphorus-rich Lowcountry soil didn't allow for the citrus farming the Draytons had mastered in Barbados. ...When they investigated, the[y] discovered that the Africans had been growing their own food... . The Africans were growing rice." Harriot, *Black AF History*, p.59.
- "In a humid climate like Carolina, it is a backbreaking prospect that fosters disease, dehydration, and exhaustion. But even in these conditions, the Draytons' stolen human class were able to persevere, saving the family from starvation—and the entire Carolina economic system from collapse—with the introduction of America's first edible cash crop." *Id.*, p. 60.

- "By 1776, South Carolina was the number one exporter of rice to England, the number one supplier of salted meat to the Caribbean, and had the highest per capita income in the British colonies. ...In the five years before the American Revolution, South Carolina had imported more enslaved Africans than all the other ports in all the other American colonies combined." *Id.*, p.65.

- "[I]n the South Carolina colonies, the male-to-female ratio would eventually reach a one-to-one ratio after plantation owners realized that African women were the ones who possessed the engineering and agricultural knowledge necessary to grow what would become known as 'Carolina Gold.'" *Id.*, p.61.

- A group of South Carolins slaves revoted "on September 9, 1739.... After crossing the Stono Bridge, they broke into a hardware store and armory that sold guns and munitions. They executed the two shopkeepers, decapitated them, confiscated the firearms, and kept things moving. ...The Stono Rebellion changed the face of slavery in the slave capital of the world and, by proxy, in America as a whole. As a result of it, whites temporarily paused the slave trade for a decade, blaming the violence on the fact that these rebels were born in Africa. ...When the transatlantic slave trade eventually reopened, they avoided the Congo-Angola region..." *Id.*, pp.71-2.

17. Georgia, founded in 1733, initially banned slavery. Under pressures from the neighboring Carolinas, for economic reasons, that ban was removed in 1750.

- "Georgia may have been the most utopian of North American colonial schemes. It was designed to turn a profit and provide defense against rival empires, but it was also a philanthropic and self-consciously idealistic project. There were to be no wars, no dispossession of Native Americans, no slavery, no lawyers, and no hard liquor—just a better life for common White people than was possible in Europe." Hämäläinen, *Indigenous Continent,* pp.202, 203.

- "By the mid-1740s the Trustees realized that excluding slavery was rapidly becoming a lost cause. In the absence of their strong leadership, there was little to prevent the Georgia settlers, with the connivance of South Carolina sympathizers, from illicitly importing enslaved Africans primarily through the Augusta area." Betty Wood, "Slavery in Colonial Georgia." *New Georgia Encyclopedia,* last modified Jul 27, 2021.

- "The lifting of the Trustees' ban opened the way for Carolina planters to fulfill the dream of expanding their slave-based rice economy into the Georgia Lowcountry. The planters and the people they enslaved flooded into Georgia and soon dominated the colony's government. In 1755 they replaced the slave code [initially] agreed to by the Trustees with one that was virtually identical to South Carolina's." *Id.*

- "Between 1750 and 1775 Georgia's enslaved population grew in size from less than 500 to approximately 18,000 people. Beginning in the mid-1760s, Georgia began to import captive workers directly from Africa—mainly from Angola, Sierra Leone, and the Gambia. Most were given physically demanding work in the rice fields, although some were forced to labor in Savannah's expanding urban economy." *Id.*

- "The circumstances of slavery in the Georgia Lowcountry precluded the possibility of organized rebellion. Yet enslaved people resisted their owners and asserted their humanity in ways that included running away as well as acts of verbal and physical violence." *Id.*

The Slave Codes

18. The colonies did not originally have laws regarding slavery, so the early arrangements were fluid. Many slaves were treated

like indentured servants. And, slaves could be freed upon being baptized. In 1662, Virginia enacted a law providing that children of black mothers would have the status of the mother, not that of the white father. Other colonies followed, despite the long standing English tradition of patriarchy. Between 1664 and 1706, six colonies enacted laws declaring that Christian baptism would not result in emancipation, following the example of France.

- *See* Yoo, *What Kind of Christianity*, pp.64-7 ("Black enslavement did not become a formal system immediately in 1619. The laws did not initially regulate slavery and determine the rights of Black persons. ...The first legal distinctions between Black and white persons in the North American colonies emerged in the 1660s").
- "In 1641, Massachusetts became the first British colony to recognize slavery as a legal institution. Connecticut followed in 1650. By 1664, Maryland had passed its own law, declaring that "'all Negroes or other [slaves] already within [the colony] And all Negroes and other [slaves] to bee hereafter imported' would henceforth be considered slaves for life, as would their children." Swarns, *The 272*, p.6.
- "By the end of the 1670s, black slaves began to replace both white indentured servants and native Americans held as slaves as Virginians' primary source of labor. As the number of slaves grew, the Virginia Assembly began to specify the difference between slaves and servants, on what basis someone could be enslaved, and the conditions and character of slave and servant labor. The law on slaves and servants, enacted by the Virginia Assembly in 1705, compiled and updated these various laws into one comprehensive legal statement. Such 'slave codes' were necessary because they were not part of the English common law that the colonists brought with them to Virginia." David Tucker, "An act concerning Servants and Slaves," *teachingamericanhistory.org*.
- "[T]he first instance of a British Slave Code in the New World was on the Caribbean island of Barbados in 1661. The Slave Codes

used on Barbados were copied and used on another island in the Caribbean—Jamaica. The British colony of Jamaica began using Slave Codes in 1664, but they were updated twenty years later in 1684." *www.historycrunch.com.*

- "The first area to establish a Slave Code was South Carolina ... in 1712. ...[I]n 1770 the colony of Georgia adopted similar Slave Codes to South Carolina. ...Florida followed suit... ." *Id.*

- Massachusetts Bay, however, approved the first slave law in the English Atlantic in 1641, partly to clarify the status of hundreds of Pequot captives in colonial households. In 1670 the colony decreed that enslaved status would be inherited through the mother." Pekka Hämäläinen, *Indigenous Continent: The Epic Contest for North America* (2022), p.151.

- "In 1662, 1667, 1682, and 1693 Virginia had passed various parts of slave codes, including the 1662 law that made enslaved status hereditary through the mother. A 1667 law declared that baptism did not free slaves. A 1682 law allowed the enslaving of Indians. A 1693 law ... added ... language that dictated that 'mulatto' children of white women and 'negro' men to be bound as indentured servants for 31 years. As Virginia entered the new century, the ... new [1705] law was the most detailed slave code the colony had produced yet... ." Slavery Law & Power, *Codiyfing Enslavement*, The Virginia Slave Code of 1705.

- In subsequent years, the Assembly passed further laws aimed at controlling slaves, for example, passing a law governing how slaves would be tried for capital crimes and to better detect slave conspiracies and revolts (1723). This same law deprived free Blacks of the right to vote. The Board of Trade in London, which oversaw the colony, raised a question about this prohibition, occasioning an exchange of letters that reveals already divergent attitudes towards Africans in the colony and the mother country. The Board of Trade wanted to know how a free man could be deprived of the vote solely because of his complexion, while the Lieutenant

Governor of Virginia replied that the colony needed to keep Africans, both slave and free, under control." *Id.*

- In Virginia, "An act concerning Servants and Slaves" (1705) imposed a clear distinction between servants and slaves, with servants being given some civic rights and protections denied to slaves. And, the categorization was based upon origin. If a servant or slave had not come from a Christian country, that person was thereafter a slave. Furthermore, the children of a mother who is a slave will also be slaves.

"IV. And also be it enacted . . . that all servants imported and brought into this country, by sea or land, who were not Christians in their native country, (except Turks and Moors in amity with her majesty, and others that can make due proof of their being free in England, or any other Christian country, before they were shipped, in order to transportation hither) shall be accounted and be slaves, and such be here bought and sold notwithstanding a conversion to Christianity afterward."

- Some provisions governed the conduct of owners, as well.

XVI. Provided always, and be it enacted, That when any person or persons convict for dealing with a servant, or slave, contrary to this act, shall not immediately give good and sufficient security for his or her good behavior, as aforesaid: then in such case, the court shall order thirty-nine lashes, well laid on, upon the bare back of such offender, at the common whipping post of the county, and the said offender to be thence discharged of giving such bond and security."

---

19. Many of the provisions sought to preserve order and security and to prevent runaways, whether servant or slave. There were even regular armed slave patrols to prevent escape or rebellion. And, acts of rebellion were met with shockingly savage brutality. Various provisions levied heavy penalties on relationships between whites and people of other races, with emphatic "Christian care and usage of all Christian servants." The Act also exempted whites from liability for violence against slaves and recognized the owners' property rights in slaves.

"XIV. ... That all servants shall faithfully and obediently, all the whole time of their service, do all their masters' or owners' just and lawful commands. And if any servant shall resist the master, or mistress, or overseer, or offer violence to any of them, the said servant shall, for every such offence, be adjudged to serve his or her said master or owner, one whole year after the time, by indenture, custom, or former order of court, shall be expired."

...

"XX. And be it further enacted, that no minister of the church of England, or other minister, or person whatsoever, within this colony and dominion, shall hereafter wittingly presume to marry a white man with a negro or mulatto woman; or to marry a white woman with a negro or mulatto man."

...

"XXXIV. And if any slave resist his master, or owner, or other person, by his or her order, correcting such slave, and shall happen to be killed in such correction, it shall not be accounted felony; but the master, owner, and every such other person so giving correction, shall be free and acquit of all punishment and accusation for the same, as if such incident had never happened... .

...

"XXVIII. Provided always, and it is further enacted, that for every slave killed, in pursuance of this act, or put to death by law, the master or owner of such slave shall be paid by the public."

- Hannah-Jones discussed at lengths the impact of fear of violence and bloody rebellion on the making of laws and enacting of statutes, and she notes the temporal relationship between incidents of violence and the enactment of "slave codes." Hannah-Jones, *The 1619 Project*, pp.18, 66, 105, 111.

    - "Following Bacon's Rebellion in 1676, where an alliance of white and Black indentured servants and enslaved Africans rose up against Virginia's white elite, the colony passed slave codes to permanently enshrine legal and social distinctions between Black and white residents that ensured that all white people, no matter their status, permanently existed in a status above all Black people."

    - "The first official slave patrol was created in South Carolina in 1704, following rumors of a planned rebellion. By the late 1720s, slave patrolling in the Carolina colony had become a fundamental part of the militia's regular duties".

    - "[In] May 10, 1740 The South Carolina Commons House of Assembly passes the Negro Act, making it illegal for enslaved Africans to move freely, assemble in groups, grow food, earn money, or learn to read and write. These restrictions come in response to the Stono Rebellion, the largest uprising of enslaved people in the colonies to date."

    - "[O]n August 21, 1831, Nat Turner, an enslaved man in Virginia who believed that slavery violated God's law and that God had selected him to lead his people to freedom, unleashed a bloody rebellion. Over the next two days, he and his followers, which included several free Black people, attacked farms and killed some sixty white enslavers throughout Southampton County. ...In the decade following Nat Turner's rebellion, as rural areas struggled to suppress the enslaved population, Southern cities concluded that the only way to protect their residents from uprisings in surrounding areas was to invest in armed patrols."

- "Many of the regulations were passed during spasms of white anxiety—like just after Nat Turner's rebellion in 1831—and then, after a while, people ignored them." Dylan Penningroth, *Before the Movement: The Hidden History of Black Civil Rights* (2023), p.18.
- A group of South Carolins slaves revoted "on September 9, 1739.... After crossing the Stono Bridge, they broke into a hardware store and armory that sold guns and munitions. They executed the two shopkeepers, decapitated them, confiscated the firearms, and kept things moving. ...The Stono Rebellion changed the face of slavery in the slave capital of the world and, by proxy, in America as a whole. As a result of it, whites temporarily paused the slave trade for a decade, blaming the violence on the fact that these rebels were born in Africa. ...When the transatlantic slave trade eventually reopened, they avoided the Congo-Angola region..." Harriot, *Black AF History*, pp.71-2.

20. In the "Old South" (the Chesapeake and the coastal areas of the Carolinas and Georgia), there evolved through the continuous interactions of slaves and owners a set of privileges and "rights" held by the slaves, not enforceable in court but supported by custom and community expectation. Generally, the slaves' duties were defined by "tasks." The parameters of the tasks were established and modified by negotiation. Time available after completion of the task was the slave's to use as he or she determined. Most slave families had plots of land that they could cultivate. What they produced or otherwise were able to accomplish in the exra hours belonged to them as their property. Some earned money by doing "extra" work or by making things to sell. They were able to buy things from local merchants.

- "For centuries, since the 1660s, masters had looked at their profits from the task system and decided it wasn't worth risking all that just to show that enslaved people didn't have rights. Instead, they negotiated over the nature of slaves' privileges: how many square feet of hoeing customarily counted as a 'task,' for example, or how many acres their allotted 'private fields' were supposed to be, who they were allowed to trade with, and so on." Penningroth, *Before the Movement*, p.6.

- "White people recognized Black rights because life's ordinary business could not go on if whites could not make contracts and convey property to Black people." *Id.*, p.xxii.
- "During slavery, it was well–established practice in many parts of the country for slaves like my forebear Jackson Holcomb to have the privilege of owning property and making bargains even though they did not have rights. The vast majority of Americans' rights and privileges were not spelled out in the Constitution. Instead, they were defined by the states... ." *Id.*, p.xxiv.
- "Many slaves, maybe even most of them, got paid incentives for "overwork" during the harvest and planting seasons. Slaveowners did not do this out of the goodness of their hearts. They did it to save money, offloading the costs of feeding and clothing their workforce onto the exhausted workers themselves. From their patches of land, slaves had to supply a significant portion of the vegetables, chickens and eggs, meat, and more that kept them alive and healthy." *Id.*, p.7.
- "On this foundation of overtime work, they created other pre-scriptive rights, of property ownership and trade. Enslaved people were key players in the South's market economy, not just as com-modities and workers, but as buyers and sellers. Country store-keepers liked selling to slaves, wrote Charles Ball, who escaped slavery in Georgia, because the slaves "always pay cash," whereas poor white customers 'almost always require credit.'" *Id.*, p.7.
- "Enslaved people sold wood and fish to steamboat captains and portering services to steamboat passengers. Some bought wagons and mules and hauled goods. Others, like my great-great-great-uncle Jackson Holcomb, bought boats and ran ferries." *Id.*, p.7.

- "Along the coast of Georgia and South Carolina and in the tobacco and iron factories of Richmond, a 'task system' assigned each enslaved laborer a certain amount of work each day, with remaining time to use as they wished." *Id.*, p.6.
- "...South Carolina's enslaved worked on the 'task system.' Enslaved people were responsible for their own food, clothing, and even their medical care. Each captive had a required amount of work they had to complete, and once they were done, they were released from their enslavers' oversight to work in their own gardens, sew their own clothes, or make their own money." Harriot, *Black AF History*, p.63.
- "On rice plantations, the high risk of catching malaria, yellow fever, or other contagious diseases meant the white people didn't bother their enslaved as much as they did on other types of plantations. *Id.*
- "The second, more familiar pattern of slavery is gang labor: lines of people moving in unison down a vast field of cotton, under an overseer's whip, from sun-up to sun-down. Here, too, the enslaved had certain privileges, which they tried to establish as prescriptive rights: the privilege not to work for their masters on Sundays, to be paid for after-hours work, and to own and market small amounts of property." Penningroth, *Before the Movement*, p.6.
- "If slaves could possess property, control it, enjoy it, and could get permission to lawfully buy and sell everything except guns, land, and liquor, then slaves could lawfully exercise most of the sticks in the 'bundle of rights' that makes property property." *Id.*, p.15.
- "It encouraged hundreds of thousands of enslaved people to think in the logic of contract, and made millions of white people used to the idea of bargaining with them. In America before the Civil War, the privileges of enslaved people weren't exceptions or deviations from the law; they were part of the law." *Id.*, p.10.
- "Property-owning, bargaining, court week, church tribunals, and plantation courts fostered a legal culture during slavery, one that

would make Emancipation a much less sharp break than historians have assumed."*Id.*, p.23.

- "[L]ife on the Cottingham plantation reflected the biblical understanding that cruelty to any creature was a sin—that black slaves, even if not quite men, were at least thinly made in the image of God. ...Those slaves who died on the Cottingham place were buried with neat ceremony in plots marked by rough unlabeled stones... . ...Even on the harshest of family-operated antebellum farms, slave masters could not help but be at least marginally moved by the births, loves, and human affections that close contact with slave families inevitably manifested." Blackmon, *Slavery by Another Name,* pp.16, 44.

- "Before Union troops arrived in Bibb County, the night hours had permitted Henry his one limited taste of freedom within the confines of chattel life. It was after sundown that the slaves of Riverbend and other farms>could slip quietly through the forests to see and court one another."*Id.*,p. 37.

- "Far from the brutality of Southern plantation life, though, enslaved Black people in Washington [D.C.] were more like indentured servants. They comprised almost a third of the population —the majority of them manumitted." Nigel Hamilton, *Lincoln vs. Davis: The War of the Presidents* (2024) p.49.

The New Nation

21. The slavery question was a disruptive controversy from the beginnings of the nation. Thomas Jefferson's plan as Governor to provide for the gradual emancipation of the slaves in Virginia met too much opposition to be put into effect, "but as he moved into the new nation's legislature, he still hoped to ensure that the western United States would be settled and governed by free, self-sufficient farmers—not an oligarchy of slave-driving planters." In

Philadelphia, a compromise was reached to enable the formation of a union, with the expectation of many that slavery would die out.

- "[A]s [Thomas Jefferson] moved into the new nation's legislature, he still hoped to ensure that the western United States would be settled and governed by free, self-sufficient farmers—not an oligarchy of slave-driving planters." Baptist, *The Half Has Never Been Told*, p.6.
- "By the time the framers began writing the Constitution, states that did not rely heavily on enslaved labor within their borders, like Massachusetts and New Hampshire, had already outlawed it. ...Pennsylvania had begun a gradual process of abolition in 1780." Hannah-Jones, *The 1619 Project*, p.258.
- The U.S. Constitution does not endorse or accept slavery and does not use the word "slave" (or "slavery"):
  - "The Migration or Importation of such Persons as any of the States now existing shall think proper to admit shall not be prohibited by the Congress prior to the Year one thousand eight hundred and eight, but a Tax or duty may be imposed on such Importation, not exceeding ten dollars for each Person." Article 1, Section 9.
  - "Representatives and direct Taxes shall be apportioned among the several States which may be included within this Union, according to their respective Numbers, which shall be determined by adding to the whole Number of free Persons, including those bound to Service for a Term of Years, and excluding Indians not taxed, three fifths of all other Persons." Article I, Section 2.
  - The "other Persons" were not "free Persons," *i.e.*, they were slaves. This provision was a compromise, and it limited the political influence of the Southern states where the slaves were located. It would have been more anti-slavery not to count "other Persons" at all, but the provision was

a compromise. "Indians not taxed" were considered to be members of other nations.

- "In the first decades of the early republic, the northern states had a significant population of slaves, which only slowly diminished through gradual emancipation laws. In the South, the percentage of the population that was enslaved was extraordinarily high: over 70 percent in most counties along the Mississippi River and parts of the South Carolina and Georgia coast." Lincoln Mullen, "These Maps Reveal How Slavery Expanded Across the United States: As the hunger for more farmland stretched west, so too did the demand for enslaved labor," *Smithsonian Magazine,* May 15, 2014.

- "...Lincoln and other Republicans embraced a tradition of antislavery constitutionalism that reached back decades. That view held that the United States was founded on the principle that all men are free, based on the Law of Nations and affirmed by the 1772 British *Somerset* case. Adherents to antislavery constitutionalism accepted slavery as protected by the Constitution where it existed at the Founding. However, they insisted that its further expansion was not only not constitutionally protected but would violate the fundamental principle of universal freedom and thus the Constitution." Adolph L. Reed, Jr., *The South: Jim Crow and Its Afterlives* (2022), p.126.

22. The slave trade into the U.S. was inactive from the 1770s until early 1800. Legal restrictions and taxes were imposed starting in 1794. The United States outlawed the importation of slaves in 1807, effective 1808. (The U.K. also banned the slave trade later in 1807.)

- Until 1800, "none of the states had reopened the African trade.... Before 1800 all introductions into the U.S. were thus illegal, even if the slaves were brought in by foreign ships. After 1800, however, Georgia and South Carolina reopened their international slave trade, and in the next eight years, these two states would introduce about 100,000 new slaves from Africa." "Abolition of the Slave Trade," *abolition.nypl.org*, 2020.

- The domestic slave exchange continued, however. It was, for example, big business in Alexandria, Virginia (part of the District of Columbia from 1789 to 1847), facilitating the reallocation of slaves. These slave exchanges were profitable businesses, generating several large personal fortunes.
- Thus, the vast preponderance of slaves in the United States in 1860 had been born here. Many were third generation Americans.

Expansion

The Northwest Territory

23. The Treaty of Paris of 1783, ending the Revolutionary War, transferred from Britain to the new American nation an enormous tract of contiguous land known as the Ohio country or Northwest Territory. This land, north and west of the Ohio River and extending to the Mississippi, had been "acquired" by the British from the French following the French and Indian War pursuant to the Treaty of Paris of 1763, and was devoid of European settlements. Thomas Jefferson persuaded Congress to adopt the Northwest Ordinance.

- *See generally* David McCullough, *The Pioneers: The Heroic Story of the Settlers Who Brought the American Ideal West* (2022), pp.6-29..
- In 1786-87, the U.S. Constitution did not yet exist, nor the Presidency. A private company was founded to propose the purchase and settlement of a part of the land across the Ohio River from Virginia (now West Virginia). The representative of the new Ohio Company, a Massachusetts pasror named Manasseh Cutler,

approached the Continental Congress seeking a contract for the purchase of the land and the enactment of a law setting out a governance scheme for the Territory. The result was the Northwest Ordinance, enacted July 13, 1787. *Id.*, pp.9-17.

- The protections for the Indians did not fair well after a confederation of 8 tribes attacked the settlors in 1790 and then defeated and decimated the forces of General St. Clair. *Id.*, pp.95-105.

24. The Ordinance provided that the Territory would be divided into between three and five states that would become part of the Confederacy, as it then was, and any successor sovereign entity. (Ultimately, the Territory became Ohio, Michigan, Indiana, Illinois and Wisconsin.) Remarkably, the Ordinance provided for freedom of religion, the promotion of public education, the protection of the property and lives of the indigenous peoples and the prohibition of slavery.

- The Northwest Ordinance of 1787 "set forth a tenet such as never before stated in any American constitution. 'There shall be neither slavery nor involuntary servitude in the said territory.' ...[T]his had been agreed to when slavery existed in every one of the thirteen states. It was almost unimaginable that throughout a new territory as large as all of the thirteen states, there was to be no slavery. ...[T]he great Northwest Ordinance of 1787 stands alongside the Magna Carta and the Declaration of Independence as a bold assertion of the rights of the individual." *Id.*, pp.29-30.

From the Northwest Ordinance

"**Art. 1.** No person, demeaning himself in a peaceable and orderly manner, shall ever be molested on account of his mode of worship or religious sentiments, in the said territory.

"**Art. 3.** Religion, morality, and knowledge, being necessary to good government and the happiness of mankind, schools and the means of education shall forever be encouraged. The utmost good faith shall always be observed towards the Indians; their lands and property shall never be taken from them without their consent; and, in their property, rights, and liberty, they shall never be invaded or disturbed, unless in just and lawful wars authorized by Congress... .

"**Art. 4.** The said territory, and the States which may be formed therein, shall forever remain a part of this Confederacy of the United States of America, subject to the Articles of Confederation, and to such alterations therein as shall be constitutionally made; and to all the acts and ordinances of the United States in Congress assembled, conformable thereto.

"**Art. 6.** There shall be neither slavery nor involuntary servitude in the said territory, otherwise than in the punishment of crimes whereof the party shall have been duly convicted: Provided, always, That any person escaping into the same, from whom labor or service is lawfully claimed in any one of the original States, such fugitive may be lawfully reclaimed... ."

"Done by the United States, in Congress assembled, the 13th day of July, in the year of our Lord 1787, and of their sovereignty and independence the twelfth."

The Southwest Ordinance

25. In 1789, North Carolina agreed to cede to the United States its western territory, which would eventually become the state of Tennessee. In 1790, Congress passed the Act for the Government of the Territory of the United States South of the River Ohio. The

Act extended the provisions of the Northwest Ordinance to the South, with the important exception of the prohibition of slavery. Georgia's cession of lands in 1802 also made reference to the Northwest Ordinance but also exempted the region from the provisions forbidding slavery. These provisions for territorial government were applied, in fact, only to Tennessee.

- "South of the Ohio, the new Congress left open a massive new region for enslavers, organizing the Tennessee Territory in 1790 by passing a Southwest Ordinance that was an exact copy of the Northwest one—except that it left out the clause banning slavery." Baptist, *The Half Has Never Been Told*, p.12.
- "In 1798, Georgia ceded its lands to the federal government, and Congress organized the land between the Chattahoochee and the Mississippi Rivers into the Mississippi Territory, with slavery included." *Id.*, p.30.

The Louisiana Purchase

26. The next acquisition of land by the United States was the Louisiana Purchase in 1803. It posed quite different governance issues because the land was already populated by French and Spanish (largely Catholic and without a tradition of parliamentary government). There were also a sizable number of slaves, many recently brought by the Spanish who had continued the slave trade. The question of slavery was, thus, resolved on a state by state basis as new states were admitted to the Republic.

- *See* McCullough, *The Pioneers*, p.149; Baptist, *The Half Has Never Been Told.* pp.47, 154.
- "Many in Congress feared that the western settlements might secede or, worse yet, fall into the arms of European empires. As Britain's Indian allies raided south from their base at Detroit, Spain claimed the English-speaking settlements around Natchez.

In 1784, Spain also closed the mouth of the Mississippi at New Orleans... ." Baptist, *The Half Has Never Been Told*, p.7.

- "In 1791, Africans enslaved in the French Caribbean colony of Saint-Domingue exploded in a revolt unprecedented in human history. Toussaint Louverture had welded bands of rampaging rebels into an army that could defend their revolution from European powers who wanted to make it disappear. Between 1794 and 1799, his army defeated an invasion of tens of thousands of antirevolutionary British Redcoats." *Id.*, p p.44-5.
- Then, "[i]n 1801, [Napoleon] sent the largest invasion fleet that ever crossed the Atlantic, some 50,000 men, to the island under the leadership of his brother-in-law Charles LeClerc. Their mission was to decapitate the ex-slave leadership of Saint-Domingue." *Id.*, p.45.
- "Napoleon had also assembled a second army, and he had given it a second assignment. In 1800, he had concluded a secret treaty that 'retroceded' Louisiana to French control after thirty-seven years in Spanish hands. This second army was to go to Louisiana and plant the French flag. And at 20,000 men strong, it was larger than the entire US Army." *Id.*, p.45.
- "By the middle of 1802, the first wave of French forces had withered away. Napoleon reluctantly diverted the Louisiana army to Saint-Domingue. Then this second expedition to the Caribbean was also destroyed." *Id.*, p.46.
- As a result, France made the U.S. "an astonishing offer: not just New Orleans, but all of French Louisiana—the whole west bank of the Mississippi and its tributaries... for a mere $15 million—828,000 square miles, 530 million acres, at three cents per acre. This vast expanse doubled the nation's size. Eventually the land from the Louisiana Purchase would become all or part of fifteen states." *Id.*, p.47.

27. William C. Claiborne was governor of the Orleans Territory from 1804 to 1812, when Louisiana became a state. Although,

Congress was planning to admit Louisiana as a non-slave state, it granted Orleans territory the same status as the Mississippi territory in 1804, which the territorial Attorney General interpreted as permitting the importation of slaves from other states. President Jefferson did not interfere. Then, in 1810, a ship full of refugees from Cuba, including numerous slaves, sought permission to land at the port of New Orleans. The Gvernor resisted, contacting Washington. But, under apparent popular support, he granted permission. The result of which was a dramatic increase in the number of slaves. Most were promptly sent to the sugar cane and cotton plantations just up the river.

- "In July 1804, ...Congress was ... planning to ban the internal slave trade from other parts of the United States to Louisiana. [But,] Congress passed a law raising Orleans to the same territorial status as Mississippi. The territory's attorney general, James Brown, a Virginian who owned a German Coast sugar plantation, pounced on the loophole this law opened. Mississippi could import enslaved people from other states. [President] Jefferson allowed the ruling on the ground to stand. Slave imports resumed." Baptist, *The Half Has Never Been Told*, p.52.
- "Many Saint-Domingue refugees had moved to Spanish Cuba. Some of these French nationals had helped to incubate the new Cuban sugar industry. But at the beginning of 1809, when Napoleon invaded Spain, the Spanish Empire retaliated by expelling the refugees from its possessions. Now a shipload of these twice-refugees had crossed the bar at the Balize, seeking asylum." *Id.*, p.53.
- "There was the problem of finding food, shelter, and employment for 9,000 people in a city that normally supported 15,000. There was the legal problem of bringing slaves. And then again, there was the fact that a third of the refugees were free people of color, forbidden to immigrate to the United States... ." *Id.*, p.54.

- "Yet over the next few days, the white people of New Orleans held meetings and wrote petitions insisting that they wanted Claiborne to admit the refugees.Sympathy drove them, but so did other forces of attraction. ...So Claiborne capitulated. The refugees poured up the river."*Id.*, p.54.
- "The refugees' slaves accounted for a full quarter of the growth of the Orleans Territory's slave population, from 22,701 to over 34,000, between 1806 and 1810, and for 16 percent of the 3,000 people sold as slaves in New Orleans between 1809 and 1811... . ...Along the river's east bank above New Orleans, on the German Coast, dozens of slave labor camps stretched back from the river in French-surveyed "long lots," narrow strips of land that ran a mile or two across cleared ground to a dense belt of forested swamps." *Id.*, p.56.

28. Most of the slaves in the Orleans territory were new to America, having arrived from the Caribbean and Africa. Toward the end of the sugar cane harvest in early January 1811, these slaves staged the largest slave rebellion to occur in the U.S. prior to the Civil War. The rebels marched toward New Orleans, intent on capturing the City. But, they were met and defeated by Federal troops. Many were subsequently executed.

- "Most of the thousands brought in the previous ten years from Africa and the Caribbean, local-born Louisianans, and a few from Virginia and Maryland. ...[At the end of the sugar cane harvest, on] Saturday, January 5, 1811, [t]he men were planning what would become the biggest slave rebellion in the United States before the Civil War.The key of the plotters' 1811 strategy was a march straight on to New Orleans. They apparently believed that they outnumbered whites by enough on the German Coast to sweep all before them." Baptist, *The Half Has Never Been Told*, p.56.

- Almost exactly three years after the Rebellion of 1811, General Andrew Jackson defeated the British at New Orleans, ending the War of 1812 and finally securing the western territories from European meddling. (Mexico gained independence from Spain in 1821.)

The Missouri Compromise

29. The Missouri Compromise of 1819 prohibited any more slave states from being carved out of the Louisiana Purchase above 36°30' north latitude.

- "By December 1818, when a petition from the Missouri Territory's whites reached Congress for statehood, ...[m]ore than 10,000 enslaved African Americans lived in Missouri." Baptist, *The Half Has Never Been Told*, p.154.
- "Representative James Tallmadge of New York ... stood up in Congress on February 13, 1819, [and] ... proposed two amendments to the Missouri statehood bill. The first banned the importation of more slaves into Missouri. The second proposed to free all enslaved people born in the new state once they reached twenty-five. And here is what might have surprised even savvy observers: as the clerk of the House counted the votes, it became clear that heavy northern support had passed Tallmadge's amendments over universal southern opposition." *Id.*, p.155.
- "In the Senate, matters were different. Over the previous decade, Congress had been admitting states in pairs, retaining a rough balance between North and South in the Senate. Southern senators turned back the House's bill and struck the antislavery clauses. In response, the House rejected the Senate's version of the Missouri statehood bill. ...In the face of [Georgia's Thomas] Cobb's implied threat of civil war, New York's Tallmadge replied that 'if blood is necessary to extinguish any fire which I have

assisted to kindle . . . I shall not forbear to contribute my mite.'"
Id., p.156.

- "[President] Adams had a startling late-afternoon conversation with Secretary of War John C. Calhoun, a South Carolinian. Calhoun predicted that the Missouri crisis 'would not produce a dissolution of the Union.' But if it should, 'Calhoun continued, the South would of necessity be compelled to form an alliance . . . with Great Britain.' [T]hat 'would be returning to the colonial state,' replied the shocked Adams, who remembered two wars with the old empire. 'He said, yes, pretty much, but it would be forced upon them.'" *Id.*, p.156.

- "The [new] bill ... barred any more slave states from being carved out of the Louisiana Purchase above 36°30' north latitude, essentially Missouri's southern border. Then southerners, plus a few northerners, voted for Missouri statehood (with slavery), while northerners passed the 36°30' restriction line. ... [T]he Misasouri Compromise as it came to be known... ." *Id.*, pp.157, 158.

Lands Taken from Mexico

30. Mexico gained independence from Spain in 1821 and became a Republic in 1824. It abolished slavery in 1829. Texas declared independence from Mexico in 1836. The subsequent war by the U.S. against Mexico in 1846 reflected a political decision to seek to expand the U.S. territories to the west and south. The plan succeeded.

- *See* Baptist, *The Half Has Never Been Told*, pp.302-4, 327-33.
- "Congress had approved the declaration of war with Mexico on May 13, 1846. A few months later, on August 8, and with war well under way, President Polk asked Congress for $2 million to fund his administration's negotiations with Mexico." *Id.*, p.327.
- "[T]he Treaty of Guadalupe Hidalgo, the result of negotiations with the representatives of defeated Mexico. In addition to

confirming Texas annexation, the treaty gave the United States 525,000 additional square miles of the conquered nation-state— 13 acres for each of the 23 million people in the Union. This was the third-biggest acquisition of territory in US history, after the Louisiana Purchase and Alaska." *Id.*, p.333.

- "Northerners in the House of Representatives tried to ban slavery from any territory taken from Mexico with a proposal called the Wilmot Proviso, but southerners killed the measure in the Senate. The issue of the extension of slavery remained unresolved when the Mexican-American War ended in 1848 with the transfer of the Southwest—including what is now California, Nevada, Arizona, Utah, and much of New Mexico, Colorado, and Texas— from Mexico to the United States." Richardson, *How the South Won the Civil War*, p.71.

31. The Compromise of 1850 authorized the admission of Texas as a slave state, the abolition of slavery in the District of Columbia, the ban on slavery in California and the rights of New Mexico and Utah to decide for themselves about slavery. And, it established the Fugitive Slave Act, putting the power of the Federal government behind the return of runaway slaves found in other states. It did not last long.

- " On Monday, January 9, 1837, John Quincy Adams took to the floor of the Capitol to decry the evils of slavery before his fellow members of the House of Representatives. The fierce debate over the petitions calling for an end to slavery would consume Congress for weeks." Swarns, *The 272*, p.110.
- "Congress addressed rising tensions by cobbling together a complicated truce, but the Compromise of 1850 would not last." Richardson, *How the South Won the Civil War*, p.71.
- "On September 20, almost ten months after the Thirty-First Congress had first been seated, Fillmore signed the compromise bills into law. Cannons boomed in Washington, DC. Crowds outside

of boardinghouses and hotels serenaded the congressional leaders, who were inside drinking themselves into stupors of relief. In December, in his message to Congress as it opened a new session, President Fillmore referred to the Compromise of 1850 as 'in its character final and irrevocable.' Around the country, both northerners and southerners seemed to be cooling down and accepting the results." Baptist, *The Half Has Never Been Told*, p.340.

- "In 1860, just before the Civil War, ten northern states barred free Black people from voting at all and four others put special restrictions on them, including restrictions on testifying against white people. Black people were not even allowed to settle in Indiana, Illinois, or Oregon. ...[W]hen the leaders of the Oregon Territory had petitioned for statehood in 1858 with a proposed constitution that said free Blacks could not settle there, testify in court, own property, or make contracts, Congress balked." Penningroth, *Before the Movement*, p.34.

The Denouement

32. As slavery was becoming increasingly uneconomic in the Old South, the practice of loaning or leasing slaves to others developed. The practice strained families through separation, but the slave owners maintained a financial stake in the health of the slaves.

- "By the end of the 1850s, a vigorous practice of slave leasing was already a fixture of southern life. Farm production was by its nature an inefficient cycle of labor, with intense periods of work in the early spring planting season and then idleness during the months of 'laid-by' time in the summer, and then another great burst of harvest activity in the fall and early winter, followed finally by more months of frigid inactivity." Blackmon, *Slavery by Another Name*, p.34.

- "Borrowing from the practices of railroads and the few other industrial systems already familiar to businessmen of the South, the Shelby Works quickly came to rely on "leased" slave labor that would prove both extraordinarily effective and resilient." *Id.*, p.49.

- "The renting of slaves, as much as anything, had taught them that masses of black laborers brought under temporary control of a commercial enterprise could be powerfully leveraged in commerce." *Id.*, p.52.

- "Leased slave laborers typically cost $120 a year near the beginning of the war, but their cost more than doubled by the crisis years of 1864 and 1865. Under terms of the contracts, owners received quarterly payments, and their slaves were provided with basic food, clothing, and shelter. If a slave escaped, it was the responsibility of the company to pay a fee for the slave's arrest and return to the ironworks. As an incentive to work hard and follow rules, slaves were permitted to earn small amounts of cash for themselves—typically less than $5 a month—by agreeing to perform extra tasks such as tending the furnace at night, cutting extra wood, or digging additional ore." *Id.*, p.49.

- "But few slave masters encouraged the forge operators to treat their valued stock with brutality, particularly when the efficiency of the slave had no bearing on his financial return to the owner." *Id.*, p.50.

- "Slaves who at Christmas reported to their owners that the managers of the ironworks had abused them often were not made available to the company again. Moreover, slaves with wives still living back at the plantations from which they had come were allowed to return home periodically, sometimes several times a year." *Id.*, p.50.

33. The nature of slave labor that accompanied the emergence of industrialization in Alabama and Georgia in the middle of the nineteenth century and the expansion into the new territories of the

Mississippi regions, based first in sugar cane then predominantly on cotton, was different from the "old" slavery. The emphasis of the owners, often multiple distant investors, was on efficiency and short-term profits, maximizing production by applying the techniques of nineteenth century capitalism. The conditions for the slaves were much harsher, even similar to those in the Caribbean Islands under the French, Spanish and Portuguese or, previously, the English.

- "The South's highly evolved system of seizing, breeding, wholesaling, and retailing slaves was invaluable in the final years before the Civil War, as slavery proved in industrial settings to be more flexible and dynamic than even most slave owners could have otherwise believed. ... Labor here was more akin to a source of fuel than an extension of a slave owner's familial circle. ...But in the setting of industrial slavery—where only strong young males and a tiny number of female 'washerwomen' and cooks were acquired, and no semblance of family interaction was possible—slaves were assets to be expended like mules and equipment. It was a model particularly well suited to mining and first aggressively exploited in high-intensity cotton production, absentee owners routinely left overseers in charge of small armies of slaves. In an economic formula in which there was no pretense of paternalistic protection for slaves, the overseers drove them mercilessly." Blackmon, *Slavery by Another Name*, p.44.

- "An increasingly efficient market for hands was the core of the process that enabled the new men of New Orleans ... to knot together a nexus of cotton, slaves, and credit. The kind of slavery that ... was emerging on the frontiers of the early nineteenth-century South was inherently new. ...[I]t led to continuous increases in productivity per person—what economists call 'efficiency.' ...The first slavery had not yielded continuous improvements in labor productivity. On the nineteenth-century cotton frontier, however, enslavers extracted more production from each enslaved person every year. ... [B]y measuring work, implementing continuous surveillance of labor, and calibrating time and torture [the whip].... enslavers... forc[ed] enslaved people to invent, over and over, ways to make their own labor more efficient and profitable for their owners." Baptist, *The Half Has Never Been Told*, pp.107, 112, 113.

- "Chesapeake slave quarters had large numbers of nonworking children and old people as well as those who did some kinds of labor and not others. But cotton entrepreneurs worked men, women, and older children together for most of the year at jobs that were identical." *Id.*, p. 119.

- "Southern enslavers had developed a harsh new labor system, different from the one commonly employed in the Chesapeake. Enslaved people were under constant surveillance, forced to work at a furious, unrelenting... ." Swarns, *The 272*, p.67.

- "But producing such vast volumes of cotton required a completely new way of working; it required backbreaking labor and punishing work schedules that bore little resemblance to what enslaved people had endured in the Chesapeake. ...On cotton plantations ... overseers carefully monitored Black people in the fields and required men, women, and older children alike to tend to the crop at a breakneck pace. To increase production, the men employed violence and savagery at levels typically unseen in the Upper South." *Id.*, p.146.

34. Serious setbacks occurred in the 1850s, both in Congress (the repeal of the Missouri Compromise) and at the Supreme Court (the *Dred Scott* decision), setting the stage for armed combat.

- "Douglas introduced the Kansas-Nebraska Act, separating the remaining unorganized part of the Louisiana Purchase—land that had been designated as free under the Missouri Compromise—into two large territories: Kansas (which included much of what is now Colorado) and Nebraska (including today's Nebraska, but also much of what is now Wyoming, Montana, North Dakota, and South Dakota). The status of slavery in those territories would be decided by the voters, though the senators' unstated expectation was that Kansas would have slaves while Nebraska would be free. Despite popular fury at the measure, Democratic president Franklin Pierce put enormous pressure on members of the House to pass it. They did, finally, on May 8, 1854." Richardson, *How the South Won the Civil War*, p.72.

- "In May 1854, Sen. Stephen Douglas of Illinois had won passage of what became known as the Kansas-Nebraska Act, which established two new territories and allowed the inhabitants of each to decide whether to permit slavery, a doctrine known as popular sovereignty. It also repealed the Missouri Compromise, which had banned slavery in all new territory north of the 36º30' parallel. The act set off a race between slaveholders and free-soil advocates... ." Erik Larson, *The Demon of Unrest: A Saga of Hubris, Heartbreak, and Heroism at the Dawn of the Civil War* (2024), pp.54-55.

- "[T]he *Dred Scott* decision, which gave slave owners everything they wanted. It declared that African Americans were not citizens and 'had no rights which the white man was bound to respect,' and that Congress could not prohibit slavery in the territories, because the Constitution required the protection of property, including slaves. ...Therefore, the Missouri Compromise, which had protected freedom in the Northwest, was unconstitutional." Richardson, p.73.

* * *

- "James Hammond had been undecided about returning to Washington for the December 1859 start of the next Senate session. ...By this point he had begun to moderate his views on secession, arguing that at least for the time being, the South would do better within the Union than outside it, provided Congress left slavery alone. But after John Brown's raid, Congress was in no mood for reasoned debate on the subject. ....Hammond felt that he had no choice but to return to Washington. He told a friend, 'I fear it would appear like shrinking from duty not to go.' He found Congress seething with sectional malice; it took the House seven weeks to at last elect a speaker. Every debate seemed to turn back to slavery." Larson, *The Demon of Unrest*, pp.68-69.

- "Given the skyrocketing value of cotton as a commodity on the world market, however, opposition had only grown to enfranchising the four million enslaved Black people in the United States—from servants to the laborers who produced and picked the cotton—in counter-voice to antislavery fanatics: an abolitionist political pressure that stirred moral passions as perhaps no other economic and social inequity in the nation. With the United States more and more polarized over slavery—indeed, both its continued existence and its possible extension into new territories—feelings on both sides of the argument had risen to hysterical, even homicidal levels." Nigel Hamilton, *Lincoln vs. Davis: The War of the Presidents*, pp.28-29.

35. The prospect of an electoral victory for Abraham Lincoln and the new Republican Party in 1869, ending 30 years of domination of the Federal government by Southern politicians prominent in the Democratic Party, precipitated a movement toward secession in the states of the Deep South. The formal process was begun as the election results were announced.

- "[Major General John] Frémont had failed to get sufficient support in '56, losing to the Democratic candidate, James Buchanan. Frémont had nevertheless polled more than 1.3 million votes: a third of all ballots cast.... . Thus, ... so-called Black Republicans had been widely seen as beginning a march toward presidential destiny. Indeed, there were many 'slavers' in the South who, in

1856, had called for secession if Frémont were elected president." Hamilton, *Lincoln vs. Davis,* p.297.

- "For the slaveholding states, [Lincolln's] election conjured the real possibility of abolition and its inevitable—and intolerable—consequence, the utter loss of control over the Black race." Larson, *The Demon of Unrest,* p. 92.

- "Many Southerners, egged on by activists known as 'fire-eaters,' reviled Lincoln as a fanatical abolitionist whom they imagined to be hell-bent on making Blacks and whites equal in all things— an intolerable prospect... . So hated was he that ten Deep South states did not even include him on the ballot." *Id.,* p.16.

- "If Lincoln won and the Republican Party took control in Washington, it would sweep out the administration of James Buchanan and the proslavery Democratic Party, which had filled most federal posts with men sympathetic to the South and its 'peculiar institution.' The Democrats had held almost unshakeable control of both houses of Congress since 1833, at times with stunning majorities." *Id.,* p.16.

- "Lincoln's election and the apprehension leading up to it inflicted a direct cost on the financial well-being of the South's leading citizens, its planters. Cotton prices fell, as did the market value of slaves, and this in turn limited the planters' ability to use them as security for mortgages and other investments. A... male who sold for $1,625 in Richmond over the preceding summer now sold for only $1,000, or 38.5 percent less. South Carolina reacted with particular fury. The day after the election, the state's most senior federal officials resigned their posts... ." *Id.,* p.20.

- "Conciliation... was becoming less and less realistic, in view of President Buchanan's spineless, dawdling timidity: his cowardly refusal to act resolutely. Even Jefferson Davis, who'd long considered Mr. Buchanan to be a friend of the South, had become critical of Buchanan's so-called leadership, which had left no one clear as to the federal government's position. Northerners, for their part, were indignant." Hamilton, pp.29-30.

36. By the time of Lincoln's inauguration in February 1861, seven states had purported to withdraw from the Union, had adopted a constitution and had selected and inaugurated a president, Jefferson Davis.

- "South Carolina taking the first step in seceding from the Union barely six weeks after the 1860 election, before the winner could even be inaugurated. Thanks to lame-duck president Buchanan's refusal to immediately use federal force to disarm seceding state militias and stop them from seizing federal installations or buying weapons, six other states—which had initially waited to see the consequences of secession—had then followed suit, with total impunity. Conciliation, of course, was becoming less and less realistic, in view of President Buchanan's spineless, dawdling timidity: his cowardly refusal to act resolutely." Hamilton, *Lincoln vs. Davis*, p.29.

- "On February 4, 1861, a convention of six seceding states of the Deep South—South Carolina, Mississippi, Florida, Alabama, Georgia, and Louisiana (Texas having seceded, too, but was still awaiting gubernatorial signature)—had begun meetings in the majestic Alabama state capitol in Montgomery: a mere forty-two delegates gathering to create a new, independent, slaveholding 'Southern nation.'" *Id.*, p.10.

- "Slavishly copying the existing U.S. Constitution, the Confederacy's new constitution would, this time however, guarantee 'the institution of negro slavery' in the South: Article IV specifically stating that 'negro slavery, as it now exists in the Confederate States, shall be recognized and protected by Congress and by the Territorial government.' ...[However,] importation of 'negroes of the African race from any foreign country,' or even from non-Confederate states, would be 'forbidden.' ... In short, slavery was to be permanent—not only for the enslaved but also for their offspring, and their offspring's offspring." *Id.*, pp.10-11.

37. The threat of secession had been used successfully for years to generate policies favorable to the South. Many in the North apparently believed that this was another bluff that could and would be resolved by further concessions. Moreover, the Federal governmental and military hierarchies were filled with Southerners and Southerner sympathizers. Yet, the new Confederate States of America selected a military man as president and he, although not favoring actual secession, focused immediately upon preparing to defend the Deep South from Union aggression. Thus, the importance of capturing Fort Sumter intact.

- "Secession had been a marvelous threat in the halls of Southern legislatures and in Congress—a useful form of political blackmail." Hamilton, *Lincoln vs. Davis*, p.9.
- "In the months—indeed years—prior to Mr. Lincoln's election, the threat of secession and war had gotten Southern slaveholding leaders such as Toombs almost all they had ever wanted, from the extension of permitted slavery in new states to the Fugitive Slave Act, the Dred Scott Supreme Court Decision, and the salutary execution of John Brown. But there was a world of difference between waving a stick and using it." *Id.*, p.145.
- "Crucial U.S. military officers were resigning in droves, including generals—despite their sworn vows to serve the very nation, the United States of America, which had trained and employed them. By March 7, 1861, for example, Colonel Samuel Cooper, the U.S. Army's adjutant general, though a New Yorker by birth, had not only resigned but had left for Montgomery, with dozens of other officers following him there—among them General Scott's own longtime aide-de-camp, Colonel George Lay—and were promoted in Montgomery to the rank of general. It had been the same at the Navy Department—where forty-three officers had resigned their commissions, while only five of forty officers at the Naval Academy remained loyal to the Union... ." *Id.*, pp.91-92.

* * *

- "As president of the Confederacy, Davis thus had no intention of using force against the rump United States. His task, as he saw it, was simply to marshal the South to defend its borders. ...The president's strategy was simple: to seize and hold as many Atlantic coast and Gulf coast forts, fortifications, and defensible positions as possible in order to resist amphibious federal attack. ...President Davis had told [General Beauregard] ...he wanted Sumter to be captured intact, if possible with its cannons unspiked, so that it could be turned immediately into a Confederate stronghold for coastal defense." Hamilton, pp.35, 81.

37. Some Southerners, including important Confederate leaders like Jefferson Davis and Robert E. Lee, did not favor secession, were ambivalent about slavery and doubted that slavery could survive. Yet, when faced with the fact of secession and the likelihood of armed confrontation, their loyalties lay with their native states rather than the Union. In fact, there was little interest in the Union by most of the people of the Deep South, who mainly wanted to be left alone.

- "James Petigru, seventy-one, a devoted unionist and former state attorney general ... voted for secession. He agreed with a friend's assessment that the state was 'going to the devil,' but in accord with honor and loyalty to home, two of the most powerful forces in the South, he felt compelled to go with it." Larson, *The Demon of Unrest*, pp.111, 116-117.

* * *

- "[Jefferson Davis] did not favor actual, rather than threatened, secession. Nevertheless he'd stood ready to defend his home state, if necessary, as a soldier." Hamilton, *Lincoln vs. Davis*, p.9.

- "[Davis] knew that the new 'nation' of the South would have to be defended and fought for—and the general determined, as a soldier, to do his best, however doomed the outcome. Privately, therefore, Davis doubted whether the South could do more than play for time, not only in terms of survival in a war, but even in the matter of slavery. ...[H]e thought secession would be followed by war, as night followed day—for the new U.S. administration, once Mr. Lincoln was in Washington, could not simply stand back and watch a third of the nation abscond. And slavery itself would not outlast such a disaster." *Id.*, pp.15-16.

* * *

- "Acting through an intermediary—Francis Blair, father of Post-master General Montgomery Blair—Lincoln offered Lee command of all Union land forces. That same day Lee learned that Virginia had seceded. For Lee this was a wrenching moment. He considered slavery 'a moral and political evil' and looked upon secession 'as anarchy.' Writing to Blair, he said, 'If I owned the four million slaves in the South I would sacrifice them all to the Union; but how can I draw my sword upon Virginia, my native state?'" Larson, p.469.
- "Had Scott and the president acted sooner in promoting Lee to the rank of U.S. general—and signaling his probable promotion, after that, to head the U.S. Army at the War Department in Washington in place of General Scott, who had privately told him he saw him as his successor—then perhaps history might have unfolded differently." Hamilton, pp.198-199.

38. Although, there were significant cultural differences and conflicting visions and values between the South and North, the opposing views of slavery were the dominate source of tensions. Southerners subsequently, after the War, made a considerable effort to rehabilitate their reputations by characterizing the rebellion as

a matter of states' rights (the "Lost Cause"); the contemporaneous record compels the conclusion that the root cause of the Civil War was slavery.

- "...[A] kind of preexisting tribal divergence between North and South that had gotten steadily worse as the North had industrialized and, thanks to open immigration, became ever more dominant—finally reaching a climax with South Carolina's secession in December of that year and Mississippi's withdrawal from the Union soon after that, on January 9, 1861." Hamilton, *Lincoln vs. Davis*, pp.55-56.
- "[T]hese planters constituted a kind of aristocracy and saw themselves as such. They called themselves 'the chivalry.' As the prominent South Carolina planter James Henry Hammond put it, they were 'the nearest to noblemen of any possible in America.' This idea was affirmed on a daily basis by the fact of their possession of, and dominion over, a subservient population of enslaved Blacks. ...Planters had once constituted the richest class in America, wrote Dennis Hart Mahan, a New York–born, Virginia-raised professor at West Point in a November 1860 letter to a friend. 'But when commerce, manufacturers, the mechanic arts disturbed this condition of things, and amassed wealth that could pretend to more lavish luxury than planting... .'" Larson, *The Demon of Unrest*, pp.5-6, 7.
- "Confederacy [was] cementing its image in the vital first months of the war as a brave, independence-seeking underdog—a Southern self-perception that would, over time, be maintained for another century and a half in the form of a mythic 'lost cause.'" *Id.*, p.364.
- "Lost Cause ideology was propagated aggressively, nationally as well as regionally, as part of southern elites' crusade advocating 'sectional reconciliation' on white supremacist terms that would undermine enforcement of black southerners' constitutional rights and give the southern ruling class a free hand in establishing

and maintaining its new order." Adolph L. Reed, Jr., *The South: Jim Crow and Its Afterlives* (2022), p.130.

* * *

- "What Seward had not addressed in his speech, and perhaps did not truly understand, was that at this point in the crisis, the thing that the South most resented was the inalterable fact that the North, like the rest of the modern world, condemned slavery as a fundamental evil. In so doing, abolitionists and their allies impugned the honor of the entire Southern white race, for if slavery was indeed evil, then the South itself was evil, and its echelons of gentlemen, the chivalry, were nothing more than moral felons." Larson, p.196.
- "What most troubled [James Henry] Hammond and his fellow Southerners was the rapid intensification of antislavery sentiment in the North, epitomized in 1831 by William Lloyd Garrison's founding in Boston of his abolitionist newspaper the Liberator. ...Many Virginians blamed Garrison's rhetoric for igniting the Nat Turner Rebellion of August 21–22, 1831, in which Turner and coconspirators killed fifty-five whites." *Id.*, pp.39-40.
- "Underlying that historic wartime confrontation, however, festered a far deeper division, a far greater issue—the matter of slavery. It was, as Lincoln later admitted, both the cause of the war and the marker of its course from the very start. Yet for different reasons both presidents attempted to 'shove it under the rug,' as the great Civil War historian James McPherson once put it, for almost a year and a half of increasingly venomous hostilities." Hamilton, p.xviii.
- "[W]hat had made secession inevitable, in Jefferson Davis's view ... was that an unbridgeable divide, a veritable abyss, had grown between the Northern and Southern people and their cultures. It was thus not enslavement, *per se* ... . Rather, it was the cultural cleft: one in which the ever-expanding, rapacious, immigrant-

infused North had become more and more economically, industrially dominant. A North that had therefore become resented, as well as feared, in the South by white people... . A South where such whites, rich or poor, were looked down upon by their Northern confrères; and a North in which the moral issue—the iniquity—of Southern slavery was used to denounce the South while masking Northern greed. Slavery ... had lined the pockets of millions of white merchants in the North... ." *Id.*, p.117.

* * *

- "[D]elegates from twenty-one states—fourteen free, seven slave—gathered in Washington for a 'Peace Convention' to try to find a way out of the secession crisis. This was set to begin on Monday, February 4, but bad weather hampered the travels of many delegates. ...[At the end of February 1861,] the Peace Convention approved a proposed Thirteenth Amendment to the Constitution to be submitted to Congress for a vote. All seven of its clauses dealt with slavery, including one nicknamed the 'Never-Never' clause, which would bar Congress from ever interfering with slavery as it existed in any state or territory in the country. The seven clauses underscored the fact that for all of the South's efforts to blame the crisis on Northern tyranny in imposing tariffs, collecting revenue, and ordaining 'internal improvements,' the crux of the crisis was in fact slavery." Larson, pp.214, 274.
- "On Wednesday, January 9, Mississippi's secession convention voted 84 to 15 in favor of immediate exit from the Union and became the second state after South Carolina to do so. The delegates were very clear about their motivation. 'Our position is thoroughly identified with the institution of slavery—the greatest material interest of the world,' they wrote in their official declaration." *Id.*, p.191.

39. Nonetheless, the magnitude and intensity of the resulting conflict was the result of folly, misjudgment, mistake, coincidence and conflicted loyalties, if not outright treason. The decision of South Carolina to secede was foolhardy, facilitated by an outbreak of smallpox causing the state convention to be moved from Columbia to the radicalized Charleston. President Buchanan took no action due to timidity or Southern sympathies. President Lincoln's belated effort to reinforce Fort Sumter was bungled or, perhaps, sabotaged. President Davis' order to attack Fort Sumter was politically unwise. Lincoln's response by calling up 75,000 men was impetuous and incendiary. The Confederacy's decision to move its capital to Richmond, Virginia, was arrogant and shortsighted. Lincoln's decision to launch an immediate attack on Richmond was militarily and politically foolish.

- "After the election, Edmund Ruffin promptly set out for South Carolina convinced that it alone had the resolve to act. ...He arrived in Columbia, the state's capital, in time to be present on November 10, 1860, when, spurred by Lincoln's victory, the legislature debated holding a special convention to decide whether South Carolina should secede from the Union." Larson, *The Demon of Unrest*, p.85.
- "The choice of Columbia had been a point of controversy. ...[T]he delegates who favored secession, among them the fire-eater Robert Barnwell Rhett, worried that Columbia might not only be central in terms of geography, but centrist also in attitude. Unionist sentiment in the state remained strong, with some prominent conservatives publicly opposed to secession, including James Petigru, seventy-one, a devoted unionist and former state attorney general... ." *Id.*, pp.110-111.
- "[A] minor outbreak of smallpox in Columbia seemed to be intensifying. On December 16, the day before the convention began, the state Board of Health had reported fourteen new cases. The radicals, fanning fears of a wider outbreak, urged

adjournment to Charleston; the delegates agreed, in the process bruising Columbia's pride. The state legislature also fled to Charleston." *Id.*, p.112.

* * *

- "It was, in retrospect, madness in the first degree: a gamble, taken with scant thought to the real consequences, and done with breathtaking alacrity by six electors, representing the six seceding states." Hamilton, *Lincoln vs. Davis,* p.11.
- "The ... claim of 'peaceable withdrawal' from the USA, moreover, was naïve. How could secession fail to have warlike consequences, given the takeover of all federal military forts and buildings in Mississippi? Seized under the threat of violence—armed insurrection—how could such actions be parsed as 'peaceable' by the federal government? Bloodshed 'would be' the inevitable consequence, Davis was well aware." *Id.*, p.14.

* * *

- "...President Lincoln was perplexed by the idea of surrendering the government's premier fortress in the South.... Lincoln unable to understand how his predecessor, President Buchanan, could have failed to reinforce the fort by employing the U.S. Navy in strength (rather than a pathetic, ill-starred, rented paddle steamer, the Star of the West, which failed to deliver provisions), while South Carolina forces, on land, had still been weak." Hamilton, p.86.
- "Even more suspicious: Why did General Scott—whose amphibious invasion of the Mexican coast with barely seven thousand troops had made U.S. military history—now balk at the idea of immediate Union reinforcement on the U.S. East Coast, given the president's inaugural vow to hold all remaining U.S. forts?

If it wasn't explicitly treasonous, it certainly smacked of it." *Id.*, p.88.

- "Lincoln's error in assigning the same warship, the Powhatan, to the two relief expeditions came to light on April 5.... He received a surprise visit from Secretary of State Seward and Navy Secretary Gideon Welles. ... Lincoln read and reread the telegram and asked if there wasn't some mistake. 'He took upon himself the whole blame... .'" Larson, *The Demon of Unrest*, p.391.

- "The secretary of state, embarrassed, promised the president he would send an immediate telegram, revoking his secret requisition of the powerful vessel. Instead, Seward deliberately delayed his new order by a day—and then signed it 'Seward' rather than 'Lincoln.' This enabled Seward's protégé, Lieutenant David Dixon Porter, already at sea, to keep command of the USS Powhatan by earlier presidential authority, signed at Seward's request. ... Lieutenant Porter had thereupon sailed the warship a thousand miles away to the Gulf of Mexico, out of contact, instead of to Fort Sumter." Hamilton, p.139.

- "In New York, Capt. Gustavus Fox, in charge of the expedition to Fort Sumter but unaware of the Powhatan confusion, speedily gathered troops, supplies, and ships. ...For reasons never made clear, Fox had no idea that the all-important Powhatan was now on its way to Florida." Larson, p. 392.

* * *

- "[W]ithout waiting or vacillating, the president, as U.S. commander in chief, bravely responded to the attack with a mobilization-by-proclamation unlike any the country had ever seen. " Hamilton, p.163.

- "On Monday, April 15, Lincoln issued a proclamation calling for 'the several States of the Union' to muster their militias and contribute a total of seventy-five thousand troops for the suppression of rebellious 'combinations' in the seceded states and to reassert the authority of U.S. law. ...The effect of the proclamation was explosive. If there had been any hope that after Sumter passions would subside and everyone would get back to their lives, that hope was now obliterated. Northern states reacted with jubilation. ... On April 17 the state's long-seated convention voted to secede. Even staunch pro-unionist William Rives voted in favor, stating, 'The Government being already overthrown by revolution, I vote 'aye.'' " Larson, pp.467, 468.

- "Jefferson Davis was knocked sideways by the news. He'd expected war, and had six thousand men under Beauregard's command to defend the East Coast. But a Union army of seventy-five thousand troops? Abraham Lincoln's response to defeat at Fort Sumter was not at all what Davis or his colleagues in the CSA had expected." Hamilton, p.172.

- "Even staunch Union loyalists in those states now cast Mr. Lincoln's impetuous presidential edict as a grave error: one that, as one stalwart Unionist in North Carolina put it, might well let 'loose on us a torrent to which we could oppose no resistance.' Another hitherto loyalist leader in Virginia, John Botts, would also mourn the 'mistake' a few weeks later, calling the president's proclamation 'the most unfortunate state paper that ever issued from any Executive since the establishment of the government.'" *Id.*, p.177.

- "Behind the scenes Abraham Lincoln did, in fact, soon recognize that his grand proclamation was a mistake in terms of the ammunition it had given his opponents." *Id.*, p.183.

* * *

- "As with President Lincoln's call-up proclamation in April 1861, the matter of Richmond-as-new-Confederate-capital in May 1861 would, over time, come to seem impetuous, ill-considered, and ultimately disastrous: a political gambit of the most myopic kind, recklessly pursued by certain individuals for their own ends in secret sessions—leaving the public in Virginia, Alabama, and across the South ignorant of its military ramifications." Hamilton, p.221.

- "Decided by a tiny, overnight, four-vote majority in the Confederate Congress—totaling only forty-four delegates—it was now formally decreed that the Congress would reconvene in Richmond on July 20, 1861. On that day, after the planned Virginia plebiscite, the Congress would be in a position to formally admit Virginia to the Confederacy—and make the city of Richmond the new capital." *Id.*, p.223.

* * *

- "The notion of a quick Union action to seize Richmond, using the 75,000 volunteers whom Mr. Lincoln had called to arms, was certainly enticing in a Washington that seemed to have found its nerve again." Hamilton, p.226.
- "'On to Richmond!' the press was already dubbing Mr. Lincoln's leaked and preferred strategy. It represented popular sentiment for action to be taken—and Abraham Lincoln, more than any member of his cabinet, was sensitive to popular opinion and voters' feelings." *Id.*, p.231.
- "The Union, the president thus solemnly declared at the fateful White House war council on June 29, would invade Virginia, across the Potomac, in full-army strength—and move on Richmond—as soon as possible. A battle that might, if they were lucky, decide the war before it really began in earnest." *Id.*, p.232.

40. The Civil War resulted in 750,000 deaths (2% of the population) and cost $5.2 billion (greater than the GDP of 1860). Slavery was ended, but at great expense. By the mid-19th century, manufacturing had begun to challenge agriculture as the main economic activity, and the War greatly accelerated the process. The North prospered. The South suffered a catastrophic economic decline.

- "...[A] war that over the course of four years would involve more than 2 million men and cost the government more than $5 billion. (The entire 1861 budget had originally been projected at $62 million.)" Richardson, *How the South Won the Civil War*, p.79.

- "Commanded by Gen. James H. Wilson, the Union army, well drilled and amply armed, split into three huge raiding parties, each assigned to destroy key elements of Alabama's industrial infrastructure. Moving unchallenged for days, the federal troops burned or wrecked iron forges, mills, and massive stockpiles of cotton and coal at Red Mountain, Irondale, and Helena, north of Bibb County." Blackmon, *Slavery by Another Name*, p.23.

- "Wilson crushed the last functioning industrial complex of the Confederacy and left Alabama in a state of complete chaos. Not three years later, the valley remained a twisted ruin. Fallow fields. Burned barns. Machinery rusting at the bottoms of wells. Horses and mules dead or lost. The people, black and white, braced for a hard, anxious winter." *Id.*, p.14.

- "Alabama ... suffered losses totaling $500 million—a sum beyond comprehension in 1865. The total value of farm property was reduced during the war from $250 million to less than $98 million, including the loss of slaves. All banks in the state had collapsed. Agricultural production levels would not match that of 1860 for another forty years." *Id.*, p.24.

- "The 'expiation' Lee had feared, what Mary Lincoln called 'this hideous nightmare,' had come to pass, killing 750,000 Americans. South Carolina alone lost 21,000 men, more than a third of the 60,000 state citizens who fought. Its planters grieved a more venal loss: The end of slavery cost them three hundred million dollars in human capital overnight." Larson, *The Demon of Unrest*, p.479.

CHAPTER VIII

Racism

"SYSTEMIC RACISM"

Racism can be ugly, especially when coupled with hatred, or anger, or fear. But, racism is also personal. People are racists. Racism is a matter of beliefs, feelings, attitudes and intentions, as well as of behavior. So, there are serious limits to what government can do about racism. Government can prohibit and combat various racist actions (like "hate crimes" or job discrimination), but not racism itself. Churches, families, maybe schools, possibly communities, but not government.

This country has a long history of discriminatory behavior—exclusion, hostility, violence and, often, compelled residential segregation—based on differences among people, whether racial or other. Such discrimination has affected Native Americans, Irish, Italians (especially, Southern Italians), Polish, Chinese, Japanese, Hispanics, Jews, and so on. (In many cases, discrimination was effected by official government action as well as private conduct.) Racists are a blemish on our society (and are present in most others).

I applaud the affirmation by communities and churches of the country's founding principles and the recent reinvigoration of the efforts fully to realize them. Those efforts are for the good of all. And, it is a worthy objective for each of us to recognize our own biases and prejudices, including racial biases. Some other reactions, however, are destructive. We badly need acceptance, tolerance and good will, and not just between races.

Now, we are talking about "systemic [or institutional or structural] racism." Generally, in ordinary usage, institutions could not be racist. They may have discriminatory consequences and their founders or leaders may have been (or may be) racists, but not the institutions. But, we now have a new definition: "Racism: The marginalization and/or oppression of people of color based on a socially constructed racial hierarchy that privileges white people." ADL (The "Anti-Defamation League", founded in 1913 to combat anti-semitism), July 2020. *See also*, John McWhorter, "The Dictionary Definition of Racism Has to Change," *The Atlantic*, June 22, 2020 ("If I had it my way ... we would allow that racism now refers to a societal state, and revive prejudice to refer to attitudinal bias").

"[The word]] racism... was coined—somewhat belatedly, you might think, given this history—not to evoke hostile white attitudes to blacks but to describe the anti-Semitism of the German National Socialists." Kwame Anthony Appiah, *The Lies that Bind: Rethinking Identity* (2016), p.123.

Some refer to systemic racism as "white privilege," but that is nonsense—it is not about anyone's privilege, but about someone's disadvantage. ("White privilege" is not based on Black, or minority, oppression.) Moreover, it is not only whites (or only white Protestants) that can be racist. I was fortunate to grow up in a two-parent household, to have caring and supportive parents, to live in a community sufficiently isolated that it was safe for children to walk themselves to school or roam the neighborhood. I was also fortunate to be tall. In all of these things, I was lucky; in none of them, was I "privileged." So, the phrase is to me a misnomer. It is not "white privilege," but the allegedly racially discriminatory effects of our history and our current system that should be the current focus.

This is a curious development. The social and moral opprobrium traditionally ascribed to racism is not appropriate for institutions or systems that happen to cause negative effects on "persons of color." So, the new emphasis would seem to reduce the seriousness of the characterization (which McWhorter would now call "prejudice"). But, it does play to the sensibilities of those who think that government benefits are the solution to most problems. It is clearly being advanced to support "compensatory" and preferential treatment.

At the same time as this new concern with "systemic racism," the degree of violence and group lawlessness has increased dramatically. For example: "Neighborhoods in some of the largest US cities erupted in gun violence over the Fourth of July weekend [2020], killing an estimated 160 people and leaving more than 500 wounded from Friday night to Sunday." "Gun violence kills 160 as holiday weekend exposes tale of 'two Americas'," *The Guardian*, 7 July 2020. And, one month later:

> "On Friday [Portland] police said 'people defied orders to disperse and threw rocks, frozen or hard-boiled eggs and commercial-grade fireworks at officers,' the Associated Press reports. Rioters also 'filled pool noodles with nails and placed them in the road, causing extensive damage to a patrol vehicle.' On Saturday night, arsonists set a fire inside the Portland police union building and rioters outside landed two officers in the hospital.
>
> ...

"Meanwhile in Chicago on Sunday night, hundreds of looters ransacked stores along the Magnificent Mile. ... The Chicago Tribune reports that some looters 'could be seen throwing merchandise into rental trucks and other large vehicles before driving away.' ...13 cops were injured."

The Editorial Board, "Mayhem Continues, Protest Narrative Crumbles: Looters rampage in Chicago and arson returns in Portland," *WSJ.com*, August 10, 2020.

It is not politically correct to refer to these recent events as "riots", so we will say that during a period of widespread racial protests, there has been murder, arson, violence and looting. (Contrary to some recent claims, incidents of racial violence in 1917 in East St. Louis; in 1919 in Chicago, Omaha and several other American cities; in 1921 in Tulsa, as well as at seaports across the United Kingdom, were referred to as "riots" and were generally condemned by government officials. These riots with whites attacking blacks were largely motivated, however, not by racism, but by competition over jobs following WW I.)

The year 2020 also saw a huge increase in homicides: "This year, 51 cities of various sizes across the U.S. saw an average 35% jump in murder from 2019 to 2020—a 'historically awful' development, says New Orleans-based crime analyst Jeff Asher, who crunched those numbers." "2020's murder increase is 'unprecedented.' But is it a blip?" *The Christian Science Monitor*, December 14, 2020.

The year 2021 was only worse. And, 2022, even worse.

Then, 2023—with the notable exception of the District of Columbia, an improvement. Tim Arango and Campbell Robertson, "After

Rise in Murders During the Pandemic, a Sharp Decline in 2023," *NY-Times*, December 29, 2023; Emily Davies, John D. Harden and Peter Hermann, "2023 was District's deadliest year in more than two decades: The city recorded 40 homicides per 100,000 residents, with victims in every ward, from babies to the elderly," *Washington Post,* January 1, 2024.

THE "SYSTEM(S)"?

What are the particular institutions today that have racially discriminatory effects? And, what specifically are their problem features?

One view was recently set forth by Raphael Bostic, the President of the Federal Reserve Bank of Atlanta, in a July 2020 Bank release:

> "[M]any of our fellow citizens endure the burden of unjust, exploitative, and abusive treatment by institutions in this country. [T]he examples of such institutionalized racism are many, and include slavery, federal law (consider the Three-Fifths Compromise our founding fathers established to determine federal representation), sanctioned intimidation during Reconstruction, Jim Crow laws in southern states, redlining by bankers and brokers, segregation, voter suppression, and racial profiling in policing."

He continues: "...To be fair, we have made some progress."

Some progress?

Bostic's list of examples of "institutional racism" are things from the distant past. Except for "racial profiling," the extent and effects of which are debatable (and discussed below), all of the things listed were banned between 50 and 150 years ago (by the Acts listed in the history set out below), all long since gone from the system. Moreover, some were not racist (like the Three-Fifths Compromise) and others were not institutional. His list is simply neither useful nor informative.

Much of the publicity for the claim came from the "1619 Project," an effectively rebutted piece of purported history, and an attempted revival of Derek Bell's "critical race theory," also largely discredited (obviously, some/many may disagree with my judgment on "critical race theory"). The public commentary is not very helpful. For example, McWhorter says "one might say that societal racism is to blame for neighborhoods with decaying infrastructure, because white flight lowered tax revenues." "The Dictionary Definition of Racism Has to Change," *The Atlantic*, June 22, 2020. Is that really a meaningful statement? Does it shed light either on the causes of the problems or on possible solutions?

Some approaches effectively define racial inequality as racism. Ibram X. Kendi, in his 2019 best-seller *How To Be An Antiracist*, includes in racism the failure to oppose policies that result in racial inequalities (which he calls "racial inequities"): less wealth, lower income, poorer health, shorter life expectancy, less home ownership, *etc*. The problem with such a single- minded focus on the impact on racial groups is not that such impact is irrelevant, but that it is unidimensional. Real public policy issues and actions are necessarily multi-dimensional and must be so evaluated. Moreover, inequality is not necessarily inequity. In many cases, unequal may be very equitable.

"[R]eality is obscured in a contemporary perspective that flattens out history and context into a simple polarity of racism/anti-racism and reduces politics to an unchanging contest of black and white. That perspective compresses historical distinctions between slavery and Jim Crow and ignores the generation of struggle, often enough biracial or interracial, against ruling class power over defining the political and economic character of the

---

post-Emancipation South, as well as ongoing struggle against and within the new order as it consolidated."

Adolph L. Reed, *The South: Jim Crow and Its Afterlives* (2022), p.130.

"[S]imple racism/anti-racism framework isn't adequate for making sense of the segregation era, and it certainly isn't up to the task of interpreting what has succeeded it or challenging the forms of inequality and injustice that persist." *Id.*, p.140.

Recent attention has largely become focused not on attitudes or intent or on actual racism, but on the lingering effects from past events in our history. So, the concern presumably is primarily for the effects on American-born Blacks descended from slaves—not first or second generation immigrants who are black or brown. These are the people who would bear the scars of our history of slavery. That category would include Condoleezza Rice, Martin Luther King, Jr., and Thurgood Marshall; but, it would not include Barrack Obama, Kamala Harris or Colin Powell. It is not a matter of race, but of ancestry and cultural heritage. Or, so the logic says.

Shelby Steele asserts that: "'Systemic racism' is a term that tries to recover authenticity for a less and less convincing black identity. This racism is really more compensatory than systemic. It was invented to make up for the increasing absence of the real thing." "The Inauthenticity Behind Black Lives Matter," *WSJ.com*, November 22, 2020.

For example, the state of Oregon established a Covid relief fund exclusively for blacks and black-owned businesses, so Hispanic businesses in similar distress are denied relief on the basis of race.

> "'Centuries of systemic and institutional discrimination —perpetuated and exacerbated by current systems—have caused economic disparities.' ... [The relief] is available not on the basis of discrimination against applicants but on the presumption that all blacks and black businesses have been discriminated against by the state."

James Huffman, "Oregon's Segregated Covid Relief Fund Is Blatantly Unconstitutional," *WSJ.com*, December. 4, 2020.

The concept of "systemic racism" suggests that any identifiable disadvantages of Blacks today must be attributed to or blamed on the "system". (Of course, racist attitudes exist toward many other groups beyond Blacks.) A recent letter to the editor of the *Wall Street Journal* (Maggie Reeves, October 13, 2020) asked the pertinent question:

> "I wonder what reasons ... exist for racial disparities in our society other than racial prejudice? The 'black underclass' and 'black elites' both want safe neighborhoods and better schools for themselves, their families, and their communities."

The writer clearly intended the question to be rhetorical only. But, it is, in fact, a real question, and one that demands a real answer.

RACIST LAW ENFORCEMENT?

Racial discrimination in the enforcement of laws is unacceptable and a clear violation of our principles. The first question is whether there is evidence of significant (not isolated) acts of such racial discrimination. If so, then the second question would be whether that evidence reflects the presence of actual racism or the results of existing systems or structures.

On this first question, however, the data is incomplete and unclear.

Take fatal police shootings. For 2017-9, white deaths from police shootings averaged 407 per year and black deaths averaged 222 per year. "Victims were majority white (52%) but disproportionately black (32%) with a fatality rate 2.8 times higher among blacks than whites. Most victims were reported to be armed (83%); however, black victims were more likely to be unarmed (14.8%) than white (9.4%) or Hispanic (5.8%) victims." Sarah DeGue, *et al.*, "Deaths Due to Use of Lethal Force by Law Enforcement," *Am. J. Prev. Med.*, November 2016.

> "Among all groups, black men and boys face the highest lifetime risk of being killed by police. Our models predict that about 1 in 1,000 black men and boys will be killed by police over the life course (96 per 100,000). ...Latino men and boys have an estimated risk of being killed by police of about 53 per 100,000, ...while white men and boys face a lifetime risk of about 39 per 100,000."

Frank Edwards, *et al.*, "Risk of being killed by police use of force in the United States by age, race–ethnicity, and sex," *PNAS*, August 20, 2019.

But, Blacks also had much more frequent encounters with police. When adjustments are made for that factor, the disparity almost disappears: "we find no racial differences in officer-involved shootings...." Roland G. Fryer, Jr., "An Empirical Analysis of Racial Differences in Police Use of Force," *law.yale.edu*, July 2016. Similarly: "A Black person in America is roughly three times more likely than a white person to be killed by police. ...In 2018, the rate of arrests for violent crime was

3.6 times higher for Black people than white people. So actually, the argument goes, Black people are underrepresented as victims of police killings, after controlling for the number of encounters... . " Aubrey Clayton, "The statistical paradox of police killings: In the numbers of fatal encounters with the cops, one kind of discrimination masks another," *Boston Globe*, June 11, 2020.

However, Clayton persuasively argues: "The inflated number of nonlethal encounters Black people experience due to racial profiling could be what shifts the balance, perversely using one kind of discrimination, overpolicing, to mask another: the greater use of deadly force against Black suspects." *Id.* (emphasis in original).

"[C]ould be"? Well, yes, it could be. But, is it?

For 2018, an analysis showed that of all persons arrested, 69% were white and 27% were black; of arrests for violent crimes, the percentages were 58% and 38%. So, blacks (13% of the population) were twice as likely to be arrested as whites and 3 times as likely to be arrested for a violent crime. For murder and manslaughter, blacks represented 53% (more than 4 times as likely as whites). U.S Department of Justice, *OJJDP Statistical Briefing Book*, "Estimated number of arrests by offense and race, 2018," October 31, 2019. For curfew and loitering offenses, blacks represented 56% (over 4 times as likely as whites), but for drunkenness, disorderly conduct and vagrancy, blacks were between 25% and 30% (2 times as likely or less). *Id.*

At the same time, "[for] non-lethal uses of force—putting hands on civilians (which includes slapping or grabbing) or pushing individuals into a wall or onto the ground, there are large racial differences. In the raw data, blacks and Hispanics are more than fifty percent more likely to have an interaction with police which involves any use of force." Roland G. Fryer, Jr., "An Empirical Analysis of Racial Differences in Police Use of Force," *law.yale.edu*, July 2016.

Are black lawbreakers just more likely to be caught? Probably not, but the question is hard to answer empirically. Yet, we can answer whether the rates of crime are the same in communities independent of racial characteristics? That answer is an unambiguous "no." In fact, "the proportion of black suspects arrested by the police tends to match closely the proportion of offenders identified as black by victims in the [FBI's] National Crime Victimization Survey." Patrick Worral, "Do black Americans commit more crime?" *Channel 4 News, Factcheck*, 27 November 2014. Moreover, it is likely that Black communities under-report crime, so the actual statistics could be even more adverse for Black communities. The same conclusions were reached in a subsequent study using the same sources of data:

> "[In 2018], black people accounted for 29% of violent-crime offenders and 35% of violent-crime offenders in incidents reported to police, compared to 33% of all persons arrested for violent crimes. ...Among the most serious incidents of violent crime (rape or sexual assault, robbery, and aggravated assault), there were no statistically significant differences... ."

U.S. Department of Justice, Office of Justice Programs, Bureau of Justice Statistics, "Race and Ethnicity of Violent Crime Offenders and Arrestees, 2018," January 2021.

Similarly suggestive: "According to the CDC, about 14,500 Americans were murdered with guns in 2017. More than half were young black men killed in metro areas, which has been the pattern for at least the last five years... " Melissa Chan, "How Likely Is the Risk of Being Shot in America? It Depends," *Time*, August 16, 2019.

Thus, a black man is 7 times more likely than a white man to be killed by a gun and, generally, by other black men. So, while Blacks are 3 times more likely to be killed by police than whites, they are 7 times more likely to be killed by guns.

The crime rates by neighborhood evidence racial disparities as well.

"African Americans and Hispanics are more likely to be victims of violent crimes—especially serious violent crimes— than are whites, although the gap has narrowed over the past 10 years... African Americans are disproportionately victims of homicide compared with whites or Hispanics. Similarly, low-income people are much more likely than others to experience crime, including violent crime."

"Neighborhoods and Violent Crime," *Office of Policy Development and Research*, Summer 2016.

However, the differences are not as great as one might expect.

I note that there is a similar racial pattern in high school disciplinary actions. "Black women were three times as likely as white women to say they'd been disciplined." Mellisa Korn, "College Common App Drops Question About Discipline, Citing Racial Disparities," *WSJ.com*, September 20, 2020. (This data is for high school students applying to college. The solution adopted is to remove the question from the application. But, the cause of the pattern is not addressed. I think that the fact of such a disparity is more alarming than any possible obstacle to college admissions that the question—or the answers—present.) More broadly, "[a] U.S. Government Accountability Oversight report from 2018 shows Black students accounted for 15.5% of all public-school students, but represented about 39% of students suspended from school." *Id*.

> "A New York Times analysis ...found that Black girls are over five times more likely than white girls to be suspended at least once from school, seven times more likely to receive multiple out-of- school suspensions than white girls and three times more likely to receive referrals to law enforcement."

Erica L. Green, Mark Walker and Eliza Shapiro, " 'A Battle for the Souls of Black Girls'," *NYTmes.com*, October 1, 2020.

Is this problem all or largely discriminatory disciplinary practices occurring across the country or something else? The *Times* article is based largely on the "victims" explanations of their "victimhood." The referenced evidence of systematic discrimination is weak. If the cause is discrimination, then what do we do? Most schools are government controlled, so political action is possible. But, if much of the cause is with the students, then solutions are significantly more difficult to design and implement.

The biggest factor in crime rates appears to be living in poverty and in disadvantaged neighborhoods. "...African Americans and Hispanics... are disproportionately involved in street crime, victimized by street crime, and brought under the control and supervision of the criminal justice system. [But,] street crimes are more characteristic of impoverished, inner city, and ghetto neighborhoods ... ." "Race and Crime—Data Sources And Meaning," *law.JRank.org*, 2020.

If we had the data, we could look at patterns based upon economic status rather than race. We might find that the patterns of crime statistics are better explained. Of course, Blacks are disproportionately represented among the poor and disadvantaged. But, we must ask: How much of the pattern in school disciplinary actions is the reflection of class or economic, not racial, differences?

So, is any of this evidence of discriminatory racial profiling? Or, does it look like responsible law enforcement, marred by the acts of "bad" or inexperienced cops?

NPR conducted an investigation. "Since 2015, police officers have fatally shot at least 135 unarmed Black men and women nationwide... . NPR reviewed police, court and other records to examine the details of the cases." Cheryl W. Thompson, "Fatal Police Shootings Of Unarmed Black People Reveal Troubling," *NPR*, January 25, 2021.

The empirical results do not suggest systemic racism:

- "At least 75% of the officers were white." About what would be expected. ("In hundreds of police departments across the country, the percentage of whites on the force is more than 30 percentage points higher than in the communities they serve... . Minorities make up a quarter of police forces... ." Caroline Cournover, "The Race Gap in America's Police Departments," *Governing*, September 4, 2014.)
- "For at least 15 of the officers, ... the shootings were not their first —or their last... . They have been involved in two—sometimes three or more—shootings."
- "At least six officers had troubled pasts before being hired onto police departments, including drug use and domestic violence. ...Several officers were convicted of crimes while on the force, such as battery, and resisting and obstructing... . More than two dozen officers have racked up citizen complaints or use-of-force incidents."
- "Nineteen of the officers involved in deadly shootings were rookies, with less than a year on the force."

So, individual "bad" or inexperienced cops appear to be much of the problem, participating in 40 of the 135 shootings.

Finally, how is any racial discrimination that exists supposedly embodied in the "system" anyway? Is the fact that police often go where criminal activity is occurring a form of "systemic racism"? Or, is the mere existence of a police force "systemic racism"? That seems to be the view behind the "defunding movement." To me, that position is completely irrational, and I suspect it is not shared by most Black households.

INCOME, HOMEOWNERSHIP AND WEALTH

For many of the comparisons below, we would have wanted to isolate the descendants of Black Americans of the 19th century. Generally, however, we cannot separate out immigrants (or their descendants). The racial categorizations are also self-selected, so the data is not confirmed by objective standards; and, that selection is based largely on choices among the outdated U.S. Census categories. *See, e.g.,* Janet Adamy and Paul Overberg, "The Census Predicament: Counting Americans by Race: The racial and ethnic categories used by the U.S. Census obscure the changing ways we think about identity and assimilation," *WSJ.com,* November 27, 2020. Currently, "[a]mong Black adults, one in eight is an immigrant. ...[And,] Americans of two or more races or ethnicities—including Vice President- elect Kamala Harris—are the country's fastest-growing demographic, and they defy labels." *Id.*

I. Income

Median household income (in 2017) was as follows:

- Asian $81,331
- White (not Hispanic) $68,145
- Hispanic (any race) $50,486
- Black $40,258

Individual Black worker's median income was $31,000.

For all women, the median was $33,280.

U.S. Census Bureau, *Current Population Survey*, 1968 to 2018 Annual Social and Economic Supplements.

We can look also at the distribution of income within each racial group. For example, comparisons of the thresholds of the top 10% with those of the bottom 10% by income shows significant differences.

"In 2016, ... Asians near the top of their income distribution (the 90th percentile) had incomes 10.7 times greater than the incomes of Asians near the bottom of their income distribution (the 10th percentile). The 90/10 ratio among Asians was notably greater than among blacks (9.8), whites (7.8) and Hispanics (7.8)."

R. Kochhar and A. Cilluffo, "Key findings on the rise in income inequality within America's racial and ethnic groups," FactTank, *Pew Research Center*, July 12, 2018.

"[I]f you divide black income into quintiles, the top quintile has now secured almost 50 percent of the total black income, which is a record. The top quintile in the white population has secured about 44 percent of the white income, which is also a record.... if you just look at the distribution of income, inequality is growing more rapidly in the black community surprisingly than in the white community.

...

"[C]ompare the income of black professors and white professors. Black professors make more than white professors. That's because we are in demand. "

William Julius Wilson, "Interview ... by Henry Louis 'Skip' Gates, Jr.," *Frontline*, November 2015.

It may be instructive also to look at differences in employment participation rates, reflecting the percentage of persons with or looking for work. That could explain some differences in household income.

"Among the race and ethnicity groups [for 2016], Native Hawaiians and Other Pacific Islanders (68.7 percent) and Hispanics (65.8 percent) had the highest labor force participation rates while American Indians and Alaska Natives (61.1 percent) and Blacks (61.6 percent) had the lowest participation rates. The participation rates were 62.9 percent for Whites, 63.2 percent for Asians, and 65.0 percent for people of Two or More Races."

"Labor force characteristics by race and ethnicity, 2016," *BLS Report*, October 2017.

This income data, based on IRS filings, excludes gains from the underground ("off-the-books") economy and gains from illegal activities such as drug trafficking and prostitution or Ponzi schemes and Medicare fraud. The underground economy is generally estimated at around $2 trillion per year (10-13% of GDP). Drug trafficking is estimated at $100-150 billion per year. ("The results show that drug users in the United States spend on the order of $100 billion annually on all four drugs.... This figure has been stable over the decade, but there have been important shifts in the drugs being purchased." "How Big Is the U.S.

Market for Illegal Drugs?," *rand.org*, 2014.) Prostitution also generates hundreds of billions of dollars. I have no estimates of the average annual take from all fraudulent activities, but it is very substantial.

If the receipt of that income is not distributed evenly among racial groups, which seems very likely, its inclusion in the calculation would alter the median and average numbers of the groups differently, perhaps noticeably so. *See* Sudhir Venkatesh, "The Underground Economy of the Urban Poor," *NPR*, October 4, 2006. For example, minorities hold a disproportionate number of the jobs in activities readily susceptible to cash payment (and tax evasion), like construction, home maintenance, gardening and housecleaning.

The income data also does not include government transfer payments or welfare and public assistance. So, the actual effective (after tax and after government benefits) income differences may be much less than suggested above.

II. HOME OWNERSHIP

The current disparity in home ownership is about 30 percentage points, with Black homeownership in the mid-40%s and non-Hispanic white homeownership in the mid-70s.

Part of the disparity between Black and white non-immigrant Americans appears to derive from national housing policies that started with the Great Depression and continued after World War II. "[F]or decades government policies explicitly helped white Americans build housing capital and denied Black Americans the same opportunity." Gerald F. Seib, "The Debate Over Systemic Racism: Why It Divides and Why It Provides Hope," *WSJ.com*, July 27, 2020.

According to Seib, these programs were not aimed to deprive blacks or minorities, but to maximize the impact of the capital committed by focusing on the "safer" investments:

> "Starting during the New Deal, the federal government ... began underwriting mortgages to allow working-class Americans to keep their homes during the Depression. But the government wanted to protect its investment by funneling funds to relatively 'safe' mortgages—and decided that homes owned by white people, in all-white neighborhoods, were safer investments than homes sold to Black people or in mixed-race neighborhoods.
>
> ...
>
> "[T]he Federal Housing Administration ... simply adopted the same policies. Then, crucially, so did the Veterans Administration... ."

The result of these programs, unfortunately, was that Blacks were left behind. Of course, even more white families (by number) were also unable to participate in and benefit from these programs than Blacks. Such results could have been avoided only by offering subsidies to those left out. But, in fact, special treatment for housing was tried:

> "[T]he Clinton administration decided to expand federal government servicing of low-income and minority borrowers through various 'affordable-housing goals.' Imposed in 1992, [they] ... requir[ed] a certain percentage of the loans ... acquired each year to have been made to borrowers in financially isolated communities or those who were at or below the median income in the communities in which they lived.
>
> ...

"By 2006, 45 percent of first time homebuyers were putting nothing down."

Daniel Press,"The Financial Crisis 10 Years Later: Fannie and Freddie Fueled the Subprime Mortgage Bubble," *Competitive Enterprise Institute,* September 12, 2018.

Those efforts largely failed in the end. There is a debate about whether these policies contributed to the housing "bubble;" but, regardless, the bubble burst by 2010. Many of the homeowners who benefitted from the underwriting lower standards lost everything. Ten years later, the Black home ownership percentage is still below where it was in 1968. ("After the foreclosure crisis that accompanied the previous recession, the black homeownership rate slid to 41% in early 2019 from 48% in early 2007." Amara Omeokwe, "Coronavirus Pandemic Threatens to Widen Racial Homeownership Gap," *WSJ.com*, September 20, 2020.)

So, timing and economic conditions mattered a lot.

A research report by the Urban Institute in 2019 attempted to determine statistically the relationship between various factors and homeownership, controlling for age and some other influences assumed to be independent of race. Jung Hyun Choi, "Breaking Down the Black-White Homeownership Gap," *Urban Institute,* February 21, 2020.

The findings were:

1. "If the household income distribution was the same for white and black households, while other household and MSA level factors remained constant, the gap between the black and white

homeownership rates ... would drop by 31 percent, or 9.3 percentage points."

2. "Compared with white households, black households are less likely to marry. If black households were married at the same rate as white households, the black-white homeownership gap ... would decrease by 27 percent, or 8.1 percentage points... ."

3. "Credit score differences: 22 percent of the gap."

4. "Differences in educational attainment do not contribute to the gap."

The remaining "unexplained" percentage of the gap was 17% or about 5.7 percentage points.

At least some 49% of the difference in homeownership is attributable to factors not directly related to possible discrimination. Only 31% is attributable to income differences, which might be at least partly the result of discrimination.

In this study, household income appeared to be only slightly more significant than marriage status in explaining the disparities in homeownership. Others have obtained similar results but placed more emphasis on the income gap: "our analysis supports the conclusion that the racial labor income gap is the primary driver behind the large and persistent difference in average wealth between black and white households." Dionissi Aliprantis and Daniel R. Carroll, "What Is Behind the Persistence of the Racial Wealth Gap?" *Federal Reserve Bank of Cleveland*, February 28, 2019. Of course, as discussed below, there is a strong correlation between household income and marital status.

III. WEALTH ACCUMULATION

"[T]he 2016 wealth gap [between whites and blacks] is roughly the same as it was in 1962, two years before the passage of the Civil Rights Act of 1964... ." Dionissi Aliprantis and Daniel R. Carroll, "What Is

Behind the Persistence of the Racial Wealth Gap?" *Federal Reserve Bank of Cleveland*, February 28, 2019.

Differences in accumulated wealth among racial groups appear to be influenced by several extraneous factors, which should be taken into account in the comparisons. One such factor is the age distribution of the population. Blacks have two thirds the percentage of persons over 54 as whites (23% v. 34%), the age group mostly likely to have accumulated wealth and to pass it to the next generation. (Hispanics have less than half the percentage of whites over 54, 15%.) Carmel Ford."Homeownership by Race and Ethnicity," *Eye On Housing*, December 15, 2017. (However, older Blacks do not have greater wealth than middle aged Blacks.)

And, as noted above and discussed below, a much smaller percentage of blacks are married, also adversely affecting wealth accumulation. (About 35% of black women are married, versus 59% of white women and 63% of Asian women. "Marital Status in the United States," *Statistical Atlas*, September 4, 2018.)

Otherwise, there are some apparent race-related (but not discrimination-related) causes of disparity in accumulated wealth based upon people's behavior on average. Two such factors are are less savings and more conservative investment activity by certain minority groups in comparison to whites.

"Racial and ethnic differences in housing equity narrow among households in the higher income quartiles, whereas differences in nonhousing equity generally widen as income increases. The widening gap in nonhousing equity stems from differences in financial asset holdings, particularly risky assets. At every income quartile and educational level, the percentage of black and Hispanic households that own risky, higher-yielding assets is considerably smaller than the percentage of white households."

Sharmila Choudhury, "Racial and Ethnic Differences in Wealth and Asset Choices," *Social Security Bulletin*, Vol. 64, No. 4, 2001/2002.

Similarly, a study using data from a single very large employer plan found:

"...[B]oth African American and Hispanic employees are less likely to participate in the 401(k) plans. Moreover, ...African Americans contribute a lower proportion of their income to their 401(k) plan on average. ...African Americans and Hispanics tend to draw down on their 401(k) balances more often. Finally, ...both African Americans and Hispanics favor safer assets within their plan options. Together these differences substantially impact the level of 401(k) balances accumulated and therefore overall wealth accumulation."

Kai Yuan Kuan, Mark R. Cullen, and Sepideh Modrek , "Racial Disparities in Savings Behavior for a Continuously Employed Cohort," *NBER*, Working Paper No. 20937, February 2015.

Separately, civil disturbances over time have taken a toll on Black wealth, both immediately in destroyed assets and over time in discouragement of investment. "This article examines census data from 1950 to 1980 to measure the riots' impact on the value of central-city residential property, and especially on black-owned property....[E]stimates indicate that the riots depressed the median value of black-owned property between 1960 and 1970, with little or no rebound in the 1970s." William J. Collins and Robert A. Margo, "The Economic Aftermath of the 1960s Riots in American Cities: Evidence from Property Values," *The Journal of Economic History*, December 2007, pp. 849-883.

Nonetheless, as of a few years ago, of the households in the U.S. with a net worth of more than a million dollars, approximately 8% were

Black, 8% were Asian and 7% were Hispanic. Some 20% of the million-aires inherited at least some of their wealth. Assuming very few of that 20% were Black, it appears that of those who made it on their own, 10% were Black.

A Caveat About Immigrants

For many of the matters discussed herein, as noted above, one would like to examine non-immigrant racial categories, because immigrant communities have important different characteristics independent of race.

    1. Many immigrants prioritize helping families at home over savings, explaining differences in savings rates and biasing comparisons of accumulated wealth.

"A significant share of immigrants all over the world send part of their paycheck back to help their families in their home countries. ...[I]t is estimated that the collective sum of remittance payments in 2017 came to $625 billion, a 7% increase from 2016.... In the United States alone, it is estimated that more than $148 billion was sent to individuals in other countries in 2017."

Niall McCarthy, "Immigrants In The U.S. Sent Over $148 Billion To Their Home Countries In 2017," *Forbes*, April 8, 2019.

See also, "Mexican workers in US are sending record money home despite coronavirus-related economic shutdowns," *The Conversation*, May 27, 2020 ("The 11.2 million people of Mexican origin living in the United States together send upwards of US $38 billion to Mexico each year.")

---

2. Also, immigrant communities have lower violent crime rate.

"Numerous studies show that immigration is strongly associated with lower rates of violent crime. One rigorous study of neighborhoods in Los Angeles in the mid-2000s, for instance, found that greater concentrations of immigrants in a neighborhood are related to significant drops in crime. Similarly, ...[analysis of] data on Chicago neighborhoods ... found that ... concentrated immigration is directly associated with lower rates of violence."

"Neighborhoods and Violent Crime," *Office of Policy Development and Research*, Summer 2016.

---

3. To some extent, the immigrant population is self-selected for success—people who have come affirmatively seeking a better life, risk-takers, people who have fled hardship or oppression and people determined to find opportunities.

"...African immigrants are more likely than Americans overall to have a college degree, and a recent study ... reveals that their labor-force participation rate is 73%, 10 points higher than that of the overall population. By some measures, Nigerians are the most successful immigrant group in the country. Fifty-nine percent have a college degree, more than double the population as a whole; and in 2018 their median household income was nearly $7,000 higher than the average."

Dave Seminara, "Africans Knock on America's Door: Why would millions want to immigrate if the U.S. is a land of 'systemic racism'?" *WSJ.com*, September 23, 2020.

But, immigration status is not an available subcategory of the data from the U.S. Census bureau or other Federal agencies.

So... ?

All of this data may reflect some types of discrimination, just not by race. Indeed, "Black Americans" are not a race. The black racial population consists of at least three distinct groups: immigrants, the middle (and upper) class and the poor (the bottom two quintiles). Our concern should be with this third group: the underprivileged, largely inner-city Blacks. Harvard sociologist William Julius Wilson explains:

> "When I said [in 1978] there was a declining significance of race, what I really meant was not that racism was declining... but ... that class was becoming more important than race in determining individual black life chances. ...[W]e had a tendency to not pay attention to some of these non-racial factors that impacted significantly on the black community."

"Interview ...by Henry Louis 'Skip' Gates, Jr.," *PBS*, November 2015.

As we have noted, the Black community is not homogeneous and that the disadvantages noted above exist mainly for the substantial bottom rung.

SOME OTHER FACTS

Here are some facts about the bottom two quintiles of Blacks.

I. Crime and Drug Use

"...There are many positive things to say about the black community. ... But if you ... don't explain why the murder rate is so high in ... inner city neighborhoods or why the drug addiction rate is so high or why the school dropout rate is so high or why individual aberrant behavior is so high in general. If you don't explain those things, you create a void... ."

William Julius Wilson, "Interview ... by Henry Louis 'Skip' Gates, Jr.," *PBS Frontline*, November 2015.

Some of the data on the disparate crime rates is outlined above. The Federal government's War on Crime and War on Drugs led to shockingly high rates of incarceration of Blacks males, but did not reduce crime. So, how do we explain "why individual aberrant behavior is [still] so high" in these disadvantaged Black communities? And, what can be done about it?

II. De Facto Segregation

"At the beginning of this century, for Blacks, the typical residential setting was southern and rural; for Whites it was northern and urban.

...

"Successive waves of Black migration out of the rural South into the urban North transformed the geographic structure of Black segregation during the twentieth century, however, **ending the regional isolation and rural confinement of Blacks.**"

Douglas S.Massey, "Residential Segregation and Neighborhood Conditions in U.S. Metropolitan Areas," *America Becoming: Racial Trends and Their Consequences*: Volume I, Chapter 13, 2001 (emphasis added).

Overall, "... there was a gradual movement of blacks to Northern areas throughout the first half of the twentieth century. And as jobs opened up in Northern industries, there was a fairly rapid increase during the 1940s, so much so that the population of blacks in certain cities quadrupled."

William Julius Wilson,"Interview."

Then,

"After 1950, Blacks and Whites not only tended to live in different neighborhoods; increasingly they lived in different municipalities as well. ...Blacks and Whites came to reside in wholly different towns and cities. ...Blacks were still unlikely to come into residential contact with members of other groups. The large ghettos of the North have remained substantially intact ...."

Massey, "Residential Segregation."

The *de facto* residential separation of races is not easily altered. For example, who moves and to (and from) where? And, how is the relocation of millions of people orchestrated? Presumably, not using the methods of China or of Stalin's Soviet Union. Moreover, mere relocation will not solve the problems.

III. Depressed Communities

These separate post-1950 Black communities have not been like many Chinatowns across the country—vibrant, active communities attracting tourism and generating economic activity—or, like Harlem, have failed to stay that way. Instead, the *de facto* segregation was accompanied by significant joblessness and high rates of crime, as discussed. These communities have been spiraling downward since the 1950s, turning into islands of despair.

Clearly, joblessness is an important part of the equation. Extensive joblessness infects the whole community.

> "[A] neighborhood in which people are poor and working is entirely different from a neighborhood in which people are poor and jobless. One of the reasons why you have had such an increase in rates of these social dislocations ranging from gang formation to drugs to violent crime is the high jobless rate."

William Julius Wilson, "Interview."

Employment has fallen in the inner cities as many companies suffered declines or closed and others moved away. So, "...disadvantaged blacks have really been hard hit by changes in the economy. The computer revolution, changes in scale-based technology. The internationalization of economic activity had combined to decrease the demand for low-skilled workers." *Id*.

> "...Among adult men (ages 20 and older) ... , Hispanics (76.6 percent) continued to have the highest employment –population ratio. Blacks (62.0 percent) had the lowest, continuing a longstanding pattern. The employment–population ratios for Asian men and White men were 72.8 percent and 69.1 percent, respectively. Among adult women, the ratios showed less variation across the race and ethnicity groups... ."

"Labor force characteristics by race and ethnicity, 2016," *BLS Report*, October 2017.

With respect to unemployment, looking at the 12 months ending October 2020, there are some oddities. For those without a high school diploma, the unemployment for whites and Hispanics were 10.1% and 10.5%, respectively, while the rate for Blacks was 15.3%. In contrast, for persons with a bachelor's degree, the white, Hispanic and Black unemployment rates were 4.8%, 6.7% and 6.1%; and, with advanced degrees, they were 3.3%, 4.2% and 4.4%. So, with more education, Blacks did as well or better than Hispanics. Eric Morath, "Disparity in Jobless Rates Suggests Black Workers Face Slower Recovery," *WSJ.com*. November 29, 2020.

The isolation of increasingly dysfunctional communities has particularly adverse effects on the children: "[L]iving in such a place, where everyday survival is often a challenge, is not conducive to acquiring the habits for success in the larger society. .... About 20% of black children (compared with 1% of white children) grow up in such places." Holman W. Jenkins, Jr., "How to Show That Black Lives Really Matter: The single best thing for young families is leaving a high-crime, high-poverty neighborhood," *WSJ.com*, July 10, 2020. In contrast,

> "[t]he few areas with small black-white gaps tend to be low-poverty neighborhoods with low levels of racial bias among whites and high rates of father presence among blacks. Black males who move to such neighborhoods earlier in childhood have significantly better outcomes. However, less than 5% of black children grow up in such areas."

Raj Chetty, Nathaniel Hendren, Maggie R Jones, Sonya R Porter, "Race and Economic Opportunity in the United States: an Intergenerational Perspective,* *The Quarterly Journal of Economics,* May 2020.

Again, the Black population is not monolithic. Joblessness and low income are much more prevalent among the urban poor. So, the pertinent questions are how to improve things in those predominantly Black communities, especially for the children, and how to help people who want to escape to do so.

IV. Lack of Two-Parent Households

One of the most serious current challenges for the Black community is the lack of two-parent, two wage-earning households, as already noted.

"More than half (58%) of black children are living with an unmarried parent – 47% with a solo mom. At the same time, 36% of Hispanic children are living with an unmarried parent, as are 24% of white children." Gretchen Livingston, "About one-third of U.S. children are living with an unmarried parent," *Pew Research Center,* April 17, 2018.

"Women of color are ... much more likely than white women to be raising children while unmarried, even though white women make up the majority of unmarried mothers. In 2016, for example, 40 percent of all births in the United States were to unmarried mothers. This included 17 percent of births to Asian or Pacific Islander women, 29 percent to non-Hispanic white women, 53 percent to Hispanic women, 66 percent to American Indian or Alaskan native women, and 70 percent of births to non-Hispanic black women."

Sarah Jane Glynn, "Breadwinning Mothers Continue To Be the U.S. Norm," *Center for American Progress,* May 10, 2019.

There is pretty wide recognition that children do better in two-parent homes. But, there are purely economic consequences as well. Marriage boosts home ownership, wealth accumulation and income levels, as well as inheritances. ("...30% of solo mothers and their families are living in poverty compared with 17% of solo father families and 16% of families headed by a cohabiting couple. In comparison, 8% of married couple families are living below the poverty line." *Id.*) Among Black families, the impact is even starker.

"Being raised in a married-couple household led the poverty rate for black children to go down 73 percent compared to mother-only households and 67 percent compared to father-only households. And, ... 31 percent of white children raised in mother-only households live in poverty, versus just 12 percent of black children living with their married parents."

Ian Rowe, "The power of the two-parent home is not a myth," *Thomas B. Fordham Institute,* January 8, 2020.

Part of the the economic benefit of two-parent families is the ability to have dual incomes. In 2012, of all married couples with children under 18, 60% were dual or two-income households, up from 25% in 1960. "The Rise in Dual Income Households," *Pew Research Center*, June 18, 2015. Many affluent families are dual income. *See, e.g.*, Cara David, "Dual income households are the norm in affluent homes," *YouGov.com*, March 08, 2018 ("Fifty-five percent of the affluent households surveyed (those with a household income of at least $150,000) are dual-income households"). For example, these various studies show that Asians have the greatest percentage of married, two-parent households, the highest household income and the lowest crime rates, well ahead of non-Hispanic whites in all categories.

This problem is not new; it was identified over 50 years ago.

> "[T]he Moynihan Report [1965] highlighted the fact that the Negro family was weakening as reflected in the growth of female-headed households, and that the growth of female-headed households would have profound negative implications for the black family, because female-headed families are much more vulnerable to problems in the larger society, much more likely to be impoverished, and much more likely to experience difficulty in socializing children to compete in the broader society. ...Single-parent families, family break-ups in the black community are problematic because of the impact on children, and that's the main thing. ... So, children growing up in these poor, female-headed families are at a disadvantage ... ."

Ben Wattenberg, "William Julius Wilson Interview," *The First Measured Century on PBS: The Other Way of Looking at American History*, 2000.

At the same time, the lack of two-parent households is not a legacy of slavery or even of Jim Crow. The percentage of two-parent households among Blacks, as reflected in the U.S. Census, exceeded that for whites consistently between 1890 and 1940. Walter E. Williams, *Race and Economics: How Much Can Be Blamed on Discrimination?* (2011), p.8 (citing Thomas Sowell's research).

William Julius Wilson points to joblessness as a cause of single-parent households.

> "[W]e found ... a strong relationship between black male joblessness and single-parent families. ...[T]hat employed fathers were two-and-a-half times more likely to marry the mother of their first child than jobless fathers. This is especially true of men under the age of thirty-five. So, in the inner city we found a very strong relationship between male joblessness and female-headed families. ...Moynihan [in1965] talked about [how]... joblessness creates problem streams in the family. It leads to family breakups resulting in increasing number of families going on welfare."

Wattenberg, "Interview."

However, the lack of two-parent households will not be cured merely by providing jobs for the currently unemployed, many of whom are effectively unemployable. The focus must be on the young-—on children and young adults. There must be hope and opportunity for the young, looking to the future.

So, is this factor a problem that can or should be addressed or is it just a partial explanation for the observed disparities?

V. Deteriorating Public Education

"[T]he black lives most at risk are the young men and women living in the nation's poorest urban neighborhoods, attending the worst-performing public schools in the U.S."

Daniel Henninger, "Reading the Trump-Biden Inkblots: Voters can't pretend a Biden presidency will help the black children trapped in failing inner-city schools," *WSJ.com*, July 29, 2020.

The consequences are clear and dramatic.

'Blacks make up just over 1% of all SAT test takers who score between 700 and 800 on the math SAT, but 24% of all math SAT test takers with scores between 300 and 390. The average black math SAT score (454 in 2020) is more than a standard deviation below the average Asian math SAT score and nearly a standard deviation below the average white math score."

Heather MacDonald, "Woke Science Is an Experiment Certain to Fail: Advancing knowledge, not imposing diversity, should be the goal of federal research funding.," *WSJ.com*, September 24, 2020.

Yet, today's response is: "many people would say that the fact that, on average, black students do not perform as highly on standardized tests as white students means that the tests are racist, in that they disadvantage black students." John McWhorter, "The Dictionary Definition of Racism Has to Change," *The Atlantic*, June 22, 2020. However, presumably no one suggests that the SATs were designed or have been utilized to discriminate against Blacks. Is the solution to this disparity to abolish the use of SATs? Really? That is a solution to what?

Can, perhaps, instead, something be done about the schools? At least, politicians could resist the union pressures against educational alternatives and experimentation and the belief that more money is the answer to what is wrong. Perhaps, they could even make changes that would actually help.

Again, citing work by Thomas Sowell, Walter Williams observed that the disgraceful state of Black schools is a relatively recent phenomenon:

> "[Baltimore's] Frederick Douglass High School of yesteryear produced many distinguished alumni, such as Thurgood Marshall and Cab Calloway, and several judges, congressmen, and civil rights leaders....[It] was second in the nation in black Ph.D.s among its alumni. As early as 1899, [Paul Laurence Dunbar High School, a black public school in Washington, D.C.] ... students scored higher on citywide tests than any of the city's white schools. From its founding in 1870 to 1955, most of its graduates went off to college. ...[Its] distinguished alumni include U.S. Sen. Edward Brooke, physician Charles Drew, and, during World War II, nearly a score of majors, nine colonels and lieutenant colonels, and a brigadier general. Today's Paul Laurence Dunbar and Frederick Douglass high schools have material resources that would have been unimaginable to their predecessors. However, having those resources have meant absolutely nothing in terms of academic achievement."

"The Tragedy of Black Education Is New," *TheDailySignal*, December 2, 2020.

Yet, there are indications of potential routes to progress.

"...[C]harter schools are not simply doing a better job than their :traditional counterparts with the same demographic groups. In many cases, inner-city charter-school students are outperforming their peers in the wealthiest and whitest suburban school districts in the country.

...

"[Moreover, quoting economist Thomas Sowell,] '[t]he educational success of these charter schools undermines theories of genetic determinism, claims of cultural bias in the tests, assertions that racial "integration" is necessary for blacks to reach educational parity and presumptions that income differences are among the "root causes" of educational differences' ."

Jason L. Riley, "Thomas Sowell Has Been Right From the Start," *WSJ.com*, July 21, 2020.

The existence of some choice and the feeling of influence with respect to one's children's education are highly desirable and are likely to lead to better results. But, public policy has been counterproductive, discouraging charter schools and discriminating against parochial schools, apparently in the interest of equality. Similarly, during this pandemic, alternative approaches to continuing education are resisted in the interests of "equality," because they may disadvantage the poorer students. Vested interests are being protected at the expense of the children. *See, e.g.,* Elliot Kaufman, "The Teachers Union's Tiny New Enemy: The behemoth National Education Association seeks to squash popular pandemic microschools," *WSJ.com*, October 14, 2020 ("It's a strange pitch from the teachers union: Microschools are dangerous—they help their students learn more! This seems like a reason to broaden access, not restrict it"). At the same time, although everyone seems to recognize that lack of in-person instruction hurts the underprivileged students more, those same vested interests resist resumption of in-class instruction even well into 2021.

When the accepted approach has resulted in decades of failure, that is not a reason for "more of the same" in bigger doses; it is a reason for change—a reason for experimentation, innovation and diversity. However, we will now experience a reassertion of the influence of the teachers' union under President-elect Biden. Let us hope that we see some improvements and gains, that more money actually does something positive.

GOVERNMENT POLICIES

The review above of various relevant factors suggests that the real problems plaguing the disadvantaged segment of Black Americans today are a lack of mobility (physical and economic), a predominance of single-parent families and largely dysfunctional communities, with high rates of crime and violence (by Blacks against Blacks). Racism simply is not the biggest problem for these Blacks nor the primary cause of their current levels of poverty.

Moreover, as noted, these problems arose long after slavery ended and even after Jim Crow. Indeed, they followed the reduction in legalized racism and the *de jure* integration after World War II. We need to identify the causes of these changes after 1950. The current narratives about "systemic racism" offer no insights into this question. We also need to know why these problems—as also previously noted, already identified and described in the late 1960s—have persisted and become more severe.

So, what has government done with respect to the well-being of these communities over the past 60 years and with what effect?

I. SOCIAL WELFARE

Over the past 55 years, since the beginning of The Great Society programs in 1964, we have spent over $20 trillion (in today's dollars) on fighting poverty. Yet, we still have poverty.

Why? Because the money was provided for current consumption, not infrastructure, and it was then spent, not saved or invested. As a result, these programs merely ameliorated the burdens of poverty, which has tended to make poverty more resilient. They reduced "poverty" (as then defined), but did not help the recipients to escape dependence on government subsidies, to become more self-sufficient and independent.

Policymakers failed to realize the extent to which making poverty more tolerable would reduce the incentives to escape poverty and would tend to increase dependency on the state.

> "The ... programs are focused on making poverty more comfortable—giving poor people more food, better shelter, health care, *etc.*—rather than giving people the tools that will help them escape poverty. As a result, we have been successful in reducing the worst privations of poverty. Few Americans live with out the basic necessities of life, yet neither do they rise out of poverty. Moreover, their children are also likely to be poor."

Michael D. Tanner, "War on Poverty at 50—Despite Trillions Spent, Poverty Won," *CATO Institute*, January 8, 2014.

As Tanner observes: "Our goal should not be a society where people struggle along in poverty, dependent on government for just enough to survive, but rather a society where as few people as possible live in poverty, and where every American can reach his or her full potential."

Similarly, Jason Riley argues that: "[g]overnment programs are no substitute for the development of human capital. If wealth-redistribution schemes lifted people out of poverty, we would have closed these gaps a long time ago. Liberal politicians and activists have little interest in addressing the ways in which black behavioral choices impact inequality." "The Race Card Has Gone Bust: America has never been fairer or more integrated, yet politicians obsess over wiping out discrimination," *WSJ.com*, July 16, 2019.

The basic social problems of disintegrating families and communities were identified by social scientists beginning in the 1960s, but minimal ameliorative actions were taken by government to address them.

"In 1965 Daniel Patrick Moynihan, then an assistant secretary of labor, issued a detailed report concluding that generational poverty among black Americans was the result not of an insufficiently generous welfare system but of the black family's dissolution. He was dismissed as a racist. Irving Kristol, James Q Wilson and others argued for decades that an unreformed welfare state hurt minority communities more than they helped... ."

Barton Swaim, "Radicals Have a Point About Racial Liberalism: They know the prevailing orthodoxy has failed. Too bad they don't recall those who predicted its failure," *WSJ.com*, August 9, 2020.

In fact, the incentive structures created by government policies aggravate and perpetuate the disparities. It appears that these isolated Black communities have been written off and are being bought off with increasing handouts.

II. RACIAL PREFERENCES

Similarly, affirmative action is largely irrelevant to Black inner-city youth. Racial preferences have aided the Black middle class in competition with the white middle class, but have done little for the really disadvan- taged. The same is true of the recent proposals to forgive student debt and of the current efforts to increase diversity on corporate boards and among CEOs. Or, the actions to increase substantially the minimum wage; whether or not such actions will increase unemployment, they clearly will not generate jobs for the currently unemployed.

Of course, affirmative action programs may have improved the educational experiences for others (of all races) by increasing diversity and broadening outlooks and these current efforts may enhance and enrich our institutions and society. (Harvard's express justification for its admission policy may be sound policy, whether it actually reflects the motivation.) But, have they helped or hurt Black Americans as a group on balance? Good queston. One answer:

> "[In the 1960s and 1970s,] ... policy makers ... blessed the creation of racial and ethnic categories and the related use of racial preferences for university admissions, employment and government contracting. The formalizing of groups, the addition of incentives to adhere to them, and the culture of victimhood that the whole scheme instilled, betrayed the colorblind promise of the civil-rights movement ...[and] all but ensured victimhood would never end."

Mike Gonzalez, "We Might Get Fooled Again," *WSJ.com*, July 9, 2020.

III. AND NOW?

So, have we learned anything?

It appears not. The new current (2021) approach is substantially to expand government social benefits, divorcing them from work and, even, from need. Minorities are helped only incidentally. The programs are squarely aimed at the middle class.

The so-called "Covid-19 Relief" bill allocated less than 30% of its spending for assistance to persons who actually suffered economically from the pandemic. Benefits went to government employees, pubic school teachers and staff of professional service organizations who generally continued to be paid while working fewer hours, often from home, saving the time and expense of commuting, and enjoying greater flexibility and personal time. And, President Biden now rewards them with a substantial pay increase. For those with government student loans, payments were suspended. Economically, all of these people are better off as a result of the pandemic; yet, they got the government "relief" funds. And, more than $100 billion went to state governments that are enjoying record surpluses. Relief? And, how much simply went to fraudsters and crooks?

Of course, millions were put out of work by the pandemic, especially in the hospitality and travel industries. But, the government provided substantially increased unemployment payments, giving many an income from not working that was greater than their income while employed and inviting massive numbers of fraudulent filings pursuant to which some 10-15% of the benefits nationwide were stolen, and even more in California. The bill even provided a tax exemption for over $10,000 of unemployment benefits per person. However, a household would have to earn about $75,000 for the year to benefit from that exemption (*i.e.*, one would have to be in the top third of all families).

Who are to be the primary beneficiaries of this bill? Not the poor, clearly.

The two quarters with the highest GDP growth in the last 40 years are 3Q 2020 and 1Q 2021. Household net worth grew 16% in the 15 months ending March 31, 2021. Even the net worth of the bottom quintile grew 2.5%. Individual savings rates have soared, credit card debt has plummet- ed and there are record unfilled job openings—all evidencing that much of the benefits went to persons not seriously in need. As a further irony, the bill appears to have fueled rapid, dramatic inflation, which will hurt savers, those on fixed incomes and most aver-age workers. Not so much those living on government benefits or the wealthy. Just the average working people.

The response? Plans to spend another $3.5-5.5 trillion! The Presi-dent assures us that the inflation is just "transitory" (so is life) and that his program will pay for itself and cost "nothing". These are deceptions of Trumpian proportions. The Build Back Better proposal is rife with budgetary gimmicks, not for overcoming procedural technicalities, as is usual; but, to deceive the American public.

The President's so-called "infrastructure" bill would have devoted less than 30% of its commitments to capital investment or infrastructure. The rest was for current consumption. And, the proposed "American Rescue" and the "American Families" plans do not even purport to focus on Blacks or on minorities or, even, on the bottom quintile, but are intended to extend government subsidy payments to more than 50% of all voters. The proposal is to do so initially at the expense of the top 1%. Of course, with this "shotgun" approach, some of the benefits will go to the needy, but at a huge cost.

These plans are simply efforts to "buy" votes. The political motiva-tion must be the belief that few Americans will have the strength to vote against continued handouts to themselves at the expense of others. Will it work? We shall see. But, I am pretty sure it would not have worked if announced in advance. If Biden had disclosed during the campaign what he would do when elected (assuming he then had any idea), he would have lost the election.

Racists and racism continue to exist and have a negative and disruptive impact on American society, but the national identity simply is no longer racist. Look at Blacks in government (mayors, police chiefs, governors, senators and, even, President and Vice-President), business, entertainment and sports or their presence at universities, in the military and among the ranks of millionaires (some hundreds of thousands) and even of billionaires (12 or 13 worldwide, at least 7 in the United States)—there are more Black millionaires in America than in the rest of the world combined.

Here are the comments by four Black American authors and educators:

- Ward Connerly: "The claim that America is 'systemically racist' is a false narrative that fuels racial paranoia, division and hatred. If we can identify specific institutions or people within them that are racist, we should confront them. If not, it doesn't serve us well to allow a false presumption of guilt to guide our conduct." "America Isn't a Racist Country," *WSJ.com*, July 24, 2020.
- Robert L. Woodson Sr.: "Those who attribute all failure of blacks in America—academic, occupational and even moral—to an all-purpose invisible villain of 'institutional racism' are betraying those they purport to represent. ... This debilitating dynamic is exacerbated by the guilt among white liberals, who approach the black community with a combination of pity, patronage and pandering." "The Resilience of the Black American," *WSJ.com*, August 6, 2020.
- Shelby Steele: "...[W]e blacks aren't much victimized any more. Today we are free to build a life that won't be stunted by racial

persecution. Today we are far more likely to encounter racial preferences than racial discrimination. Moreover, we live in a society that generally shows us goodwill—a society that has isolated racism as its most unforgivable sin." "The Inauthenticity Behind Black Lives Matter," *WSJ.com*, November 22, 2020.

- Walter Williams: The difficulties of poor Blacks are not due to racial discrimination but are "self-inflicted ... or a result of policies, programs, and regulations emanating from federal, sate and local governments." *Race and Economics: How Much Can Be Blamed on Discrimination?* (2011), p.10.

I suggest that the continuing problems are not the result of current racism nor, even, of historical racism. They are significantly the result of the well-intentioned but misguided or naive governmental social policies that permitted and even encouraged the expansion of bad behavior. Such programs include social welfare in a wide variety of forms, public housing and racial preferences. These policies have created a culture and preserved a societal structure that disadvantage minorities, especially Blacks. These policies have eroded the values of family and community.

The current obsession with systemic racism is not helpful. It is a false narrative that deflects attention from the real struggles, further discourages ambition and self-reliance and indulges those who want to feel guilty. The principe problems affecting inner-city Blacks, identified above, were not caused by systemic racism, and they will not be solved by the diminution or even elimination of "systemic racism."

There are two ways to reduce inequality: pull up the disadvantaged or pull down the successful. The latter is certainly easier to accomplish; and, unfortunately, there is considerable political support for that approach, especially in education. "If it is not available to all, it should not be available to any." Really? Progress is almost always incremental, in steps, "Trickle up" (and "trickle down") is evident and effective in many spheres of life. We will always have a bottom 10% and a bottom quintile. (And, a top 1%.) The important issue is how fluid and dynamic those groups are. Inequality causes ambition in some have-nots and envy in others. It is no surprise which ones tend to succeed and which ones tend to flounder. There need to be opportunities to succeed, and to fail. We want equal opportunity; but, inequality In outcome is not necessarily inequitable nor equal outcomes, equitable.

From the politicians' standpoint, a hand-out is much easier to offer than a hand-up. Sadly, it is also often easier to accept, and it can become addictive. One thinks of the movement to de-criminalize drugs—the likely result would be fewer criminals but not fewer addicts. This approach is a perversion of paternalism—it is not "paternal", but patronizing—and it is patronization at its worst. Patronization and indulgence soothe the consciences of the privileged. They also are approaches that are politically easier to design, adopt and support. But, such approaches exacerbate and perpetuate, not ameliorate, the problems.

What is also needed is that which we often call "tough love," consisting of ample support coupled with high expectations and a clear emphasis on personal responsibility—opportunities combined with consequences, opportunities to succeed and to fail. So, government, especially Federal government, is not well-suited to address these problems. It has great difficulties (practical and legal) with accountability and differentiation. The better approach is through private actions, by both charitable and for-profit entities. Government may provide support and incentives. Correction of the problems will probably have to be incremental, person by person and family by family. We cannot simply improve permanently everyone's lot across the board by sweeping governmental action.

Some promising government avenues for improvement are: (i) incentives for the employment of persistently unemployed persons in the inner cities, (ii) policies that provide incentives to individual savings and productive investment by underprivileged families, (iii) targeted programs to assist young families in escaping the inner-city neighborhoods and (iv) increased choice and flexibility in grade school and high school education. These are matters for state and local governments—not for the Federal government. And, such steps would be surprisingly inexpensive.

But, the real need is for the creation of healthy neighborhoods communities. For example, it appears that "on April 1, 2010, 44 percent of the low-income black men from the Watts neighborhood of central Los Angeles were incarcerated. On the other hand, just 6.2 percent of the men who grew up with similar incomes in the Compton neighborhood were incarcerated on that day. Compton is just 2.3 miles from Watts." David Brooks, *The Second Mountain* (2019), p.273. That is something only local governments and local groups can do.

Remarkably, since 2015, there have been some improvements.

> "Between 1963 and 2012, unemployment averaged ... 11.1% for blacks. ...[I]n January 2017, the black jobless rate was 7.5%. ... [I]t dipped to 5.3% in August 2019, then fell to a record-low 4.7% in April of this year. ...[T]he black employment rate of 58.9% is only 1.5 percentage-points lower than the white rate of 60.4%, which is a historically narrow racial gap. ...Second, labor-force participation rates for black workers, which have tended to trail those of white workers, now surpass them slightly. The trend started before the pandemic and has been noticeable for most of the past year. In June 2020, 62.2% of working-age blacks were employed or looking for a job, versus 61.9% of whites."

Jason L. Riley, "Liberals Can't Comprehend Black Economic Progress," *WSJ.com*, July 11, 2023.

"JIM CROW" AND LATER

Without doubt, the circumstances immediately following Emancipation created a highly incendiary racial situation. Some 4 million people who, and most of whose parents and grandparents, had known nothing but slavery were set out on their own. The Federal government, struggling to win the War, had no plans for how this historically unprecedented event could be managed. So, these 4 million people, with few resources and little relevant training, were just set loose.

"[I]n 1865 there was no strategy for cleansing the South of the economic and intellectual addiction to slavery." Douglas A. Blackmon, *Slavery by Another Name: The Re-Enslavement of Black Americans from the Civil War to World War II* (2008), p.41.

"[N]orthern whites who pushed for full citizenship for black freedmen operated under naive assumptions. Many believed that once schools and wages were extended to liberated slaves, they could be quickly and fully assimilated into U.S. society. ...But no society in human history had attempted to instantly transform a vast and entrenched slave class into immediate full and equal citizenship. ...The cost of educating freed slaves and their children came to seem unbearably enormous, even to their purported friends." *Id.*, p.235.

Starting early in the century, there had been considerable discussion about the possible colonization of some remote region with freed slaves. The idea germinated the American Colonization Society and actually led to the formation of Liberia on the West Coast of Africa.

"[T]he Grain Coast was suggested as a suitable home for enslaved people in the United States after their emancipation. In 1818 two U.S. government agents and two officers of the American Colonization Society (founded 1816) visited the Grain Coast. After abortive attempts to establish settlements there, an agreement was signed in 1821 between the officers of the society and local African chiefs granting the society possession of Cape Mesurado. The first group of formerly enslaved people, led by members of the society, landed in 1822.... . They were followed shortly by Jehudi Ashmun, a white American, who became the real founder of Liberia. ...In 1839 Thomas Buchanan was appointed the first governor. On his death in 1841 he was succeeded by Joseph Jenkins Roberts, the colony's first Black governor, who was born free in Virginia in 1809... ."

Svend E. Holsoe, Donald Rahl Petterson, and Abeodu Bowen Jones, "Liberia," *Encyclopedia Britannica*, 14 March 2024.

It is conceivable that a massive relocation plan of that type could have been designed and implemented, but the courage demonstrated by Black Union soldiers and outspoken opposition from leading Blacks convinced Abraham Lincoln to abandon the idea.

At the same time, about 5 million white survivors in the Confederate States were effectively turned out, also to fend for themselves. Their sons and fathers had been killed or maimed, their wealth had disappeared, their economies and supporting infrastructure had been destroyed and they, like their Black neighbors, faced a difficult winter with inadequate food supplies.

"[H]ow white southerners perceived the destruction of the South they had known. Physical and financial devastation, death and grief, followed by a transforming struggle to survive and rebuild. ...[T]he story also underscored the terrifying vulnerability whites like the Cottinghams discovered in being forced to place the fate and future of Moses' family in the hands of a descendant of Africa."

...

"Redefined by war, grief, deprivation, death, and emancipation, America was faced with the challenge of repairing and reordering a collective house-hold. ...Across the South, white southerners were baffled. What to do with freed slaves... ? They could not be driven away. Without former slaves—and their steady expertise and cooperation in the fields—the white South was crippled."

Blackmon, pp.28-9. 39.

This fraught situation was aggravated by the discernible differences in appearance between the two groups and the legacy of economic segregation and segregation by social status.

"[T]he end of the war had left the white Cottinghams at a point of near desolation. ...The threat that Elisha's former slaves would come to own his plantation—that he and his family would be landless, stripped of posses-sions and outnumbered by the very creatures he had bred and raised—was palpable." *Id.*, pp.17-8.

"The last desperate rallying calls of the Confederacy had been exhorta-tions that a Union victory meant the political and economic subjugation of whites to their black slaves." *Id.*, p.18.

"The loss of slaves left white farm families such as the Cottinghams, and even more so those on expansive plantations with scores or hundreds of slaves, not just financially but intellectually bereft.

...The Cottinghams had not even the cash to buy cotton seed and corn, much less the labor of the former slaves they had so recently owned. ...A sense of paralysis was pervasive among whites." *Id.*, pp.26, 28.

"[H]ow white southerners perceived the destruction of the South they had known. Physical and financial devastation, death and grief, followed by a transforming struggle to survive and rebuild. ...[T]he story also underscored the terrifying vulnerability whites like the Cottinghams discovered in being forced to place the fate and future of Moses' family in the hands of a descendant of Africa." *Id.*, pp.28-9.

"Redefined by war, grief, deprivation, death, and emancipation, America was faced with the challenge of repairing and reordering a collective household. ...Across the South, white southerners were baffled. What to do with freed slaves... ? They could not be driven away. Without former slaves—and their steady expertise and cooperation in the fields—the white South was crippled." *Id.*, p.39.

Nonetheless, through the utilization of existing skills, industriousness and luck, many whites and Blacks began to prosper.

"Since Reconstruction, Black homeownership had climbed rapidly: from about 43,000 Black families in 1870 to some 506,590 in 1910—nearly one in four Black families nationwide. America's 218,972 Black farm-owners owned more land than ever before or since: more than fifteen million acres, practically all of it in the South. ...Soon, Black business districts sprang up in nearly 'every Southern city' to sell homes, sewing machines, dressers, carpets, books, washstands, funeral policies, and more to the farmers, maids, and laborers who were joining America's consumer economy in ever greater numbers."

Dylan C. Penningroth's *Before the Movement: The Hidden History of Black Civil Rights* (2023), p.204

"What Black families achieved during Jim Crow was astounding: from the fifteen million acres of land and $1.1 billion worth of farm property to the tuition they paid to Black churches, colleges, and more." *Id.*, p.223.

Immediately following the removal of Federal troops, the former Confederate States adopted laws that imposed the segregation and differential social status that had existed under slavery. These laws clearly inhibited the exercise of political rights by and the participation in government of Black residents, but they did not dramatically alter daily life.

Then...

Subsequent events included: The 13th Amendment in 1865, the 14th Amendment in 1868, and the 15th Amendment in 1870. (Note, the 19th Amendment, granting women the vote, was only ratified in 1920.) But, there was a step backwards, following the Hayes versus Tilden election of 1876. It is called The Compromise of 1877.

> "The Compromise of 1877 was an informal agreement between southern Democrats and allies of the Republican Rutherford Hayes to settle the result of the 1876 presidential election and marked the end of the Reconstruction era.
>
> ...

"The Democrat agreed not to block Hayes' victory on the condition that Republicans withdraw all federal troops from the South... . [P]romises to protect civil and political rights of blacks were not kept, and the end of federal interference in southern affairs led to widespread disenfranchisement of blacks voters."

History.com, March 17, 2011 (updated November 27, 2019).

Following the Tilden/Hayes election compromise of 1877, the absence of the Federal government to enforce the agreement made and the Southern states' repudiation of their commitments allowed evil to take control in the Southern states. The "Jim Crow" era did not just impact the recently emancipated slaves.

"The breadth of white venom toward freed slaves—and the decades of venality that followed it—belied the wide spectrum of perspectives on slavery shared by white southerners before the war." Blackmon, p.39. "A century later, this was the paradox of the post-Civil War South—recognition of freed slaves as full humans appeared to most white southerners not as an extension of liberty but as a violation of it, and as a challenge to the legitimacy of their definition of what it was to be white. ...Even among those who had been troubled by—or apathetic toward—slavery before the war, there was scant sympathy for the concept of full equality." *Id.*, p.41.

"The resistance to what should have been the obvious consequences of losing the Civil War—full emancipation of the slaves and shared political control between blacks and whites—was so virulent and effective that the tangible outcome of the military struggle between the North and the South remained uncertain even twenty-five years after the issuance of President

Abraham Lincoln's Emancipation Proclamation. ...In the first decades of that span, the intensity of southern whites' need to reestablish hegemony over blacks rivaled the most visceral patriotism of the wartime Confederacy."

Id., p.42.

There were a lot of free Blacks in the South at the time of the Civil War, and they held property.

> "There were a quarter million free Black people in the South by 1860, and they owned nearly $8.8 billion of property (in 2021 dollars)—some 60,045 acres in Virginia alone—twice as much per household as their parents had held. A few free people of color owned slaves, who sometimes were their wives and children, sometimes not."

Penningroth, *Before the Movement,* p.29.

Despite the restrictions on daily life and the threats of violence, the Black southerners aggressively pursued their property and contract rights commercially and through the courts. White lawyers were perfectly happy with Black clients, if they could pay or had claims that could support contingency fees. "[I]n growing numbers, across the country, Black people during Reconstruction vastly expanded their use of the courts, and aired out their opinions about the legal process and about lawyers. Some hired white lawyers to work for them. Others hired Black lawyers... ." *Id.,* p.77. "What Black families achieved during Jim Crow was astounding: from the fifteen million acres of land and $1.1 billion worth of farm property to the tuition they paid to Black churches, colleges, and more." *Id.,* p.223.

"Five years after the Civil War ended, 4.8 percent of the South's Black families, or about 43,000, owned real estate. Over the next fifteen years, as whites sold land to Blacks on credit, that figure steadily rose. ...First, whites were already used to seeing slaves have property, and it was not a very big step from the idea that slaves could have property to the notion that ex-slaves could have property rights. Second, the formal rules of property law itself demanded some amount of respect for Black rights. Property law is conservative."

...

"Since Reconstruction, Black homeownership had climbed rapidly: from about 43,000 Black families in 1870 to some 506,590 in 1910—nearly one in four Black families nationwide. America's 218,972 Black farm-owners owned more land than ever before or since: more than fifteen million acres, practically all of it in the South. ...Soon, Black business districts sprang up in nearly 'every Southern city' to sell homes, sewing machines, dressers, carpets, books, washstands, funeral policies, and more to the farmers, maids, and laborers who were joining America's consumer economy in ever greater numbers."

Penningroth, *Before the Movement*, pp.80, 204.

"When freedom came in 1865, it started a new chapter in an ongoing story of Black legal life. Many if not most freedpeople had dealt with law and legal rules during slavery, and now, for the first time, they could try to enforce their claims in a court of law. Because now they had civil rights—the fundamental rights that belonged to all free men."

...

"What really underpinned whites' respect for free Black people's civil rights was a stronger version of what underpinned the privileges of slaves: the fact that so much private law was so closely entwined with community opinion and woven in such a way that repudiating Black rights would have unraveled their own rights. Or, put another way: it did not threaten the racial order to recognize free Black people's rights of everyday use."

...

"[W]hite lawyers and judges and other local officials took real Black families quite seriously, investigating their family trees, identifying and notifying heirs of their rights. They did not do this out of pity or a sense of duty toward faithful old 'servants.' They did it because the rules of property law demanded it. White-owned businesses and individuals had a stake in the orderly resolution of Black inheritance because Black landowners were links in the chain of title that anchored everyone's property rights."

...

"[T]he evidence from county courthouses suggests that Black people went to the trial courts during Jim Crow even more than during Reconstruction. They were less likely to sue than whites, but not drastically less. ...With few exceptions, Black people's legal activity did not challenge white supremacy in any substantive way. Black people routinely had contract dealings with white people, but most of their lawsuits were against other Black people... ."

*Id., pp.*26, 31, 114, 151.

Something happened during the first quarter of the twentieth century: America seemed to become actively racist. We had a practicing racist as President (Woodrow Wilson, 1913-21), we institutionalized racial categorizations (the segregation of the Federal bureaucracy under President Wilson), we experienced horrific community violence against Blacks across the states (1917-22) and we enacted radical new social assistance programs (under FDR in the 1930s) that were available mainly only to "white" Americans.

"[T]he Jim Crow order had a specific and relatively brief life span. It was not completely consolidated until the end of the first decade of the twentieth century. ... And during the roughly three decades or so between the regime's consolidation and its slow, painful unraveling, the system was placed under considerable strain and reorganized internally by the Great Migration of black people out of the South or to cities within it, the Great Depression and the New Deal, the emergence of the industrial unions of the Congress of Industrial Organizations (CIO) and the war. And in large and small ways, black people never stopped challenging its boundaries and constraints—from the struggle over its imposition to its eventual defeat. From that perspective, the segregationist order was never stable."

Adolph L. Reed, *The South: Jim Crow and Its Afterlives* (2022), p.115.

"Lost Cause ideology was propagated aggressively, nationally as well as regionally, as part of southern elites' crusade advocating 'sectional reconciliation' on white supremacist terms that would undermine enforcement of black southerners' constitutional rights and give the southern ruling class a free hand in establishing and maintaining its new order. It ... was propounded as historical fact by prominent intellectuals like Columbia University historian William A. Dunning and Woodrow Wilson—Princeton historian, political scientist and president, New Jersey governor, and eventual US president."

Id., pp.130-131.

"[T]the core of the Jim Crow order was a class system rooted in employment and production relations that were imposed, stabilized, regulated, and naturalized through a regime of whhis underscores the point that the core of the Jim Crow order was a class system rooted in employment and production relations that were imposed, stabilized, regulated, and naturalized through a regime of white supremacist law, practice, custom, rhetoric, and ideology."

Id., p.140.

Why did that racism take such a virulent turn? A combination of the following:

Human Nature

Racism seems to be a likely consequence of in an interactive world. The distrust and suspicion of outsiders was probably an adaptive characteristic favored by evolution. People who look different or act differently may be a threat to a group's security either through violence or disease. The outsiders may also be competitors for scarce resources. In addition, when difficulties arise, humans tend to look for scapegoats. So, racial differences would be expected to be vulnerable spots in human relations, to be overcome through favorable experience and education or exacerbated by unfavorable experience and education. In adition, resentment, economic or physical inssecurity and feeling disrespected or judged can bring out harsh reactions. Of course, we must include humankind's propensity for violence, which I cannot really understand.

Science

We should also consider the role played by science. The social applications of Darwinism and the attention focused on eugenics certainly must have had an impact on attitudes and opinions and affected discussion.

"Then science was conscripted to do the dirty work of white supremacy as social Darwinism held that race hierarchy was nature's will. Evolutionary theory and a sham science of eugenics and phrenology justified the wealth gap in the nineteenth century."

...

"[I]nstead of the Bible, white supremacists turned to Darwin. Social Darwinist theories of 'survival of the fittest' created a more virulent and hostile

---

strand of racism than had existed under slavery. Evolution-based theories cast the racial hierarchy as an inevitable by-product of natural selection."

...

"The justification used to enforce this order was not economic. Rather, racial Darwinism convinced Americans that blacks were less-evolved humans... ."

Mehrsa Baradaran, *The Color of Money: Black Banks and the Racial Wealth Gap* (2017), pp.6, 64, 68.

"It is important to appreciate that within the U.S. and European scientific communities these ideas were not fringe but widely held and taught in universities. The report of the Eugenics meeting was the lead story in the journal Science on October 7, 1921, and this opening address was published, in its entirety, beginning on the first page of the issue."

Steven A. Farber, "U.S. Scientists' Role in the Eugenics Movement (1907–1939): A Contemporary Biologist's Perspective," *Zebrafish*, December 2008.

It seems that the societal response following the exposure of the Nazi atrocities was to ban the discussion of these subjects and to condemn the proponents. If this purportedly science-based view was really a significant contributor to the racist attitudes, then the most effective response would have been a science-based rebuttal. Instead, the principal effort was to crush it with morality based denunciations, successful most likely only because of the repugnance of the conduct of Nazi Germany and its position as the enemy in a brutal war.

The problem is that the failure to meet the arguments fully on the merits leaves lingering, even if unspoken, doubts. It may have been the most appropriate approach at the time, but we may (perhaps) have reached a sufficient distance to permit an analysis on the merits. By that I mean, recognize that at least some of those proponents were acting in good faith, assess the scientific merits of the theories and arguments and investigate what effects that work had on public opinion.

I note that science is still being used (or, misused) in discussions of race. Wilkerson asserts (p.66):

"The epic mapping of the human genome and the quieter, long-dreamt-of results of DNA kits ordered in time for a family reunion have shown us that race as we have come to know it is not real. ...Two decades ago, analysis of the human genome established that all human beings are 99.9 percent the same."

But, chimpanzees and bonbons share an estimated 99.8% of DNA with us; pigs, an estimated 98%. Very tiny differences in DNA can cause very dramatic differences in the length and quality of life. I do not think that science itself establishes Wilkerson's conclusion.

"[I]t is simplistic to put an actual figure on the amount of genetic material we have in common, says animal geneticist Professor Chris Moran from the University of Sydney's Faculty of Veterinary Science. ...'[I]f you compare the protein-encoding portion of our DNA we have a lot in common with a lot of mammals. ...[B]ut if you compare rapidly evolving non-coding sequences from a similar location in the genome, you may not be able to recognise any similarity at all. This means that blanket comparisons of all DNA sequences between species are not very meaningful.'"

"Do pigs share 98 per cent of human genes?" *ABC Science* [Australia], May 3, 2010.

Economic Conflict

The country suffered economic hardship and severe competition for jobs at the end of WW I. There was a decided emergence of isolationist attitudes. There were increasing "class" conflicts and violence over unionization. Fluctuations in the business cycle appeared to be becoming more severe, with recessions more frequent and deeper. Industrial conflicts and violence erupted in the 1890s with the Homestead and Pullman Strikes of 1892 and 1894. Labor unrest surged in 1919. The Bolshevik Revolution of 1917 injected a new element—Communism —into the growing labor/management conflict.

The Great Migration

What has come to be called the Great Migration saw hundreds of thousands of Blacks relocate to urban centers, often in the North, from 1915 through the 1920s, perhaps a million Southern Blacks, attracted by employment opportunities that emerged during WW I. Significantly, the Black migrants located among friends, relatives, acquaintances, acquaintances of people they knew or of people who were known by people they knew. Subsequent discriminatory practices helped perpetuate segregated housing.

This was a volatile and violent period in American history. Ultimately, the Jim Crow period raises two fundamental questions, the same questions we had come to ask about Nazi Germany:

- How could evil so overwhelm those communities?
- Why did the rest of the nation fail to take action?

In the South: Was it racial hatred? Fear? Resentment/Revenge? In the North: Exhaustion? Self–interest? Protectionism? Racism?

Of course, we are looking at a variety of types of actions. "Separate but equal" may be shortsighted and incorrect, but it was not necessarily evil at the time. The wrong in segregation is not in the separation but in the stigma and the inequality. In contrast, rape, murder, terrorism, physical brutality are simply evil.

What was needed following the end of the war was a kind of Marshall Plan for the South like the United States undertook for Europe following WW II. Of course, there was no historical president for such a policy. The norm was for the victor to demand "reparations" from the loser, not provide him financial support.

Much of the subsequent tragedy would have been avoided had the nation undertaken to rebuild the South and provide ways forward for the destitute and displaced. The idea of "40 acres and a mule" would have been a constructive investment and should have applied to every propertyless family regardless of race. It was the right time to implement colorblind government policies. Such an approach would not be based on the concept of compensation (for past injuries) but on relief of suffering and the creation of opportunity (the future): A wise approach given that the goal had been to preserve the Union. Everyone had an interest in the economic recovery of the South. But, human nature was not that mature.

We, as a nation, missed more such opportunities, for varied reasons.

"There's a different narrative of race and racism in America—a story of missed opportunities to achieve a colorblind state. Key chapters in that story include the founding of our republic on the backs of slaves, the ratification of a weaker version of the Fourteenth Amendment ..., a Supreme Court decision that upheld the constitutionality of racial segregation (Plessy), another Supreme Court decision that fell short of affirming colorblindness (Brown), the betrayal of colorblindness at just the moment when the civil rights movement was enjoying its greatest success, and the rise of race consciousness... ."

Coleman Hughes, *The End of Race Politics: Arguments for a Colorblind America* (2024), p.153.

The Twentieth Century

"The progress of blacks from the Civil War to World War II, in some respects was fairly rapid because ...Blacks were just overwhelmingly impoverished. By the time of World War II, however, you ... saw the development of a growing working class population, so much so that they probably represented at that time about 25 percent of the black population. And you saw a dwindling number of truly lower class blacks."

Ben Wattenberg, "William Julius Wilson Interview," *The First Measured Century on PBS: The Other Way of Looking at American History,* 2000

"[WW II] opened up job opportunities in factories because of the labor shortage, and blacks experienced fairly rapid mobility during that time. And it also ... hastened their entry into blue-collar positions... . I'm talking about factory jobs in urban areas, even in Southern cities blacks were working... ."

"Interview of William Julius Wilson by Henry Louis 'Skip' Gates, Jr.," *Frontline,* November 2015.

Also,

> "Unlike any prior U.S. attorney general, [Attorney General Francis Biddle (1941-45)] recognized the federal government's duty to admit that African Americans were not free and to assertively enforce the statutes written to protect them. ...Two years later, President Harry Truman's Committee on Civil Rights recommended bolstering the anti-slavery statute to plainly criminalize involuntary servitude. In 1948, the entire federal criminal code was dramatically rewritten, further clarifying the laws against involuntary servitude. ...Finally, in 1951, Congress passed even more explicit statutes, making any form of slavery in the United States indisputably a crime."

Blackmon, *Slavery by Another Name*, pp.378, 381.

Further Federal government actions sought to reduce discrimination, including :

- Executive Order 9981 (desegregating the military) 1948
- *Brown v. Bd. of Education* 1954
- The Civil Rights Act of 1964
- The Voting Rights Act of 1965
- The Fair Housing Act of 1968
- The Hate Crimes Prevention Acts of 1999 and 2009.

"...[A] politically formidable 'defining contradiction' 'that all men are created equal'—came into existence through the Declaration of Independence. ... As for the notion that the Declaration's principles were 'false' in 1776, ideals aren't false merely because they are unrealized, much less because many of the men who championed them, and the nation they created, hypocritically failed to live up to them. Most of us, at any given point in time, are falling short of some ideal we nonetheless hold to be true or good." Bret Stephens, "1619 Chronicles," *The New York Times*, October 9, 2020.

The surprising fact is that despite three decades of Jim Crow, the black families, communities, churches and schools remained strong. Then, following the end of the Jim Crow era, these institutions all began to fall apart. Why? It cannot be blamed on the War on Drugs or the War on Crime since the deterioration preceded, and gave rise to, those Wars (which certainly failed to improve the situation).

What happened? And, what can be done?

A NEW RACISM

"We are stuck in a vicious cycle of appeasement by one side and goalpost shifting by the other."

Coleman Hughes
The End of Race Politics
(2024), p.133.

This is a troubling time for my generation. The year I was born, President Truman ordered the desegregation of the U.S. Armed Forces (July 26, 1948, Executive Order 9981, creating the President's Committee on Equality of Treatment and Opportunity in the Armed Services and mandating the desegregation of the U.S. military). Also, "[i]n 1948, the entire federal criminal code was dramatically rewritten, further clarifying the laws against involuntary servitude. ...Finally, in 1951, Congress passed even more explicit statutes, making any form of slavery in the United States indisputably a crime." Douglas A. Blackmon, *Slavery by Another Name: The Re-Enslavement of Black Americans from the Civil War to World War II* (2008), p.381.

The background of my childhood included the Civil Rights marches and demonstrations across the South; of my teens, the powerful image of Assistant U.S. Attorney General Nickolas deB. Katzenback nose to nose with a defiant George Wallace at the entrance to the University of Alabama in 1963 and the enactment of The Civil Rights Act of 1964 ending Jim Crow throughout the country.

Nick Katzenback was a big man with a large head but not what one would call a physical person. When I knew him almost 20 years later, his most striking characteristics (besides his intelligence) were his kindness and his projection of absolute calm.

In the year I turned 60, the country elected its first Black president.

I have lived through a very different world than had my grandfather born in 1899.

To be clear, race and racism were rather abstract, distant concepts for me growing up. My grandparents were quite prejudiced, but toward Catholics. Actually, not Catholics, but the Catholic Church. I think that one of their big concerns was that one of their grandchildren would marry a Catholic. My father had commanded a mortar platoon of Black soldiers in Italy during the war (before desegregation), but I did not know that until I was a teenager. My mother's parents became resentful when the value of their home fell, wiping out their retirement savings, as their neighborhood became integrated. My parents were apparently quite open minded.

In college and, then, at the law firm, I observed and, as hiring partner, participated in so-called affirmative action. I thought it made sense. Society would benefit from increasing interaction among races and some individuals with strong potential would get the opportunity to prove themselves that deficient education and cultural disadvantages would otherwise have denied them. (By the way, I did not limit my exceptions based on race.) But, this was a short-term and very limited "patch," a band-aid, affecting only the most exceptional individuals. The real solution would be in addressing and reducing the deficiencies that create the disadvantages.

In any event, I entered my mature years believing, like many, that the issues of race and racism were well on the way out, really things of the past.

I retired in 2011 and lived in England from then until mid-2015. I returned to the States to discover the beginnings of the new racism. It seemed that colorblindness was no longer the "gold standard" as my generation (of, I think, all races) had believed. Instead, we have: "Race" (as central to U.S. life and history), "White privilege", "Systemic racism", "Black Lives Matter", "Reparations."

"Our country has never been colorblind. Given the lengthy history of state-sponsored race-based preferences in America, to say that anyone is now victimized if a college considers whether that legacy of discrimination has un-equally advantaged its applicants fails to acknowledge the well-documented 'intergenerational transmission of inequality' that still plagues our citizenry."

Justice Jackson's dissent, *Students for Fair Admissions v. Harvard*, 600 U.S. 181 (2023).

"[N]one of the actions we are told Black people must take if they want to 'lift themselves' out of poverty and gain financial stability ... can mitigate four hundred years of racialized plundering."

...

"At the center of those policies must be reparations. It does not matter if your ancestors engaged in slavery or if you just immigrated here two weeks ago."

Nikole Hannah-Jones, *The 1619 Project: A New Origin Story* (2021), pp.471, 472.

What the hell happened?

Over the next few years, I tried to educate myself about this new point of view. I read and read. And, I was not very impressed and certainly not persuaded. I have written critiques of many of the books and have presented my thoughts on several of the relevant topics. Of course, the inadequacies of the arguments of the proponents do not establish the incorrectness of the proposition. So, I decided to address the issue directly.

I just read Coleman Hughes book—*The End of Race Politics: Arguments for a Colorblind America* (2024)—and I found that his straight forward presentation, generally avoiding the overblown rhetoric of those whose positions he criticizes, helped me organize my thought. (He refers to what I had characterized as the new racism as "neo-racism.") I agree with much of what Hughes has to say, but I have reservations about two of his conclusions: that the new racism is based upon retribution and that its appearance was caused by smartphones and social media.

As to the first, he is surely correct about the unfortunate consequences of the seeking of retribution (*id.*, pp.156-7), but I doubt that he is correct about the motivations behind or the goals of the "neoracist."

> "[T]he law of retaliation, the principle of taking an eye for an eye, is a simplistic and outmoded way to think of justice, one that leads to interminable hatred generation after generation. ...Discriminating against white people in the present doesn't erase the injustice of discrimination against black people in the past. It doesn't decrease the sum total of injustice in the world. ...Any act of injustice adds to the sum total of injustice in the world."

Hughes, pp.120, 121, 122.

I do not know these people, so I can only guess about motivations; but, I doubt that it is a desire for retribution. Hughes notes that the outspoken advocates of this view probably do not want a prompt solution, since that would curtail their career prospects (*id.*, pp.132, 176). We need not be so cynical; however, I do think that the objective is money (rather than revenge).

Hughes argues that Blacks today are not injured by past racist practices and that income differentials today are not likely caused by discrimination (*id.*, pp.116-8). However, he does not address one of the arguments made—that Blacks would be wealthier today if their ancestors had been better off, because they would have inherited wealth. Now, that is a highly speculative argument and, whatever its merits with respect to possible statistical averages, an impossible basis on which to assert claims for individual entitlements or injury. (I discuss the "wealth gap" in another essay.) So, I agree with Hughes about the invalidity of claims for "reparations." Yet, that seems to be what is really at issue.

As for the second point, Hughes looks at Gallup poll results showing that people's feelings about race relationships began to turn negative in 2013 and have continued steadily down ward since. He observes that 2013 was something of a watershed moment for video phones.

"The more plausible explanation is that 2013 is about the time that a critical mass of Americans had two pieces of tech: camera-enabled smart-phones and social media. ...Neoracist ideas were able to take advantage of this development in a way that other ideas could not. ...Anything that appeals to our tribal identities, us versus them narratives, or historical grievances travels fast." *Id.*, pp.93-94.

Well, I am sure that smartphones and social media have substantially inflamed and spread the racist sentiments, but what was the cause?

Justice, Looting and Violence

"Why did some poor people
take to the streets and others not?
How to explain why some cities where conditions
were wretched remained calm while others
with better conditions experienced disturbances?
Why do poor whites not riot?"

Steven M. Gillon
"Why the 1967 Kerner Report ... Suppressed Its Own
Expert Findings"
History.com, June 8, 2018 (updated January 31, 2019).

1965 and 1967

Hughes claims that the race riots in 1965 and 1967 caused an abandonment of the "colorblind" principle.

> "Why the sudden pivot away from colorblindness? The answer has to do in part with the race riots that rocked cities like Detroit and Newark in the mid-1960s—especially during the summer of 1967. Many Americans were shocked to see black people rioting at the very moment when it seemed that the civil rights movement had achieved its greatest successes. They expected that the movement's success would have the effect of quelling civil unrest, but it did just the opposite. In the resulting confusion and dismay, people lost faith in the colorblind principle."

Hughes, pp. 57-58.

I doubt that. My personal observations as a college student at the time were that the issue commanding attention was the war in Vietnam. I think that many viewed the riot in Watts in 1965 and the similar urban disturbances in 1967 as reflections of particular local conditions in a few cities and some copycat responses. The Kent State shootings on May 4, 1970, were perceived as much more of a direct threat to our way of life.

The Kerner Commission

President Johnson appointed the Kerner Commission to investigate the causes of the 1967 riots. In 1968, the Commission issued its final report finding that the cause of the riots was "white racism." Curiously, when the group of social scientists engaged by the Commission provided a preliminary report, the Commission rejected it and ordered the destruction of the report. This event can be misinterpreted. As I read the materials, the project of the researchers was terminated not because of their conclusions, but because the work was taking way too long (the report was decidedly an incomplete, tentative first draft) and it was likely to produce overly nuanced results. The Commission wanted a prompt and decisive Report, and the conclusions and recommendations were already emerging from the negotiations among the Commissioners.

"The commission's executive staff was not interested in ambiguity; it needed to produce a final document that would garner the signatures of 11 commissioners and, hopefully, gain the support of the White House. As a result, the staff ordered all copies of Harvest destroyed and dismissed all but one of the social scientists. Instead, the final document the commission submitted blamed the disturbances on 'white racism' and the economic disadvantage that it caused."

Gillon, "Why the 1967 Kerner Report," June 8, 2018.

The final report:

"...was a provocative statement about the problems that shaped racial conditions in urban America. The report described the riots as the outgrowth of racial inequality and oppression rather than as acts of political or criminal agitation. .

...

"[T]he commissioners devoted almost all of their attention to institutional forces, such as unemployment and housing discrimination."

Julian E. Zelizer, "Fifty Years Ago, the Government Said Black Lives Matter: The radical conclusions of the 1968 Kerner Report." *Boston Review*, May 5, 2016.

President Johnson was unhappy with the Report, presumably because it failed to praise his quite remarkable legislative accomplishments.

"President Lyndon Johnson constituted the Kerner Commission to identify the genesis of the violent 1967 riots that killed 43 in Detroit and 26 in Newark ..., while causing fewer casualties in 23 other cities. ...[I]n March 1968, the Kerner Commission ... declar[ed] white racism—not black anger—turned the key that unlocked urban American turmoil. ...'White society,' the presidentially appointed panel reported, 'is deeply implicated in the ghetto. White institutions created it, white institutions maintain it, and white society condones it.'"

Alice George, "The 1968 Kerner Commission Got It Right, But Nobody Listened," *The Smithsonian*, March 1, 2018.

"President Johnson, who was facing a tough reelection campaign and struggling with whether he should even be running, was unhappy with the findings... . He felt that the report had not given sufficient credit to his Great Society for alleviating racial inequality and that it called for programs, such as higher taxes, that were politically impossible."

Zelizer, "Fifty Years Ago," May 5, 2016.

The Report was not particularly well received and had minimal impact. "[T]he report's findings were received differently by white and black Americans. In mid-April, ... 53 percent of white Americans polled rejected the commission's claim that white racism was to blame for the riots, while 58 percent of African Americans agreed with the findings." *Id.*

The cancelled preliminary report was published in 2018. Robert Shellow, *The Harvest of American Racism: The Political Meaning of Violence in the Summer of 1967* (2018). "One of the original researchers later found a copy in an archive with the word 'Destroy' stamped on the cover page." *Id.*, p.vii. The preliminary report is clearly a draft in progress. One of the authors has since said "one hastily put together, underdeveloped, and, although data-rich, poorly integrated report." Shellow, *The Harvest*, p.134. The last chapter (Chapter 7), apparently authored by one person, Lou Goldberg, is completely disconnected from the prior six analytical chapters. ("Our mistake, my mistake, was to let the chapter go without a meticulous review, something I belatedly realized at the time." *Id.*, p.121.) Yet, it was the center of most of the controversy and is what has been quoted and summarized in the subsequent commentary.

A few quite interesting observations appear in the analytical chapters:

1. The course of the disturbances was heavily influenced by strategic and tactical choices made by the police. The level of violence and property damage could probably be controlled by more sophisticated and informed approaches to crowd control.
2. The smaller disturbances had significant political content, often with specific objectives being pursued. "In a number of other cities disturbances took the form of political confrontation, in which goals and processes were more explicit, form and structure more evident." Shellow, *The Harvest,* p.28. For the major

disturbances in the largest cities (Watts, Detroit and Newark), the situation was more ambiguous.

3. The actions of the rioters was directed against local businesses owned by whites and not against whites generally. "The focus of Negro antagonism in the riots is white authority and white property: mainly the police and white stores. Their antagonism is directed at white dominance over Negroes rather than at white people *per se*. The impulse toward indiscriminate attacks on whites has been notably absent." *Id.*, p.98.

4. The participants were predominately young (15 to 30), but otherwise reflected the Black population generally, not disproportionately consisting of the poorest or least educated residents. *Id.*, pp.54, 67, 70.

5. The disturbances were not caused by outside agitators, foreign or domestic, and were not particularly influenced by the more radical Black movements. "Objective examination indicates that they are very low on the list of causal factors in the recent disorders." *Id.*, p.36.

6. The participating youth typically felt alienated from their elders and excluded from political influence: "[T]he ingredients of a revolt by the militant young against their more conservative elders, a tension that had been brewing for some time... ." *Id.*, p.30.

7. "One factor that needs to be emphasized as a major source for aggressive ghetto upheavals, political rebellions, and anticipatory white responses is leadership competition within the Negro community." *Id.*, p.35.

8. "The social scientists ... found no direct relationship between poverty and rioting. Their studies had found poor African Americans were no more likely to participate in the disorders than their middle-class neighbors. Rioters were not, by all the evidence, disproportionately poor or disengaged from the communities around them. ...Those most likely to riot shared one characteristic —they had experienced or witnessed an act of police brutality." Gillon, "Why the 1967 Kerner Report," June 8, 2018.

To me, these facts do not suggest the conclusions of the final chapter or of the actual Report. Instead, they suggest that improvement was possible through incremental reforms addressing the issues of concern and through increased civil participation by the young people as they age. The handful of large urban ghettos, however, probably would have benefited from more significant and costly intervention. Subsequent studies indicate that the disturbances tended to occur in the poorest communities and that those communities have continued to be the most impoverished.

"... [B]lack neighborhoods that directly experienced riots were populated with residents that had lower incomes, lower educational levels, experienced higher unemployment, and had higher incidence of welfare usage than other black neighborhoods that were not directly affected by riots... . ...[T]hese level differences across riot and non-riot affected black neighborhoods persist over time... ."

Marcus Casey and Bradley Hardy, "50 years after the Kerner Commission report, the nation is still grappling with many of the same issues," *Brookings.edu*, September 25, 2018.

Fifty years later, the 1960s riots took on a different significance in some revisionist histories.

"Black youth were organized in their liberation of goods from stores as one car would drive up and break out the windows and drive away while subsequent cars drove up to seize and load merchandise. Essentially, the burning occurred after the store was emptied. Black youth used citizens band radios and payphones to coordinate efforts. ...Black youth engaged in urban rebellion to dispense retaliatory violence. One teenage girl was quoted as shouting, 'White men, you started all this the day you brought the first slave to this country.'"

M. Keith Claybrook, Jr., "Remembering, Rethinking, and Renaming the Watts Rebellion," *Black Perspectives [AAIHS]*, August 13, 2021.

This commentary suggests two different characterizations of the event—a response to particular, localized experiences of police brutality and exploitation by neighborhood merchants or, alternatively, an attack on the white race.

Note that the riot by a white mob in Tulsa in 1921 was directed against Blacks and black-owned businesses and property, while the later Black riots destroyed primarily Black neighborhoods. The Tulsa riot began with an armed confrontation between hundreds of Blacks and perhaps 2000 whites over a threatened lynching—a far more explosive situation than the events that sparked the 1960s riots. The white mob promptly moved to attack the prosperous Black neighborhood, presumably the source and object of white resentment. In the subsequent Black riots, the mobs attacked local businesses, presumably because they were perceived to have been exploiting the community. They were not typical race riots.

The 1992 L.A. Riot

"Early on March 3, 1991, an intoxicated parolee named Rodney King led police on a high-speed car chase... . His subsequent beating ... was caught on video... . ...All four officers were acquitted of charges... . The response was immediate, as protesters took to the streets....The final tally for the L.A. riots included 2,000 injuries, 12,000 arrests and 63 deaths attributed to the uprising. Upwards of 3,000 buildings were burned or destroyed and 3,000 businesses were affected as part of the $1 billion in damages sustained by the city, leaving an estimated 20,000 to 40,000 people out of work."

Editors, "Los Angeles Riots," *History.com*, April 18, 2017 (updated April 20, 2021).

The O.J. Simpson Trial 1995

"It was one of those 20th-century moments when you realized race is here to stay as an unending factor, an unyielding actor in American life. White and black saw two different realities. Whites: All the evidence points to his guilt, he's one of the most admired men in America, race isn't the story here. Blacks: This is what you do to black men, you railroad them on cooked-up evidence, there's plenty of room for doubt. ...It showed in some new and unforgettable way the divided country. "

Peggy Noonan, "America in the Age of O.J. Simpson: His case gave rise to a new kind of fame and left Americans of all races cynical about the law," *WSJ.com*, April 11, 2024.

Black Lives Matter 2013

Systemic or institutional racism was being discussed by some social scientists in the late 2000s (2007-2009), but it became widely discussed only in the mid-2010s (2013-2015). Critical Race Theory arose in law schools in the 1980s but did not get much public attention until the 2010s.

> "Critical Race Theory was first developed by legal scholars in the 1970s and '80s following the Civil Rights Movement. It was, in part, a response to the notion that society and institutions were 'colorblind.' CRT holds that racism was not and has never been eradicated from our laws, policies, or institutions, and is still woven into the fabric of their existence."

The Legal Defense Fund Website.

Black Lives Matter was formed in 2013 in response to the acquittal of Trayvon Martin's murderer.

"Black Lives Matter Global Network Foundation, Inc. is a global organization in the US, UK, and Canada, whose mission is to eradicate white supremacy and build local power to intervene in violence inflicted on Black communities by the state and vigilantes."

...

"Black Lives Matter is an ideological and political intervention in a world where Black lives are systematically and intentionally targeted for demise. It is an affirmation of Black folks' humanity, our contributions to this society, and our resilience in the face of deadly oppression."

Black Lives Matter Website.

More Violence

Campus protests erupted in 2015. "The passion that ousted the heads of the University of Missouri after protests over racial discrimination on campus is spreading to other colleges across the country, turning traditional fall semesters into a period of intense focus on racial misunderstanding and whether activism stifles free speech." Anemona Hartocollis and Jess Bidgood, "Racial Discrimination Protests Ignite at Colleges Across the U.S." *The N.Y. Times*, November 11, 2015.

So,

The change to which I am referring is the movement toward blaming not past wrongdoings, but current circumstances, with approbation placed on a racial group of today, in this case, white Americans, and the conclusion that that group is morally inferior, unworthy. That is racist.

The argument against colorblindness and in favor of race-based policies (and politics) seems to be based upon five untruths and two highly debatable beliefs. The falsehoods are that: (i) any racial disparity is the result of racial discrimination, (ii) the two hundred year struggle against slavery and, then, racial discrimination was conducted almost exclusively by Blacks, (iii) all whites enjoy a privileged position in American society, (iv) little progress has been made by Black Americans and (v) there is little Blacks themselves can do to improve their position in the American society or economy. The questionable propositions are that (i) more discussion about and focus on race is good and (ii) discrimination against whites and white values will benefit Blacks.

The five falsehoods are factual propositions as to which there are substantial empirical evidence of their incorrectness and little if any evidence in support. The two presumptions are more value judgments than factual statements, so they are debatable. Now, the human appeal of this viewpoint is pretty obvious. It absolves one of blame for the past, denies any responsibility for the future, provides a clear scapegoat, grants permission to hate and to act badly, makes one the center of attention and strengthens one's bargaining position and provides the possibility of windfall gains. It had to be pretty tempting, when the opportunity presented itself.

When did the change occur and what was the cause? As for the timing, one would need to identify a measure by which to decide that a change has now occurred. Opinions are altered by experience and as a result of persuasion and, sometimes, through calculation. I suspect that the new racism emerged when it became clear that white guilt was a more potent tool than violence.

A NOTE ON "THE 1619 PROJECT"

I had not read the *New York Times Magazine* of August 2019, so I decided to read the subsequent book about the 1619 Project: Nikole Hannah-Jones, The New York Times Magazine, Caitlin Roper, Ilena Silverman, and Jake Silverstein, *The 1619 Project: A New Origin Story* (2021). These are some comments. (There are more in the Sources section below.)

We are told that the point of Daniel Patrick Moynihan's 1965 *The Negro Family: The Case for National Action* was "that Black mothers were responsible for the disintegration of the Black family and the consequent failure of Black people to succeed in America" due to "Black women's dangerous maternity resulting from an unbridled sexuality." We are told that crediting the Country with the emancipation of the slaves is detrimental because it demeans the role played by blacks. Saying that blacks are responsible for their own lives is detrimental because it suggests that their failures are their fault. The public recognition of progress is detrimental, because it allows whites to feel absolved and to ignore how much more needs to be done. And, non-monetary assistance is detrimental because it is patronizing. *See* Ibram X. Kendi (contributor), *The 1619 Project,* p.434.

"[I[n the context of the Cold War, the government used racial progress rhetoric to prop up the United States as the world's leading democracy. ... American officials grew increasingly concerned that a public projection of racism against its own citizens would cause the United States to lose the support of people of color abroad ... while increasing their support for joining forces with the USSR."

Ibram X. Kendi (contributor), *The 1619 Project,* p.434.

Douglas Blackmon presents a more charitable characterization of these events:

"President Franklin D. Roosevelt instinctively knew the second-class citizenship and violence imposed upon African Americans would be exploited by the enemies of the United States. ...Biddle—especially when faced with the harsh but truthful depiction of black life as it would be suddenly projected through the propaganda of Japan and Germany—fundamentally grasped that African Americans, no matter how condescendingly he viewed them, had been denied the compact of freedom forged in the Civil War. "

Slavery by Another Name, p.377.

But, "[i]t was a strange irony that after seventy-four years of hollow emancipation, the final delivery of African Americans from overt slavery and from the quiet complicity of the federal government in their servitude was precipitated only in response to the horrors perpetrated by an enemy country against its own despised minorities." *Id.,* p.382.

The "Remedy"

It is in connection with these questions that *The 1619 Project,* for example, becomes most depressing. Apparently, there is nothing that the black community can do:

> "[H]undreds of years of state-imposed hardship and unequal treatment made such success nearly impossible for most Black people.... . [N]one of the actions we are told Black people must take if they want to 'lift themselves' out of poverty and gain financial stability ... can mitigate four hundred years of racialized plundering."

Hannah-Jones, *The 1619 Project,* p.471.

But, why then do the problems arise so starkly only in the late 1950s and 1960s?

"This new trend, beginning a century after Emancipation, can hardly be explained as 'a legacy of slavery' and might more reasonably be explained as a legacy of the social policies promoted by the anointed ... Whatever factors caused the changes, these were clearly twentieth-century factors, not 'a legacy of slavery.' ...[B]oth poverty and dependency were declining for years prior to the Johnson administration's 'war on poverty.' Black income was rising, not only absolutely but relative to rising white income. In the five years prior to passage of the Civil Rights Act of 1964, blacks were rising into professional and other high-level positions at a rate greater than in the five years following passage of the Act. Nationwide, Scholastic Aptitude Test scores were rising, venereal diseases were declining sharply, and the murder rate was at an all-time low."

Thomas Sowell, *The Vision Of The Annointed,* pp.81, 218.

Now, it seems, equal rights are not sufficient. What is required is money. Hannah-Jones asserts that the source of the disparities in wealth are not differences in income or spending practices or savings rates. The source is the head-start whites enjoyed in the accumulation of wealth.

"[T]he lack of wealth that has been a defining feature of Black life since the end of slavery. Wealth, not simply securing equal rights, is the means to security in America. ...[I]t is white Americans' centuries-long economic head start that most effectively maintains racial caste today."

Id., p.456.

She claims that that disadvantage can only be cured with reparations.

"At the center of those policies must be reparations. It does not matter if your ancestors engaged in slavery or if you just immigrated here two weeks ago. Reparations amount to a societal obligation in a nation where our Constitution sanctioned slavery, Congress passed laws protecting it, and our federal government initiated, condoned, and practiced legal racial segregation and discrimination against Black Americans until half a century ago."

Id., p, 472.

She is not talking about "40 acres and a mule," which might have given a chance of independence and self-sufficiency. She is talking about a monetary windfall.

Is the implicit assumption that redistributed monies would reduce violence, crime, gang warfare, vandalism, drug use and single parent families? That it would improve discipline, academic achievement, community spirit, civic commitment? If so, what reasons are there to think that such reparations would result in such long-term differences? Do we find support in the experiences of lottery winners or professional athletes or from the results of over 50 years of government antipoverty programs?

No.

"Black median household income in 1950 was about half that of white Americans, and today it remains so. More critical, the racial wealth gap is in relative terms about the same as it was in the 1950s as well. The typical Black household today is poorer than 80 percent of white households. 'No progress has been made over the past 70 years in reducing income and wealth inequalities between Black and white households ... .'"

Hannah-Jones, *The 1619 Project*, p.470.

Or, is the belief just that money (not behavior) is all that matters? That the disparity in wealth is the only problem? That we can/should ignore everything else?

Then, what about the "head start" allegation itself?

Wealth is accumulated by countries, by organizations, by individuals, but not by races. How much of the average white American's wealth is attributable to parental gifts and inheritances? I do not know. But, I know that there are many well off immigrants who arrived with nothing and who provided significant support to the families left behind. They had no head start. I know that I started out when I finished at Cambridge with $20,000 in debt, no savings, no automobile, no furniture and no housing. My current net worth does not derive from gifts or inheritance. Not to deny that I had advantages. I had a loving, caring extended family; parents who instilled discipline, responsibility and ambition and who valued education; healthy food, shelter and an education. I was also blessed with good genes. Those things were my "head start," not material possessions accumulated by my ancestors during their 200 years here before me.

The most ridiculous claim?

> "Reparations are not about punishing white Americans, and white Americans are not the ones who would pay... .
> ... [I]t is the federal government that would pay."

Hannah-Jones, *The 1619 Project*, p.472.

Right. It is our children and grandchildren, Black and white and other, who would pay.

Final Thoughts

A final question suggested by this extensive condemnation of the country's formation and history is: Should the Founders have confronted and disposed of the issue of slavery in 1787? That is, instead of negotiating compromises that united the 13 states in the expectation that slavery would gradually die out, should the North have insisted on the abolition of slavery on a fixed and relatively short schedule as a condition of Union?

Or, alternatively, should the North have rejected the Missouri Compromise in 1819? If it had on either occasion, there are two (barely) plausible outcomes. Perhaps, the South would have relented and agreed. The likely next step would have been the sale and export of the marketable slaves, perhaps to Spanish and French territories. Then, the colonization of the rest, either abroad or in a remote corner of North America. Presumably, a large number of the additional 3.5 million people that were slaves in 1860 would simply not have been born. The then existing slaves would have had different and probably shorter lives.

Of course, much more likely, the South would have refused. Presumably, the result would have been two new countries, one slave-holding and one not. How would each new country have fared and evolved?

"If the Confederacy had been a separate nation when the Civil War began, it would have ranked among the richest in the world. ...As the historian Steven Deyle writes in *Carry Me Back: The Domestic Slave Trade in American Life*, the monetary value of the enslaved population in 1860 was 'equal to about seven times the total value of all currency in circulation in the country, three times the value of the entire livestock population,...twelve times the value of the entire U.S. cotton crop, and forty-eight times the total expenditures of the U.S. federal government that year.'"

...

"But the Revolution left the colonies broke and vulnerable. Incomes plummeted in the final decades of the eighteenth century, and if the states could not come together to form a national government, they would be susceptible to foreign invasion and economic collapse."

Hannah-Jones, *The 1619 Project*, pp.111, 167.

In addition, the lands acquired from Britain as part of the Treaty of Paris of 1783 would presumably have been split. The original Northwest Territories, an area greater in size than the 13 colonies, would then have become part slave holding rather than all free as it was under the Northwest Ordinance. It is hard to guess what the subsequent events would have been. What about the subsequent expansion of the U.S., acquiring territory from Spain and France? Would it have happened? To which nation would it have belonged?

It is difficult to argue that the world would have been better under these alternative scenarios. Of course, the Northern states could be claiming the moral high ground today. Would that make things better? Would today's problems then be less?

Not likely.

CHAPTER IX

Climate Change

CLIMATE CHANGE

AND PUBLIC POLICY

The discussion herein bears only a tenuous relationship to much of what appears in the media as the controversy about climate change. The reason is that most of the media commentary and debate ignores the issues that are central to the determination of sound public policy, while the advocates on all sides promote largely political and emotional agenda advancing personal agendas and interests.

Although, the effects on the environment of gases in the atmosphere have been the subject of scientific inquiry since at least the second half of the nineteenth century,[1] the issue of carbon emissions took on a particular urgency in the twenty-first century. The 2007 report of the United Nation's Intergovernmental Panel on Climate Change ("IPCC") sounded a strident alarm with dire predictions of the likely future consequences of a continuation of our established patterns of energy production and use. Considerable public debate and media coverage has followed.

In early 2014, a committee of the American Association for the Advancement of Science released a report entitled "What We Know." The report set out no new science; instead, it purported to summarize what we already knew and to urge the need for action in language accessible to the lay person. *See, e.g.,* Justin Gillis, "Scientists Sound Alarm on Climate," *The New York Times,* March 18, 2014. That report contained the now often quoted assertion that "about 97% of climate scientists have concluded that human-caused climate change is happening."

As we shall see, that conclusion amounts to very little.

Since 1850-1900, the rate of carbon emissions has been rising as a result of population and economic growth and the accumulation of greenhouse gases in the environment has been increasing. We also are relatively certain that this accumulation has had a detectable impact on global temperatures. But, the real questions are: what are the consequences that are likely to occur in the future as a result of continued carbon emissions and what, if anything, can be done about them? It matters very little for issues of policy what the climate would have been like today or in 50 years if we had never generated carbon emissions. Similarly, there is also no real point in bemoaning how much climate change we have or will experience due to carbon emissions in the past. What we want to know specifically is what the future will hold if we do nothing versus what would happen under alternative policies designed to achieve some reasonable and realistic objectives in reducing emissions.

Then, we can have a debate about the potential costs and benefits of the alternatives.

Unfortunately, most of the public debate so far has been framed in terms of conflicts between believers in science and "science-deniers." That dichotomy is both unproductive and misleading. One reason is that, when it comes to policy, science never is and never can be "certain."

And, that is certainly the case with respect to the issues that matter here. The other important reason is that most really important policy decisions are not about science (as set forth in a prior essay).

As always, we are confronting the world we think we know versus the world of the future, about which we can only speculate. The issues are ones of "policy," of the weighing of costs and benefits, of economics and of risk assessment. Thus, it is a matter for serious, reasoned analysis of the facts, the risks, the assumptions and the uncertainties and for dispassionate, critical thinking about our values and priorities.

SOME BACKGROUND

NATURAL CYCLES AND CHANCE EVENTS

- We know with relative certainty that the Earth has gone through regular periods of significant warming and cooling over at least the last million years, and we believe (based upon the historical patterns) that the Earth is currently going through one of the periods of warming as part of its normal cycles.
- There is also compelling evidence that the more severe of these cycles have had very significant impacts on the distribution of life on the planet, on the existing species of animals and on the emergence of new species.
- "Near the end of the Ordovician period, around 444 million years ago, a sudden cooling ... led to sharp falls in temperature and initiated shifts in deep ocean currents, as well as declines in sea level that shrank habitats for marine planktonic and nektonic species. That cooling produced one pulse of extinction; another came when temperatures moderated, sea levels rose and ocean current patterns stagnated, with a resultant sharp fall in oxygen levels. ...[A] process that ultimately brought about the extinction of 85 per cent of all species. ...This was just one of several spectacular episodes that wiped out life for all but a small proportion of

living organisms." Peter Frankopan, *The Earth Transformed: An Untold History* (2023), p.28.

- There is strong evidence that so-called greenhouse gases can contribute to the warming of the Earth independent of the natural cycles. In fact, it appears that greenhouse gases have on at least one occasion resulted in severe climate change and mass extinction (the Permian-Triassic extinction). The emissions in that example, some 250 million years ago, appear to have been the result of volcanic activity.

- A regional mass extinction due to climate change some 160 million years ago appears to have been the result of "polar wander" or shifting tectonic plates. *See* Maya Wei-Haas, "Earth's odd rotation may solve an ancient climate mystery: A geologic change might have plunged lush landscapes into arid zones, killing off an array of creatures—and it might happen again one day," *National Geographic*, November 14, 2019.

- "The single most famous moment of large-scale transformation in the past, however, was caused by an asteroid strike that impacted the earth 66 million years ago on the Yucatan peninsula, near what is now the town of Chicxulub in Mexico, and led to the demise of the dinosaurs. ...[T]he outcomes included 10–16 ° C cooling in mean surface air temperature on land and sharp drops in seawater temperatures, especially at shallower depths—and mass extinction of plant and animal life." Frankopan, *The Earth Transformed*, p.30.

- "In 1991, ... a major eruption of Mount Pinatubo in the Philippines injected twenty megatons of sulphur dioxide into the atmosphere which was then oxidised to form stratospheric particles of sulphate aerosols; these then propagated, increasing the opacity of the stratosphere. Among the startling results was a reduction of direct sunlight by 21 per cent and a reduction in insulation that led to an averaged global temperature cooling of about 0.5º C." Frankopan, *The Earth Transformed*, p.11.

- "Then there are other events that could have severe effects on human life on earth. These include solar winds that have major impact on earth's magnetosphere, solar storms that could destroy power-grid transformers... . Then there are risks of lunar flooding which NASA expects to occur in the mid-2030s when the lunar cycle amplifies rising sea levels to create increasing high-tide floods that surge in low-lying regions, and earthquakes which can cause major disruption... . But by far the biggest risk to global climate comes from volcanoes." Frankopan, *The Earth Transformed*, p.650.

- "Based on paleoclimate and historical evidence, it is likely that at least one large explosive volcanic eruption would occur during the 21st century. ...Such an eruption would reduce global surface temperature and precipitation, especially over land, for one to three years, alter the global monsoon circulation, modify extreme precipitation and change many [other factors]." Working Group I contribution, *Sixth Assessment Report of the Intergovernmental Panel on Climate Change*, August 7, 2021, at SPM-32 ("AR6").

- "[A] big underwater eruption of Hunga Tonga-Hunga Ha'apai in Tonga on 15 January 2022 was reported around the world, less well covered was the scientific analysis of what had happened. The eruption had more explosive force than a hundred simultaneous detonations of the atomic bomb dropped on Hiroshima in 1945. A plume of ash and dust was forced into the atmosphere, reaching higher than any other on record, with volcanic heat and superheated moisture from the ocean acting like 'hyperfuel for a mega-thunderstorm', according to NASA scientists— which generated almost 600,000 lightning strikes in three days." Frankopan, *The Earth Transformed*, p.651.

IMPACT ON HUMANS

- "Such [climate] events were spectacular and devastating. They also each played a part in the extraordinary series of flukes, coincidences, long shots and serendipities that ultimately brought about the rise of humankind... ." Frankopan, *The Earth Transformed*, p.31.

- In fact, environmental upheavals may have led to the emergence of *Homo sapiens* as the dominant bipedal species. *See* Maya Wei-Haas,"Surprising leap in ancient human technology tied to environmental upheaval: Sediment core evidence reveals the critical factors that may have given rise to strikingly complex behaviors some 320,000 years ago, around the time the first members of our species appeared," *National Geographic*, October 21, 2020 ("Scientists have long pointed to changes in climate, such as the onset of wet or dry periods, as the key driving force behind the adaptation of our early ancestors").

- "One key point in the history of our species came around 130,000 years ago with a sudden and dramatic reorganisation of global temperatures, sea level and weather which were modulated by changes in ocean circulation and deep-water ocean CO_2 storage." Frankopan, *The Earth Transformed*, p.46.

- We also have evidence of the significance of the impact of climate change on societies in specific geographical regions. For example, recent research reported in *Geology* has supported the hypothesis that climate change resulting in a prolonged drought was responsible for the disappearance of the large metropolises in Pakistan and India over 4,000 years ago. University of Cambridge, "Decline of Bronze Age 'megacities' linked to climate change," *Research Bulletin*, 27 February 2014.

- Similarly, Cambridge Gates scholar Mary Beth Day has uncovered evidence that the Cambodian city of Angkor, the largest preindustrial city in the world, collapsed 600 years ago because of climate change. University of Cambridge, "Ancient lessons for a modern challenge," *Research Bulletin*, 20 January 2012.

- Archaeologist Judith Bunbury has been engaged in a long-term study of the impacts of gradual and sudden climate change in Egypt over the past 10,000 years, noting the relocation of populations and economic activity in response. She states: "It's clear from our work in Egypt that there was climate change going on all of the time, and this affected different people in different ways. Resources weren't stationary, so they had to keep moving. ... Some wrote literature about how terrible it was, others just accepted it and moved, and others developed new technologies...." University of Cambridge, "Climate change: it's all happened before...," *Research Bulletin*, 22 October 2013.

• Temperatures went up "some 11,900 years ago. ...[T]hey did so extremely quickly, going up by more than 10 ° C in sixty years. ...The end of the Younger Dryas marked the start of a new period, first named the Holocene... . The onset of a long period of warmer, stable conditions corresponded with some profound changes in demographic expansion, settlement patterns and innovations—the most significant of which was the emergence of agriculture." Frankopan, *The Earth Transformed*, p.58.

IMPACT OF HUMANS

• We know that every year over 200 billion tons of carbon are removed from the atmosphere by growing plants; some 200 billion tons are added back through decomposition, digestion and respiration. Human activity directly adds another 10 billion tons (or 5%). Matt Ridley, *The Rational Optimist*, p.346. Volcanic activity, forest fires and other natural events also contribute emissions to the atmosphere. So, human activity directly makes only a small contribution to the total amount of greenhouse gases in our atmosphere. But, human activity is a net contributor that, at least to some extent is within our control.

• "[I]n the late 1500s and early 1600s, ...a global drop in surface air temperatures occurred—part of the 'Little Ice Age'—which natural forces can't explain. Quite likely, European expansion in the Americas played a role. With perhaps 90 per cent of the indigenous population eliminated by the effects of conquest and infectious disease, forests reclaimed regions in which terraced agriculture and irrigation had been practised for centuries. In Mesoamerica, Amazonia and the Andes, some 50 million hectares of cultivated land may have reverted to wilderness. Carbon uptake from vegetation increased on a scale sufficient to change the Earth System and bring about a human driven phase of global cooling." David Graeber and David Wengrow, *The Dawn of Everything: A New History of Humanity* (2021), p.258.

- Human impact on the climate includes far more than carbon emissions. "Cities intensify human-induced warming locally, and further urbanization together with more frequent hot extremes will increase the severity of heatwaves (very high confidence). Urbanization also increases mean and heavy precipitation over and/or downwind of cities (medium confidence) and resulting runoff intensity (high confidence). In coastal cities, the combination of more frequent extreme sea level events (due to sea level rise and storm surge) and extreme rainfall/riverflow events will make flooding more probable (high confidence)." AR6, at SPM-33.

- "Dirty air is not simply the result of fossil fuels being burned for energy; it also comes from open-air burning of rubbish. An estimated 40 per cent of global waste is burned in the open air ...,
...human-made mass—such as concrete, construction materials and metals—was equal to about 3 per cent of global biomass a century or so ago, today it exceeds it." Frankopan, *The Earth Transformed*, p.22.

- However, not all human activity and emissions cause warming. For example, from the late 19th century to 2010, "other human drivers (principally aerosols) contributed a cooling of 0.0°C to 0.8°C, natural drivers changed global surface temperature by −0.1°C to 0.1°C, and internal variability changed it by −0.2° C to 0.2° C. It is ... extremely likely that human-caused stratospheric ozone depletion was the main driver of cooling of the lower stratosphere between 1979 and the mid-1990s." AR6, at SPM-6.

- "[O]ur species is not alone in transforming the world around us, for other species of biota—that is to say, flora, fauna and micro-organisms—are not passive participants in or simple bystanders to a relationship that exists solely or even primarily between humans and nature. ...Each is actively involved in processes of change, adaptation and evolution—sometimes with devastating consequences." Frankopan, *The Earth Transformed*, p.26.
- "Nature is not a harmonious, benign and complementary concept that preserves balance, for ecosystems have always been trans-formed and reshaped by many non-human forces." Frankopan, *The Earth Transformed*, p.39.

And,

The effects on climate of the accumulation of carbon in the atmo-sphere to date will continue for many centuries, even if all further greenhouse emissions were to cease tomorrow.

- "A thousand years from now—30 human generations—more than half the heat-trapping carbon-dioxide that humanity has pumped into the atmosphere since the beginning of the In-dustrial Revolution will still be there. Twenty thousand years from now, ... a third of that CO_2 will remain." Jonathan Shaw, "Controlling the Global Thermostat: Coming to terms with cli-mate change's relentless, long-term fallout," *Harvard Magazine*, November-December 2020.
- Similarly, even with minimal further emissions, "it is virtually certain that global mean sea level will continue to rise over the 21st century. ...In the longer term, sea level is committed to rise for centuries to millennia due to continuing deep ocean warming and ice sheet melt, and will remain elevated for thousands of years ... ." AR6, at SPM-28.
- "If global net negative CO_2 emissions were to be achieved and be sustained, the global CO_2-induced surface temperature increase

would be gradually reversed but other climate changes would continue in their current direction for decades to millennia ... ." *Id.*, at SPM-39.

Yet,

"[W]hile the last eleven millennia have not been uniformly clement or favourable, they have been less unstable and variable than at many times in the past. While contending with potentially catastrophic global warming in the course of the twenty-first century should not be downplayed, current projected rises of 1.5–2 ° C are modest in the grand scheme of climatic change, not only in the history of the earth but in that of humans too, and look paltry indeed compared to the very many and regular double-digit rises and falls that have occurred in the past."

Frankopan, *The Earth Transformed*, p.60.

SUMMARY

At a minimum, history teaches us that warming and cooling of the planet generally and climate change affecting particular areas are certainly not unnatural nor are the consequences necessarily all bad. We know that climate changes have and will continue to impact human populations. We also know that human activity contributes to climate change. And, finally, we know that global warming as a result of past carbon emissions will continue for the foreseeable future, regardless of our public policies.

What is the relevance of these facts? Not much, except for context. This context should make clear that what is involved in the matter of manmade climate change is not the fate of Earth. It is not nature, not the world, not the existence of life. It is where we have chosen to live, how we have chosen to live, the investments we have chosen to make in altering our environment. Those are the things being threatened. by climate change.

The climate is changing, and always has been. Human activity (generating greenhouse gases) affects the climate. However, the impacts of human activity on climate are small relative to the climate system as a whole, so the variability attributable to such activities may be insignificant compared to natural variability. *See* Steven E. Koonin, "Climate Science Is Not Settled," *The Wall Street Journal*, September 19, 2014.

Humankind may be at risk or, at least, our world as we now know it, but not the planet nor "nature" nor life on Earth.

CLIMATE SCIENCE

We look to climate science to try to predict what the timing and severity of the current warming cycle is likely to be, given the current conditions. In addition, we would like that science to tell us the extent to which human activity is contributing to that change. What we really need to assess is the likely differences it would make if man-made carbon emissions were to be less than what is now expected (based upon current forecasts and known technology) by some potentially feasible amount? So, does climate science have the answers?

THE IPCC ASSESSMENTS

The IPCC Fifth Assessment Report (AR5) was issued in late 2013 and early 2014. (The full-length reports were published by Cambridge University Press.) There are reports from each of three Working Groups (WG1, WG2 and WG3), each of which has a Summary for Policymakers ("SPM"), and a Synthesis Report based upon the work of the three groups. These documents could be seen to represent the state of climate science as of the date of the reports.

The Working Group I part of The IPCC Sixth Assessment Report was issued in August 2021 ("AR6").

> "[I]mprovements in observationally based estimates and information from paleoclimate archives provide a comprehensive view of each component of the climate system and its changes to date. New climate model simulations, new analyses, and methods combining multiple lines of evidence lead to improved understanding of human influence on a wider range of climate variables, including weather and climate extremes. ...The effort was made to estimate temperature change attributed to total human influence, changes in well-mixed greenhouse gas concentrations, other human drivers due to aerosols, ozone and land-use change ..., solar and volcanic drivers, and internal climate variability."

AR6, at SPM-5,8.

The AR6 Summary stresses its efforts to assess all forms of human influence on climate, often referring to "human-induced" changes, and touts the use of "new" models, analyses and methods. Interestingly, the report indicates that but for greenhouse gas emissions, we could be experiencing global cooling. AR6, at SPM-7.

Because the full Sixth Assessment Report report was not out yet, I focus below on AR5. I quote from AR6 above. Other excerpts from AR6 are included below, in brackets.

There are several general observations to be made about AR5. It was less alarmist in many respects than AR4 issued in 2007. It was also somewhat more informative. For example, it provided percentage quantification of the assessments, so one had a firmer idea of what it meant for something to be "likely" or "highly likely." In addition, WG2 concluded that there was little clear evidence of adverse impact upon human health from changes to date, acknowledged that various expected adverse effects were not clearly established by the evidence and forecast that the longer term economic effects of climate change would be only between 0.2% and 2.0% of gross output or income (compared to very much larger previous forecasts). WG2, at SPM-4-8, 19. Repeatedly, the WG2 Report also observed that the adverse impacts of climate change will be felt much more strongly by the poor and by the less developed societies. *E.g., id.,* at SPM-6 to 7, 20.

WG1 sets out the evidence concerning the impact of human activity on climate. The key conclusions concern the forecast of climate sensitivity to greenhouse gases, traditionally expressed as the number of degrees of temperature increase caused by a doubling of the concentration of those gases. The sensitivity estimate matters because it is the link between forecasts of the level of future greenhouse emissions and the change in temperature. In other words, one can evaluate different policies in terms of their effects on emissions which can then be translated, using the sensitivity estimate, into expected differences in climate change.

WG1 expressly acknowledged that the 15-year period from 1998 through 2012 showed essentially no warming. It attributed that fact to phenomena—natural variability—that can occur in shorter periods of time but do not alter long term trends. *Id.,* p.5. Yet, based upon that actual experience of the past fifteen years, WG1 lowered the bottom end of the forecast range from 2.0C to 1.5C. The top end, however, remained at 4.5C. WG1, at SPM-16.

The estimates set forth are for equilibrium climate sensitivity ("ECS"), which would be the change that would occur from a doubling of greenhouse gases once all of the adjustments in the climate system had worked themselves out—a period that may be a thousand years. Thus, the ECS could never actually be measured, because other important changes will inevitably occur before equilibrium can be reached. A modified version of ECS looks at a period of 100-150 years.

The "best estimate" of ECS (equilibrium climate sensitivity) went from 3.0 C in 1979 (a National Academy of Science report), to 2.5 C in AR1 in 1990, back to 3.0 C in AR4 (2007). No "best estimate" was given in AR3 (2001) or, now, in AR5 (2014). Lewis and Crok, "A Sensitive Matter," p.19 (Table 1).[2] The reason for the decision in AR5 was set out in footnote 16: "No best estimate for equilibrium climate sensitivity can now be given because of a lack of agreement on values across assessed lines of evidence and studies." What that footnote appears to recognize is that estimates based upon the current observed historical data are not consistent with the forecasts from the climate models being used.

The decision not to publish a "best estimate" has been subject to sharp criticism by some climate scientists and commentators, who assert that the current "best estimate" would be lower than the previous "best estimate" of 3 C, perhaps as low as 1.75 C. *See* Nicholas Lewis and Marcel Crok, "A Sensitive Matter: How the IPCC Buried Evidence Showing Good News About Global Warming," *The Global Warming Policy Foundation*, Report 13, March 5, 2014; Matt Ridley, "Climate Forecast: Muting the Alarm," *The Wall Street Journal*, March 27, 2014. Such a reduction in the "best estimate" would be a significant development and would undercut many of the policy recommendations of the IPCC. If the current 'best estimate" is less than 2.0C, then the "science" would indicate that the threat is less than previously expected for a given increase in greenhouse gas.

AR6 reports: "The equilibrium climate sensitivity is an important quantity used to estimate how the climate responds to radiative forcing. ...The AR6 assessed best estimate is 3° C with a likely range of 2.5°C to 4°C (high confidence), compared to 1.5° C to 4.5° C in AR5, which did not provide a best estimate." AR6, at SPM-14. So, the best estimate is again 3.0° C, with an increase in the bottom and a reduction in the top of the range.

Another relevant measure is transient climate response ("TCR"), which looks at the temperature change when the concentration of gases doubles. The estimate of TCR by WG1 in AR5 is a likely range of 1.0 C to 2.5 C. *Id.*, p.16. This is the estimate most comparable to historical observations. The estimated range for TCR has steadily declined from the range of 1.1 C to 3.1 C set forth in AR3 (2001). *See* Lewis and Crok, "A Sensitive Matter," p.15.

> "In the IPCC AR3, it was argued that TCR, rather than ECS, was a more relevant metric of model response to increasing CO_2. ...[T]he overall magnitude of TCR was thought at that time to be more comparable to the time scale and magnitude of the response in the real world over the 21st century. In addition, there were factors that complicated the calculation and interpretation of ECS that were emerging by the late 1990."

Gerald A. Meehl, Catherine A. Senior, *et al.*, "Context for interpreting equilibrium climate sensitivity and transient climate response from the CMIP6 Earth system models," *Science Advances*, Vol. 6, no. 26, 24 June 2020.

AR6 "reaffirms with high confidence the AR5 finding that there is a near-linear relationship between cumulative anthropogenic CO_2 emissions and the global warming they cause. Each 1000 $GtCO_2$ of cumulative CO_2 emissions is assessed to likely cause a 0.27° C to 0.63° C increase in global surface temperature... . This is a narrower range compared to AR5... ." At SPM-36.

Of course, greater levels of emission because of greater expected economic activity and/or population growth than previously forecast could create a greater threat despite the possible lower climate sensitivity. And *vice versa*.

Somewhat curiously, climate sensitivity estimates had not changed much since the first estimate in 1979.[3] A major new five-year study by the World Climate Research Program, however, utilizing three independent sources—historical records of temperatures and CO_2 levels, paleoclimate records of prehistoric temperatures (like sediment samples, coral reefs and tree rings), and satellite observations—undertook to narrow the range of climate sensitivity. The researchers appear to have succeeded:

"Very low sensitivities are ruled out by cloud physics and by the understanding from the instrumental and paleo periods. Very high sensitivities would require the understanding of clouds to be wrong in the other direction, aerosols to have a much stronger cooling effect than we thought, and our understanding of paleoclimate changes to be off."

Scott K. Johnson, "Major study rules out super-high and low climate sensitivity to CO_2," *ARSTechnica*, July 22, 2020.

"So the likely range for equilibrium climate sensitivity ends up at 2.6-4.1° C, with the most likely answer just a hair above 3°C. ... That's considerably narrower than the old 1.5-4.5° C range." *Id.*

AR6 claims to find evidence that extreme weather is a result of global warming: "[E]very additional 0.5° C of global warming causes clearly discernible increases in the intensity and frequency of hot extremes, including heatwaves (very likely), and heavy precipitation (high confidence), as well as agricultural and ecological droughts in some regions (high confidence)." AR6, at SMP-19.

THE MODELS

The assessments described above are in large part based upon models that are vastly more complicated than mere extrapolations from historical evidence. And, there are serious difficulties in reconciling historical evidence with the models.

The starting point in the process is to identify patterns of climate change over some reasonable historical period. Then one can attempt to develop models that would "explain" those changes, that is, models that would generate "predictions" consistent with what happened when applied to past periods. We do not really care very much what the causes were of what happened in the past; however, there is no other established means of predicting what will happen in the future. The assumption is that if a model cannot reconstruct the past, then it seems unlikely that it could accurately predict the future. At the same time, the successful reconstruction of the past (with the benefit of hindsight) is no guarantee of reliability in predicting the future.

Several elaborate models of climate change have been created. At this time, they all seem still to be inadequate for predicting the future, since they have generally appeared to overestimate the change in global temperatures that has occurred over the past 10 to 15 years. *See, e.g.,* Richard McNider and John Christy, "Why Kerrey Is Flat Wrong on Climate Change," *The Wall Street Journal,* February 19, 2014. At the same time, the thawing of the Arctic ice cap seems to be occurring faster than earlier models predicted (although, the ice cap increased in 2013).[3] Efforts to alter the models to capture the Arctic phenomenon have increased the apparent over- estimations for the rest of the Earth. *Id.*

Curiously, the deep atmosphere global temperatures (up to 75,000 feet above the surface of the Earth) have not gone up much, but ice in the Northern Hemisphere has been melting rather quickly (while ice in Antarctica has been increasing). *See, e.g.,* Jason Samenow, "Antarctic sea ice hit 35-year record high Saturday," *The Washington Post,* September 23, 2013 (reporting on the new NASA report); Guy Williams, "Why is Antarctic sea ice growing," *Skeptical Science,* 12 December 2013.

Sea ice is the thin layer that forms on the surface of the sea, which is different from glaciers or ice caps. The sea ice does not affect sea levels in the ocean, whereas land ice does. Antarctic land ice is apparently decreasing. *See, e.g., id.;* "Is Antarctica losing or gaining ice?" *skepticalscience.com,* 2018.[4] However, the thicker shelf-ice at the edges of the land mass does "slow down the movement of ice flowing from the interior of the continent out to sea. The smaller they are, the less they hold back the flow and the faster ice on land can reach the ocean. That extra ice is what drives increases in sea levels." Daniela Hernandez, "Satellite Study Reveals Wide Scale of Melting Ice Shelves in Antarctica," *WSJ.com,* August 10, 2020.

One might suspect that the explanation of what is happening is, at least, much more complex than is captured in the theory of global warming and, perhaps, that the loss of Arctic ice is due to something other than increased carbon dioxide in the atmosphere. Indeed, "CFCs [chlorofluorocarbons] are likely what's caused the Arctic to warm...

faster than the rest of the planet... . CFCs are, after all, potent greenhouse gases. One shred of optimism: since the phase-out, CFCs have been on the decline, so perhaps this Arctic amplification soon will be, too." Victoria Jaggard, "What's the Ozone Hole Got to do with Warming?" *National Geographic,* February 5, 2020. "Gases that deplete the ozone layer could be responsible for up to half of the effects of climate change observed in the Arctic from 1955 to 2005." Giuliana Viglione, "Ozone-depleting gases might have driven extreme Arctic warming: The far north is heating up twice as fast as the global average," *Nature.com,* 20 January 2020.

Recent results of many of the models are particularly puzzling. "[L]ast year, unnoticed in plain view, some of the models started running very hot. ...The scientists involved couldn't agree on why—or if the results should be trusted." Eric Roston, "Climate Models Are Running Red Hot, and Scientists Don't Know Why: The simulators used to forecast warming have suddenly started giving us less time," *Bloomberg Green,* February 3, 2020. In fact, "one factor might have caused the recent unusual results: clouds. It turns out simulated clouds often cause headaches for climate modelers." *Id.*

In short, there seem to be many important factors affecting the Earth's climate that the models miss or misapply. And, there are many unknowns:

- Particulates in the atmosphere reflect sunlight back, reducing warming. Changes in activities due to economics or regulations or various natural events, like volcanic eruptions, will affect the amount of particulates present. Similarly. "[c]louds in particular are hugely important. For example, high-altitude, wispy clouds act more like greenhouse gases than shade umbrellas, while low, fluffy clouds can reflect a lot of incoming sunlight back to space." Scott K. Johnson, "Major study rules out super-high and low climate sensitivity to CO_2: Five-year effort represents important progress on four-decade-old questions." *ARSTechnica*, July 22, 2020.[5]

- Our understanding of the impact of changes in the level of greenhouse gases is also hampered by the limitations on our understanding of the oceans and how they will change and thereby affect the climate. We simply have inadequate knowledge of the several other natural feedback systems that can mute or amplify the climate's response. "... [T]he decreasing range of TCR over generations of models, contrasted with the recent increase in range of ECS ..., likely involves processes connected to ocean heat uptake, a better quantification of which would require improved temperature observations through the full depth of the global ocean ..., as well as increased understanding of various feedbacks in the climate system." Gerald A. Meehl, Catherine A. Senior, *et al.*, "Context for interpreting equilibrium climate sensitivity and transient climate response from the CMIP6 Earth system models," *Science Advances*, Vol. 6, no. 26, 24 June 2020.

- And, there are serious gaps in our understanding of the physical dynamics of glaciers. "Thwaites Glacier [in Western Antarctica] is a scientific twofer. ...It contains enough fresh water to raise global sea levels by more than a foot and a half, and it braces the entire West Antarctic Ice Sheet, which could raise sea levels by almost 10 feet if it pooled away. But Thwaites is also ... physically mysterious. In its enormous size and ominous future rest the answers to some of the biggest unresolved questions in climate science.'" Robinson Meyer, "The New Video of One of the Scariest Places on Earth: For the first time, scientists have a clear view of the line where the giant Thwaites Glacier is leaking water into the ocean," *The Atlantic*, January 30, 2020.

The predictions of models are now being treated as empirical data, which they clearly are not. Of course, no empirical data about the future is available.

All we have is data about the past and the present. How good is that? Moreover, the results of simulations of the present are now being used to generate simulations of the past. The results of both sets of simulations are used to generate simulations of the future. *See* AR6, *e.g.,* at SPM-3 to 7.

THE DATA

It is clear that there are some pretty serious challenges in measuring climate change for the planet as a whole. Obviously, one can compile data on temperatures, rainfall, and so on for a specific geographical region and can keep track of physical changes in the region that might impact the data. As recent news reports make clear, the short-term weather patterns in various regions will likely vary pretty dramatically. Some areas will be experiencing unusual cold; some, unusual heat; some, floods; some, droughts. For example, for the year April 2013 to March 2014, England experienced an unusually cold spring; summer came weeks late; the winter was mild but January saw the greatest rainfall on record. Over the same period, California and the American Southwest suffered from a severe and prolonged drought. The American Southeast experienced a snow and ice storm of "historic proportions" in February 2014. New York City and much of the Midwest had an unusually cold winter, with exceptionally large and frequent snow storms. In the summer of 2015, several of the Midwestern States experienced record rain fall, accompanied by highly unusually flooding; France and Italy had record heat waves; and parts of Australia experienced their first ever (recorded) snow fall.

Hot years or cold years?

In 2019, France (and much of Western Europe) experienced a summer of record heat. The American Northwest had an enormous snow storm bringing record snowfall (with accumulations of up to three to four feet) and record low temperatures in September 2019. In early November, much of the United States experienced additional record low temperatures. In late November, the northern half of the country faced an "unprecedented" winter storm disrupting Thanksgiving travel. Yet, NASA has announced that 2019 was the "second hottest year on record. It barely edged out 2016, the previous warmest year. ...And the last decade was the warmest decade." Evan Gough, "According to NASA, 2019 Was the Second Hottest Year on Record," *Universe Today*, January 20, 2020. But, as Gough explains: "The global mean surface temperature is an abstraction in some ways, because the temperature rise is not the same everywhere. In the contiguous 48 US states, the temperature was the 34th highest on record. But there's little comfort in that. The Arctic region is warming about three times faster than the rest of the world."

And, in January 2021:

> "NASA and the European Union's Copernicus Climate Change Service announced that Earth's average global surface temperature in 2020 tied 2016 as the warmest year on record. Independent studies by the National Oceanic and Atmospheric Administration and a private climate-analysis group called Berkeley Earth found that 2020 was slightly colder than 2016 but warmer than every other year since 1850."

Robert Lee Holtz, "World's Ice Is Melting Faster Than Ever, Climate Scientists Say," *WSJ.com*, January 25, 2021.

So, how, in fact, does one collect data on the planet as a whole? One would probably say take measurements in many places all around world, using consistent methodology and standardized equipment. Of course, you need to collect the same data year after year for many years, decades or even centuries. (It is obviously too late to go back to do it or to redo it.) Then, climate scientists have to develop definitions to be applied to all of the data from various regions (how to combine and weigh the disparate results) to determine whether in the aggregate there has been global warming (as so defined). Yet, there is still uncertainty.

For example, one would presumably determine changes in the temperature of the oceans by using multiple thermometers to take water temperatures in many, many locations. That is essentially what scientists have done (but, overall, there have not been consistent measurements collected over decades). Indeed, the most common method of measurement has been by sailors taking buckets full of sea water and taking their "temperature". *See, e.g.*, Rebecca Hersher, "How Much Hotter Are The Oceans? The Answer Begins With A Bucket," *NPR*, August 19, 2019. Among other problems, the temperature of the water changes quickly after collection, depending upon the bucket size and the air temperature.

A 2018 study reports:

> "... that between 1991 and 2016 the oceans warmed an average of 60 percent more per year than the [IPCC] panel's official estimates. ...[H]owever, [t]he researchers used a new approach that derived ocean temperatures by measuring the levels of carbon dioxide and oxygen in the atmosphere. Those gases dissolve in ocean waters, but the amount the ocean can hold depends on its temperature."

Kendra Pierre-Louis, "Taking the Oceans' Temperature, Scientists Find Unexpected Heat," *NYT.com.*, October 31, 2018.

Which is more accurate, the direct measurements or the measurements by inference from the atmosphere? Are either reasonably correct? Of course, the methodological problems are eased somewhat by the fact that one need only to determine the changes over time not the absolute temperature levels.

But, there are still issues. For example, some climate scientists in 2015 concluded that the apparent slow-down in global warning was the result of errors made in the way global warming was measured—when the data is "corrected," the warming trend reappears. *See, e.g.,* Justin Gillis, "Global Warming 'Hiatus' Challenged by NOAA Research," *The New York Times,* June 4, 2015 (the data issues focus on the measurement of the temperature of seawater by sailors collecting buckets of sea water and measuring the temperature of the water in the buckets with thermometers). Other climate scientists have challenged these tentative conclusions. It also seems that the revisions to the data proposed significantly reduce the apparent warming since 1880, while also reducing the amount by which the warning seems to have slowed down in the last 15 years. *Id.*

Our models necessarily take data from the past (which is all that we have) and project that data into the future. The assumption (almost certainly wrong) is that the future will be like the past. Thomas Malthus, in the 18th century, predicted the continual return of mankind to a mere subsistence level of existence, because population growth was exponential while agricultural productivity growth was arithmetic. In the early 1970s, we supposedly faced a catastrophic worldwide population explosion, be- cause of the steady exponential growth rate of the world's population. In both cases, the mathematics were impeccable, but the assumptions about the facts (in the future) were simply wrong. *See, e.g., id. See also,* Laurence B. Siegel, *Fewer, Richer, Greener: Prospects for Humanity in an Age of Abundance* (2020) (the title of this book, like its organization, is a bit misleading: the evidence presented suggests that "richer" leads to "fewer" and then, eventually, to "greener").

Eric Roston, in the article cited above, notes: "To a degree, every scientist suspects their model is wrong. There's even an aphorism about this: 'All models are wrong, but some are useful.'" Michael Crichton, in a speech 15 years ago, reviewed numerous examples of alarmist predictions by scientists during the twentieth century that turned out to be false (such as the "nuclear winter," the food shortage and the population explosion), commenting:

> "I have to say the arrogance of the model-makers is breathtaking. There have been, in every century, scientists who say they know it all. Since climate may be a chaotic system ... these predictions are inherently doubtful, to be polite. ..[E]ven if the models get the science spot-on, they can never get the sociology. To predict anything about the world a hundred years from now is simply absurd. ...You tell me you can predict the world of 2100. Tell me it's even worth thinking about. Our models just carry the present into the future. They're bound to be wrong. Everybody who gives a moment's thought knows it."

"Aliens Cause Global Warming", *Caltech Michelin Lecture,* January 17, 2003 (emphasis added).

Not convinced?

Just look at the dramatic yet unpredictable changes between 1920 and 2020, or 1820 and 1920, or even 1720 and 1820. And, of course, as most of us are keenly aware, the pace of change has been increasing "exponentially" (whatever that means). In the end, we might question the actual usefulness of computer models attempting to forecast very far into the future.

EXAMPLES OF THE CHALLENGES

One example.

Let's take a conceptually simple example, relatively free of the problems of technological change and other issues of forecasting: What is the net relationship between trees (and plants generally) and climate change?

Trees absorb carbon from the atmosphere as they grow, but they release carbon when they die and decompose (or are burned). Warming temperatures and more CO_2 in the atmosphere promote tree growth, causing the trees to grow faster. Faster growth means greater carbon aborption. But, faster growth may also mean shorter lives for the trees, resulting in faster release of carbon. *See* University of Cambridge, "Amount of carbon stored in forests reduced as climate warms," *Research*, 15 May 2019 ("As the Earth's climate continues to warm, tree growth will continue to accelerate, but the length of time that trees store carbon, the so-called carbon residence time, will diminish"). So, older, slower growing trees generally live longer, but they also absorb less carbon per year. Separately, the green leaves of trees absorb more of the Sun's heat than do other, lighter ground cover (like snow, especially), which reflects more sunlight. *See* Gabriel Popkin, "How much can forests fight climate change?" *Nature*, 15 January 2019. Well, so what is the net impact of trees?

There are similar issues about the assumed rate of absorption of carbon from the atmosphere by plants generally. Growing plants pull from the atmosphere tremendous quantities of carbon (while rotting plants return the carbon). Thus, the rate of deforestation and other reductions or increases in the quantities of plant life are relevant to the results obtained from the models. At the same time, there is some expectation that the increasing levels of carbon dioxide and higher temperatures will spur plant growth in the near term. But, increasing prevalence of drought conditions may reduce the amount of vegetation, reducing the capability to absorb carbon and even increasing the rate of release of carbon back into the atmosphere. There is also the possibility that at some point, higher temperatures will result in the saturation of the aggregate ability of plants to absorb additional carbon, which could result in a sudden surge in greenhouse gases and more rapid climate change. *See* University of Cambridge, "4 degree temperature rise will end vegetation 'carbon sink,'" *Research*, 17 December 2013.

Then, there are also questions about other impacts on the environment of plant growth stimulated by rising levels of CO_2, such as on the availability of water for human use. *See* Stephen Leahy, "Thirsty future ahead as climate change explodes plant growth: Rising CO_2 levels and a warmer earth means plants will grow bigger and have longer to suck the land dry. That's bad news for human water supplies," *National Geographic*, November 4, 2019. Consider this explanation given by Leahy:

> "Climate change affects the growth of plants in three ways. First, as CO2 levels increase, plants need less water to do photosynthesis. This well-documented effect was long thought to mean that there would be more fresh water available in soils and streams. But a second effect counters that: A warming world means longer and warmer growing seasons, which gives plants more time to grow and consume water, drying the land. ...[The] third effect: As CO2 levels rise, it amps up photosynthesis. Plants in this hotter, CO2-rich environment grow bigger, with more leaves. That means when it rains there will be far more wet leaves creating more surface area for more evaporation to occur."

So, more CO_2 means less water use per average-sized plant. But, more CO_2 also means more and bigger plants, using more water. And, more and bigger leaves means more evaporation. But, more plant growth means more CO_2 pulled from the atmosphere. Yet, more leaf coverage means more heat absorption and more evaporation!

Pretty complicated.

Two other examples: Bacteria and microbes. Really?

Bacteria and other micro-organisms are among the tiny particles that seed the formation of crystalline structuring of water that create snow-flakes and ice crystals as the first stage in most rainfall, as well as all snow and hail. Bacteria that are able to withstand the intense ultra-violet light and lack of nutrients in the upper atmosphere could travel throughout the world in airborne colonies. These bacteria affect weather patterns, so the changing of a regional microbiome (for example, through agri-culture) or changes in particular microbiomes that occur as a result of climate change may affect the weather in such regions or elsewhere. Ferris Jabr, "It's Buggy Out There," *The New York Times Magazine*, February 13, 2015. How does one model this relationship?

And,

> "The first active leak of methane from the sea floor in Ant-arctica has been revealed by scientists. The researchers also found microbes that normally consume the potent green-house gas before it reaches the atmosphere had only arrived in small numbers after five years, allowing the gas to escape."

Damian Carrington, "First active leak of seabed methane discovered in Antarctica," *The Guardian*, 21 July 2020 ("The research also has significance for climate models, which currently do not account for a delay in the microbial consumption of escaping methane"). [6]

A SUMMARY COMMENT

Steven Koonin observes that the important questions have not been answered by science to date and the widespread belief that climate science is settled "distorts our public and policy debates" and "has inhibited the scientific and policy discussions that we need to have." "Climate Science Is Not Settled," *The Wall Street Journal,* September 19, 2014. The simple, stark fact is that "climate science ... is not yet mature enough to usefully answer the difficult and important questions being asked of it." *Id.*

THE BIG QUESTIONS

Let us assume that we could predict with reasonable reliability the causes and processes of climate change under current conditions. Several important questions still arise:

- First, absent some change from the *status quo,* what are the conditions that are likely to exist at various times in the future? For example, what daily and seasonal temperatures do we predict? What, if any changes, in acidity will occur? What will the pattern of rainfall be? Will there be flooding (for example, from rising sea levels)?
- Second, taking some reasonable estimate of what it might be possible to change about the current trends, such as reductions in the aggregate expected future amount of greenhouse gases in the atmosphere, what are the conditions that would be likely to exist at the same times in the future?
- Third, what are likely to be the impacts on environment, agriculture, existing species of plants and animals, man-made

infrastructure and facilities of both sets of future conditions (under the first scenario and under the second scenario)?

- Finally, what is the array of feasible policy actions that could be effectively implemented, especially on a global basis?

Then, there are related big questions. I discuss six below.

But, first, note: the feared adverse consequences simply may not be avoidable merely by curtailing future carbon emissions: "[T]emperatures will continue to increase progressively... Unless the process can be reversed—not just slowed—the globally transformative effects of human-induced warming will thus extend across a geological time scale that has come to be known among scientists as the anthropocene... ." Jonathan Shaw, "Controlling the Global Thermostat: Coming to terms with climate change's relentless, long-term fallout," *Harvard Magazine*, November-December 2020. So, it may be that engineered projects to recapture carbon and to alter the environmental dynamics are the only hope. *See, e.g., id.*; Daniel Schrag and David Keith, "Can Solar Geoengineering Help Fight Climate Change?" *Harvard Magazine*, Podcast, October 16, 2020.

And, a comment about recent (2020) events. Interestingly, in the second quarter of 2020, we experienced a natural (unplanned and unintentional) experiment. A dramatic decrease in global economic activity due to a pandemic has resulted in a decrease in carbon emissions, a reduction in pollution, clearer skies, cleaner water, the presence of fish (and jellyfish) in Venetian canals, the visibility of the Himalayas from the Indian state of Punjab, and much less road congestion. *See, e.g.,* "Coronavirus: Air pollution and CO2 fall rapidly as virus spreads," *BBC.com*, 19 March 2020; "'We can see the Himalayas for the first time in 30 years'—from India to Venice, the beautiful side effects of the coronavirus pandemic," *The Telegraph*, 9 April 2020; Jim Carlton, "Coronavirus Offers a Clear View of What Causes Air Pollution," *WSJ.com*, May 3, 2020 ("With factories and vehicles idle, nitrogen dioxide levels hit lows not seen since the early 20th century; 'We didn't know was how significantly it could drop'"). We also are seeing the takeover of National Parks (and even city streets) by native wildlife. Nature is reasserting itself much faster than we ever would have expected. See, e.g., "7 ways the earth has gotten better since the coronavirus shutdown," *The Philadelphia Inquirer*, April 22, 2020. We may have the unique opportunity actually to examine the environmental consequences of certain changes in our economies and our behavior. This event may also give us insights into the human costs of various such changes.

Now, the related overarching questions.

1. WHERE WILL THE PREDICTED NEGATIVE IMPACTS MOST LIKELY OCCUR?

What would seem to matter as far as public policy is what will be happening in specific geographical regions, not mere changes in some global average. So, we need to answer the above questions with respect to specific geographic regions, not with global averages. Clearly, these issues have meaning only in a local context. We would want not only to identify the impacts but also to place values or costs on them or, at least, on the differentials identified. Thus, the identification of the specific regions to be affected is crucial. Thus, the actual analysis will be even more complex than the public debate suggests.

One question is what impact global warming is having and will have on regional weather patterns. In 2012, *National Geographic* featured on its cover a story with the question "What's Up With The Weather?" Accompanying the customary spectacular photographs, the author described the apparent dramatic increase in extreme weather events during the twenty-first century. They ranged from "Record Floods" to "Endless Drought", from "Summer in March" to "Snowmageddon." Peter Miller, "Weather Gone Wild," *National Geographic*, September 2012, at 30-65. Global warming seems to have increased the amount of water evaporation which, in turn, contributes to making the normal weather patterns more extreme. Of course, there may be other explanations.

Some of the rather severe recent weather patterns in the United Kingdom and the United States seem to be as a result of changes in the path of the jet stream possibly caused by climate change. It has been proposed that the warming trend in the arctic region has altered the relationships in atmospheric temperatures around the Northern Hemisphere so as to allow the jet stream to wander or meander, bringing unusual and potentially prolonged weather patterns. *See, e.g.*, Pallab Ghosh, "Wavier jet stream 'may drive weather shift,'" *BBC News*, 15 February 2014. The current drought in California, however, may just be a typical cyclical phenomenon unrelated to climate change. *See* Justin Gillis, "Science Linking Drought to Global Warming Remains Matter of Dispute," *The New York Times*, February 16, 2014 (reporting that there is no consensus among scientists nor any definitive evidence linking the drought to global warming).

For the east coast of the United States and the Carribean, there are significant questions about the relationship between climate change and hurricanes. "[E]xperts say it has been challenging to draw conclusions with limited data. While many scientists agree that global warming is responsible for more rainfall in these storms, and has no effect on storm frequency, there is no consensus on a link between warming and the storm intensification and wind strength." Denise Chow and Andrew Williams, "This year's Atlantic hurricane season was worse than normal, but it wasn't nearly as destructive as much of the last 10 years: While scientists say global warming is to blame for wetter storms, no consensus exists for such a link to storm strength," *NBC News*, December 10, 2019 (emphasis added).[7]

The point of importance here is simply that the particular effects of climate change in different areas are likely to be quite different and difficult to forecast. In short, the nature and amount of the expected impact of global climate change varies by region, as do the likely costs and benefits of that change. Yet, the ability of climate science to predict regional impacts is quite limited.

2. COULD EXPECTED DAMAGE FROM THE PREDICTED NEGATIVE IMPACTS BE AMELIORATED?

With respect to each of the impacts identified, are there other steps that could be taken to ameliorate the negative effects? If so, what would be the costs of those steps? These analyses will necessarily be focused on bits and pieces.

Certainly, one should want to assess the potential costs of means of ameliorating or avoiding the costs of climate change as an alternative to trying to avoid the change itself. The costs of the policies of intervention would be avoided, and some significant portions of the predicted damage of the climate change could be minimized. I suspect that projects that could help cope with the changing conditions could be achieved at relatively reasonable cost and utilizing already available or easily realized technology.

It has been estimated that the number and costs of major weather disasters for the period 1996-2011 was almost twice that of the period 1980-96, in standardized dollars. Peter Miller, "Weather Gone Wild," *National Geographic*, September 2012, pp.54-5. The author observes, however, that the numbers reflect the fact that "more people are located in harm's way." Greater concentrations of people, more buildings and, often, more expensive buildings are being located in highly vulnerable places (like the coastlines). "Instead of defending themselves against climate change, many communities appear to be leading with their chin." *Id*. at 52. Similarly, Phil Klotzbach, of Colorado State University, has been quoted as saying: "even if you think climate change is a hoax, hurricanes are going to do more damage because we've built up coastlines and so there are more people in harm's way." Chow and Williams,

"This year's Atlantic hurricane season was worse than normal, but it wasn't nearly as destructive as much of the last 10 years," *NBC News*, December 10, 2019.

One could adopt zoning and building regulations that reduce the future risks of climate change. Similarly, if one predicts that a current residential area would be flooded by rising sea levels, destroying homes for hundreds or thousands of families, it would be worth investigating what the feasibiilty and cost would be of constructing dykes, sea walls and drainage systems sufficient to preserve those homes. It would also be worth estimating what it would cost to relocate those families, in human terms as well as in material resources.

There are a host of possible adjustments that can (and will) be made. For example, "'[a]s the climate changes, you can either move the farm or you can change the plant. It's easier to change the plant,' says Hanna Neuschwander, communications director at World Coffee Research, a nonprofit research firm that is coordinating scientists' efforts to engineer coffee varieties that can thrive in higher temperatures." Patience Haggin, "What Rising Temperatures Mean for Coffee-Bean Farmers," *WSJ.com*, October 9, 2019. Indeed, it would seem to be sensible to investigate the means of reducing the impact of climate change as a first step, if for no other reason, because of the likelihood that climate change will be experienced to some significant degree regardless of efforts made to reduce greenhouse gases. Indeed, even to the extent that the policies can only delay and not avoid the damage, these steps may be particularly significant.

3. WHAT ARE THE LIKELY EFFECTS OF INNOVATION/ TECHNOLOGICAL CHANGE ON THE PREDICTIONS?

While it may be interesting to be able to predict what the future would be if nothing changes, the one thing we know for certain is that there will be change, and change in many things. For example, is it likely that new non-carbon or low-carbon sources of energy will be developed over the next 25 or 50 years? The answer, based upon history, would have to be a resounding yes.

The real issues have to do with the costs and the scalability of those technologies. Will they become economic, and will they be capable of delivering some significant portion of the world's emery needs? Again, history suggests that the most likely answer to both questions is yes. *See* Matt Ridley, *The Rational Optimist*, at 139-56, 191-200, 217-43 (Ridley chronicles several of the truly spectacular successes of technology, combined with division of labor, specialization and trade, in expanding the world's food supply and its industrial production, creating a far, far wealthier and healthier human population than most people could imagine even in the nineteenth century).

Dramatic improvements in battery technology are already being realized. *See, e.g.*, Chris Hall, "Future batteries, coming soon: Charge in seconds, last months and power over the air," *Pocket-lint.com*, 7 October 2020. "The battery boom could erode demand for crude oil and by-products such as gasoline—as well as for natural gas... . While mining materials and manufacturing batteries produces some greenhouse gas emissions, analysts believe shifting to batteries in the auto and energy sectors would reduce emissions overall... ." *WSJ.com*, February 5, 2021.

Generally, renewable energy sources have already become cost-effective and often cheaper than traditional sources. *See, e.g.*, Amory B. Lovins and M. V. Ramana, "Three Myths About Renewable Energy and the Grid, Debunked," *Yale Environment 360*, December 9, 2021.

And, here is another type of example.

"This planet is home to about 1.5 billion cows, which collectively produce a lot of gas. In fact, they create more greenhouse gas emissions than planes, trains and automobiles combined." "Adding Red Seaweed

To Cow Feed Could Cut Bovine Flatulence," *NPR (WAMU 88.5)*, December 2, 2020. Of particular concern is the production of methane (CH_4) by cows and sheep during digestion, since methane has 28 times the greenhouse effect of carbon dioxide. Robert Talbot, "Methane Is A Powerful Greenhouse Gas, But Where Does It Come From?" *Forbes*, September 29, 2017 (The increase in methane is not the result of increased oil and gas production; "it appears that increasing agriculture and human population is a more likely scenario"). But, "[r]esearch shows that a specific type of seaweed can cut cows' methane production by up to 98%." *Id.* So, we can stop eating beef and cheese, drinking milk and wearing wool and leather or, perhaps, we could starting feeding cows (and sheep) some tropical red seaweed (specifically, *Asparagopsis taxiformis*). Small amounts of this seaweed also improve the digestive process leading to healthier cows. Commercial production of the product is already beginning. See Jeff Kart, "Hawaiian Seaweed Makes Cows 90% Less Gassy," *Forbes.com*, November 21, 2020.

Or,

> "[R]ecent research shows that raising or lowering the altitudes of less than 2 per cent of aircraft flights could reduce the climate impact inflicted by vapour trails made up of hot exhaust gases as they meet cold, low-pressure air—since this tiny minority are responsible for 80 per cent of the radiative forcing in the atmosphere by altering the balance between radiation emitted by the sun and heat emitted by the earth, resulting in changes in the climate."

Frankopan, *The Earth Transformed*, p.645.

In short, the desired benefits might be much more easily achieved through innovation than through coercive policies.

4. WHAT ARE THE LIKELY IMPACTS OF CULTURAL CHANGE?

Separately, we should ask what relevant changes in societal values and practices will occur over time as more societies become richer? They will almost certainly occur. The issues are what and when?

For example, it is likely that carbon emissions will follow the pattern of the population explosion, viewed as a major threat in 1970 —the mathematics of exponential growth were beyond dispute, but the assumptions about the world were wrong. We should expect that carbon emissions will continue to fall in the developed countries and then do so elsewhere as the less developed countries become more prosperous. *See, e.g.*, Laurence B. Siegel, *Fewer, Richer, Greener* (2020).[8] And, "[t]here are other ways that economic development supports the environment. ...[I]f economic development spreads the blessings of greater freedom and greater education to more of the world, popular demands for cleaner air, cleaner water and the protection of nature will only grow." *Id*.

But, in the meantime, the less developed countries will need cheap energy (fossil fuels) to become prosperous. What is the timing of this likely development?

5. WHAT ARE THE LIKELY COSTS (AND BENEFITS) OF IMMEDIATE CORRECTIVE ACTIONS?

If we had good models of climate change and reasonable predictions of technological developments, we could, in theory, assess the potential costs to the Earth of a continuation of man's current behavior relative to what would be likely to occur if the growth of such emissions were curtailed. We could then compare those avoidable costs (*i.e.*, benefits) with the estimated costs of programs that would reduce the emissions.

The questions we would be trying to answer are: What would the world be like in 100 years if we do nothing? What would it be like if various possible changes were made? Are the differences resulting from the policy changes likely to be permanent or only temporary? That is, would our efforts avoid or merely delay the occurrence of the consequences? And, what would be the costs to society of making those various changes? With the answers to these questions, one could have a sensible debate about what to do.

It is important to remember that the carbon emissions at issue are largely the result of activities that have provided great benefits to large portions of world's population in the form of economic prosperity and material wellbeing. Changes in those activities as a result of policy-making will have costs in the form of the losses of benefits that would otherwise be enjoyed. In addition, of course, there will be the more direct costs of the policies as well. Moreover, governmental regulation carries substantial transaction costs beyond the impact of the rules themselves, much in terms of bureaucratic overhead, inevitable mistakes in policy implementation and, unfortunately, corruption.

Furthermore, alternatives to fossil fuels have costs as well, in terms of the resources used, other impacts on the environment and the possible disruptions of implementation. *See, e.g.,* Charlie McGee, "Wood Pellets Draw Fire as Alternative to Coal: A lawsuit says European policy on using pellets will increase greenhouse-gas emissions; 'burning gas would release far less carbon dioxide,' expert says," *WSJ.com*, Aug. 7, 2019; Mark P. Mills," If You Want 'Renewable Energy,' Get Ready to Dig: Building one wind turbine requires 900 tons of steel, 2,500 tons of concrete and 45 tons of plastic," *WSJ.com*, August 5, 2019; Russel Gold, "Building the Wind Turbines Was Easy. The Hard Part Was Plugging Them In," *WSJ.com*, June 22, 2019 ("We have 21st-century technology to produce the power, but we still have a 20th-century power grid that can't move it from the windy and sunny parts of the country to the urban markets. The American power grid isn't set up for it"); Chris

Martin, "Wind Turbine Blades Can't Be Recycled, So They're Piling Up in Landfills: Companies are searching for ways to deal with the tens of thousands of blades that have reached the end of their lives," *Bloomberg Green*, February 5, 2020.

Indeed, in 2021, the International Energy Agency ("IEA") issued a report on the process of transition to "green" energy, warning that it might not be attainable:

> "An energy system powered by clean energy technologies differs profoundly from one fuelled by traditional hydro-carbon resources. Solar photovoltaic (PV) plants, wind farms and electric vehicles (EVs) generally require more minerals to build than their fossil fuel-based counterparts. A typical electric car requires six times the mineral inputs of a conventional car and an onshore wind plant requires nine times more mineral resources than a gas-fired plant. ...The prospect of a rapid rise in demand for critical minerals—in most cases well above anything seen previously—poses huge questions about the availability and reliability of supply."

"The Role of Critical Minerals in Clean Energy Transitions: Part of World Energy Outlook," *IEA Flagship Report*, May 2021, Executive Summary.

Efforts to achieve the transition will result in an increase in green-house emissions for years. The report also identifies additional serious challenges to the transition in terms of adverse environmental impact and energy security, further warning: "Tackling the environmental and social impacts of mineral developments will be essential, including the emissions associated with mining and processing, risks arising from in-adequate waste and water management, and impacts from inadequate worker safety, human rights abuses (such as child labour) and corruption." *Id.*

The costs and benefits will not all be readily measurable dollar terms. One would need to find a way to value benefits such as the preservation of potentially endangered species, the protection of existing communities and the avoidance of adverse impacts on life style. One would also need to find a means of valuing the costs of reduced economic growth and restrictions on various amenities that we, especially in the developed world, currently take for granted.[9]

6. WHO WILL BEAR THE COSTS (OR ENJOY THE BENEFITS) OF ANY SUCH CORRECTIVE ACTIONS?

In evaluating alternative policy responses, there is necessarily more involved than just comparing the total estimated costs with the total estimated benefits. The costs and benefits would not be shared equally across the world's population. Indeed, some of the more substantial costs in terms of reduced economic activity would fall primarily upon the less developed and less wealthy societies.

It is, perhaps, ironic that the IPCC reports stress the prediction that the adverse impacts of climate change would fall more heavily on the poor and on the less developed societies. Ironic because, at the same time, it seems likely that the costs of policies to mitigate greenhouse emissions would also fall disproportionately on the same constituencies. (Cheap energy and lavish exploitation of raw materials have been important sources of the rapid industrialization of the developed world.) And, many of the benefits of such policies (especially the intangible ones) would fall disproportionately on the wealthier societies. How does one account for the disparate impacts of a policy that reduces carbon emissions? Can these impacts be offset by mere transfer payments?

Also, it should not be surprising that it appears that climate change ranks very low on the lists of concerns of the world's poorest inhabitants. Food, shelter, sanitation, cheap energy, medical care, education, jobs and numerous other basics of a healthy and happy life are far more urgent and significant to those who do not have those necessities. *See, e.g.*, Bjorn Lomborg, "This Child Doesn't Need a Solar Panel," *The Wall Street Journal*, October 21, 2015 (referencing a United Nations survey of over 8 million people in which those from the poorest countries ranked action on climate change last among a list of 16 public policy goals.)

That is not to say that policies to address climate change necessarily come at the cost of assistance to those suffering from other, more immediate challenges, but resources are limited and some of the policy remedies for climate change do have implications for other aspects of people's lives.

SO... ?

Matt Ridley sets forth his conclusions as follows:

> "I find ... the probability of rapid and severe climate change is small; the probability of net harm from the most likely climate change is small; the probability that no adaptation will occur is small; and the probability of no new low-carbon energy technologies emerging in the long run is small. Multiply those small probabilities together and the probability of a prosperous twenty-first century is therefore by definition large."

The Rational Optimist, at 347 ("[it is] very probable that the world will be a better place in 2100 than it is today").

CONCLUSIONS?

Obviously, the answers to all of these questions would be only a part of a bigger, interrelated calculation that would attempt to accumulate the costs and benefits of alternative policy approaches. And, any global policy would also need to deal with the serious issue of the distribution of the resulting costs and benefits among the world's current and future generations. But, in the end, we need to face reality. The fact is that we will never be able actually to obtain the answers to any, let alone all, of these questions. At best we will have approximate, incomplete and dated answers. And, we will have to deal with people and nations.

Underlying any attempt to find solutions will be the ugly face of uncertainty. All of our predictions about the process of climate change and of the consequences of every action that might be taken will be necessarily be subject to uncertainty to varying (but probably unknown) degrees. The point is that all policies "carry costs, risks and questions of effectiveness;" moreover, "nonscientific factors inevitably enter the decision. These include our tolerance for risk and the priorities that we assign to economic development, poverty reduction, environmental quality, and intergenerational and geographical equity." Koonin, "Climate Science Is Not Settled," *The Wall Street Journal*, September 19, 2014.

It is important to note that the discussion set out above certainly does not, in my view, demonstrate that human-induced climate change is not real nor that it is not a threat. The arguments here concern the types of actions that could rationally and reasonably be taken in response to what concededly is a problem. The point is that many of the proposed cures are likely worse than the disease or will, on balance, make the world worse off than it would be if nothing were done. We are talking about public policy after all. Moreover, we may have already passed the "tipping point"—the point of no return, absent technology to reverse the accumulation of greenhouse gases (carbon recapture).

In addition, we will always need carefully to assess the feasibility and achievability of any proposed solution or means of reducing emissions. The challenge is especially acute because the causes and sources of emissions are global. The action of one nation is unlikely to make a difference, unless it becomes an example followed by many others. How can we assure the serious commitment of China, now the largest source of carbon emissions by far? Or, of India and Russia, numbers three and four?[10]

In addition, of course, many countries face other pressing concerns.[11]

In the end,

> "It goes without saying, or at least it should do, that the world will keep spinning on its axis and rotating around the sun, however many of us—or however few of us—are around to witness and enjoy it. ...[I]t will be nature, rather than human action, that ultimately brings net emissions towards zero. It will do so through catastrophic depopulation, whether through hunger, disease or conflict."

Frankopan, *The Earth Transformed*, p.658.

ENDNOTES

1. In February 1861, John Tyndall gave a lecture at the Royal Society in London reporting on his recent studies of the role of heat-absorbing gases in the atmosphere on global temperatures. Peter Moore, "The Great Victorian Weather Wars," *The New York Times*, August 7, 2015.

2. The range has been 1.5 C to 4.5 C in each report, except for 2007 (4AR) when it was 2.0 C to 4.5 C. The IPCC then went back to the prior estimated range. Lewis and Crok, "A Sensitive Matter," at 19 (Table 1). In AR6, the range is 2.5C to 4.0C. That is considerably narrower.

3. David Rose, "And now it's global COOLING! Return of Arctic ice cap as it grows by 29% in a year," MailOnline, 8 September 2013 (reporting on the corrected figures from the NSIDC—National Snow and Ice Data Centre—showing that the Arctic ice cover had increased significantly from the prior year, apparently due to a cool Arctic summer in 2013 and noting that the BBC had reported on 12 December 2007 the forecasts of the disappearance of Arctic sea ice by the summer of 2013). But, the winter of 2013-14 was warmer than usual in the Arctic (while colder in the eastern United States), resulting in slower growth of the sea ice, leaving the extent of ice in February to be the fourth lowest recorded by satellite data since 1979. (February 2005 was the lowest on record). NSIDC, "In the Arctic, winter's might doesn't have much bite," *Arctic Sea Ice News & Analysis*, March 3, 2014. The sea ice in the Bering Sea was down somewhat, but had been at record levels in recent years. "On July 15, Arctic sea ice ex- tent stood ... below the record for July 15, set in 2011. This places extent at the lowest level for this time of year on the satellite record. ... By contrast, extent north of Alaska is near the 1981 to 2010 average for this time of year." NSIDC, "Siberian downward slide," *Arctic Sea Ice News & Analysis*, July 15,2020.

4. "In the last decade, Antarctic sea ice has experienced both its highest and lowest extents in the satellite record [starting in the late 1970s]. The years 2012, 2013, and 2014 brought record highs; 2017 and 2018 brought record lows. Starting in 2016, Antarctica sea ice extent was mostly below the 1981–2010 average. ...Long story short: Climate change has a discernible influence on Arctic sea ice, but it has a complicated, messy influence on Antarctic sea ice." Michon Scott,

"Understanding climate: Antarctic sea ice extent," *NOAA Climate.gov*, April 28, 2020.

5. "Because the higher ECS values in some models are related to cloud feedbacks and cloud-aerosol interactions, a major research question that needs to be pursued is what is the actual nature and magnitude of cloud feedbacks in general and cloud-aerosol interactions in particular." Gerald A. Meehl, Catherine A. Senior, *et al.*, "Context for interpreting equilibrium climate sensitivity and transient climate response from the CMIP6 Earth system models," *Science Advances*, Vol. 6, no. 26, 24 June 2020.

6. The reason for the emergence of the new seep remains a mystery, but it is probably not global heating, as the Ross Sea where it was found has yet to warm significantly." *Id.*

7. "David Nolan, a professor in the Department of Atmospheric Sciences ... said slow-moving hurricanes are not altogether unusual, ... it can be just a matter of bad luck. Nolan said he agreed that global warming is driving increased rainfall but added that it has been harder to draw links between hurricanes and other effects of climate change. ...[I]t has been suggested that global warming could strengthen storms by making the strongest hurricanes even more intense. But so far, ... there has been no evidence that such a trend exists." *Id.*

8. Indeed, the declining population growth rate is continuing:

"For some time, demographers have been scaling back forecasts of future population growth, but they may not have gone far enough. A new University of Washington study... predicts some startling changes over the course of the century. Instead of the global population reaching between 9.4 billion and 12.7 billion by 2100 (as estimated in the 2019 United Nations World

Population Prospects report), the new study suggests it will peak at 9.7 billion in 2064 and then decrease to about 8.8 billion by 2100."

Walter Russell Mead, "Snooze the Climate Alarms: A new study predicts population will drop sharply as developing economies grow," *WSJ.com*, July 27, 2020.

9. "[N]ew research ... found that emissions from global air travel [accounting currently for only 2.5% of manmade carbon emissions] may be increasing more than 1.5 times as fast as the U.N. estimate. ... 'Airlines ... are becoming more fuel efficient. But we're seeing demand outstrip any of that,' ... ." Hiroko Tabuchi, "Worse Than Anyone Expected': Air Travel Emissions Vastly Outpace Predictions," *The New York Times*, September 20, 2019.

10. The 2019 climate conference lasted two weeks yet produced no agreements on actions. *See, e.g.*, Brady Dennis and Chico Harlan, "U.N. climate talks end with hard feelings, few results and new doubts about global unity," *The Washington Post*, December 15, 2019 ("a handful of higher-emitting countries squared off against smaller, more vulnerable countries. Negotiators were at loggerheads while crafting rules around a fair and transparent global carbon trading system, and they pushed the issue to next year. Fights also dragged on about how to provide funding to poorer nations already coping with rising seas, crippling droughts and other consequences of climate change"). Other issues in contention include the allocation of the costs among the more developed and less developed countries.

11. Secretary of State John Kerry urged Indonesia to combat climate change, noting the potentially devastating effects it may have on that country, but he could identify no specific steps that Indonesia could take, only programs [that] would help protect its ports and

infrastructure from the consequences of global warming. *See* Michael R. Gordon and Coral Davenport, "Kerry Implores Indonesia on Climate Change Peril," *The New York Times*, February 16, 2014. Kerry's meeting with President Susilo Bambang Yudhoyono was reportedly canceled because the President was focused on relief efforts following a deadly volcanic eruption. *Id.*

POLITICAL SOLUTIONS?

There are no political solutions to climate change.

If a crisis is averted, it will be because of technology, *i.e.*, innovations. But, political actions can help or hurt the situation. Nonetheless, some action seems like a prudent precautionary measure, given the uncertainty of the predictions on all fronts. And, "it's entirely possible to envision climate-related policies that would meet a cost-benefit test. Investing in basic science and research is almost always high-return." Holman W. Jenkins, Jr., "How Greens Humiliate Themselves," *The Wall Street Journal*, October 30, 2018.

SUBSIDIES

President Biden's "go to" solution
(for everything): Buy votes.

There are four major disadvantages to using subsidies to try to reduce greenhouse gas emissions.

First, they lower energy costs, promoting total energy usage.

"Clean energy subsidies have two countervailing effects. First, they make clean energy less expensive, thereby creating incentives for agents to produce energy with clean sources. ... Second, clean energy subsidies reduce the price of the energy composite [increasing total energy usage]. This additional effect is also governed by the share of clean energy in the energy composite... . [I[n the quantitative model we have put forward, these two effects roughly cancel out. Subsidies as large as 75% yield only a minuscule reduction in CO_2 emission and temperatures. We conclude that clean energy subsidies are not an effective way to combat global warming."

José-Luis Cruz and Esteban Rossi-Hansberg, "The Economic Geography of Global Warming," *NBER Working Paper No. 28466*, February 2021.

Second, they incite the allocation of resources, especially entrepreneurial efforts, towards the collection of government payments rather than innovation aimed to profit from addressing the problem. For example, subsidies for the purchase of EVs largely drive up the prices charged for the EVs relative to gasoline powered vehicles. (Just like university tuition responding to subsidized student loans and health insurance premiums soaring under Obamacare.)

Third, subsidies encourage fraud. As with most government payments, subsidies attract corruption. The larger the payments, the greater the attraction.

And, fourth, politicians are deciding where resources will be committed.

These drawbacks are serious. Government subsidies generally provide very poor "bang for the buck." And, they almost always result in waste and misallocations of resources. The main advantage of subsidies is that they are politically much easier to enact. For the average voter, subsidies just mean transfers from one group of wealthy people to another. Thus, I would eliminate the various subsidies for alternative fuels and for electric vehicles (mainly enjoyed by the relatively wealthy and the manufacturers). I note that performance-based payments, which are rewards for success, avoid the more serious drawbacks.

REGULATION

President Obama's favorite:
Avoiding the messy process with Congress.

Regulation carries heavy costs for enforcement—inspections, testing, enforcement actions. But, the bigger problem is the perils of unintended consequences. An example: The regulation of tailpipe emissions. In the 1970s, the U.S. imposed emission rules for vehicles, allowing greater latitude for trucks.

"[In 2010,] the Obama administration's EPA used the same logic to carve out an additional and similar exception for large vehicles based on their 'footprints'—the area between their wheels."

...

"Since then, truck and SUV sales have exploded far beyond ranchers and others who actually need such vehicles for their work. SUVs, which a decade ago made up one-third of new vehicle sales, now account for three-fifths.... And car sales have plummeted, from about half of new vehicles sold to just one in five. ...Automakers, meanwhile, can sell larger SUVs and trucks because these smaller "trucks" bring down the overall emissions of the vehicles they sell—helping them comply with federal tailpipe emissions rules."

...

"[T]he rise of these heavier vehicles has not been kind to the planet. A February report by the International Energy Agency ... pointed out that SUVs consume about 20 percent more oil (as fuel) than the average medium-size non-SUV car. The world's 330 million SUVs released 1 billion tons of carbon in 2022.... . If SUVs were a country, they'd rank sixth for emissions in the world, just behind Japan."

"The US Wants to Close an 'SUV Loophole' That Supersized Cars: A new proposal from the EPA would make it less attractive for auto-makers to build big vehicles," *Wired*, April 14, 2023.

"A modest increase between 1973 and 1991 (from 12.9 mpg to 19.6 mpg). No change between 1991 and 2004.... . A modest increase between 2004 and 2008 (from 19.6 mpg to 21.8 mpg). A minor increase between 2008 and 2017 (from 21.8 mpg to 22.3 mpg). [Now, 25 mpg (2022).]"

...

"SUVs reached a record 45% of the market in model year 2021, and pickups increased to 16% market share. The trend away from sedan/wagons ... and towards vehicle types with lower fuel economy and higher CO2 emissions has offset some of the fleetwide benefits that otherwise would have been achieved.... ."

The EPA Automotive Trends Report, 2022.

"The rise of the SUV as the world's pre-eminent car has been so rapid that the consequences of this new status—the altered patterns of urban life, air quality, pedestrian safety, where to park the are still coming into focus. ...But it's increasingly clear that SUVs' most profound impact is playing out within the climate crisis, where their surging popularity is producing a vast new source of planet-cooking emissions. ...Last year, the International Energy Agency made a finding that stunned even its own researchers. SUVs were the second largest cause of the global rise in carbon dioxide emissions over the past decade, eclipsing all shipping, aviation, heavy industry and even trucks, usually the only vehicles to loom larger than them on the road."

Oliver Milman, "How SUVs conquered the world—at the expense of its climate," *The Guardian*, 1 September 2020.

A CARBON TAX

Personally, like Holman Jenkins of the *Wall Street Journal*, I favor taxes on fossil fuels and on activities that generate greenhouse gases, *i.e.*, a "carbon tax." Perhaps, also, a "methane tax" on livestock (increasing the cost of meat) and on natural gas production (based upon estimated leakage).

"Natural gas, long seen as a cleaner alternative to coal and an important tool in the fight to slow global warming, can be just as harmful to the climate, a new study has concluded, unless companies can all but eliminate the leaks that plague its use. It takes as little as 0.2 percent of gas to leak to make natural gas as big a driver of climate change as coal, the study found.

...When power companies generate electricity by burning natural gas instead of coal, they emit only about half the amount of planet-warming carbon dioxide. In the United States, the shift from coal to gas, driven by a boom in oil and gas fracking, has helped reduce carbon emissions from power plants by nearly 40 percent since 2005."

Hiroko Tabuchi, "Leaks Can Make Natural Gas as Bad for the Climate as Coal, a Study Says," *NYT.com*, July 13, 2023 (updated July 19, 2023).

I would do so on the traditional economic theory of externalities. Certain activities have known and identifiable (but not necessarily quantifiable) adverse effects on others. Where those effects are born by society generally, it is reasonable to impose a fee on the activities in question in order to shift some of those burdens to those receiving the benefits, in effect bringing those costs into the price paid. The fees would generate revenue that could be used to compensate society for the burdens being imposed (if not "revenue-neutral"). And, the cost of fossil fuels to its users would better reflect the costs to society.

Of course, those fees are also very likely to cause a reduction in the activities on which the fee is imposed, by making them more expensive relative to alternatives. The tax would create economic opportunities in achieving reductions of energy use, in general, and the use of fossil fuels, in particular. This approach has the advantage of relying on the market to make continuous, dynamic adjustments to changing circumstances and of providing incentives for corrective behavior.

"In sum, the main effect of a carbon tax is to delay dirty energy consumption, by spreading its use over time; less current consumption but more future consumption. The more protracted path for CO_2 emissions has stark implications for the evolution of global temperatures: It flattens the temperature curve. A carbon tax of 200% leads to an evolution of average global temperatures that is as much as 4^0 C lower in the first half of the 22nd century... ."

José-Luis Cruz and Esteban Rossi-Hansberg, "The Economic Geography of Global Warming," *NBER,* Working Paper No. 28466, February 2021.

A carbon tax ultimately will impose burdens on the less well-off. For example, in airline travel, the planes have become much more efficient, reducing emissions per passenger mile, but the number of people flying has soared, as plane travel has become affordable to the average person. In the case of fossil fuels (like gasoline), the increased taxes are likely to be regressive, imposing a greater burden on the average family than on the wealthy. The financial impact could be offset by transfer payments; but, in the end, if there is to be a reduction in the burning of fossil fuels, that reduction will have to be, at least initially, at the expense of those who would otherwise be doing the burning. At a minimum, those persons would have to do less burning. In other words, the working poor need to drive less, and any compensation cannot simply be used to maintain the levels of prior activities. (This plain fact poses a real problem for Democrats.)

Obviously, a carbon tax would not alleviate the global problem unless widely adopted among the nations. Some pressure might be exerted on reluctant nations through tariffs that would indirectly collect the tax, but the free-rider problem will likely persist. That fact presents a policy dilemma that may not be so easy to resolve but cannot be ignored. However, we can afford some number of free riders (as all societies do). And, as technological and cultural changes occur, other nations are likely to follow the leaders.

A carbon tax has sometimes been described as an "insurance policy," which of course it is not. I think of it as simply hedging one's bets. Hedging can often be a sensible public policy choice, to reduce risks modestly at a moderate cost, especially in the face of uncertainty.

So, in short, is it better to incentivize human ingenuity (i) to seek to reduce carbon emissions or (ii) to seek to reap government benefits? Where do we want the talent directed?

"However it's designed, carbon pricing stands out as a unifying model, which aligns the incentives of investors, business, and government to decarbonize industry and finance green technology... ." Lynn Forester de Rothchild, "Why The World Must Set a Price on Carbon: At the COP28 climate conference nations missed an opportunity to set a global price on carbon—a key tool for ensuring a just transition," *Time*, December 20, 2023.

Conclusion

"In 2008, after the Obama Democrats won full control in Washington, Al Gore had an epiphany: Unpopular, tax-like measures were no longer necessary. The climate problem could be solved with subsidies. Who doesn't like a handout? A proposed oil tax disappeared from the Obama campaign website. Overnight, the Democratic focus went from climate policy to climate pork."

Holman Jenkins, "Biden's Climate Is Serious—About Green Pork," WSJ.com, July 17, 2020.

The Biden Administration is now in a bind. The subsidies have not reduced carbon emissions (the rather dramatic reductions in the U.S. have come largely from the increased use of natural gas—enabled by fracking). Biden needs something that appears dramatic, but does not place burdens on the working-class voters. So, no carbon tax. Instead, he acts to obstruct North American oil and gas production (the obvious "bad" guys), while simultaneously encouraging OPEC to expand production so gas prices do not go up. What a plan! Carbon emissions are unaffected, more money flows from the U.S. to the OPEC nations (including Russia), yet Green "Brownie" Points are earned.

A "win," just not for the American people.

Surprised? Why?

"Every time government intervenes in unpredictable energy markets, politicians get it wrong."

...

"Take the Fuel Use Act of 1978. The young Sen. Joe Biden and Rep. Al Gore were among those who championed the act, which mandated the use of coal to generate electricity because so-called experts were sure the U.S. was running out of oil and natural gas. ...Then in 1980 the Carter administration spent billions of dollars on renewable-energy subsidies and even a business called Synthetic Fuels Corp. that went bankrupt six years later. When Ronald Reagan let the market work by deregulating energy, oil production soared and prices tumbled. No one worried about running out of oil anymore. ...That is, until Barack Obama came into office. In 2011, when gasoline prices rose, Mr. Obama said that 'we can't just drill our way out of the problem.' ...So instead Mr. Obama spent millions on now bankrupt propositions such as the solar-energy company Solyndra."

Harold Hamm, "Washington Has Energy Production All Wrong: Biden was wrong to back a 1978 law mandating the use of coal, and he's wrong to push solar and wind now," *WSJ.com*, August 6, 2023.

Climate "Justice"

The use of the word "justice" here is misguided and counterproductive. But, it is widely used, nonetheless, partly for that very reason.

I.

Over the last 20 years, there have been discussions about how we might provide compensation to victims of climate change, particularly in the U.S. The basic problem is that unlike localized pollution, no particular source is the cause of the injury. One suggestion for the U.S. is the establishment of a no-fault compensation fund, where claimants must show direct injury and would surrender their legal claims for those injuries. *See, e.g.,* Melissa Farris, "Compensating Climate Change Victims: The Climate Compensation Fund as an Alternative to Tort Litigation," *Sea Grant Law and Policy Journal*, Vol. 2, No. 2 (Winter 2009/2010).

Importantly, funding would be sought from ongoing emitters of greenhouse gasses, constituting a cost of continuing to emit.

> "A CCF should be designed to provide a no-fault compensation scheme with the dual purpose of (1) **ensuring fair compensation to climate change victims** and (2) **shielding fossil fuel-dependent industries from crushing liability and possible insolvency.**...Funding for the CCF remains a challenging factor. As a starting point, however, the CCF could emphasize a 'polluter pays' principle in which **fossil fuel-dependent industries contribute to the fund as an incentive to limit liability.** "

Id. (emphasis added)

Of course, such a funding mechanism is similar to a "carbon tax," which I favor. The producers of fossil fuels would face higher costs and the consumers of fossil fuels would face higher prices. As a result, use would go down, producers' profits would be reduced and production would decline. Thus, fewer emissions of greenhouse gasses.

II.

In 2022, the United Nations adopted a different approach.

> "In a historic first, countries have agreed to set up a fund to help pay for the devastating impact of climate change on poorer nations.... . [T]he final agreement [was] reached at the United Nations environmental summit, known as COP27, in the Egyptian Red Sea resort city of Sharm el-Sheikh. ...The creation of a fund was approved by almost 200 countries ..., after the European Union and other nations were left disappointed at the lack of an agreement to reduce the burning of fossil fuels in the first place. ...Wealthier nations had previously rejected the proposals for creating a specific loss and damage fund at the last climate change summit in Glasgow, Scotland."

Mithil Aggarwal, "Historic compensation fund approved at U.N. climate talks," *Associated Press*, Nov. 19, 2022.(emphasis added).

A supporting organization explained:

> "Yeb Saño, Head of the Greenpeace delegation attending the COP[,] said: 'The agreement for a Loss and Damage Finance Fund marks **a new dawn for climate justice.**

> ...

> [T]hese negotiations have been marred by attempts to **trade adaptation and mitigation against loss and damage.** ... Moving forward into discussion of the details of the Fund, we need to ensure that **the countries and corporations most responsible for the climate crisis make the biggest contribution.'"**

Laura Bergamo, "COP27 Loss and Damage Finance Fund a down payment on climate justice," *Greenpeace Canada*, 20 November, 2022 (emphasis added).

This "Loss and Damage" fund is explicitly divorced from the reduction of greenhouse gas emissions. It would only help pay for, not reduce, the impact of climate change. The fund is supportable on the same grounds as any other disaster relief and, perhaps, foreign aid.

The efforts, however, to tie funding to prior benefits from the use of fossil fuels or prior greenhouse gas emissions ("laying blame") seem misguided and detrimental to me. Certainly, some countries grew and prospered based on access to cheap fossil fuels, but others stagnated despite access to cheap fossil fuels. No one is to blame; and, everyone benefited from the resulting technology that provided abundant food supplies, modern medicine, mobile phones, the internet, as well as enormous improvements in global standards of living. Moreover, there is no way to attribute causation where the problem is not anyone's emissions, but the aggregate of all.

The relief provided to suffering nations will not ameliorate the climate crisis. Paying to prevent deforestation would be useful, but helping the smaller nations to employ "clean energy" would have a truly *de minimus* effect. Those nations should not now be denied cheap fossil fuel. And, those nations will enjoy the new technology as it becomes economic. The real problem is the expanding emissions from large countries that is continuing to occur even after the deleterious effects have been recognized. From China, India and, even, Australia.

However, if this approach would reduce the politics and increase the likelihood that assistance would be proportional to need, I would be in favor. What we do not need is a fight among potential beneficiaries over the fund or politicians using it for their purposes. Can the UN devise a workable, non-corrupt method of distribution? Who knows?

III.

Another approach was recently revealed:

"The world's top court will for the first time advise on countries' legal obligations to fight climate change, following a UN resolution on Wednesday. The International Court of Justice will now prepare an advisory opinion that could be cited in climate court cases. The motion came from Vanuatu, a low-lying Pacific island nation facing peril from rising sea levels. ...Governments may learn that not curbing warming gases breaks international law. Courts in countries around the world may take their lead from the decision, and it may shape UN negotiations on climate change, and impact decisions by fossil fuel companies on their long-term investments."

Matt McGrath, "Climate change: World's top court to weigh in," *BBC News*, March 29, 2023.

This development could be quite constructive, if it is not politicized. I am assuming that we could get a statement of the obligations and responsibilities of nations with respect to serious externalities going forward (not judgments on past actions). The opinion might also give guidance on enforcement. I like approaches that provide incentives.

Even an advisory opinion will provide standards for judging behavior and can influence future actions. It could reduce offenders' ability to obfuscate, to dissemble, to evade, thereby focusing public pressure within and without individual countries.

IV.

In December 2023, COP28 was held in Dubai, with almost 200 countries patticipating and 100,000 registered attendees, some 70,000 of whom showed up. It reflects some interesting developments.

1. The Loss and Damage fund "was formally established to offer money to countries that have suffered irreparable economic losses and damages. The money pledged to that fund was modest: around $700 million. The United States committed $17 million, which one climate campaigner from India, Harjeet Singh, called 'paltry' compared with other countries. The United Arab Emirates and Germany committed $100 million each." Somini Sengupta, "Four Takeaways From the COP28 Climate Summit," *NYT.com*, December 13, 2023.

2. There are a large number of lobbyists present, reflecting that climate policy has been recognized to be a political activity in which large amounts of money will be lost and gained.

See Rachel Sherrington, Clare Carlile and Hazel Healy , "Big meat and dairy lobbyists turn out in record numbers at Cop28: Food and agriculture firms have sent three times as many delegates to the climate summit as last year," *The Guardian*, 8 December 2023.

"More than 100 world leaders at this year's United Nations climate summit agreed to make their farm and food systems a key part of their plans to fight climate change, seeking improvements in a sector that accounts for about a

---

third of planet-warming emissions." Melina Walling , "Agriculture gets its day at COP28, but experts see big barriers to cutting emissions," *The Washington Post*, December 9, 2023.

"Cop28 organisers granted attendance to at least 475 lobbyists working on carbon capture and storage (CCS), unproven technologies that climate scientists say will not curtail global heating... ." Nina Lakhani, "At least 475 carbon-capture lobbyists attending Cop28," *The Guardian*, 8 December 2023.

"Fossil fuel interests have infiltrated the conference in other ways, including a record 2,456 fossil fuel lobbyists in attendance, according to Kick Big Polluters Out, as well as four times the number of oil and gas-affiliated industry officials attending compared to last year." Peter Wade, "COP28 Climate Summit President Has 'Direct Conflict of Interest,' Al Gore Says," *Rolling Stone*, December 10, 2023.

3. Sharp divisions appeared over the official position to be taken as to the future of fossil fuels. Some say that a phase out should be declared, the OPEC nations oppose it and some less developed nations argue that a phase out should be in stages, starting with the wealthy nations and with themselves being last.

"A coalition of more than 80 countries including the United States, the European Union and small island nations are pushing for an agreement at COP28 that includes language to 'phase out' fossil fuels, the main source of greenhouse gas emissions that scientists blame for global warming. They are coming up against tough opposition led by the oil producer group OPEC and its allies."

...

"The conference has yielded a slew of other commitments from countries to hit targets like tripling renewable energy and nuclear power deployments, slash coal use and curb emissions of the powerful greenhouse gas methane. The International Energy Agency (IEA) on Sunday said these pledges—if honoured—would lower global energy-related greenhouse gas emissions by 4 billion metric tonnes of carbon dioxide equivalent in 2030. While the figure is substantial, it represents only about a third of the emissions gap that needs to be closed in the next six years to limit warming to 1.5C above pre-industrial levels, as agreed to in the 2015 Paris Agreement, the IEA said."

David Stanway, Gloria Dickie and Kate Abnett, "Big divisions loom over fossil fuels as COP28 talks head into final phase," *Reuters*, December 10, 2023.

"India's environment minister, Bhupender Yadav, on Saturday demanded 'equity and justice' in U.N. climate negotiations, holding that rich countries should be leading global climate action. The comments underlined India's long-held position that, as a developing country, it should not be a forced to cut its energy-related emissions—even as it is the world's third-biggest emitting country after China and the United States."

Gloria Dickie, "India at COP28 insists on 'equity' in climate talks," *Reuters*, December 9, 2023.

The opposing view does not challenge the threat from greenhouse emissions, but the conclusion that fossil fuels should have no future role as an energy source, arguing that what we need to reduce are emissions not fossil fuel use itself. Sufficient abatement technologies could enable the dramatic reduction of greenhouse gasses and the continued use of fossil fuels. As a logical matter, this position is correct. There is also no logical reason to make a decision now. But, the symbolic and emotional aspects predominate the debate.

It is not surprising that nations whose wealth depends on oil oppose a declared phase out of their source of revenue. However, they should begin to accumulate cash and explore diversification. In addition, it would be fair and costless to allow the underdeveloped nations to continue to use fossil fuels as long as they want. Technological advances should enable them to skip over some stages of development, like cellular telephone technology allowed various nations to bypass the land based service and avoid the investment in lines and poles.

4. The final declaration, approved by 198 countries and territories, commits parties to "transitioning away from fossil fuels in energy systems, in a just, orderly and equitable manner ... so as to achieve net zero by 2050 in keeping with the science."

The last minute changes to gain the support of Saudi Arabia consisted of replacing "phase out" with "transitioning away from," having the declaration refer to uses "in energy systems" rather than all uses and the use of the word "just" to modify the "manner" of implementation, not the "transitioning" itself.

The result is a statement addressed to ameliorating the dangers and not placing blame. Of course, that result was not what some wanted. For the activists and less developed nations, the focus is on "justice," which apparently requires the placement of blame and transfer of money.

"[M]any in the developing world ... say any commitment to phasing out fossil fuels must be 'fair, funded, and fast', with the rich polluting countries transitioning first. ...Mohamed Adow, the director of the ... thinktank Power Shift Africa, said **the money was key.** ...African countries would be willing to side with the rich world but only if they received assurances that their transition to renewable energy would be fully funded... ." Fiona Harvey and

Nina Lakhani, "Last-ditch attempt to forge fresh Cop28 deal after original rejected," *The Guardian*, 12 December 2023 (emphasis added).

5. The E.U., the U K. and, perhaps, the U S. are planning to impose a type of "carbon tax" on goods imported from countries that are high producers of greenhouse emissions. The goal is to create a more level playing field for domestic producers who are incurring greater costs as a result of efforts to reduce such emissions.

"A European Union plan to tax the carbon pollution emitted to make goods imported from countries like India and China has sparked a debate at the United Nations climate conference in Dubai, as poorer countries fear such tariffs will harm livelihoods and economic growth."

...

"A recent study by the U.N. Conference on Trade and Development found that a tax of $44 per ton of carbon emitted would slash pollution from the supply chain by half. It also estimated that rich countries would make $2.5 billion from the tax, but poorer countries might lose up to $5.9 billion."

...

"Sen. Sheldon Whitehouse of Rhode Island and Rep. Suzan DelBene of Washington, both Democrats, on Wednesday reintroduced legislation to create the "Clean Competition Act" that would similarly set a fee on imports from high-carbon emitting producers."

Gauray Saini, Press Trust of India, Sibi Arasu, Jamey Keaton, "The EU wants to put a tax on emissions from imports. It's irked some other nations at COP28," *A.P.*, December 10, 2023.

Presumably, these are directed at India and China. As such, they may make some marginal reduction in carbon emissions and could tend to promote some action from India and China to reduce their use of coal.

Some, like U.S. Senator Sheldon Whitehouse, view such tariffs as part of "climate justice." *Id*.

> "Whitehouse said such measures would generate revenues for climate justice and improve the pathway toward 'climate safety'... . ...'I have zero remorse about CBAM from a climate justice point of view,' he said, insisting that his legislation would both grant exemptions to the least-developed countries and focus on the worst polluters in any given industry."

Go figure.

CHAPTER X

Abortion

"FIRST THINGS"

I did not take a class with Hadley Arkes while I was at Amherst College; although, I knew him pretty well since he was effectively a *de facto* member of the Economics Department (presumably, because it was the one bastion of conservative to moderate thinking at the time).

At some point, I did read at least part of his book *First Things: An Inquiry into the First Principles of Morals and Justice* (1986). *First Things* is a work of moral philosophy, in which Prof. Arkes sets out and defends his positions. I cited it as a source for a handful of propositions of philosophy in my own book three decades later, *Limits of Science? Important Things We Do Not Know About Nearly Everything* (2016), I used Prof. Arkes and his book as a source. I did so largely as a matter of convenience. There were other options for the same points.

Background

Shortly after writing my book (just before publication), I became aware of substantial on-going criticism of Prof. Arkes among members of my class at Amherst, which was celebrating its 45th reunion. The vitriolic comments were directed mainly at his positions in opposition to homosexuality, gay marriage and abortion. So, I rethought my choice of authorities. In criticizing Prof. Arkes, these classmates pointed to statements in which he supposedly equated homosexuality with other forms of behavior that were uniformly perceived as immoral or uncivilized. (These statements were not in his book but in more recent writings of articles and commentaries.)

I assumed that Prof. Arkes was using an established form of logical argument to attack the proposition at issue (*reductio ad absurdum*). The argument is that if the proposition at issue can be reduced to a proposition broadly perceived to be absurd without crossing any principled lines of distinction, then the propositional issue must be incorrect (or, in this context, immoral). (More typically, the argument is presented in the form that a proposition is true when its negation leads to an absurdity.)

While, in some sense, since the advocate is saying that he sees no principled distinction between the propositional issue and the absurd or immoral proposition, he may be said to be arguing that they are equivalent; but, I think he is really posing to the reader the question of identifying the principled distinction—where to draw the line. To me, that is an important difference. The invited response is not the condemnation of the author, but the answer to the question. However, his essays were admittedly quite blunt or worse.

In any event, all of this led me to go back and reread *First Things*. I wanted to see what I thought of the arguments he made therein. Not so much, it turns out. But, then again, I had also criticized his arguments in *Limits of Science*.

The opening argument

In his book, Prof. Arkes builds his argument for "necessary truths" on the following construct: He asks, is the proposition "there is no truth" a statement that is true or false? If it is false, then there must be some things that are true. If, instead, that statement is true, we then will know that there is at least one statement that is "true" and, given that, there may well be more. Thus, Arkes says, it must be the case that there are some "truths".

How satisfying is that logical exercise? To me, not very. To say that it is "true" that "there is no truth" does not obviously lead to the conclusion that there is "truth." Indeed, if there is "truth," then the proposition must be false. More importantly, however, if it is the case that "there is no truth," then it is not meaningful to demand that one declare whether that proposition is true or false. The reason is that if there is no truth, then the distinction between true and false is meaningless. If "truth" does not exist, then the adjective "true" is simply inapplicable.

Prof. Arkes also argues that it is a matter of "necessity" that "two contradictory propositions cannot both be true." He treats that proposition as a matter of *a priori* truth, that is, something we know to be true independent of our life experiences, "knowledge," with which we are born. This "law of contradiction" plays a significant role in his subsequent arguments. He repeatedly attempts to show that each of various positions inevitably lead to a contradiction, which he claims disproves those positions.

I have a problem here as well. I have trouble seeing how the "law of contradiction" can exist or have meaning independent of or before language. The reason is that the propositions must be set forth, and they can only be set forth in language. I can imagine that *Homo*, pre-language, could have understood that two inconsistent states could not exist simultaneously. For example, something cannot be both alive and dead, or it cannot be both day and night. However, contradictory propositions must be set forth in language.

So, can something simultaneously both "exist" and "not exist"? Can something both "be" and "not be"? Can something be both "true" and "false"?

Presumably, Prof. Arkes says definitely not. Well, apart from the fact that modern particle physics and quantum mechanics can be interpreted as providing affirmative answers to all three questions, these questions can only have meaning in "context." The answers will depend upon what the "something" is, on the perspective of the observer or multiple observers (possibly with different perspectives) and upon the meaning of the words in quotation marks (exist, be, true) and their supposed opposites. This is not so mysterious; it is the stuff of which many riddles are made.

The application

Next, Arkes asserts that the fundamental moral principles are "necessary truths" because of the related propositions that man is capable of reasoning (the basic elements of logic) and man has a moral sense, that is, a recognition of the difference between right and wrong. In other words, man uniquely among known living species is able to reason about moral propositions and to understand the concept of "justification." That characteristic, he asserts, entitles human beings to special treatment. For example, based upon the assumption that all people are "created equal," it is morally wrong to deprive a human being of life or liberty or, presumably, property without "justification"—without a logical explanation founded on a concept of justice or of right and wrong.

Prof. Arkes also seems to suggest that one can establish the existence of a necessary truth based upon an argument that failure to see that principle as a truth puts one on a slippery slope that will lead to clearly unacceptable results. The proposition would be that if conduct A is acceptable, then there may be no logical basis of distinction to assert that conduct C or D is not acceptable. But, this proposition simply states the question of whether there is a basis of distinction; it does not answer it.

I agree that man is (apparently) uniquely capable of reasoning about matters of morality. But, I can only say that that is true once man has the concept of morality or right and wrong. Is that initial concept a "necessary truth"? My dispute is not with the notion of *a priori* knowledge (or even so much with the "law of contradiction"). I accept that we are born with the concept of causation, with a sense of the meaning of space and spatial relationships and with the notion of time. But, of relevance here is the question whether man is born with a moral sense, the concept of right and wrong, good and evil? As to that question, I find myself quite uncertain. Does the concept of the moral arise from our genetic makeup or from our cultural and societal experiences? Interestingly, one can "explain" the emergence of many of these *a priori* understandings or constructs on evolutionary bases, as characteristics capable of giving an advantage in survival and reproduction. Can the same be said for morality?

I can imagine some convoluted explanations about how a sense of "right and wrong" provided an evolutionary advantage for *Homo sapiens,* but it does not seem very compelling. A better approach to an explanation seems to lie in the area of community and societal organization. As man began to live in groups, it would make sense that a set of rules concerning behavior would give a group advantage in the struggle with other groups over limited resources. In fact, law and morals could even have played an important role in the family group; although, I would think that the given power hierarchy in the family could be sufficient. In any event, the suggestion here is that the source of morality may not be in the capacity of man to reason, but in the strong incentives for man to live in communities, in being a social animal. If so, would that take morals outside of "necessary truths" and place it in the category of a construct of society? Alternatively, its appearance as part of community life could be genetic, facilitating successful reproduction not directly but as a result of the success of the group.

It may be that child psychologists can answer the question of whether the moral sense is innate or culturally derived (and, perhaps, they have already done so). But, if this issue depends upon a factual investigation, then it is "contingent" and not "necessary." As such, matters of fact seem to be fundamentally different from what we have discussed as *a priori* knowledge. On the other hand, we identify moral reasoning as a distinguishing and unique characteristic of mankind. Presumably, were we to discover some other life form that also engaged in moral reasoning, the moral principles that apply to humans should be extended to that other life form.

Actually, I have recently read a book by a leading social psychologist, Jonathan Haidt, that addresses some of these issues. The book is *The Righteous Mind: Why Good People Are Divided by Politics and Religion* (2013). Based on the results of a host of empirical studies, Haidt asserts that the sense of morality appears to be an innate human characteristic, but the details of what is right and wrong are derived from the culture in which the individual is raised. Thus, e.g., the scope of morality is much narrower in Western, individualistic societies than it is in Eastern, family and community-centered societies. As he says: "We're born to be righteous, but we have to learn what, exactly, people like us should be righteous about" (*id.* p. 31).

In addition, Haidt explains that these studies demonstrate that typical moral reactions to events arise instinctively. Thereafter, the person may engage in logical reasoning about that reaction, but the reasoning is most often an effort to articulate a *post hoc* justification for the moral judgement already made, not an effort to reach a judgement. This is not "moral reasoning" as Arkes use the concept.

I have already noted that the existence of an innate sense of morality could have an evolutionary basis arising out of man's social being. Similarly, specific moral rules could have "evolved" in the competition among alternative cultures. Obviously, however, these supposedly empirically- based conclusions are at odds with the philosophical views of Arkes (and Kant).

I do not actually know where to go with this line of thinking. But, it does seem to me that a credible case can be made that what Arkes calls "the first principles of morals and of justice" arise as a matter of logic from what we as a society have decided to identify as distinguishing characteristics of humanness. But, if that is the basis of the principles, then the principles presumably could change as the societal consensus changes. This approach is in direct conflict with Arkes.

The conclusion

Moving forward, Prof. Arkes observes that if these moral principles arc necessary truths, then it is insufficient to say that "I will live by these principles but leave to every other person the decision as to what to do." The reason is that if they are truths, then logic demands that everyone be expected to abide by them (recognizing that there will be individuals who decide to break the rules). Obviously, society has many rules. But, that fact certainly does not establish that those rules are based on necessary truths, just as the fact that a principle is not reflected in a law of society does not mean that it is not a necessary truth.

As an aside, I would note that Arkes' conclusion about the need to impose moral rules on others is not a necessary implication of religion. For example, I do not understand Christianity to advocate that its views of right and wrong be imposed on others by law. Its religious teachings, as I understand them, are directed to the individual and to the individual's personal salvation; they are not to be forced on people but to be chosen by them. Christ's well known injunction "Render unto Caesar..." reflects the distinction between the world of government and law and that of the spirit and morality. The advice "Feed the hungry, clothe the naked" was not addressed to the State or to the governing powers, but to individuals who were urged to give of themselves (not to redistribute the property of others).

Prof. Arkes' conclusions seem more in the nature of "natural law." As I understand it, "natural law" is based on the assumption that actual laws do or should reflect that which is morally right. But, what is the basis of that assumption? I did not find "natural law" jurisprudence very persuasive when I took the course 45 years ago with Lon Fuller. I still do not.

THE ISSUE OF ABORTION

Prof. Arkes devotes his final two chapters to the matter of abortion. I have considerable sympathy with his concern about the subject. It is difficult to articulate why the "taking" of the life of a newborn infant moments after birth (even through the failure to feed or provide shelter) can lead to charges of murder or manslaughter, yet doing so through affirmative action only weeks earlier may be perfectly legal. Nonetheless, I again have issues with his arguments.

He frames the question in terms of when the new life can be said to become "human," identifying various characteristics of the unborn fetus and looks at how those characteristics, when existing in a living person, are treated in the law. He notes that the law provides protection to persons with severe disabilities, retardation, mental illness, on life support and with other conditions that limit or prevent the display of characteristics that we would generally identify as part of being a full human.

Then, he says, why should the unborn sharing some of these characteristics be subject to having his or her life taken "without justification"?

By looking to the accepted legal standards, Prof. Arkes seems to assume that what is and has always (or often) been protected by the law are rights that are "necessary" as a matter of moral principle. Yet, that assumption seems to be resting on somewhat flimsy grounds. We know that the law sets forth many rules that have no or little moral content. In addition, legal rules are often shaped by pragmatic considerations, such as the benefits of having a "bright line." Finally, some of these legal rules have changed and continue to change overtime. For example, we have seen already, and it seems likely that we shall see further, some significant changes in the laws concerning suicide and assisted suicide.

So, if the question is when does an unborn child become a "person" or become "human," I do not find Prof. Arkes references to the legal treatment of various categories of individuals who have been born as very useful. In fairness, he does also discuss the difficulties of basing the test on various biological or developmental characteristics or stages. Scientific progress has pushed the conclusions of many of those tests earlier and earlier in the pregnancy. Of course, the embryo is "human" biologically from the beginning. I just do not think that this is the right question.

The right to choose

Most proponents of abortion frame the issue in terms of the right of the woman to make decisions about her own body. The law generally provides considerable latitude with respect to what one legally can do to one's own body, such as cosmetic surgery, decorative mutilations, and the like. In addition, although the law generally prohibits suicide, people are normally permitted to engage in extraordinarily reckless and dangerous activities where the likelihood of death or the risk of serious injury to health is significant. This argument is sometimes augmented by the assertion that in relation to the mother the unborn fetus it is really a parasite. Presumably, the suggestion is that a person has the right to eliminate a parasite, whenever the person so chooses. The "viability" standard implicitly reflects this categorization.

The law in other areas

With respect to the question of the obligations of the woman to the unborn child, I note that the law generally provides very few duties or obligations of one person to come to the assistance of another. For example, one has no legal duty to feed a starving person (and, it is generally ille- gal to steal food in order to save one's life or the lives of one's children), to assist an injured person, to rescue a drowning child or otherwise to inconvenience oneself or put oneself at risk for the sake of another. The exceptions occur where there are special relationships between the two persons, like parent and child, teacher and student or doctor and patient. Indeed, certain obligations are imposed on parents with respect to their own children or others in their guardianship, once those children have been born; but, that seems to beg the question.

More pertinent perhaps are various criminal laws that can be applied to the conduct of a mother-to-be that causes the death of the unborn children, conduct like drug use, attempted suicide or reckless driving. *See. e.g*, Anna North "She had a stillborn baby. Now she's being charged with murder. Her case is part of a nationwide problem, advocates say," *Vox*, November 8, 2019. These laws in some 38 states and in Federal statutes apply to domestic partners and even strangers whose actions cause the death of the fetus. Most of the laws have been enacted in the last 40 years, changing the prior legal standards presumably to provide more protection to pregnant women and their families. *See, e.g.*, Sandra L. Smith, "Fetal Homicide: Woman or Fetus as Victim? A Survey of

Current State Approaches and Recommendations for Future State Application," *William & Mary Law Review*, Volume 41, Issue 5, 2000.

However, these laws are now being criticized as part of the attack on all legal restrictions on abortion, because of their possible applicability to such acts. It is anomalous, at least, that a partner's action that causes the loss of an unborn child can be charged as murder whereas action by the mother with the same result is legal.

I think that we need a comprehensive rethinking, and then rewriting, of all of these laws.

One could phrase the question in terms of whether the woman has an obligation to take certain actions or to refrain from certain actions with respect to her own body in order to preserve another life, in this case that of her own unborn child. You might object, "But, abortion is generally an affirmative action designed and intended to end the life of the unborn child". Yet, perhaps, there are principles we can formulate based upon affirmative action versus non-action and on intent. Certainly these concepts are prevalent in our existing laws. Of course, such an approach is certainly different from that advocated by Prof. Arkes.

Justification

It is possible that a relatively broad consensus could be reached on justification, even if one acknowledges that an embryo is a "human life" at a very early stage. The life or health of the mother it is clearly a factor that could constitute "justification." So could be conception occurring through rape or lack of consent. For different reasons, for pregnancy resulting from incest or where there appear to be signifIcant abnormalities. (Prof. Arkes does not find these examples to be "sufficient" justification, but I do not see how he could claim that those conclusions to be "necessary truths.")

I note that "justification" in other contexts does not necessarily turn on blaming the victim. For example, self-defense looks at the reasonable beliefs of the one who killed, not at the blame-worthiness of the one who was killed. And, I believe that some degree of pragmatism is inevitably required in the application of the standards of "justification," whatever they are. For example, it is obvious that any "justifications" would be vacuous if the abortion has to occur within four or six weeks of conception. In addition, the application of the standards must be objective and the outcomes recognizable.

So, it may be that articulation of the "justifications" could satisfy the views of most of the people not on the two extremes.

Where to Now?

All of this discussion is in a slightly different and more abstract context than the issue that gets the most publicity: whether the majority of voters in any particular jurisdiction can place legal limits on what a woman can do with an unborn fetus or a potential life.

One would think that there should generally be fairly wide discretion left to the political process. We recognize that the community has the right to curb actions contrary to the common interest and to protect its members (especially, those who cannot protect themselves). But, we acknowledge that there are fundamental human rights that cannot be abridged. So, how do we define the rights of the individual in relationship to the rights (and responsibilities) of the community? Maybe a resolution of the tensions between individual and community interests can be fashioned in terms of the concept of "justification" discussed above.

Unfortunately, rational and civil debate has been difficult. Certainly, much harm has been done by the value-burdened language used by both sides in "framing" the issue. And, of course, in the U.S. for some 50 years, the matter of abortion has been largely in the hands of the Federal courts, so most of these questions have been sidelined. If the question is neither when does life begin nor when does life become human, then it must be when is human life to be protected by society. What are the proposed answers to that question?

There simply does not seem to be a principled position among the prochoice advocates that acknowledges morality. If we were to be given a proposed answer, then we could start an actual dialogue. A consensus might emerge. Note that in Europe, "abortion is legal in most countries, usually with limits that are more strict than America's and generally as a result of democratic choice." The Editorial Board, "Europe's Abortion Lesson: How democracies compromised on the issue after political debate, not judicial fiat," *WSJ.com*, May 8, 2022.

However, I do think that it is clearly preposterous to assert that a woman's right freely to elect to have an abortion is clear-cut as a moral matter. A moral sensibility requires, at least, the belief that there are some things that matter more than "me." If one acknowledges that moral principles are relevant to human behavior and that human life is "special," then the issue of abortion necessarily involves serious and troubling questions not susceptible to easy answers.

I suppose that that assertion itself would offend many pro-choice advocates, a fact that troubles me in and of itself.

DOBBS V. JACKSON WOMEN'S HEALTH

There are three separate types of issues relating to abortion: the morality, the legality and the Constitutionality.

On the first, I have trouble imposing an answer on someone else, in part, because I believe that moral assessments are hard (impossible?) to base only on objective, observable acts. The person matters. His or her perceptions, intentions, state of mind are all relevant in assessing the moral dimensions of any act. The second category, in contrast, requires objective, identifiable and observable criteria providing for the application of rules. It is also a political matter, to be determined ultimately by the people. The third category is in some disarray. There is the issue of when the Constitution attaches. I would assume at birth, but it is an open question. Then, there is the issue of limits to the impositions a government can place on individual freedom of action.

I have opinions on what those limitations on government ought to be. For example, I think personal sovereignty over one's body should control for at least the first trimester of pregnancy. But, it has been too long since I studied Constitutional Law for me to argue a Constitutional basis. Yet, what should be the point at which a life is protected? My personal view is not at conception. Indeed, I accept the use of the morning-after pill as just another form of birth control, subject only to regulation for safety concerns. At the other end, for the rare late term abortion, I think sufficient reasons should be required, and I would make the provider legally responsible, not the woman. I believe that the government has a legitimate and substantial interest in protecting the yet–to-be born, an interest that increases as a pregnancy advances. I view that interest as being very insubstantial or nonexistent during the fragile, uncertain first three months of a pregnancy and as becoming very significant after "viability."

The new opinion, *Dobbs v. Jackson Women's Health*, is quite unfortunate.

For example, "the state interest in protecting fetal life plays no part in the majority's analysis. To the contrary, the majority takes pride in not expressing a view 'about the status of the fetus.' The majority's departure from *Roe* and [*Planned Parenthood v.*] *Casey* rests instead—and only—on whether a woman's decision to end a pregnancy involves any Fourteenth Amendment liberty interest... ." Dissent at 26.)

Still, I think *Roe v. Wade* was a poor decision. The majority in *Dobbs* rather effectively demolishes it, but it is an easy target. Indeed, even the dissent chose not try to defend *Roe*, focusing on *Casey*. However, *Casey* is not a persuasive opinion on the underlying issue of the Constitutional right. It was a 3, 2, 4 opinion. and is most relevant on the *stare decisis* question.

I would have sided with the Chief Justice. The basic underlying Constitutional question was not actually presented by *Dobbs*, despite the positions of the litigants. The Missouri statue could have been upheld on its own terms. The majority said "Why put it off?" Of course, the answer, given by the Chief, is because that that is good, sound jurisprudence. To resolve only the actual issue presented and only that. Unfortunately, *Roe* had made the same mistake in overreaching to espouse a broad Constitutional right. The minority in dissent was put in an impossible position by the Chief Justices' concurrence. Unless one of the majority five would also join, they would be voting against *Roe* by joining him and still would lose on the underlying right. (Of course, I do not know how the dynamics played out, but I would be highly critical of Justice Kavanaugh if he made a decision to refuse to go along with the liberal three in joining the Chief.)

In *Dobbs*, in any event, the majority placed far too much emphasize on the traditional standard for a right to be implied under the Fourteenth Amendment: "the Court has long asked whether the right is 'deeply rooted in [our] history and tradition' and whether it is essential to our Nation's 'scheme of ordered liberty.'" (Majority at 12.) There are significant situations where that standard makes no sense, especially if the "right" is too narrowly defined. This is such a case. The majority asks whether "abortion" was a right well established in our history and finds it was not. Of course not. As the dissent points out: "*Casey* similarly recognized the need to extend the constitutional sphere of liberty to a previously excluded group. The Court then understood, as the majority today does not, that the men who ratified the Fourteenth Amendment and wrote the state laws of the time did not view women as full and equal citizens." *Id.* at 23.)

It makes no sense to ask if a woman's right to elect to terminate a pregnancy was well established in 1780 or 1868. The question should not be focused on "abortion". The proper inquiry would be with respect to analogous rights of white men or, in 1776, of white male property owners. Analogous rights would be those related to men's control over their own bodies and over their choice of livelihoods and their homes, issues like surgery, medical treatment, sterilization or forced labor. Conscription might also be viewed as similar to coerced motherhood. And, suicide.

The important point is that these and other lines of inquiry could have been pursued in a case actually presenting the fundamental question. Perhaps, the outcome would have been the same, but the arguments and analyses would not have been. The Court should have waited for a case that asked whether women ever have a right to terminate a pregnancy. Say, where a woman was made pregnant without her consent or even over her objections and resistance (like by rape). Make her also a minor. Can the state constitutionally prohibit that girl from terminating that pregnancy? I would hope not.

As already stated, I think personal sovereignty over one's body should control for at least the first trimester of pregnancy. I do not think abortion should be considered murder by the mother under any circumstances. (Actually, I do not think that the killing of a young child by a parent should be considered as "murder" either, but it should be a serious crime.) I also do not favor treating the securing of an abortion as a crime under reasonable circumstances. But, the performance of an abortion after 24 weeks without proper justification should be a crime, comparable to murder.

Nonetheless, I object to calling abortion a "right." It is something that society may (and, I think, should) tolerate as part of a choice about pregnancy, but not something for which society should offer approval or encouragement.

The harder question is the large middle ground which was at issue in *Dobbs*. For the period after 13 weeks, I do not have a test or standard to put forward. I would be comfortable leaving that question to the voters.

Of course, the ruling was met with dramatic overreactions. One political party saw the prospect finally of a winning issue, based on outrage, not on the merits of a position. The result of *Dobbs* would not be changed by the mid-term national elections (or the next Presidential election). But, anger might win votes, being cast in revenge, to get even. So, we hear the cries of the "end of democracy," an "authoritarian state," the loss of "freedoms and our personal autonomy," *etc*. Irrational or just cynically manipulative? But, the ruling only returned the issue of abortion to the people, to the voters in each of the 50 States. It was *Roe* and other "substantive due process" decisions that were anti-democracy and authoritarian, where the majority of 9 justices overrode the will of the people. *Dobbs* took away nothing from the people.

One may be quite unhappy with the laws that ultimately will result because of the recent Court decisions. But, most of these Supreme Court decisions have returned power and policymaking to the States and the U.S. Congress. In other words, to the people. It is pretty difficult to call that an "assault on democracy," at least, with a straight face (and, certainly, with a pure heart).

CHAPTER XI

Now and Later

I have been waiting to wake from this nightmare before attempting to address the issues below, but I think I must acknowledge that, in fact, Donald Trump was elected to be President. However, I cannot reconcile that fact with my world view. So, after explaining my problem, I will continue by pretending it never happened. My problem is imagining how so many Americans could have voted for him.

One could say it is just "those Republicans," but Trump is hardly a Republican and he twice got far more votes than there are party members. I know that elections are about choosing among the alternatives presented. In 2016, the alternative was understandably undesirable to many people. I certainly never would vote for her. But, I did. When the polls in Virginia tightened, I felt compelled to do my part to try to avoid a Trump election.

"Romney described the situation bluntly. 'The way I look at this choice,' he said, 'is that you can choose an awful person or awful policies. It's one or the other. And your choice will depend on which you consider more important.'"

McKay Coppins, *Romney: A Reckoning* (2023), p. 267.

But, in 2020, I do not believe many could have suspected Biden would be as bad as he has turned out to be. I also refuse to believe that the motivation for most was racism. (Actually, I think Trump himself is not a racist, as such. He views everyone as exploitable.) I do not think the primary motive was anti-immigration either; although, adverse views of how illegal immigration was being handled would be part of it. I suspect, but cannot prove, that profound unhappiness with our political leaders and with the smug elitism of the members of the establishment explains most of his votes. Sort of a protest or rebellion.

The middle finger.

Yet, it is still unsettling that so many Americans could be so disillusioned as to vote for such a man.

The Court

I have been pleased to see the Supreme Court restoring democratic rule by returning power to the States and restricting the Executive's use of administrative regulations and Executive proclamations to circumvent Congress, a development that had escalated under Presidents Obama and Biden. The People rather than the experts will determine more policy. (It hard to explain the Democrats' persistent attachment to government by experts, in light of its abysmal record starting with President Kennedy, other than as a result of a fundamental distrust of the People.)

I.
June 2023

At the very end of its 2022-23 session, the Supreme Court issued three decisions reflecting bitter disputes between the conservative majority and the three liberal Justices, displayed in the multiple opinions running hundreds and hundreds of pages.

Concerning the first decision, Heather Cox Richardson declared, in her weekly newsletter from abroad, that "in today's decision the current right-wing majority on the court demonstrated that it is willing to push that (right-wing) political agenda at the expense of settled law... ." I think Heather Cox Richardson got it exactly backwards in her summarizing sentence. It should read: "in today's decision the current [left-wing minority] on the court demonstrated that it is willing to push that (...[left-wing]) political agenda at the expense of settled law... ."

Admittedly, Justice Sotomayor tried to base her dissent on *stare decisis,* but has to resort to snippets and "reading between the lines" to do so, and then makes a political appeal. Justice Jackson freely proclaims that she is not addressing precedent but something else. "My goal here has been to highlight the interests at stake and to show that holistic admissions programs that factor in race **are warranted, just, and universally beneficial**" (n.105). It is not a judicial opinion, but a political script.

As for Richardson, even lawyers can let their preconceptions distort their perceptions. For historians, it is virtually a requirement. I think psychologists call it "projection."

The three decisions dealt with affirmative action, public accommodations /freedom of speech and student loan forgiveness. Each had a standing issue, discussed below. The decisions have generated considerable controversy and apparent angst among the vocal liberal loyalists. Dramatic overreactions. Accustom to judicial activism creating new and expanding rights over the past 50 years, the reappearance of stricter interpretation is like an ice-bucket soaking.

The Jackson Dissent

I submit that the praise for Justice Jackson's dissent is a reflection of the fact that it is not a judicial opinion but a political speech, appealing not to reason but to feelings, designed to arouse passions. Much easier and more fun to read.

Unlike judicial opinions, less than 20% of the citations are to the record on appeal or to judicial precedent. They are mainly journal articles (and some pretty old ones too). The dissent does not attempt to establish that a particular result is compelled by the record and applicable precedent. Indeed, it argues that the result should be dictated by factors previously declared by the Court to be not cognizable for that purpose (societal disadvantages) and fails even to acknowledge the existing precedent controlling when remedial actions based on race are permissible.

The dissent even elects to forego the traditional decorum and civility that customarily governs the Court's conduct, resorting to sarcasm (which I think weakens the presentation, but I am not the intended audience). It disrespectfully refers to Justice Powell's decisive opinion in *Bakke*, one of the key decisions under consideration, as: "based, apparently, on nothing more than Justice Powell's initial say so—it drastically discounts the primary reason that the racial-diversity objectives it excoriates are needed... ."

Compare what Justice Sotomayor says about the precedent:

> "Two decades after *Brown*, in *Bakke*, a plurality of the Court held that 'the attainment of a diverse student body' is a 'compelling' and 'constitutionally permissible goal for an institution of higher education.' 438 U. S., at 311–315. Race could be considered in the college admissions process in pursuit of this goal..."

...

"Later, in the *Fisher* litigation, the Court twice reaffimed that a limited use of race in college admissions is constitutionally permissible if it satisfies strict scrutiny. ...[F]or more than four decades, it has been this Court's settled law that the Equal Protection Clause of the Fourteenth Amendment authorizes a limited use of race in college admissions in service of the educational benefits that flow from a diverse student body."

Sotomayor, J. dissent.

Justice Jackson continues, sarcastically: "[T]he Court surges to vindicate equality, but Don Quixote style—pitifully perceiving itself as the sole vanguard of legal high ground when, in reality, its perspective is not constitutionally compelled and will hamper the best judgments of our world-class educational institutions about who they need to bring onto their campuses ... ." And, she closes with a particularly snarky comment about "bunkers", presumably referencing the footnote in Chief Justice Robert's opinion of the Court observing that the circumstances of the military academies were not before the Court, which the dissent repeatedly refers to as an "exemption":

"The Court has come to rest on the bottom-line conclusion that racial diversity in higher education is only worth potentially preserving insofar as it might be needed to prepare Black Americans and other underrepresented minorities for success in the bunker, not the boardroom (a particularly awkward place to land, in light of the history the majority opts to ignore)."

What the Court said in a footnote was: "No military academy is a party to these cases, however, and none of the courts below addressed the propriety of race-based admissions systems in that context. This opinion also does not address the issue, in light of the potentially distinct interests that military academies may present... ."

Most remarkably, this dissent repeatedly urges that we ignore the Constitution and "let the experts and the evidence" decide:

> "The only way out of this morass—for all of us—is to stare at racial disparity unblinkingly, and **then do what evidence and experts tell us is required** to level the playing field and march forward together, collectively striving to achieve true equality for all Americans."

> ...

> "[T]he Court's myopic misunderstanding of what the Constitution permits will impede **what experts and evidence tell us is required (as a matter of social science)** to solve for pernicious race-based inequities that are themselves rooted in the persistent denial of equal protection."

What can that even possibly mean?

And, how could it be done? Under what authority? And, by which experts and using what evidence? Obviously, not the record evidence. And, the factual history recited contains no evidence concerning the effects of this affirmative action with respect to the concerns outlined. Has it reduced income or wealth inequalities? Disparities in health and wellness, in life expectancies? In home ownership? No. The facts about individuals are not available (confidentiality). So, the dissent just presumes that the benefits are ..., what, self-evident?

Moreover, does it not occur to Justice Jackson that experts do not agree on the causes of the problems or the nature of the solutions?

Missing from the dissent's historical summary are two important facts. First, during the first 100 years after Emancipation, the former slaves and their descendants made remarkable progress (admittedly, starting from a very low base), despite Jim Crow. Second, from the mid-60s to today, the trends for many of the cited parameters have been negative, despite sustained and massive government assistance. Should that not suggest to the objective observer that the "experts" are not doing so well?

"[I]t's hard to overstate the monopoly control that career Democrats asserted over public policies affecting the lives of black Americans [for the past 60 years]. ...What is there to show for this social-welfare monopoly? Put plainly: The Democrats' stewardship of urban black America—its education, housing and family well-being—has been a policy and moral failure. ...No one will gainsay that the original Great Society was well-intentioned. But a political and psychological characteristic of the liberal administrative state ... is they never changed course no matter the evidence before their eyes. And past some point, the catastrophe for black family cohesion and education was so embarrassing that by internal Democratic consensus, it became virtually a nonsubject."

Daniel Henninger, "Scapegoating the Supreme Court: Democrats said decades ago they alone would run policies for black Americans. Now comes the blame game," *WSJ.com*, July 5, 2023.

Of course, we now judge government policies on their moral credentials, not their results.

I admit that I was more focused on what Justice Jackson's dissent lacked than on what it had, reacting to the statement of Heather Cox Richardson. I guess I just assumed that her history was a repeat of the ones I have read over the past year. Yet, I do not see it as an appeal to reason where it takes no position on how the Court should have ruled or what anyone should do. A cry of anguish intended only to inflame passions.

Frankly, in my opinion, the dissent is an embarrassment.

Affirmative Action

Racial categorizations were addressed by Justice Thomas in his concurring opinion and elaborated on (somewhat pedantically, as is his wont) by Justice Kavanaugh. They expressed strong skepticism. Indeed, the meaninglessness of the categories was a part of why the discrimination based thereon was not justifiable (*i.e.*, it did not in fact foster the type of diversity that would be beneficial for education).

Of course, those racial categories were used by the universities (and the Federal government). And, the initial discrimination against Asians was directed at "the Mongol or yellow race."

How can we change the world for the better? Does anyone really think that continued affirmative action by a handful of elite colleges and universities will improve things? Initially, I viewed affirmative action as symbolically significant and positive. After 60 years, it has, in my opinion, become symbolically a negative. And, it never really addressed the underlying problems. I practiced affirmative action as hiring partner for many years, because I thought it could make a difference in that world. I similarly tried to be a mentor to my associates. But, preferential admission to an elite university? Hardly. Perhaps, the Supreme Court decisions doomed affirmative action from the start; although, I think the Constitution limits the possibilities. My view is that affirmative action had long outlived any usefulness and was having negative effects. It was a meaningful expression of support initially, but was such no longer.

I wish that colleges and universities could be allowed to make their own decisions on admissions. One would hope that such freedom would result in greater variety and innovation in approaches to admissions practices. Perhaps, in a better world. But, we have seen that in this world, such freedom can lead to widespread racial or religious discrimination. History suggests that we cannot count on "the better angels of our nature."

Loan Foregiveness

As to the merits, I found the dissent pretty apt. On balance, however, I think that the majority gets the better on pure statutory interpretation (first, the existence of specific, but inapplicable, language addressing loan forgiveness and, second, the fact that the action did not actually waive or modify any of the loan program's terms and conditions). Just barely the better interpretation. Yet, I agree with the dissent that it would have been better for the majority to have found an argument more closely to the real problem, which was that the justification for the action was obviously a sham.

The loan payment modifications were a rational response to the pandemic, given all of the uncertainty.

The General Counsel for the Secretary had earlier opined that Biden's loan forgiveness plan was illegal. It was clear that this was a matter that should go to Congress, but the President presumably was afraid of dissent within his own party. So, even after it has become known that most Americans had become economically better off, not worse off, because of the pandemic and after the emergency was over (and, just a few weeks before he so declared), the Secretary invokes the HEROES Act to forgive the student loans of all persons "affected" by the pandemic with incomes in the bottom 2/3s.

"Despite a year when inflation pushed prices to new heights, Americans are still better off now than before the pandemic, with nearly 10 to 15 percent more in their bank accounts than in 2019... ." Abha Bhattarai, "Americans are still better off, with more in the bank than before the pandemic: Bank account balances are 10 to 15 percent higher than they were in 2019, new data shows," *WSJ.com*, July 17, 2023.

Perhaps, the Court could have concluded that the authorization under the Act extended only to persons whose ability to pay was "adversely affected" by the emergency.

In any event, the issue should now be before Congress, where it has always belonged.

Standing

Here, standing was contested by the dissenting Justices only in the student loan case.

In the affirmative action case, the plaintiff was a membership organization with members who were allegedly affected. The only new question was whether the general rule concerning membership organizations applied only where the members pay the expenses of the organization. The Court said no. The website case is a bit stranger because it was decided on largely facts stipulated by the parties. The Court had all relevant information. It is well established that a credible threat of enforcement action constitutes grounds for standing. In fact, the 10th Circuit had ruled against the plaintiff but found standing. The doctrines of membership standing and credible threat of enforcement standing both evolved in cases furthering so-called liberal causes, so the minority could not challenge standing based on those grounds.

The student loan case is more questionable. Only one plaintiff need have standing. The Court, like the 8th Circuit before, concluded that the State of Missouri did because of the financial impact on its instrumentality MOHELA. Everyone agreed that MOHELA would have standing if it had sued, but the party was the State. So, the question was whether the State could sue based on injury to its agent. (MOHELA had the legal and financial capacities to sue, but it did not.) I was not persuaded by either argument about precedent. I would need to study the cases and the record to decide.

Conclusions

These decisions are all quite narrow and will have little direct effect.

I also believe that these three decisions will also have little impact on subsequent Court actions. The website case is clearly based upon personal expressive communication. It might extend to advertising agencies and public relations firms. Not much else. The student loan case is one of a kind (although, I do think the Court will continue to curtail the "Imperial executive"). And, race-based government action had been pretty well limited already.

II.

July 2024

I am surprised and disappointed by the recent decision concerning Presidential immunity:

> "We conclude that under our constitutional structure of separated powers, the nature of Presidential power requires that a former President have some immunity from criminal prosecution for official acts during his tenure in office. At least with respect to the President's exercise of his core constitutional powers, this immunity must be absolute."

Donald J. Trump v. U.S., [July 1, 2024] 603 U.S. [   ] (2024).

I find it unnecessary, unwise and unsupported. The well-done dissent by Justice Sotomayor is far more persuasive as to the historical record than the majority opinion by Chief Justice Roberts.

Moreover, I think that the majority is quite wrong in its central factual assumption that being subject to possible criminal prosecution is likely to create greater disruption to the exercise of Presidential duties than would being subject to civil lawsuits for damages.

"Trump contends that just as a President is absolutely immune from civil damages liability for acts within the outer perimeter of his official responsibilities, *Fitzgerald*, 457 U. S., at 756, he must be absolutely immune from criminal prosecution for such acts. Brief for Petitioner 10.

"Criminally prosecuting a President for official conduct undoubtedly poses a far greater threat of intrusion on the authority and functions of the

> Executive Branch than simply seeking evidence in his possession, as in Burr and Nixon. The danger is akin to, indeed greater than, what led us to recognize absolute Presidential immunity from civil damages liability—that the President would be chilled from taking the 'bold and unhesitating action' required of an independent Executive. … Potential criminal liability, and the peculiar public opprobrium that attaches to criminal proceedings, are plainly more likely to distort Presidential decisionmaking than the potential payment of civil damages."

However, the last 50 years have shown the disruptive and costly impact of civil liability litigation, especially with contingent fees. There is a record of excess and abuse not found with criminal prosecutions. Ask any current CEO whether there is more disruption to and interference with their businesses from the threat of criminal prosecution or from the threat of civil litigation with document discovery, depositions and damage claims.

I think that as a factual matter the answer is clear. *See, e.g.*, Richard Vanderford, "'Nuclear' Jury Verdicts Rise Alongside American Anger," WSJ.com, July 8, 2024 ("Chubb, one of the world's largest insurers, intends to appoint a full-time executive to handle what it sees as a mounting problem of inflated verdicts...").

Of course, there are also the safeguards for criminal defendants that are emphasized in the dissent. And, the President's communications with his staff and administration officials could be adequately protected by privilege and evidentiary rules preventing their introduction into evidence.

Without this (faulty) assumption, the Court's precedential analysis collapses.

In the end, are we really concerned about deterring "'bold and un-hesitating action'" that arguably violates the criminal laws? Should we not worry more about encouraging such conduct?

Reading the syllabus gives a much moderate impression than does the opinion. The difficulty is that the majority opinion went too much into the factual allegations, and the dissents compounded the problem with extreme hypotheticals.

"When he uses his official powers in any way, under the majority's reasoning, he now will be insulated from criminal prosecution. Orders the Navy's Seal Team 6 to assassinate a political rival? Immune. Organizes a military coup to hold onto power? Immune. Takes a bribe in exchange for a pardon? Immune. Immune, immune, immune."

...

"Let the President violate the law, let him exploit the trappings of his office for personal gain, let him use his official power for evil ends."

SOTOMAYOR, J., dissenting

"Immunity can issue for Presidents under the majority's model even for unquestionably and intentionally egregious criminal behavior. Regardless of the nature or the impact of the President's criminal conduct, so long as he is committing crimes 'pursuant to the powers invested exclusively in him by the Constitution,' *ante*, at 7, or as needed 'to carry out his constitutional duties without undue caution,' *ante*, at 14, he is likely to be deemed immune from prosecution."

JACKSON, J., dissenting

Why would criminal conduct be activity within the scope of a President's exclusive power and authority? Why should it be possible to immunize an act merely by asserting that it was done to protect public safety or for foreign affairs? If actual motives are sheltered from scrutiny, it would still be possible to assess the acts themselves under a "reasonable person" standard.

By the way, I do think the majority is correct that the issue of immunity is a threshold matter that needs to be decided before trial. I also agree with the concurring opinion of Justice Barrett that if certain acts are to be immunized, evidence of them should still be admissible if relevant to other charges.

THE YEAR 2024

So far, 2024 is looking like a very, very strange year. The U.S. stock market is soaring, increasing inequality. Russia, China and North Korea are strengthening their bonds, forging a new Axis of Evil confronting the Western democracies, one that India seems tempted to try to join. Yet, Iran has elected an apparently much more moderate government. The United Kingdom voted overwhelmingly to remove an incompetent government that had run out of ideas and replace it with a purportedly newly more-centrist government that seems to have no ideas; while the France electorate threatened to move dramatically away from an activist government to a newly more-centrist, far right party. Central and South America continue to struggle to find a balance between social justice and economic growth/prosperity, hindered by corruption. And, the United States?

Well...

I.

Early 2024

"US culture is an incubator of 'extrinsic values'."

George Monbiot
"To beat Trump, we need to know why Americans keep voting for
him. Psychologists may have the answer"
The Guardian, 29 January 2024.

"Psychologists may have the answer," but George Monbiot does not.
Indeed, I find this article rather silly. An extreme oversimplification,
obviously, but the extrinsic/intrinsic distinction is not relevant to the
issues with which we should be concerned. This columnist undoubtedly relishes a theory that makes Trumpism "a" (or, perhaps, "the") end
stage of unfettered capitalism and free markets, but he fails to explain
why ambitious, selfish, successful people or, alternatively, unsuccessful
tycoon wannabes would be drawn to vote for Trump. Arguably, they
would be more tolerant of his character flaws, but that is different from
supporting him.

Monbiot is suggesting that persons consumed by extrinsic values are
or will become like Trump, but simple observation shows that not to
true. Separately, does an alleged significant shift from intrinsic values
toward extrinsic values, if it has occurred (which I doubt), appear to
capture what is happening today?

Not for me.

I think something significant has occurred. It is not an increase in
ambition and greed or in materialism; it is the emergence of self=ob-
session, self-worship and self-indulgence, reflected in the selfie, social
media and reality TV. This disease has spread rapidly and broadly, a

global pandemic. Gone is respect for duty, restraint, humility, sacrifice and service. This change has made a Donald Trump tolerable if not acceptable and, even, if not desirable. But, why the votes?

I found myself spiraling downward emotionally during the last few months of 2023. I was increasingly distressed by world events (which have only gotten worse), but I realize that I was particularly knocked down by the political situation in the United States. It was causing me anguish and creating a feeling of hopelessness, of sinking out of control.

Curiously, I am now much better. What has changed?

I think two things, one my conception of what is happening and the other a decision about what I will do. First, I have accepted that tens of millions of people want to vote for Donald Trump. I cannot understand why or how. It is truly shocking to me, to the core. But, I refuse to vil-lainize those people. I think one must presume the good faith of voters (absent clear evidence of corruption or fraudulent conspiracy). And, I recognize that a commitment to free elections requires a gracious (or, at least, civil) acceptance of the results. But, I am disappointed. (And, I cannot help but feel disgusted by the decisions of failed candidates to endorse Trump. I consider that to be the clear elevation of personal ambition far ahead of the public interest.)

Second, I resolved that, henceforth, I shall vote for, and only vote for, candidates who I think are suitable for the office and likely to do a good job. No more selecting "the lesser evil" nor voting against someone. I know that I will, in the process, arguably "waste" my vote. However, I do not consider it a waste. It is a protest. It is more constructive and positive than just not voting. (I am increasingly irritated by negative campaigning. I would like to hear why someone should be elected for reasons other than to block someone else's election. Yet, I know what we will hear from the candidates and pundits.)

It appears that we will experience an unprecedented election, one in which each party nominates the one candidate that the other party's candidate might be able to defeat—likely, almost any moderate Democratic (or Republican) could defeat Trump, and almost any moderate Republican (or Democrat) could defeat Biden. Indeed, one might summize that each party is resisting the selection of a strong candidate for fear of inciting the other party to select an even stronger candidate. Remarkable. And, disappointing.

I am not exactly suggesting that these are necessarily the actual motivations of anyone, but the situation does reflect a kind of paralyzing equilibrium that may lead to a most unfortunate electoral contest in November. The egos of both Trump and Biden desperately want to be President again. Trump's avid supporters will give him the nomination; Biden's position as incumbent will give him the nomination.

However, "[i]f Mr. Schumer and other Democratic power-brokers truly thought ... that Mr. Trump would abrogate the Constitution and bring about an autocracy... , they wouldn't give him a boost for the sake of marginal political gain. They are willing to give him a boost, again and again, because they don't believe their own predictions about a second Trump term. They rather enjoyed his first one."

Barton Swaim, "Why Democrats Can't Quit Trump," *WSJ.com*, March 31, 2024.

Also,

"Amid all the talk of Mr. Biden's physical and mental impairment, however, an important point bears remembering: He would be in a far stronger electoral position, infirmity and all, if he didn't make so many stupid decisions. Put Mr. Trump out of your mind, if that's possible, and consider only

---

Mr. Biden's performance as a political leader. It's almost unfailingly bad. It always has been."

Barton Swaim, "Biden's Worst Liability Isn't His Infirmity: It's his judgment. He has a special talent for making the worst possible choice out of all available options." *WSJ.com*, July 2, 2024.

I blame Biden. As he made clear in his State of the Union speech February 7, 2024, he is determined to pursue reelection with no offerings and no overtures to the other side or, even, to the middle. He is oblivious to his limitations and vulnerabilities. His arrogance and self-centeredness are real dangers. I cannot blame Trump any more than I could blame a rabid animal. And, of course, as hard as it is to believe, millions of voters expressed their preference for Trump over a variety of alternatives. Biden is deciding for and by himself. (Presumably, some voters prefer Biden over other potential candidates, but we have little idea of how many there are beyond his family members.)

Perhaps, Biden cannot help himself either. I do not really comprehend pathologies. Robert Sapolsky may be right that no one should be blamed for their actions; that we are all just slaves to our destinies. *See Determined: A Science of Life without Free Will* (2023).

If that is so, then:

> "I commend[] mirth, because a man hath
> no better thing under the sun,
> than to eat, and to drink, and to be merry."

Ecclesiastes 8:15.

But, I cannot really believe that. It is contrary to my most fundamental instincts. We must be (or, at least, must believe that we are) are responsible for our actions and decisions.

I think history will judge Biden harshly.

"[If only] Mr. Biden had found the wisdom and self-restraint to do as he originally implied—*i.e.*, free himself from frantic careerist calculation and embrace the role of one-term president. (After all, careerist calculation looks especially shabby from a politician visibly past retirement age and ready for the pasture.) But credit Team Biden with one... .They rightly saw that any Republican nominee not named Trump might give voters rein to vent their throw-the-bum-out instinct. To avoid Jimmy Carter's fate, they would make sure voters could only rid themselves of Mr. Biden by surrendering to Mr. Trump. This bet may yet pay off for Mr. Biden, if not the country. Should he lose, it also sets him up to rocket to the bottom of the presidential standings, permanently displacing the luckless James Buchanan as America's worst president."

Holman W. Jenkins, Jr., "EV Tariffs and the Inanity of Bidenism," *WSJ.com*, May 14, 2024.

Were the only issues domestic, I could still be pretty relaxed. We survived Trump once, we should be able to again. Our system of checks and balances is probably stronger today than five years ago. We will likely survive Biden's domestic policies too. (Although, inflation and the budget deficit will challenge our future, four more years will have a *de minimise* additional adverse impact.) The problem is foreign affairs. The world seems more dangerous now than at anytime I can remember—and, I remember family fallout shelters and crawling under our school desks as part of emergency drills. Neither likely candidate is even remotely up to the task ahead. I think age alone disqualifies both;

although, both of their temperaments and characters are totally unsuitable, regardless of age.

But, what can I do except worry?

I will probably need to "write in" someone. Now, I have to figure out how to do so without hands that work. But, here in February, November seems so far away.

II.

July 2024

What a month.

Following his revealingly poor debate performance, President Biden was inundated with a swelling chorus of calls for him to withdraw his candidacy and release his delegates. Among the devoted, there was a frenzy of speculation and debate over who should replace him. Curiously, I saw almost no support for Vice President Harris. Her unpopularity in the polls undoubtedly was part of the cause of the reaction, but I noticed the unmistakable recognition that she also was quite underqualified. The President, meanwhile, adamantly and repeatedly insisted that he would run (and win).

Trump then sufferers an assassination attempt, providing a boost in his popularity. Tragically, a bystander is killed. Trump receives the nomination of the Republican party. He inexplicably selects a totally unsuitable Vice presidential candidate. That choice is especially troubling given Trump's age. (People say that the Vice Presidential candidate does not matter. But, I remember that I—and, I was to learn, my mother—decided not to vote for McCain because of Sarah Palin.)

Once Trump is tthe official candidate, Biden suddenly announces his withdrawal. Was it planned in advance? If so, how far in advance and by whom? How much lying occurred?

I suspect that the timing reflects the difficulties of agreeing on the replacement. Harris was widely recognized as a weak candidate but a failure to nominate her would clearly alienate at least part of the base. (Not that they would vote for Trump, but they might stay home.) Her selection 4 years ago based on gender and race could not be rescinded or admitted. So, there was really no choice. Of course, this result was easily foreseeable since Biden was a one-term President. (Indeed, it gave me some comfort in voting for Biden, knowing that the Democratic Party would be saddled with a weak candidate in 2024 if he won.) What I did not expect was the power of Donald Trump. The future of the country would likely look much brighter today if Trump had won in 2000.

The party loyalists came out in her support. Two things stand out.

One is the frenzy with which they have expressed their enthusiasm. I have been a bit annoyed, having just followed their excitement over other possibilities. (Of course, it is understandable, and I think that the display of enthusiasm primarily reflects how much anxiety they were feeling about President Biden.) The second is Harris' decision to focus her campaign on her base. This seems stunningly misguided, at first blush. She clearly already has them. Why not appeal to the middle and do so on the merits?

III.

The Campaign

We get a campaign based not on policies, programs or, even, ideology, but on personality (bubbly?), gender/race and meaningless/misleading slogans.

For, example, we are told that Harris stands for "freedom" and, secondly, "democracy."

Ah, freedom. Freedom of speech, freedom of religion, freedom from crime, freedom to use your property as you wish, freedom to take responsibility for your life? Well, no. Freedom to terminate a pregnancy, freedom to express your sexual and gender identify and freedom from certain economic hardships, even if self-created. But then, at least, self-determination and the ability to choose your own political leaders? Actually, no again. The People did not choose her as their candidate for the highest office; she was chosen by a handful of individuals, and we do not even know who they are.

Her policy positions? Her vision?

I understand that it would be harder for her to fake moderation than it was for Biden sheltered in his basement—she would have to say something of substance and answer questions. Doing so would offend someone. So, Harris has explained no policy positions. She has expressed views on only a few questions, ones on which she reverses positions she firmly advocated in 2020 that are seen as politically unpopular in a few "swing states." The explanation? None. Only the repeated assurances that while her positions changed, her "values" have not.

Okay. So what are her values? So far, we do not know.

One might be tempted to attribute the nondisclosure as a result of cynical political strategizing, like one could suspect that the Biden conduct over reelection was part of a scheme concocted somewhere within a Democratic Party that recognized it was stuck with Harris and that Trump might be the only opponent (of either party) that she could beat. I am really skeptical of such conspiracy theories, because I do not think people are clever enough or prescient enough to plan complicated conspiracies. Successful conspiracies, like destiny, appear only in hindsight (or in television scripts).

Last night was the Harris /Trump debate. Viewed as a two-player competitive game (like tennis or boxing), Harris was the clear winner. She successfully provoked Trump, causing him to rant about subjects she selected, none relevant to the interests of the country. This tactic was successful not because it exposed who Trump is, which was already well known, but because it caused Trump to fail to pin her down any policy positions.You need to include a score for answering the questions asked. On that Harris gets a zero. With the assistance of cooperative moderators, she has managed to continue to disguise herself and avoid voter scrutiny by evading almost every question. And, that was her choice. After de,railing Trump, she could have talked to us. Despite the moderators' bias and Trump's collapse, she could have shown us respect.

An English friend (of my generation), Carolyn Holleyman, commented on a draft of this section as follows:

"This is such an interesting reflection. We get reports from the BBC every day on what is happening in the US, but it's through our filter. It's good to get your take on it. Isn't it amazing how vague the policies are; it's the same at our end. It's almost as if the politicians say 'Let's get ourselves in (not necessarily elected) first, then introduce our policies when it's too late to get us out.'

...

"Harris's non-disclosure of her vision? Maybe not a conspiracy, but definitely deliberate and convenient waffliness. Immigration (the voters' huge concern) and racism were strangely absent from the debate... . ...You say Harris 'disguised herself'. What a good way of describing all our current politicians' statements! ... So the truth is sacrificed. I think that within the bosom of her family, Harris knows very well who she is, but on the public stage she is covering her options. It's not very honest, really."

Peggy Noonan observed:

"Ms. Harris won shallowly. I mean not that she won on points, or that it was close—it wasn't, she creamed him—but that she won while using prepared feints and sallies and pieces of stump speech, not by attempting to be more substantive or revealing. When you address questions in a straightforward way and reveal your thinking, you are showing respect. You're showing you trust people to give you a fair hearing and make a measured decision. Voters can see it, and they appreciate it. They feel the absence of these things, too, and don't like it. ... She got away with a lot of highly rehearsed glibness and often seemed slippery. Sometimes you have to slip and slide in politics but slipperiness doesn't wear well."

"A Decisive but Shallow Debate Win for Harris: Trump showed he isn't up to the job. But her lack of substance won't escape the voters' notice," *WSJ.com*, September 12, 2024.

Her supporters are giddy— with relief. The curious, skeptical voters are no better off than they were on Monday. (Of course, she was able to stand up to Donald Trump. But, does anyone think that Trump represents the type of adversary she would confront as President? Still, it could certainly been worse.)

One point of substance—her apparent intended approach to the problem of high prices. Like President Biden, she appears not to recognizes, or refuses to acknowledge, that high prices and inflation are the result of too much demand relative to available supply. Her solution of distributing financial assistance to those suffering from high prices might provide some very temporary relief, but the real impact will be to increase demand, leading to even higher prices and the need for even more financial assistance, which will further boost demand, which will.... Harris has also floated the idea of some kind of price controls. That approach would reduce supply, leading to shortages, rationing and black markets. Great.

She could have learned that lesson during the Biden inflation we have still not quelled, or from numerous recent historical examples, like how increased financial aid and student loan availability led to the escalation in the costs of higher education several times that of the general cost of living (and a crisis of student debt). The problem is that government benefits are too tempting a pretend solution for politicians seeking votes.

I think that the reason we do not know who Kamala Harris is is because she does not know. And, her advisors have not decided (or have not yet told her).

Does she have thoughts on any of the serious issues? I do not suppose that we will find out before the election. Perhaps, she and her team have no thoughts on these issues. Or, perhaps, the progressive wing sees a once in a lifetime chance to win a national election by keeping quiet, praying that Trump's antics drive enough voters toward her out of desperation. He is certainly doing a stunning job of answering those prayers.

We face some extremely significant challenges: the increasingly tense confrontations with Russia, China, North Korea and Iran; inflation and a threatened recession; a ballooning deficit; an embarrassingly dysfunctional immigration policy and deteriorating public education. Yet, Harris talks about abortion, transgender rights and more entitlements.

I want no part of this farce.

(So, I still confront the question of how to do a "write in" when you cannot write?)

IV.

The Election

Was the outcome the result of racism and/or sexism? Well, Harris was selected as Vice President based on race and sex. The Democratic leadership was compelled to nominate her for President because of race and sex. I am sure that racism and sexism explain some number of the votes for Trump—and some number of the votes for Harris. So, what was the net impact? We could alternatively ask would a white male with comparable experience and as tenuous a claim to the nomination (not chosen by the voters) have done better.

Not in my judgment.

Although controversial, Clinton had abundant relevant experience and had proven herself a leader. Harris had little of the first and failed to demonstrate the second. Biden was (mistakenly) perceived as a sorely needed healer. That Clinton and Biden outperformed Harris can be easily explained without resorting to racism.

I consider the Democratic Party (that is, whoever determines the Party's strategies) to be the cause of our current mess. Biden would have de-fanged Trump had he governed from the middle and committed to a single term. Then, the Democratic voters could have/would have selected their own candidate in primary elections. Under those circumstances, I believe that Trump would not have run or, if he had, would have lost (in either the primaries or the general election). The undemocratic strategies to gain and retain power backfired.

Dedicated Democrats are grasping at phantoms to salvage their core beliefs. Some even claim that the Inflation Reduction Act was a bipartisan infrastructure bill passed in order to avoid a recession! Delusional or dishonest? Probably, just in denial. Nonetheless, I am again shocked that people apparently actually voted FOR Trump.

UNWRITTEN

I realize that looking at my writings from a distance one could easily conclude that I do not consider racism, global warming or inequality to be problems. That would be incorrect. However, I do recognize that my understanding of the nature of those problems and my views of possible solutions differ from the accepted elite-liberal consensus. I have pretty much said everything I have to say about climate change, but there are still "books" I wanted to write about racism and inequality. Yet, I lack the strength to do the appropriate research and analysis. So, those books remain unwritten. Here, based on my reading and writing to date, however, is a summary of what I currently think those books would say.

I.

Darwinism and Race

I have expressed above (*supra*, pp.343-4) the opinion that Social Darwinism and eugenics need to be discussed on the scientific merits, not just condemned on moral grounds. "[T]he societal response following the exposure of the Nazi atrocities was to ban the discussion of these subjects and to condemn the proponents. ...[That] may have been the most appropriate approach at the time, but we may (perhaps) have reached a sufficient distance to permit an analysis on the merits. By that I mean ... assess the scientific merits of the theories and arguments... ."

The points of such an analysis would probably be, more or less, the following:

1. To the extent one attempts to define race genetically, one must rely on the existence of clusters of overlapping traits. There are no definitive or dispositive markers.

"Once out of Africa, these populations remained isolated from one another—separated by mountains, oceans, or great distances. ...[E]ach group's gene pool evolved in response to the unique selection pressures of its environment. The legacy of these genetic differences is still visible and measurable today. Although each of us is genetically unique (barring identical twins), each of us also belongs to clusters of similar genomes whose similarity stems from the major out-of-Africa migrations that occurred tens of thousands of years ago. These clusters are not sharply separated from one another. They overlap a great deal, and therefore the boundaries between them are blurry."

Coleman Hughes, *The End of Race Politics: Arguments for a Colorblind America* (2024), pp.4-5.

"Racial identity is willed or imposed, or both; it has no foundation outside of social experience. Nor, therefore, is racial ancestry or heritage a real thing... . There are no racial imperatives that demand expression of particular attitudes, behavior, or social practices." Adolph L. Reed, *The South: Jim Crow and Its Afterlives* (2022), p.77.

"The vast bulk of our genetic material is shared with all normal human beings, whatever their race. ...Ninety percent of the world's genetic variation is found in every so-called racial group." Kwame Anthony Appiah, *The Lies that Bind: Rethinking Identity* (2016), pp.119-120.

2. "[G]enes are not inherited in racial packages." Appiah, p.121.

"Once you grasped the Mendelian picture, ... you could see an alternative to the idea of a racial essence. There need be no underlying single something that explained why Negroes were Negroes or Caucasians Caucasian. Their shared appearance could be the product of genes for appearance that they had in common. And those genes need play no role in fixing your tastes in poetry or your philosophical ideas."

Id., p.119.

---

3. All genetic traits occur following normal distributions represented by Bell curves.

"Most people, of course, are in the middle of the range, displaying mixtures of reciprocity, pure generosity, and greed. Why do people range across such a wide spectrum? Perhaps all of us are capable of being saints or sinners, depending on the temptations and threats at hand. Perhaps we are predisposed to being nastier or nicer by our genes. "

Steven Pinker, *The Blank Slate: The Modern Denial of Human Nature* (2002, 2016), p.260.

"[T]here are patterns of genes in human populations—which is a fact about groups—not because there are distinctive sets of genes shared by the members of a race, which would be a fact about individuals." Appiah, p.120.

---

4. As a result, variations in the means or averages between groups are irrelevant to the assessment or prospects of individuals in either group. There will always be some members of any group that will be ranked higher (and lower) than many members of other groups.

"If various characteristics are to a non-trivial extent determined by genetics (say, height, body type or athletic ability, or, more relevant here, intelligence, temperament, self-discipline or ambition), then not only will individuals differ to varying degrees, but groups of people with genetic similarities greater than average (families, stable communities, isolated populations, races, tight knit religious groups) will vary statistically from one another. ...Importantly, however, nothing much can be said about any particular individual. He or she may have had a greater or lesser probability *ex ante* of being smarter or taller than someone else, but after-the-fact, they either are or are not."

Supra., pp.42-3.

5. Genetic diversity is highly beneficial; excessive inbreeding is seriously detrimental.

"The new version of Darwin and Spencer's great theory, which includes both competitive and cooperative evolution (phylogenetic and ontogenetic learning), tells us that for fundamental reasons there is **strength in diversity**." Bobby Azarian, *The Romance of Reality: How the Universe Organizes Itself to Create Life, Consciousness, and Cosmic Complexity* (2024), p.124.

See also, James Woodford, "Modern rose hybrids have a worrying lack of genetic diversity: Intensive breeding since the 19th century has created thousands of varieties of rose, but a reduction in genetic diversity could leave them vulnerable to diseases and climate change," *New Scientist*, 25 April 2024.

6. Individual performance is only partially determined by genetics.

7. Finally, the genetic future of the species will be safe, The more able will not be outcompeted by the less able for resources and, thus, disappear—they will survive, even if increasingly outnumbered.

"It is entirely possible in a modern, industrialized nation for the less able to out-reproduce the more able, especially if the survival rates are not too disparate—a reversal of the model of Darwinian evolution. [Not that I am concerned about the genetic future of the species from this phenomenon (unlike things like increasing pollution or toxins causing more frequent mutations). The more able will not be outcompeted by the less able for resources and, thus, disappear. They will survive, even if increasingly outnumbered. These stronger genetic makeups will still be here, ready to resurge following the next apocalypse, just as in *The Walking Dead*. And, as in that TV series, some of the capable will be good and some will be evil.]"

Supra., p.53.

These propositions constitute a strong rebuttal of eugenics .

II.

Racism without Race

I know that there are people who base judgments on race alone, but I think the number and significance of those people diminished dramatically during the twentieth century. I suggest that since at least the 1960s, racism has been less and less about race and more about behavior, lifestyle and cultural characteristics. Indeed, even Presidents Lincoln and Teddy Roosevelt apparently found education, courage and deportment to outweigh race.

"[Fredrick] Douglass understood that Lincoln's ideas about Black people changed over the course of the war. The president had been deeply moved by the valor of the Black men who'd helped save the Union and had been influenced by Black men such as Douglass, whom he held in high esteem. ....In his final speech before his assassination, Lincoln expressed an openness to enfranchising a limited number of Black men—particularly educated men and those who'd fought in the war."

Nikole Hannah-Jones, *The 1619 Project: A New Origin Story* (2021), p.26.

"Principles of fair play told Roosevelt that nothing should inhibit the individuals in any group who have the ability to achieve great success. The extraordinary achievements of black men such as Washington were dramatic proof of this to Roosevelt. But at the same time, Roosevelt believed that, collectively, no one should or reasonably could deny the obvious racial superiority of whites over all others."

Douglas A. Blackmon, *Slavery by Another Name: The Re-Enslavement of Black Americans from the Civil War to World War II* (2008), p.163.

"While the Jim Crow order was explicitly and definitively about race, at the same time it was fundamentally not really about race at all. What at first blush appeared to be white elites' distinction between black locals and outsiders was a class distinction."

Id., p.86.

In my years of young adulthood, I perceived danger not from race but from dress and group behavior. The cultivated appearance of a tough, violent persona was the warning. It is hard for me to think this prejudice unacceptable. It was certainly rational and justified by what we observed in the streets and on the subways ofNew York City in the 1970s. Was it fair? That is hard to answer. However, one's dress and manner have traditionally been considered displays of respect or disrespect. People are free to choose to rebel or to refuse to conform, but what is obligation of others to minimize the consequences of one's choice?

The level of crime and drug trafficking in the inner cities by 1970 was of major concern. The "story" today is that the Republicans made it a political issue. Of course they did play to it, but drug-related crime was a political issue, a serious one, because drug-related crime was a serious societal issue and concern both in the suburbs and in the inner cities. It is fair to criticize the government efforts to address the problem, but it is ridiculous to claim today that the wrong was the political use of the issue rather than the destructive behavior that was occurring.

The increased militancy of the Black communities in 2013 onward and the rather sharp criticisms leveled by both Blacks and whites against the establishment heightened emotions and placed race as a central factor in the national dialogue. *See supra.,* pp. Nonetheless, the emerging national divide was not based on race, but on political philosophies. Well, perhaps not so much political philosophies as lifestyle and asserted values, increasingly polarized by group social pressures and social media. A significant portion of the population has been labeled as inferior, as less intelligent, less enlightened, less human, as "deplorables." Very reminiscent of the expressions of Jim Crow sentiments.

Racism without race. And, a view greatly exasperated, and used, by Donald Trump.

It is graduation season and commencement ceremonies are occurring across the country. President Biden delivered a commencement speech to the graduating class at Moorhead University. It was filled with overly indulgent self promotion (an astonishingly frequent use of "I" for a commencement speech).

He said:

"You all know and demonstrate what it really means to be a man. Being a man is about **the strength of respect and dignity**. It's about showing up because it's too late if you have to ask. It's about giving hate no safe harbor and leaving no one behind and defending freedoms. It's about standing up to the abuse of power, whether physical, economic, or psychological. It's about knowing faith without works is dead."

President Biden's Morehouse College Commencement Address, May 19, 2024 (emphasis added).

Quite right. If he meant it.

But, the immediately preceding sentences were:

"[T]his is what we're up against: extremist forces aligned against the meaning and message of Morehouse. And they peddle a fiction, a caricature what being a man is about— tough talk, abusing power, bigotry. Their idea of being a man is toxic. I ran into them all the time when I was younger. They got—all right, I don't want to get started. (Laughter.)"

Respect and dignity? No, denunciation, demonization and distain.

The self-congratulatory hypocrisy of the self-anointed morally superior class.

For a sharp contrast, consider this account of the contemporaneous words of the retiring President of Notre Dame addressing that graduating class:

> "Father John Jenkins, the [Notre Dame] university president for the past 19 years, is stepping down this summer. On Sunday he apologized to the graduating class that they had him rather than Taylor Swift or another exciting celebrity as their commencement speaker. Then he turned serious and urged them to pursue the values of toleration and openness to others and to resist the temptation to demonize others: **'The invitation to vilify an opponent is so seductive,** perhaps because it can seem like a confirmation of our own virtue. If we speak only to those with whom we agree, **our contempt for the evil opposition can seem like a sign of our own moral superiority.'"**

Gerard Baker, "Higher Ed Has a Progressive Disease. Can It Be Reversed?" *WSJ.com*, May 20, 2024 (emphasis added).

As Bill Maher recently remarked: "Today, 94% of adults are cool with interracial marriage; it's interparty marriage that's a deal breaker. In 1960, only 5% of Americans had a negative reaction to the idea of marrying someone from a different political party; now it's 38%." "Red and Blue America Can't Just Go Their Separate Ways," *WSJ.com*, May 17, 2024.

A fine state of affairs.

III.

Extreme Wealth

I have written about the inevitability of inequality and the benefits therefrom. *Supra.*, Chapter IV. However, we have levels of wealth held by a small percentage of people that are neither inevitable nor socially beneficial. How much is too much? One could argue that anything more than a billion dollars of assets for a single family unit is more than can be justified. But, I think that in today's environment, we should categorize as extreme wealth family holdings of more than 10 billion dollars.

If we conclude that no strong case can be made in support of extreme wealth, can we also conclude that such wealth is injurious to society? I am skeptical of many of the common arguments, like too much political influence and social unrest. I think that they are overblown and factually incorrect. However, I think that there is a problem in that these extremely wealthy individuals have control over a percentage of national and global investment funds that is inconsistent with a pluralistic market economy. These few individuals decide the allocation of too much of the total capital investment.

The composition of wealth

We can put some rough numbers on the features of interest. The total global net non-financial assets in 2023 had a value of about $510 trillion, a rather dramatic increase from 2000.

"The real economy balance sheet has $520 trillion in real assets, such as machinery and equipment, infrastructure, buildings, natural resources, and intellectual property, or IP. These are mirrored on the liability side as net worth."

...

"At the global level, real assets constitute net worth, while aggregate financial assets and liabilities net to zero... ."

...

"The global balance sheet and net worth more than tripled between 2000 and 2020. net worth grew from $160 trillion to $510 trillion."

Lola Woetzel, Jan Mischke, Anu Madgavkar, Eckart Windhagen, Sven Smit, Michael Birshan, Szabolcs Kemeny, and Rebecca J. Anderson, "The rise of the global balance sheet: How productively are we using our wealth?," *McKinsey & Company*, 2024.

Of that total, about half is residential real estate. Only about 20%, or $100 trillion, represents productive capital assets.

"The value of residential real estate including land amounted to 46 percent of global net worth in 2020, with corporate and government buildings and the land associated with them accounting for an additional 23 percent. Other fixed assets like infrastructure, industrial structures, machinery and equipment, intangibles, and mineral reserves—the types of assets that typically drive economic growth—made up only one-fifth of real assets or net worth, ranging from 15 percent in the United Kingdom and France to 39 percent in Japan... ." *Id.*

There are about 2,700 households (individuals or families) with assets worth a billion dollars or more (the top being around $180 billion). Those billionaires hold assets worth $14.2 trillion—about 10% of the total.

"There are now more billionaires than ever: 2,781 in all, 141 more than last year and 26 more than the record set in 2021. They're richer than ever, worth $14.2 trillion in aggregate, up by $2 trillion from 2023 and $1.1 trillion above the previous record, also set in 2021." *Forbes Billionaires 2024*, "The Richest People In The World".

Of that group, there are some 200 households with more than $10 billion each, holding assets totaling about $7 trillion. Thus, 200 households control almost 7% of the world's capital investment, and fewer than 3,000 households control almost 14%. That is a rather high level of concentration of control. Other measures give comparable results.

"The scale of inequality between the income quintiles grows at the top. The top 20% group has over four times as much wealth as the fourth 20%, which has close to double the wealth of the third 20%. The second 20% has around 1.3 times as much wealth as the bottom 20%. [T]he top 1% has more than half the wealth of the rest of the top 20% collectively.

"The top 1% has more in stocks and mutual funds as the rest of the top 20% combined.... . The differences in scale continue down the income quintiles. The top 20% has more than 10 times as much wealth in stocks/mutual funds as the next 20%. The fourth 20% has three times as much wealth in stocks/mutual funds as the middle income quintile. Those in the second and bottom 20% have similar wealth in stocks and mutual funds... ."

USAFacts Team, "How this chart explains Americans' wealth across income levels: The top 1% of households in America represent 26% of total US wealth," *USAFacts.org*, March 28, 2023. [The charts show that the top 20% hold $30 trillion in stocks and mutual funds, while everyone else holds about $4.5 trillion.. The top 1% holds over $15 trillion.]

Most of the increase in net worth since 2000 came from increases in asset valuations, especially in real estate, caused largely by falling interest rates, and not from an increase in assets, such as through new capital investment.

"Net worth has tripled since 2000, but the increase mainly reflects valuation gains in real assets, especially real estate, rather than investment in productive assets that drive our economies."

...

"Of the net worth gains tied to real estate at the global level, some 55 percent derived from higher land prices, while 24 percent was attributable to higher construction costs. The remaining 21 percent was a result of net investment—that is, construction of new homes or improvements to existing ones less wear and tear."

McKinsey & Company.

Most governments now have negative net worth, with debt exceeding asset value. McKinsey concludes that increased global investment is a priority need.

"Real assets are critical to the global economy. Returns on those assets account for about one-quarter of GDP directly. Growth in real assets also complements labor in driving productivity, which in turn drives economic growth. ...[R]edirecting capital to more productive and sustainable uses seems to be the economic imperative of our time, not only to support growth and the environment but also to protect our wealth and financial systems."

Id.

Taxation

And, what about taxes?

1. I have previously set out a proposal for the revision of the U.S. system which would both broaden the tax base and increase the effective income tax collected from the highest income individuals. I do not think, however, that these reforms would have much effect on inequality or extreme wealth. The primary reason is that extreme wealth generally arises from ownership of the results of entrepreneurial activities and appreciation in asset values that are not realized income so are not taxed as income until sold. Thus, for example, Sweden, despite high income tax rates, has experienced a significant wealth inequality and has a large number of billionaires.

"Sweden has a global reputation for championing high taxes and social equality, but it has become a European hotspot for the super rich. ...Recent research from Örebro University concluded that the media image of Swedish billionaires is predominantly positive ... . 'As long as the super-rich are seen to embody the ideals of the neoliberal era, such as hard work, taking risks, and an entrepreneurial attitude, the inequality behind this is not questioned,' says media researcher Axel Vikström."

Maddy Savage, "The rise of Sweden's super rich," *BBC News, Stockholm,* 6 May 2024.

---

2. Proposals to change the system to tax unrealized appreciation in assets threaten to undermine economic growth and entrepreneurial success by forcing the sales of assets to pay the taxes. And, it would be only fair also to recognize unrealized losses. The result would be complicated and costly. One possible alternative approach would be to make the borrowing of money secured by assets an income realization

event, comparable to a sale of an interest in the assets. At least, the taxpayer would be receiving money with which to pay the tax.

3. The other approach to reducing wealth through taxation is to change the estate tax system. Progressive rates is one possibility—say, amounts in an estate greater than $100 million could be taxed at 50%, amounts greater than $500 at 70%. Another approach would be to eliminate the stepped-up basis in assets at death. Then, the appreciation would get taxed as income at some point, when realized. One consequence would be that if the estate sold appreciated assets to pay estate taxes, income tax tax would be due on the realized gain. Thus, for example, the sale of assets with a gain of $100 million would be subject to the capital gains tax, at say 20%, and the remainder, $80 million, would be subject to the estate tax, at say 40%, for a combined tax rate of 52%.

4. What about the proposed wealth tax? It is like the property tax. A key source of controversy would be valuation. Even for marketable securities, issues would arise with respect to large holdings. (Would a hypothetical sale be expected to depress the price and by how much? Could there be a control premium?) And, such a tax would encourage tax-avoidance activities.

France has a wealth tax. It is successfully avoided by the wealthy through holding financial assets outside of France and buying property in France with large mortgages. The banks appear to be the main beneficiaries of the tax. The mortgage rates are reasonable enough, but the banks require life insurance bought from captive insurance companies at rates about three times the market.

Anyway, for purposes of this discussion, the most significant fact is that a wealth tax of 1% to 3% simply would not materially reduce extreme wealth.

So,

It is superficially easy to imagine a tax on excess wealth, but it is difficult to imagine how the resulting tax revenues could be utilized to promote greater dispersion of investment decision-making. Having government invest most of the revenues, say in infrastructure, would further increase, not decrease consolidation of decision-making.

Since the source of most of extreme wealth is economic rents, redistribution after the fact, even if fully anticipated, should not distort the allocation of productive resources, while still allowing market pricing to allocate consumption. This was the rationale of Henry George's proposal to tax away essentially all the gains in the market values of land in *Progress and Poverty* (1879).

The solution for this problem is not a redistribution of wealth from the top .001% to the bottom half, either. The distribution per capita or to the needy would reduce invested capitalgnificant inflation or boand increase consumption (or fuel significant inflation or, most likely, both), because the recipients would spend the funds rather than invest them, most likely hampering economic growth. So, the preferable redistribution would be within the top two quintiles. That would support capital investment while broadening substantially the number of people making investment decisions. One. approach would be to use the additional tax revenue collected to supplement voluntary private contributions to IRAs and other restricted retirement plans.

CHAPTER XII

Who We Are To Be

WHO WE WERE

We are a nation that emerged not from geography or ethnicity or conquest, but from choice. As observed by Francis Fukuyama, the United States is the successful example of a "creedal" nation, a nation based upon a commitment to a recognized creed, reflected in a set of foundational documents and principles. The idea is that people of different ethnicities, religions, family traditions and, perhaps, even languages can bond together to form a successful nation based upon common commitment to shared civic and political values. *The Origins of Political Order* (2011).

The founding settlors were quite diverse, representing very different religions, cultures and societal positions; although, most were from the United Kingdom and Western Europe, and most were Christian. The differences, however, were significant enough that wars had been fought over them in the Old World and that they were the source of significant conflict in the New.

The colonies became a nation because they collectively chose to be one, and their people fought and died to do so. The new nation was established on a handful of documents declaring the basis of this new enterprise. The fundamental commitments were to individual liberty, private property, freedom of religion, separation of church and state, and equal justice and protection under the law, coupled with a deep distrust of government and of any concentration of power.

The fact is that the United States is special and has been been a role model and an inspiration around the world. The United States has been a voice for human rights, a force against genocide, and a proponent of individual freedom, even if many of our efforts have been misguided or bungled. Founded on a set of unprecedented ideals and struggling to live up to them, we have set an example and established a standard. Our imperfect and unsuccessful efforts to live up to and realize fully those aspirations does not negate the standards but elevates them, makes them more human and more relevant.

> "[T]he American founding couldn't be perfect from the start; it had to progress toward its goal. ...Prudence is the faculty that deals with imperfection in order to form, as the Preamble put it, a "more perfect union." **To make progress effectively and democratically, prudence seeks and finds necessary accommodations in compromise.** Not all compromises are successful, but the successful ones deserve to be accepted, and those who had the prudence to make them should be honored... ."

Harvey C. Mansfield, "The 'Systemic Racism' Dodge," *WSJ.com*, September 18, 2020 (emphasis added).

Not everyone stayed to be part of the experiment during the 19th century. (But, many, many others came willingly, even eagerly.) Of course, some had little choice—*e.g.*, slaves and indigenous peoples. After the Civil War, some former slaves left. but most chose to stay. Subsequently, millions more came voluntarily to become part of this New

World. Yet, a new nation created by and for diverse people accepting a common creed required land. Unfortunately, it came from (was taken from) the original occupants. However, when the colonists arrived, North America was a sparsely populated wilderness. The large, thriving civilizations that had existed in 1492 had been decimated and some even eliminated by the pandemics brought from the Old World.

There have been moments of true dignity in our history. Peggy Noonan describes one such:

> "The armies of the North and South, in blue and gray, were massed uneasily beyond the house. ... Some of Lee's officers had urged him not to surrender but to disband his army and let his men scatter to the hills and commence a guerrilla war. Lee had refused. ...Grant asked his aide Ely Parker, an American Indian of the Seneca tribe, to make a fair copy of the surrender agreement. When Lee ventured, 'I am glad to see one real American here.' Parker memorably replied, 'We are all Americans.'."

"America's Most Tumultuous Holy Week," *WSJ.com*, April 14, 2022.

(This exchange is also quoted by Heather Cox Richardson, *Democracy Awakening: Notes on the State of America* (2023), p.211, and sourced to Heather Cox Richardson, "We Are All Americans: Ely Parker at Appomattox," *We're History*, April 9, 2015.)

And, "..[a]s he turned to leave, Grant came out to the steps and saluted him by raising his hat. Lee reciprocated and rode off slowly to break the news to the men he'd commanded." Lee's parting words to his troops: "'Leave the result to God. Go to your homes and resume your occupations. Obey the laws and become as **good citizens** as you were soldiers." *Id.* (emphasis added).

The strength of the country came from the diversity and hard work of its inhabitants. The people were largely God-fearing and God-worshipping. Common characteristics were self-reliance, industriousness and neighborliness. There was an emphasis on being good citizens. Ironically, today, diversity refers to race, gender identification and sexual preference. I am referring, instead, to a diversity of views, of ideas, of interests and abilities, of backgrounds, experiences and traditions, or economic circumstances.

America's embrace of demonstrated—not presumed (based upon birth)—ability and merit provided opportunity to many.

> "It was thanks to the radical meritocracy and audacious dynamism of institutions like Goldman [Sachs] that we were able to dismantle so much of the authority of elite power structures that restrained us from fulfilling our potential. The past 50 years have been marked by the genuine eradication of barriers to opportunity for the underprivileged regardless of ethnicity, sex, sexual orientation or anything else. This is how we were genuinely starting to fulfill the promise of equality."

Gerard Baker, "If Western Civilization Dies, Put It Down as a Suicide," *WSJ.com*, April 17, 2023.

WHERE WE ARE

Start with a question. Think of all the people you have encountered in life. Is the biggest or most important difference among them race? For me, the answer is an unambiguous "No." There are other differences that are profoundly more significant and much more relevant. Another question. Take a close look around you. Is the biggest, most important problem facing this country race (or "White Privilege")? Again, "No."

How about violence and lawlessness? Or, fraud and corruption? Or, addiction (overdose deaths now exceeding 100,000 per year), or teen suicide (on the rise), or malnutrition, homelessness, severe poverty, child abuse, domestic abuse? Or Russian aggression, potential Chinese aggression, the threat of nuclear war. We face some serious challenges. Why single one out for so much attention?

The continuing surge in violence is quite troubling. So, is the rise in shoplifting and other crimes against individuals. But, I am most concerned by the apparent increase in theft from the government. Criminal tax evasion seems to be increasing—failure to report income and the hiding of assets. I am much more aware of Medicare and Medicaid fraud now. And, of aggressive Ponzi schemes. (The reason may be that I receive a legal news report called *Law360 White Collar*, which chronicles new developments in white collar crime.) It is regularly surprising to me.

New 2022 plans for the IRS to become more aggressive are estimated to "yield more than $200 billion in revenue. ...The Joint Committee on Taxation, Congress's official tax scorekeeper, says that from 78% to 90% of the money raised from under-reported income would likely come from those making less than $200,000 a year. Only 4% to 9% would come from those making more than $500,000." The Editorial Board, "The IRS Is About to Go Beast Mode" *WSJ.com*, August 2, 2022 (emphasis added).

Tax evasion is not the sole province of the rich.

We have had welfare and Social Security fraud for years, but that always seemed rather "small potatoes". The conduct involving the Covid relief programs set a whole new standard for anti-community behavior. Between abuse of the special unemployment payments and the PPP, we experienced the largest fraud in American history, with an estimated total stolen approaching $750 billion. While the populous cried out for more assistance in the crisis, thousands stole the benefits from those in need. Individual greed trumping community. Reporter Sean Woods, in a long piece about the fraud, describes an interview with one fraudster:

> "IN A SMALL CITY with some rough neighborhoods, I meet up with a woman I'll call Danni. ...[D]uring the pandemic, she says, she stole money from the state and federal government. ...When the pandemic hit, she went right to work: following her local elected officials online for info, and applying for unemployment and rental assistance as soon as it was offered. She says it helped that she moved fast and got in early. She used stolen identities acquired from street connections to apply for more and more unemployment relief from the feds. She claims to have made tens of thousands of dollars; sending out as many as 40 to 50 requests using different IDs, getting a handful of hits for every batch of claims she sent in... .She didn't go for huge sums and was satisfied with not getting too crazy and attracting attention. Still, she says, she'd never seen so much cash in her life, and feels like she was due. 'It's reparations!' Danni tells me."
>
> ...
>
> "Danni's gone back to her usual side hustles, but the next time there's a crisis, she's got a playbook. And if the government isn't prepared, ... well, **she'll hit them up all over again. It's fast becoming the American way.**"

Sean Woods, "The Trillion-Dollar Grift: Inside the Greatest Scam of All Time," *Rolling Stone,* July 9, 2023 (emphasis added).

Prophetic?

WHO WE WOULD BE

Is the goal of America to become "one people?" No. "One people" does not embrace diversity; it depends upon uniformity and conformity. *E Pluribus Unum* does not refer to the formation of "one people," but to the formation of one community, one nation, out of multiple peoples. The coming together of peoples for a cause, for a vision, for a nation.

I previously tried to outline what constitutes being a good citizen. As I then noted, in the very early days of this country, George Washington wrote: "the Government of the United States gives to bigotry no sanction, to persecution no assistance, requires only that they who live under its protection should demean themselves as good citizens, in giving it on all occasions their effectual support." The question for the future of this nation is what percentage of the population still believes in being a good citizen and in helping one's neighbors or, more importantly, is prepared to try to be a good citizen. The Greatest Generation is largely gone. My generation is fading. There are challenges facing our youth, including the decline in the roles of family, of the Church and of voluntary associations. Social life is increasingly online. That is a loss. In-person communities ask, as well as give. Offering and accepting help are expanding and deepening experiences. Taking is a narrowing, inward experience. I worry that today's youth will not learn the meaning or experience the richness of community. Today, we do not hear much about "stronger backs." The focus is on "lighter loads." One might say that we are living in The Age of the Lighter Load.

Being good citizens (as propounded by George Washington and Robert E. Lee)? Do we still have the will? The shared vision? The courage? Do we even have the desire? Can we still strive to be people who "demean themselves as good citizens, in giving [this nation] on all occasions their effectual support"? Obey the law, pay your taxes, support our founding principles and be neighborly?

Sound too hard?

We seem to be increasingly divided, by political party, by race, by economic status, by geographic location, by sexual orientation and identification, by ideology, by sense of entitlement versus sense of obligation, by moral standards, by educational status and so on. Where is the community? Have we just become warring factions? Numbering in the dozens? And, increasingly polarized and hostile, and the discourse, increasingly uncivil? So, what happens?

President Trump, then President Biden, saw the prospects of political gain in the diviseness, and both enthusiastically embraced the opportunity. Each sought to build a coalition of self-perceived "victims," of those who obsessed over what they might get from, never asking what they might give to, others. With such leaders, we do not need enemies. But, enemies, we have. Russia, China, Iran, North Korea, the Taliban, ISSIS. Then, the watching opportunists, waiting to take sides. And, we are not doing well.

"'It's a matter of personal conscience,' he tried to explain in an interview in June. 'Presidents have an impact on the nature of our nation,' he said in another, 'and trickle-down racism and trickle-down bigotry and trickle-down misogyny—all of these things are extraordinarily dangerous to the heart and character of America.'"

Coppins, *Romney*, p.181.

"If we are losing, it is because we are losing our soul, our sense of purpose as a society, our identity as a civilization. We in the West are in the grip of an ideology that disowns our genius, denounces our success, disdains merit, elevates victimhood, embraces societal self-loathing and enforces it all in a web of exclusionary and authoritarian rules, large and small."

Gerald Baker, "If Western Civilization Dies, Put It Down as a Suicide," *WSJ.com*, April 17, 2023.

So, where to now?

"We need new leaders to cultivate the American spirit and restore institutional integrity: in the Pentagon, to put war fighting and deterrence first; in schools, to teach civics and America's exceptional story; in business, to reaffirm the principles of merit and capitalism; and across society, to create a new national commitment to citizenship. ...Perhaps the military recruiting crisis is the lagging indicator of America's cultural collapse. Or maybe it's the canary in the coal mine, an early warning that it is time to rescue American exceptionalism. What we do next as citizens will decide."

David McCormick and James Cunningham, "The Military Recruitment Crisis Is a Symptom of Cultural Rot," *WSJ.com*, April 14, 2023.

Of course we need new leaders, and we need it across the board. But, the new leaders are unlikely to be much better than their constituents.

"Amid threats from abroad, Americans need to start demanding more from their elected officials. We need a country-over-party agenda. We need the **moral courage** to do what's right. We need more statesmen and fewer partisans. **We as citizens must want and demand it.**" Don Bacon, "The Other

Party Isn't the Enemy: I support Donald Trump, but I'm an American before I'm a Republican," *WSJ.com*, September 9, 2024 (emphasis added).

I fear that the country will become increasingly divided, not between liberals and conservatives, but between the "good citizens" and the rest, between the contributors and the free riders, between the producers and the consumers. (And, of course, the leeches—the cheats, the thieves, the fraudsters. We have always had them, but it seems to me to have gotten much worse. There certainly are many more opportunities to steal, from the growing number of government benefit programs to the staggering increases in electronic interconnectiveness (the Internet). These opportunities facilitate anonymity as well as distance from the victims. Certainly more comfortable than mugging or burglary or, even, stealing your neighbor's Social Security checks.) The test, then, will be whether the protections against majority rule will survive. If so, the country should too. If not, the grand experiment is likely to end.

Is this analysis harsh? Yes. Elitist? Probably. Incorrect? Ah, that is the question.

How do we support and sustain communities? Or, families? Is it the responsibility of, or even a proper (or feasible) role for, government, whether local or national or international? In the end, is it not just a matter of participation? And, does that not depend upon individuals and the exercise of their capacity for relationships? Perhaps, the moral underpinnings of the nation can be slowly recaptured by the people. But, does that require a renewed nationalism? It is easy to be melodramatic (or sanctimonious) about these subjects.

The challenge is to figure out what, if anything, to do. Are the old traditional values simply lost forever? If not, how can they be revived? If so, can something constructive be created in their place? And, how can that happen? A people (and each person) needs something that commands loyalty, whether it be a nation state, a religion or a brother/sisterhood, with a code of honor.

What about rational discourse about the type of society in which we want to live? That does not seem likely. Instead, we have moralistic posturing. The decisions are likely to get made pursuant to traditional politics—through unprincipled efforts to obtain power. Rationality is in some disrepute today. Moral superiority is the game. As Thomas Sowell called it: "Self-congratulation as a basis for social policy."

"Just as citizens should grasp the basics of history, science, and the written word, they should command the intellectual tools of sound reasoning. These include logic, critical thinking, probability, correlation and causation, the optimal ways to adjust our beliefs and commit to decisions with uncertain evidence, and the yardsticks for making rational choices alone and with others. These tools of reasoning are indispensable in avoiding folly in our personal lives and public policies."

Steven Pinker, *Rationality: What It Is, Why It Seems Scarce, Why It Matters* (2021), p.xv.

There is some hope offered by immigration. Immigrants may again revitalize America. People willing to take risks, make sacrifices, even jeopardize their lives in pursuit of a better life and more opportunities. New arrivals are more likely to recognize and value America's exceptionalism. With their talent and motivation, they may help to preserve (or restore) it. But, will that be enough? Or, will they also be corrupted by our new way of thinking and acting?

I do not see how we go back to the past. We need something forward looking that inspires and elicits commitment and a willingness to sacrifice. What could that be for today's secular, multi-cultural, multinational, cosmopolitan elite? Or, are they as a group simply a lost cause? If so, then the prospects of a more global and inclusive community seem bleak.

Comments on (Some) Sources

Some of my readings that are reflected in the essays above made me feel the need to respond directly (ones with which I significantly disagreed). So, I have done just that. My critiques are set forth in this chapter.

Introductory Note

Based on two very different things I have been reading, it appears that the new trend is to assure authors whose work one criticizes that there is nothing personal intended.

> "I can be bristly, acerbic, arrogantly judgmental, hostile, and unfair in how I critique them. But despite that, I am majorly averse to interpersonal conflict. In other words, with a few exceptions that will be clear, none of my criticisms are meant to be personal."

Robert M. Sapolsky, *Determined: A Science of Life without Free Will* (2023), p.512.

"I trust that readers of the present essay will understand that criticism, even harsh criticism, of the reasoning contained in a scholarly work in no way constitutes a personal attack on the author. In the same way, I look forward to criticism, even harsh criticism, of my own reasoning, and trust that it will be offered in the same spirit."

Alan Sokal, "'White Empiricism' and 'The Racialization of Epistemology in Physics': A Critical Analysis,* *Journal of Controversial Ideas,* 2023.

I would think that obvious with respect to any scholarly writing, but I suppose that the degenerate nature of today's political discourse and the prevalence of the cancel culture make those attempting rational analysis to be a bit on the defensive. It seems odd to offer justification for engaging in critical analysis, but the following statement by Alan Sokal in the article just cited (puportedly paraphrasing an essay by George Orwell which is actually about language, not content) is about as good as it can get:

"Why, then, do I think it important that the ideas expressed in this article be openly debated—important enough to bother writing a detailed critical analysis?

"My worry is the one articulated by George Orwell ... in his celebrated essay 'Politics and the English language': that sloppy thinking engenders further sloppy thinking; and that the uncritical acceptance of ideas, not because the reasoning is sound (or even examined) but because the conclusions are politically congenial, leads to a further degradation of thought."

"The 1619 Project"

**"What would it mean to reframe
our understanding of U.S. history
by considering 1619 as our country's origin point,
the birth of our defining contradictions,
the seed of so much of what has made us unique?"**

Nikole Hannah-Jones,
The New York Times Magazine,
Caitlin Roper, Ilena Silverman, and Jake Silverstein,
The 1619 Project: A New Origin Story
(2021), p.xxii.

New, maybe, but "origin" of what?

Reading *The 1619 Project: A New Origin Story* (2021), one cannot help but quickly notice that the claimed inspiration for and claimed conception of the Project are fundamentally flawed. Hannah-Jones begins from her great surprise to learn what happened in Jamestown in 1619 and her conclusion that its relative obscurity is the result of an "intentional" effort to hide the facts. *The 1619 Project*, pp.xix, xx ("I knew immediately, viscerally, that this was not an innocuous omission. ...Even as a teenager, I understood that the absence of 1619 from mainstream history was intentional").

Her conclusion assumes (i) that the event was of significant historical significance and (ii) that there was something to be achieved by suppressing knowledge of it. Neither necessary assumption is established in the book and neither seems plausible. I note that Charles Mann, years earlier (in 2011), made similar comments about 1619 to the "discoveries" that were "announced" in 2019 by Hannah-Jones.

"[T]he colony left a big mark: it inaugurated the great struggles over democracy (the colony established English America's first representative body) and slavery (it brought in English America's first captive Africans) that have long marked U.S. history."

...

"Within weeks of each other, Jamestown had inaugurated two of the future United States' most long-lasting institutions: representative democracy and chattel slavery. Not that the colonists paid attention to these landmarks— they were too busy exporting Virginia leaf."

Charles C. Mann, *1493: Uncovering the New World Columbus Created* (2011), pp.84, 122.

The arrival of enslaved Africans at the new settlement of Jamestown in 1619 was, in fact, not the first slavery in North America. A hundred years earlier, Spanish newcomers enslaved indigenous Americans from Florida and the Caribbean islands. Native Americans, in turn, enslaved Spanish intruders. Starting even earlier, Native Americans enslaved other Native Americans.

The sales of those Africans in 1619 may have been the first or largest incidence of African-slave trading in North America, but it was an unplanned and isolated event. It certainly did not establish "an institution" of slavery (or of anything else) and was not a "seed" from which an institution grew. And, the colonists? They were preoccupied with survival and their relations with the indigenous population.

John Winthrop's vision of the "city on a hill" was still 10 years in the future and hundreds of miles north.

"[W]e shall be as a City upon a Hill,
the eyes of all people are upon us;
so that if we shall deal falsely with our God
in this work we have undertaken
and so cause him to withdraw his present help from us,
we shall be made a story and a byword
through the world...."

The "institutionalization" of that vision was another 150 years in coming.

"During the 18th century, the experiment deepened, as Americans began to speculate that they could form the first democratic nation in modern times. Intense experimentation went on from the 1760s to 1787, as Americans adapted and invented forms of government fit for the scope of their needs, the gaping hole of their inexperience, and the high and intense expectations for their future.." R. Sós, *thehistoricpresent.com.*

The pragmatic decision of the Virginia Company was also not a "seed" that grew to take over the colonies. Although, she does not reference it, "[s]o many colonists poured in that the company [the Virginia Company] realized they could not be controlled entirely from across the ocean and created an elected council to resolve disputes—the first representative body in colonial North America. Its opening session lasted from July 30 to August 4, 1619." Mann, *1493*, p.121. Then, "Barely three weeks later a Dutch pirate ship landed at Jamestown. In its hold was '20. and odd Negroes'—slaves taken by the pirates from a Portuguese slave ship destined for Mexico." *Id.*

"In their hurry to extract tobacco profits, the [colonists] had been clamoring for more workers. ...The Africans had arrived at harvest time. Without a second thought colonists bought the Africans in exchange for the food the pirates needed for the return trip to Europe. Legally speaking, the ... Africans may not have been slaves—their status is unclear... ."

Id., pp.121-2.

These events themselves were trivial, as well as unnoticed, barely even hints of what was to come.

Some "Nits" (or More)

1. Throughout, Hannah-Jones uses words manipulatively. Such use of language is for polemics, not history. For example, she treats as facts the assertions that the first several Presidents and most members of the Supreme Court until the Civil War were "enslavers" ("enslavers dominated the presidency in the decades after the founding and would dominate the U.S. Supreme Court and the U.S. Senate until the Civil War") and that "all thirteen colonies engaged in slavery." Hannah-Jones, *The 1619 Project*, p.xx.

"Enslavers"? Language enables distinctions that facilitate communication. An "enslaver" is one who enslaves or makes a slave of another person. There were enslavers—African chiefs and kings who sold captives, European slave traders, Southern colonial lawmakers who categorized children as slaves. But, it diminishes communication to label slave owners as "enslavers." Simiilary, what does it mean for a colony to "engage in slavery"? A colony could have been engaged in slavery, if it had owned or traded slaves. But, that is not what she means. She means only that slavery existed in all 13 colonies.

"By the time the framers began writing the Constitution, states that did not rely heavily on enslaved labor within their borders, like Massachusetts and New Hampshire, had already outlawed it. ...Pennsylvania had begun a gradual process of abolition in 1780." Hannah-Jones, *The 1619 Project*, p.258.

A colony or other governing body could have three types of law on slavery: none (as was the case initially); ones declaring slavery illegal (as was to happen in many of the new States) and laws that "institutionalize" slavery (like the so-called slave codes gradually adopted in Southern colonies). It is this third category that deserves the critical attention (and is discussed below).

"Some historians of slavery in the United States, as well as some government agencies and educational organizations, have recently urged substituting the words 'enslavement' and 'enslaved person' for 'slavery' and 'slave, which they contend rob historical figures of any identity beyond the dehumanizing one imposed on them. Similarly, they urge substituting 'enslaver' rather than 'slaveowner' and 'owner,' which are said to obscure the violence and immorality that enslaved people suffered. But often, the words 'slave' and 'slaveowner' and 'former slave' convey exactly what I mean to say. ...Slavery in the United States was built on the exploitation of slaves' humanity. Their humanity does not need to be restored. It should be taken as given."

Dylan C. Penningroth, *Before the Movement: The Hidden History of Black Civil Rights* (2023), pp.xxvii-viii.

2. One of the stranger claims is that Virginia joined the Revolution in order to protect slavery from interference by the British.

In fact, the British did not interfere with slavery until after the fighting started and did so explicitly as a threat to deter Virginia from joining the rebellion. In the event, the British actions added to the colonists' grievances, the incitement of violent insurrections. It may be that some substantial numbers of Virginians would have stayed loyal to the Crown if the British had not used the banishment of slavery as a weapon, but that is very different from rebelling in order to preserve slavery.

"The fighting had not yet reached the Southern colonies when, in April 1775, seeking to suppress the rebellion, Virginia's royal governor, John Murray, the Earl of Dunmore, warned the colonists that if they took up arms there, he would 'declare Freedom to the Slaves, and reduce the City of Williamsburg to Ashes.' Enslaved people did not wait for Dunmore to make good on that threat. By the hundreds they liberated themselves and ran to the British troops."

...

"[On] November 7, 1775 In the face of a growing Patriot insurgency, Lord Dunmore ... issues a proclamation offering freedom to all enslaved people held by colonists sympathetic to the Patriot cause in return for their joining the British Army. More than eight hundred enslaved men escape to Dunmore's lines and enlist, wearing uniforms with the motto 'Liberty to Slaves.'"

Hannah-Jones, *The 1619 Project,* pp.14, 124.

" ...[T]he governor formed the eponymous Lord Dunmore's Ethiopian Regiment, a British military unit composed of African freedom fighters." Michael Harriot, *Black AF History: The Un-Whitewashed Story of America* (2023), pp.82-3.

---

3. She even implies that the Constitution's ban on the slave trade was a cunning move to enrich existing slave holders and was very detrimental to the enslaved, noting that the end of the transatlantic slave trade increased the value of existing slaves and led to the breakup of slave families when slaves were sold by owners who did not need them

to those who did. Yet, the importation of slaves had been suspended in 1770 and the ban was set out in Constitution 20 years before it took effect in 1807.

"[T]obacco growing had depleted the soil, and landowners ... were turning to crops that required less labor.... . That meant they needed fewer enslaved people to turn a profit. White Virginians, therefore, stood to make money by cutting off the supply of new people from Africa and instead filling the demand in the Deep South for enslaved labor by selling their surplus laborers to the cotton and sugar forced-labor camps in Georgia and South Carolina."

Hannah-Jones, *The 1619 Project*, p.21.

---

4. She graphically details the central role that the production of sugar from sugar cane played in the expansion of slavery. Yet, sugar cane was not produced in the colonies. The relevance here? She says that sugar underwrote the "financing" of the colonization of North America. All she means is that the colonies engaged in lucrative trade involving products produced by slave labor, often elsewhere. "[B]lood was spilled, more than anywhere else, in the production of sugar." She also notes that sugar is currently destroying the health of America's poor black communities.

"[C]ane required tremendous coerced and coordinated human labor in warm climates and on fertile land. Arab enslavers from as far back as the eighth century are credited with spreading sugar plantations throughout the Mediterranean basin of southern Europe and North Africa... . Spain and Portugal had already begun to put enslaved Africans to work growing sugar-cane on the Atlantic islands off the coast of North Africa... ."

...

"American colonists ... traded directly with England, delivering mainland commodities produced by enslaved labor, such as rice, tobacco, and cotton, as well as flour and lumber... . [T]he climate of these regions favored other crops, such as tobacco, indigo, rice, and cotton."

Hannah-Jones, *The 1619 Project*, pp.75, 80.

"[T]he heart of the plantation economy was French and British. In the 1780s, the French slaveholding islands held the largest concentration of slaves in the Euro-American world—about 700,000—compared with 600,000 in the British possessions, and 500,000 on the plantations in the southern United States. ...[T]he proportion of slaves rose as high as 90 percent of the total population of Saint-Domingue in the 1780s... . [W]e find comparable levels in the rest of the British and French West Indies... . These are the highest levels ever observed ... in the world history of slaveholding societies... . [D]uring the same period slaves represented between 30 and 50 percent of the population of the southern United States ... ."

Thomas Piketty, *A Brief History of Equality* (2022), pp. 68-69.

Whether the blame lies with the African "elites" who sold other Africans into slavery, the English who transported them or the Portuguese and French who ran the sugar cane plantations, it is strange to assert that the United States is the culprit in this story.

5. Perhaps, the most striking claim is that our form of government with its separation of powers and checks and balances, even our tax system, was designed to preserve slavery and the wealth of the slaveholders.

"What pro-slavery advocates feared most was democracy itself: that Northern majorities would use the power of the federal government to dismantle slavery. This fear shaped our political institutions in ways still felt today. To protect slavery, Southerners fought for and won several provisions that all but ensured that majoritarian rule over the South would be impossible. ...[T]he United States government is characterized by political inaction—and that was by design. ...America's present-day tax system, however, is regressive and insipid in part because it was born out of political compromise steered by debates over slavery. This generates inequality and enables large corporations to avoid paying their fair share—or any share."

Hannah-Jones, *The 1619 Project*, p.170.

This obsessive bias treats the Federalist Papers (and most political theorizing from Plato's Republic onward) as a sham or charade. But, there are reasons to fear pure democracy; there are reasons to avoid unfettered power held by anyone. The protection of slavery is not everything.

Many have praised the political wisdom of the Founding Fathers. And, the subsequent history demonstrated their genius. The U.S. has been stable and long-lived. It has become the world's wealthiest and most influential country, leading in scientific achievement, technological advance and cultural influence—not the dismal failure Hannah-Jones describes.

Indeed, "[Frederick] Douglass ... believ[ed] that a stronger political argument could be made not by condemning our founding document for supporting slavery but by claiming that slavery was antithetical to the Constitution and that the Constitution was, in fact, as he would go on to argue, a 'glorious liberty document.'" Hannah-Jones, *The 1619 Project*, p.19.

The "institutionalization" of slavery

"[T]ransformed into an institution
unlike anything that had existed in the world before[,]
Chattel slavery was not conditional but racial.
It was heritable and permanent, not temporary... ."

Hannah-Jones
The 1619 Project, p.12.

The legal status of slaves as property was not unique to the colonies and the treatment of slaves as the property of the owners was not historically unusual or unprecedented. It was part of the legal systems in England and France, both of which provided compensation to slave owners when they abolished slavery in the 1830s and 1840s (and France demanded reparations from Haiti in exchange for independence)

"[T]he law of abolition passed by the British Parliament in 1833 put in place full compensation for property owners. Relatively sophisticated scales were drawn up on the basis of the slaves' age, gender, and productivity... . [S]ome 20 million pounds sterling, or about 5 percent of the United Kingdom's national income at the time, was paid to 4,000 slaveholders."

...

"A similar compensation was paid to slaveholders after the French abolition of 1848... . [I]t was impossible to proceed otherwise once slavery had been enshrined in a legal framework."

...

"Although in 1825 France finally agreed to accept the country's independence ..., that was only because Charles X had obtained from the Haitian government a commitment to repay to France a debt of 150 million gold francs to indemnify the slaveholders for the loss of their property."

Piketty, *A Brief History of Equality*, pp. 76, 7-8, 72.

What was new, almost unprecedented, was an interest in the raising of slave children and, perhaps, the breeding of slaves. As observed by David Graeber and David Wengrow: "Most human beings need a good deal of care and resources, and can usually be considered a net economic loss until they are twelve or sometimes fifteen years old. It rarely makes economic sense to breed slaves—which is why, globally, slaves have so often been the product of military aggression... ." *The Dawn of Everything* (2021), p.188.

But, there were exceptions. In the later part of the seventeenth century,

"Moulay Ismail had hit upon the idea of breeding slaves early on in his reign. He found mulattos to be the most trustworthy of his servant-slaves and often forced his white slaves to wed black women in order to replenish his household of loyal half-castes. ...Such bizarre breeding programs were by no means unique to Morocco. Mixed-blood slaves were also reared in Algiers, in order to increase the stock of half-caste servants of the regime."

...

"[As for his private army of Black bodyguards,] [t]heir number was constantly replenished by the great breeding farms and nurseries that Moulay Ismail had established outside Meknes. He visited these nurseries each year and would take back all the ten-year-olds to Meknes."

Giles Milton, *White Gold: The Extraordinary Story of Thomas Pellow and Islam's One Million White Slaves* (2004), pp.129., 150.

The reasons for this American anomaly—what factors altered the economics, why American slave owners allowed slave families—would be interesting to analyze. Presumably, the nature of Southern plantations and plantation life made a difference. The less harsh climate and work conditions probably were significant. (Where a slave's life expectancy is 7-10 years, one would want only adults.)

Perhaps, the relative lack of isolation from the broader community, a greater variety of tasks for slaves, the business strategies of the owners and/or different values of the owners's families made the difference. What emerged was a system that made slave families economically viable. The acceptance of certain privileges for slaves, like their own plots of land, private property, leave for childbirth and infant care and time off for caring for the sick, the disabled and the elderly, enabled the transfer of much of the costs of care and feeding from the owners to the slaves. Was that actually further exploitation of the enslaved? Or, did it provide some sense of independency and agency?

got too old or too disabled to work anymore—and slavery left huge numbers of Black people physically disabled every year. Partly to guard against such cost shifting, state governments all over the country put up roadblocks to manumission."

Penningroth, *Before the Movement*, pp.7, 9.

Seriously?

It was African diseases that made African chattel slavery economically desirable in the Southern colonies. Yet, Hannah-Jones propounds a theory that the creation of chattel slavery was driven by a demonization of the Negro woman, by sex, sexual exploitation and sexism: "Black women were crucial to the racial-classification system established by white colonists to maintain and manage slavery. The colonial legal apparats treated them as innately unrapeable and their children as innately enslaveable, while the culture justified that barbarity by slandering them as lascivious Jezebels." Hannah-Jones, *The 1619 Project*, p.60. None of this triggers a feeling of insight in me, but I am not qualified to assess it. These are questions for multidisciplinary expertise. For anthropologists, economists and historians; maybe also, for sociologists and psychologists.

But, in all events, the consequences were dramatic. Slavery did not decline even as the importation of slaves was restricted, suspended, then prohibited. Indeed, there were some 4 million slaves in the States by the time of the Civil War (and 500,000 free blacks), up from 700,000 slaves in 1790.

"Colonization"

"...Lincoln decided that the same document that would emancipate millions of enslaved people in rebel territory would also call for them, once free, to voluntarily leave their country and resettle elsewhere. This idea, known as 'colonization,' had been circulating since the 1790s, and counted among its proponents presidents ... Jefferson and James Monroe."

...

"The American Colonization Society (ACS) [was] founded in 1816. ...By 1832, every Northern state legislature had passed resolutions endorsing colonization."

Hannah-Jones,
The 1619 Project, pp.23, 225.

The colonization movement with respect to former slaves is certainly understandable. The slaves had been brought here forcibly, held against their will. They did not support the American Revolution, but fled to the British. They tried to escape to Spanish Florida and had violently rebelled. Why would one think that they would want to stay if given a choice?

"Over the course of the war, thousands of enslaved people would join the British—far outnumbering those who joined the Patriot cause. ...Just as enslaved people during the Civil War fled to the side they thought offered the best chance of freedom and inspired the Emancipation Proclamation... ."
Hannah-Jones, *The 1619 Project*, pp.13-4.

"[N]early twenty-five thousand Black people unenslaved themselves, most of whom joined the British forces. In Charleston, many became part of Clinton's infamous all-Black military unit, the Black Pioneers. ...In the South,

As it turned out, when emancipation became a possibility, the freed and enslaved demonstrated their choice with their lives in fighting for the Union. In the following years of Reconstruction, the formerly enslaved exhibited both the desire and the aptitude to participate in government.

"Few were interested in leaving the country. Instead, most would have fervently supported the sentiment of a resolution against Black colonization put forward at a convention of Black leaders in New York some decades before: 'This is our home, and this our country. Beneath its sod lie the bones of our fathers.... Here we were born, and here we will die.'"

Hannah-Jones, *The 1619 Project*, p.26.

"In his final speech ..., Lincoln expressed an openness to enfranchising a limited number of Black men—particularly educated men and those who'd fought in the war." *Id*.

The historical judgment?

"Douglass understood that Lincoln's ideas about
Black people changed over the course of the war.
The president had been deeply moved by the valor
of the Black men who'd helped save the Union and
had been influenced by Black men such as
Douglass, whom he held in high esteem."

Hannah-Jones,
The 1619 Project, p.26.

"Lincoln's positions on slavery, colonization, and
emancipation shifted with the winds of political
and military expediency stirred by the Civil War.
But when it became a military necessity to save
the Union, Lincoln issued and signed the
Emancipation Proclamation. While the proclamation
opened the door to enrolling around 180,000 Black
soldiers in the Union army, it ended up freeing fewer
than 200,000 Black people on the day it was signed."

Ibram X. Kendi
The 1619 Project, p.431.

The frustrating question is why President Lincoln strenuously refused for so long to make the conflict about slavery. Did he erroneously assess the likely public reaction? Did he fail to see the likely military consequences? Was he simply psycologically unable to reverse or revise his original strategy? Was he just obsessively worried about where the freed people would go after the war? All we can say with some confidence is that he did not favor the perpetual continuation of slavery in the United States. One may debate whether President Lincoln's apparent vacillations over emancipation and colonization reflected evolving views, indecisiveness or just political maneuvering, testing and measuring positions, manipulating expectations; but, the end result was real.

"Un-Whitewashed History"

Michael Harriot's *Black AF History: The Un-Whitewashed Story of America* (2023), is a lively read. Harriot piles the sarcasm pretty high, but does not bury the story. The sarcasm is generally amusing and often insightful, but Harriot does tend to get carried away by his agenda. His more extreme statements range from seriously misleading to absurd.

Here are some examples:

1. "In the rare case this story is told, it is cast as a tale of happenstance and coincidence, but of course, it is actually one of deception, trickery, and greed." *Id.*, p.24.

He suggests that the arrival of the first African slaves in Virginia in 1619 was not happenstance; but, his recitation of the facts establishes that it was. Through innuendo, Harriot creates the impression that the delivery of slaves to Jamestown was somehow planned ("How did they know they would be welcomed?"). Once the English pirates had seized the Spanish ship and taken part of the human cargo, they needed to try to sell the captives quickly and they obviously could not go to a Spanish port. Harriot points out that they were not welcomed in Jamestown, although they did sell their captives. He identifies no evidence pointing to premeditation, noting only the fact of a relationship between the pirate captain Daniel Elfrith and Jamestown's Deputy Governor Samuel Argall.

2. "[T]he Jamestown project was saved. This is what made the land worth something. The enslaved labor was worth more than tales of gold and diamond trees." *Id.*, p.24.

He claims that it was the arrival of slaves in 1619 and 1620 that enabled the successful cultivation of tobacco in Virginia, ignoring that the labor used for tobacco production during the 17th century in Virginia was almost entirely indentured servants from England and that the substitution of African slaves occurred largely after 1700 and after the cultivation of tobacco had become a commercial success and was significantly due to their greater disease reststance.

3. "**Henrique asked one of his African servants captured during the Reconquista how to build these ships and avoid sea beasts. ...[H]e informed them that the sea thugs weren't killing white people; it was the wind! Using this new knowledge, Henrique assembled a few local cartographers ...Henrique's boys drew charts of the ocean currents and cornered the exploring market by mastering the 'trade winds.'**" *Id.*, pp.29-30.

He mocks the Portuguese prince Henry the Navigator, suggesting that the insight into the importance of the trade winds was obtained from an African slave, but it was Henry that caused and oversaw the creation of maps of ocean currents and trade winds that gave Portugal the dominant trading position in the Western hemisphere.

4. "**When the African negotiator paraded out the prisoners, those 150 captives included Europeans, Jews, Berbers, and some Africans. Gonçalves scanned the diverse parade of prisoners and asked himself which ones would make the best slaves. Then he chose the Black ones.**" *Id.*, p.39.

In 1441, two Portuguese explorers and traders, Nuno Tristão and Antão Gonçalves, accidentally discovered that the trade in human beings could be quite lucrative and that there were slave traders in Africa ready to sell slaves to the Portuguese. Harriot describes one supposed instance where the Portuguese were offered a variety of slaves of different origins and that they chose "the Black ones." He provides no source, so we have no context. However, it is unlikely that the selection was based on "race," as he implies, since "race" was not a recognized categorization in the 15th century. As he latter notes, "The discovery of personal whiteness among the world's peoples is a very modern thing—a nineteenth and twentieth century matter, indeed. The ancient world would have laughed at such a distinction. ...For most of human history, the term 'race' didn't exist. It emerged in the late sixteenth century to describe a type of thing... ."

5. "Africans had already ventured to America, slaughtered natives, and built plantations. ...Esteban, became a legend in places that wouldn't be called 'America' for at least two centuries. Not only did he explore more of the North American continent than Lewis or Clark, but he did it before most of the Jamestown settlers were even born. ...[He] discovered more of America than Christopher Columbus, Ponce de León, and Leif Erikson combined... ." *Id.*, pp.43-7, 48-51.

Harriot offers only one example of a Black man being a conqueror in the New World, who accompanied Ponce de Leon and other Conquistadors on their adventures. "Juan Garrido was the first documented African American. ...[I]n 1503, at fifteen years old, Garrido joined explorer Juan Ponce de León's expedition to the New World, landing on Hispaniola. ...Garrido ... hooked up with a new white friend, conquistador Hernándo Cortés, and joined the Spanish conquest of Mexico." The other example is "Mustafa Azemmouri, who went by the street name Esteban," who Harriot characterizes as an explorer like Lewis and Clark, but who in fact did most of his traveling as a slave following his owner, Lucas Vásquez de Ayllón. "Esteban supposedly met his death during this journey in 1539 at the hands of the Zuni, a tribe near the border of Arizona and New Mexico. Some non-European scholars, however, believe he may have convinced the Zuni into helping him fake his death so he could finally be a free man." These observations are not to minimize the accomplishments or skill and courage of these two men, but to correct Harriot's extravagant claims about the events.

6. "Jackson ... would enjoy the United States' one military advantage—the Brits were attacking a region that was now well equipped for quelling an uprising. When Jackson sounded the alarm for volunteers, over a thousand well-armed Louisianans grabbed their guns and rushed to his aid. They were better trained than the federal forces, and were prepared to fight. The paranoia during a slave rebellion made plantation owners in the area take their militia duties seriously." *Id.*, p.126.

Harriot implies that the success of Andrew Jackson in the Battle of New Orleans was a result of the slave revolt four years earlier, because it caused the Louisiana planters to arm and train and that those men made the difference. While the purchase of guns apparently increased in the region during those four years, there is no evidence that that made the difference. Upon arrival, Jackson declared martial law and ordered the enlistment of the local population in the defense of the city. His army of 4,500 consisted of "Tennessee and Kentucky frontiersmen, Louisiana militia, New Orleans businessmen, Free Men of Color, Choctaw Indians, smuggler Jean Lafitte and his privateers, sailors, marines, and United States troops." *The American Battlefield Trust.* Jackson won the battle through a surprise night attack followed by a strategic retreat to a position behind "Jackson's Wall"—a mile long, seven-foot high earthen embankment he had had constructed across the isthmus.

"The British attack got underway before sunrise on the morning of January 8, 1815. On the British left, Keane's infantry penetrated an unfinished redoubt, only to be brought to **a grinding halt in front of the New Orleans**

Rifles and the 7th U.S. Infantry. Maj. Gen. Samuel Gibbs's column advanced against the American left center where his **ranks were decimated by Tennessee and Kentucky militia**."

The American Battlefield Trust (emphasis added).

"On January 8, 1815, the British marched against New Orleans.... . Pirate Jean Lafitte, however, had warned the Americans of the attack, and the arriving British found militiamen under General Andrew Jackson strongly entrenched at the Rodriguez Canal. In two separate assaults, the 7,500 British soldiers under Sir Edward Pakenham were unable to penetrate the U.S. defenses, and Jackson's 4,500 troops, many of them expert marksmen from Kentucky and Tennessee, decimated the British lines. In half an hour, the British had retreated, General Pakenham was dead, and nearly 2,000 of his men were killed, wounded, or missing. U.S. forces suffered only eight killed and 13 wounded."

History.com, "The Battle of New Orleans," *A&E Television Networks*, updated February 4, 2021.

7. "[E]nlisting free Black recruits and emancipating slaves was not his own idea. Hunter often consulted with a battlefield nurse who had been helping slaves flee to freedom, enlarging Hunter's crew of renegade soldiers.. ...The famed conductor of the Underground Railroad [Harriet Tubman] was instrumental in Hunter's success in the South." *Id.*, p.168.

Harriot apparently seeks to give credit for the Emancipation Proclamation to Harriet Tubman, suggesting that she gave the idea of freeing and recruiting runaway slaves to General David Hunter, whose actions then forced President Lincoln finally to act. Although, Tubman was a valuable paid spy for General Hunter and served as a liason with escaped slaves, the first declaration that escaped slaves were contraband

and freed from their enslavement was made by General Benjamin Butler in May 1861. Congress passed the First Confiscation Act in August 1861, treating runaway slaves as "contraband," becoming proprety of the Union for the duration of hostilities. Nigel Hamilton, *Lincoln vs Davis,* pp.308-4. Then, General John C. Fremont ordered the emancipation all slaves in Missouri owned by Confederate soldiers fighting against the Union there, but his order was rescinded by President Lincoln. Fremont's order, nonetheless, received considerable public attention and the support of Secretray of War Cameron. See id., pp.300-1. Presumably, Lincoln formally demanded the retraction of Frmont's order because of his dogged conviction that such action would drive away the border states and many voters and his concern over a very real practical problem—what to do with the freed slaves after the war ended. The President seemed never to appreciate the likely impact of the moral significance of emancipation. *See Id.*, pp.291-5.

Curiously, Jefferson Davis had also confronted and rejected the strategy of granting freedom to any slaves willing to support the Confederacy, which in late 1861 was starting to gain support within his political and military leadership. Davis recognized that such a policy would both increase his military resources and gain favor among the European nations, the support of which the Confederacy had actively but unsuccessfully been seeking from the beginning. *Id.*, pp.368-70.

In May 1862, General Hunter issued General Order No. 11. In September 1962, President Lincoln issued the preliminary Emancipation Proclamation, which had been drafted early that summer. It gave 100 days for rebelling states to surrender. In January 1863, Lincoln issued the final Proclamation.

"Frémont was appointed a major general of Union troops in Missouri after the American Civil War began, ... [I]n August 1861 he ordered the confiscation of the property of Missourians in rebellion as well as the emancipation

---

of the state's slaves. President Abraham Lincoln, believing those actions to be premature and fearing that they would alienate border states, relieved Frémont of his command shortly thereafter."

The Editors, "John C. Frémont", *Encyclopedia Britannica*, 1 December 2023.

"[Benjamin F. Butler] was appointed a major general on May 16, 1861, being one of the first appointed by President Abraham Lincoln. He first saw action at the battle of Big Bethel, where he was defeated. He then commanded Fort Monroe, where Butler became the first to identify slaves who ran away into Union lines as 'contraband of war,' despite the Fugitive Slave Act of 1850."

...

"[I]n August 1861, [David] Hunter was appointed to major general. On November 2, 1861, he was appointed commander of the Western Department until March of 1862. Within four months, Hunter was transferred to the Department of the South with the X Corps.

...

"As commander of the Department of the South, Hunter began to enlist enslaved peoples, forming the 1st South Carolina (African Descent). He also issued General Order No. 11 on May 9, 1862, which stated that all enslaved peoples in Georgia, Florida, and South Carolina were permanently free. General Order No. 11 upset those in the border states, who were slaveholding states in the Union."

The American Battlefield Trust.

8. "[T]he Emancipation Proclamation—enshrined in white history as the document that kick-started the freeing of slaves—was essentially a formality[,] ... a performative gesture by a president who didn't have the authority, intentions, or backbone to free the people he had deemed inferior." *Id.*, p.170.

The Emancipation Proclamation was not a "formality;" it was a dramatic symbol. It altered the perceptions, the expectations and the hopes of people across the continent. As such, it was highly significant, and it was recognized to be so universally at the time. "From the antislavery constitutionalist standpoint, the only basis for direct federal interference with slavery in the states where the institution was protected was 'military emancipation, which Republicans repeatedly threatened to use to suppress a proslavery rebellion. Ironically, secessionists provided the opportunity to do just that." Adolph L. Reed Jr., *The South: Jim Crow and Its Afterlives* (2022), pp.126-127.

9. "The War Department and Congress eventually came around to Hunter's line of thinking, and formally enacted legislation through the two Confiscation Acts. The first Confiscation Act, signed on December 2, 1861, authorized Union troops to seize rebel property, which of course included slaves. The act authorized the troops to consider slaves as contraband but did not specify their status. The second Confiscation Act of 1862 clarified the position of the escaped slaves... ." *Id.*, p.169.

"Eventually"? By the end of 1861—a matter of a few months.

10. "[T]he reason for its impoverishment today is that America and France instituted what is possibly the most racist economic foreign policy that ever existed, and upheld it for over two centuries. ...[T]he decline of Haiti's wealth was an entirely American proposition, beginning in America's greatest superstore—the slave market. ...Haiti is poor because it was forced to pay 90 million francs, the contemporary equivalent of $21 billion as of 2020, including billions in interest to the City Bank of New York. You probably know the bank by its current name: Citibank." *Id.*, pp. 98, 99, 101.

Harriot implies some coordinated effort or conspiracy between the United States and France to exploit Haiti, but again offers no evidence of such. France recognized the independence of Haiti in 1825 in exchange for Haiti's agreement to pay reparations to France for the loss of its slaves. The payments were funded by French banks. The resulting burden on the Haitian economy was devastating. The arrangements were facilitated by Haitian government corruption. The involvement of the United States only began in 1915.

> "Although in 1825 France finally agreed to accept the country's independence and to put an end to its threats to send troops to invade the island, that was only because Charles X had obtained from the Haitian government a commitment to repay to France a debt of 150 million gold francs to indemnify the slaveholders for the loss of their property."

Thomas Piketty, *A Brief History of Equality* (2022), p. 72.

"In 1820, following the deaths of both Christophe and Pétion, forces from the southern half of Haiti led by General Jean-Pierre Boyer, a mulatto, invaded the north and reunited the country. During his two decades as president, Boyer vigorously defended Haitian sovereignty through a combination of military confrontation and negotiation with the European powers. In 1822 Boyer invaded Santo Domingo, expelling the Spanish and imposing a 22-year occupation of the neighboring nation. Toward the end of his tenure, Boyer negotiated a payment to France of 150 million francs (later reduced to 60 million francs) as indemnity for the loss of the colony. In exchange, France recognized the Republic of Haiti and restored trade relations."

www.nationsonline.org.

"In an 1875 loan, the French bankers took a 40 percent cut off the top. Most of the rest went to paying other debts, while the remainder lined the pockets of corrupt Haitian officials who, historians say, enriched themselves at the expense of their country's future."

Eric Nagourney, "The Ransom: 6 Takeaways About Haiti's Reparations to France," *NYT.com*, May 20, 2022.

The American slave market ("America's greatest superstore") caused none of Haiti's problems.

"Under French colonial rule, nearly 800,000 slaves arrived from Africa, accounting for a third of the entire Atlantic slave trade. Many died from disease and the harsh conditions of the sugar and coffee plantations. Statistics show that there was a complete turnover in the slave population every 20 years. Despite these losses, by 1789 slaves outnumbered the free population four-to-one—452,000 slaves in a population of 520,000."

www.nationsonline.org.

"...Haiti's riches could only be exploited by importing up to 40,000 slaves a year. For nearly a decade in the late 18th century, Haiti accounted for more than one-third of the entire Atlantic slave trade. Conditions for these men and women were atrocious; the average life expectancy for a slave on Haiti was 21 years. Abuse was dreadful, and routine... ."

Jon Henley, "Haiti: a long descent to hell," *The Guardian*, 14 January 2010.

And, the problem of corruption continued.

"Haiti's leaders have historically ransacked the country for their own gain. Elected legislators have spoken openly on the radio about accepting bribes and oligarchs sit atop lucrative monopolies, paying few taxes. Transparency International ranks it among the most corrupt nations in the world.

...

"Nearly a century later, ... the country's prospects looked good. For the first time in more than 130 years, Haiti was unburdened by crippling international debt. That was in 1957. For the next 28 years, Duvalier and his son shared a dictatorship notorious for corruption and brutality. Professionals fled the country. A desperate country became still more desperate, and the Duvaliers looted hundreds of millions of dollars. Haiti was perhaps poorer than ever."

Nagourney, *NYT.com*, May 20, 2022.

In 2024, the country is again being controlled by violent criminals.

"Haiti's National Police, the last visible semblance of a state in a country where gangs have killed and uprooted thousands from their homes, have ceded control over most of the nation's capital save for the vacant presidential palace, the international airport and the Central Bank." Kejal Vyas and Ingrld Arnesen, "Haiti's Police, Outgunned and Outmanned, Struggle to Thwart Gangs," *WSJ.com*, April 26, 2024.

If one removed the quoted material identified above and deleted the more aggressive *ad hominems,*[*] the first 14 chapters would be a pretty good history book.

E.g.: "The criminal enterprise called America is nothing but a self-perpetuating white supremacy machine," or "If American exceptionalism exists, perhaps it lies in this country's remarkable ability to conjure up 'something else' to sate its appetite for Black bodies" or "White supremacy is the defining characteristic of America's politics ... white supremacy has been the organizing principle of American politics before America even existed." *Id.*, pp.206, 213, 356.

"The Second Slavery"

"From 1783 ... to 1861, the number of slaves
in the United States increased five times over,
and all this expansion produced a powerful nation."

Edward Baptist
The Half Has Never Been Told
(2014, 2016), Introduction.

My brother recommended that I read Edward E. Baptist's *The Half Has Never Been Told: slavery and the making of American capitalism* (2014, 2016), because it would broaden my views. I did; it did not. (At least, not in the way my brother intended.)

It is really two (or three) books.

One is derived from and inspired by the first hand recollections of former slaves, set out in a number of autobiographical accounts and hundreds of interviews. These stories are quite interesting. As Baptist says: "Slavery has existed in many societies, but no other population of formerly enslaved people has been able to record the testimonies of its members like those who survived slavery in the United States." The other, shorter, book consists of his argument that slavery was the basis of the development of capitalism in the United States and the source of the country's astonishing prosperity. I discuss that "book" below. (The effort to connect the two books, according to the author, took considerable time, but his vision was that it was all one, self-reenforcing story that needed to be so told. His attempt to do so resulted in long, repetitive sections of, perhaps, a third book.) The two books do touch each other on one point. The stories suggest that slavery in Georgia and then the Southwest (the Mississippi territory) was much more brutal than what had existed in Virginia and Maryland. He makes the "old slavery" sound almost benign.

"Throughout the history of slavery in the Southeast, infants and mothers had typically been sold, given, moved, granted, and deeded together. The infant followed the mother in condition, since the womb was "slave" and the child of a slave mother was thus also the enslaved property of her owner."

...

"In older slave regions like the Chesapeake, ... a secret way of doing or making was a treasure that gave an enslaved man or woman a kind of leverage in his or her dealings with enslavers. ...Chesapeake slave quarters had large numbers of nonworking children and old people as well as those who did some kinds of labor and not others. ...Enslaved people shared possessions, but they also used them to mark out boundaries, forming relationships and structures out of both contention and cooperation. ...Though scarcer on the southwestern frontier than back East, possessions shouted all the louder, because they now had to assert an identity for people who had not known one since birth."

...

"In counties along the James, the Roanoke, and the Potomac, African grandparents, great-grandparents, and even further-back parents had, over the decades and centuries since they had survived the Atlantic slave trade, created the traditions and networks that enabled enslaved families to survive. They had even thrived, living longer and raising more of their own babies to healthy adulthood."

Id., pp.106, 113, 119, 149, 153, 179.

In the second "book," he builds his argument on what he calls the "second slavery." This effort is disappointing. Like other conspiracy theorists, Baptist broadly attributes motivation and assumes that subsequent consequences were all both predicted and intended. Baptist seems not to recognize mixed motives or the necessity for and benefits of compromise; the difficulties of policy and decision-making in the ever present face of uncertainty and risk; the significance of chance or the ambiguities of human motivation.

So, he characterizes the turbulent early history of the new country as all about slavery. It was not. In fact, the driving force behind the events he stresses was speculation over land, not slaves. The United States had a lot of "available" land. And, a lot of speculation, fraud and corruption sprouted and flourished over the acquisition of that land, drawing many prominent citizens, skilled conmen or swindlers and many "suckers." The succession of major expansions of the nation's territories fueled the frenzy. But, unlike prior speculative bubbles (the Dutch tulip mania of the 1630s or the South Seas Company of the 1710s) or the subsequent ones (the UK railroad boom of the mid-nineteenth century or the US stock market in 1929), this boom did not irrevocably collapse (but the "second slavery" boom did), probably because of the regular massive additions of new territory.

He also seems to feel a need to establish that slavery was a part of American capitalism.

It was. But, so what? He says:

"For some fundamental assumptions about the history of slavery and the history of the United States remain strangely unchanged. The first ... is that, as an economic system—a way of producing and trading commodities—American slavery was fundamentally different from the rest of the modern economy and separate from it."

Id., loc.260.

I am not aware that this is an important issue or what its significance is suppose to be. But, I think that again Baptist has it backwards. Capitalism engulfed and embraced slavery, which led to the emergence of a new, more brutal form of slavery, one that Baptist labels "the second slavery" and Douglas Blackmon called "industrial slavery."

The word capitalism is used very broadly. To be more accurate, concepts and practices we generally identify with industrialization, such as specialization, scale economies, discounting (to reflect the relationship of time and value) and cost accounting, were imported into the new slavery, as were the techniques of capital aggregation and allocation that we associate with capitalism. The useful and perhaps necessary accompaniments to free market price determination, arbitrage, speculation, opportunism and the focus on short-term profits clearly appeared. The impacts of capitalism (the private ownership of capital and of the means of production) on the creation of businesses and, even, industries, on innovation and on economic growth were not as relevant.

The question that interests me instead is whether slavery made a material contribution to the prosperity of twentieth century America. It seems to me that there are two possible arguments. One is that the value of unpaid labor was somehow captured and preserved for the benefit of future Americans. The other is that the current prosperity would not have occurred without slavery. Both are tough to establish.

Baptist effectively concedes that the "first slavery" (that of the Chesapeake Bay) was not a significant contributor to the long term national wealth. "The great continent would incubate a second slavery **exponentially greater in economic power than the first.**" *Id.*, p.49 (emphasis added).

"After the American Revolution—which seemed at the time to por-tend slavery's imminent demise—a metastatic transformation and growth of slavery's giant body had begun instead."

...

"Back on the east side of the mountains, meanwhile [by the 1780s], slavery in the old Virginia and Maryland tobacco districts was increasingly unprofitable, and even some enslavers were conceding that enslavement contradicted all of the new nation's rhetoric about rights and liberty."

...

"In Maryland's decaying tobacco economy, enslavers were allowing many African Americans to buy their freedom. The free constituted 5 percent of the state's 111,000 people of African descent in 1790, and 22 percent of 145,000 by 1810."

Id., loc.390, pp.2, 8, 16.

So, he focuses on a "second slavery" consisting of the sale of slaves from the eastern seaboard for transportation to the new Territories. How many went to the new slave camps along the Mississippi to produce cotton? Perhaps, about 500,000 out of some 3-4 million slaves in North America. Baptist repeatedly refers to one million slaves being affected, but his and others' data suggest otherwise. *See, e.g., id.* p.2.

"[By] 1820, whites had already transported more than 200,000 enslaved people to the South's new frontiers in the years since 1790... . ...In the 1820s, migrating enslavers and new traders moved approximately 35,000 enslaved people from Maryland and the District of Columbia; 76,000 from Virginia; and 20,000 from North Carolina... . ...In the course of a mere four years, from 1833 through 1836, 150,000 enslaved people were moved from the old states to the new." *Id.*, pp.112, 180, 256.

"[T]he slave population spread westward to the lands opened for settlement by the Louisiana Purchase, the dispossession of the Indian nations of the Southeast, the war with Mexico, and the distribution of public lands. Slavery spread rather than grew because it was an agricultural rather than industrial form of capitalism, so it needed new lands. ...Historian Steven Deyle estimates that between 1820 and 1860 at least 875,000 American slaves were forcibly removed from the Upper South to the Lower South' ...[and] that 'between 60 and 70 percent of these individuals were transported via the interregional slave trade.'"

Lincoln Mullen, "These Maps Reveal How Slavery Expanded Across the United States: As the hunger for more farmland stretched west, so too did the demand for enslaved labor," *Smithsonian Magazine*, May 15, 2014.

Baptist even seems to want to claim that slavery was responsible for the Louisiana Purchase. First, he attributes the drive for territorial expansion to a desire to expand slavery. That is simply backwards. The availability of new lands created the demand for slaves, leading to the development of the mechanisms to transfer slaves from the old South to the new Southwest. Second, he credits the Slave Revolt in Haiti (the French Caribbean colony of Saint-Domingue) with enabling the Purchase. ("Even today, most US history textbooks tell the story of the Louisiana Purchase without admitting that slave revolution in Saint-Domingue made it possible." *Id.*, p.49.)

It undoubtedly improved the terms of the deal for Napoleon's troops to have been diverted from landing in New Orleans and then decimated by the rebels, but is not accurate to say it was the cause. In any event, this example is hardly relevant to the question whether American slavery was the source of America's wealth.

He asserts: "The returns from cotton monopoly powered the modernization of the rest of the American economy, and by the time of the

Civil War, the United States had become the second nation to undergo large-scale industrialization." *Id.*, loc.331. In support, he cites the emergence of increasingly sophisticated financial instruments, increases in credit, the flood of capital into the various sectors of the cotton business and the development of a highly efficient market for the relocation of slaves to where the demand was greatest. These market responses surely aided the "second slavery" but were not caused or created by it. Similarly, the enormous industries that emerged around the use of cotton drove the demand for more cotton and, therefore, more slaves.

"The interlinked expansion of both slavery and financial capitalism was now the driving force in an emerging national economic system that benefited elites and others up and down the Atlantic coast as well as throughout the backcountry."

...

"After sale on the Liverpool cotton market, they went by canal barge to Manchester's new mills. Textile workers—often former operators of hand-powered looms, or displaced farmworkers—opened the bales. Using new machines, they spun the cleaned cotton fibers into thread. Using other machines, they wove the thread into long pieces of cloth. Liverpool shipped the bolts of finished cloth, and they found their way into almost every city or town in the known world, including this one. Cotton cloth was why New Orleans was booming,"

Id., pp.33, 78.

But, it is not meaningful to say that the wealth created was "caused" by slavery; it was the market and capitalism that caused the creation of wealth, given the existence of cotton. A partial analogy (recognized by Baptist) is that of fossil fuels and industrialization. "(Eventually, fossil fuels would enable windfall profits parallel to those stolen from enslaved labor)." *Id.*, p.323. One can acknowledge that fossil fuels greatly facilitated industrialization, but to say that they "caused" it misses the important parts of the picture. Indeed, for example, "by 1790, British inventors had begun to create new machines that spun cotton into thread at a rate that human hands could not approach. A new class of factory-owning entrepreneurs emerged. They extracted massive profits from textile manufacturing, but textile revenues also boosted and transformed the entire British economy." *Id.*, p.80.

Baptist emphasizes the increases in the productivity of the enslaved cotton pickers, reaching output per capita not subsequently achievable by paid laborers. He attributes this achievement to the use by overseers of "torture" in the form of continuously revised individual quotas (upwards) combined with savage physical punishment for failure to achieve the quotas. The treatment of these slaves was certainly terrible, but the claim that it significantly increased efficiency seems, at least, debatable. Clearly, picking cotton with both hands was an acquired skill, and long practice enabled certain people to excel at it.

Baptist then asserts that the increases in per capita output was the source of the wealth that propelled the country's growth. Yet, one of the ironies of competitive markets is that greater supply tends to lead to lower prices and improvements in productivity tend to get capitalized into the price of the input. So it happened here. As Baptist notes that:

> "[I]n 1820, the average price of a male 'hand' between twenty-one and thirty-eight years of age had been $875... . In 1824 that average had fallen to $498. By 1829, prices had risen again, to an average of $596. In fact, if we compare slave prices to cotton prices multiplied by the output of cotton per enslaved person ... we can see that by the 1820s the price of slaves had begun to track closely with the revenue generated by the average cotton hand... ."

Id., p.173.

The increases in the price of slaves ameliorated the losses of the old state slave owners who had seen the value of their slaves drop significantly. And, then, the exploding cotton market collapsed in 1837 (as bubbles are wont to do), wiping out cotton-based wealth here and abroad.

The "Panic of 1837"

"In November 1836, the [Bank of the United States] began to call in all its loans. ...[Biddle] deliberately induced a massive recession.... . Businesses closed down. Factories and workshops stood idle. The slowdown threatened devastation to heavily leveraged planters and cotton merchants. Interest rates offered to the brokers who flocked to New Orleans every fall to buy the cotton harvest rose to 25 percent. Cotton purchases dropped, pushing the recession up the rivers into the Crescent City's vast watershed."

...

"The Bank of England, the source of credit for British cotton-buying firms in Liverpool, began to get nervous. In late 1836, it began denying credit to those firms ... . [T]he annualized price of short-term business loans in Liverpool skyrocketed to 36 percent, making it impossible for cotton brokers to buy even as the full tide of the 1836 crop swept in. Cotton prices began a free fall that only ended in July 1837, when a dead-cat bounce took it to 6 cents a pound. In the meantime, collapsing British merchant firms had pulled each other down as they fell. ...And Le Havre, France's main cotton exchange, shut down completely. ...As soon as the news reached the Mississippi's mouth, arrays of interlinked debtors and creditors began to cascade down. One after another in the last week in March, the ten largest cotton buyers in New Orleans announced that they were insolvent. The smaller firms were next. By the first week of May, no one in New York could borrow, collect debts, or carry out business at all."

Id., pp.253, 273.

Meanwhile, the industries of the North continued to grow and grow.

"After the South's economy grew into a bubble, and then exploded, the North recovered while the South floundered. And the main reason for the North's quicker recovery was that northerners had reinvested profit generated from the backs of the enslaved in creating a diversified regional economy.".

...

"Between 1820 and 1860, New England textile mills increased their average capital investment by 600 percent. enabling the typical textile worker of 1860 to make cloth five or six times more quickly than his or her counterpart of 1820. By the late 1830s, northern textile manufacturing was creating new spinoff industries as well. The machinists who built and repaired textile machinery not only improved power looms and spindles, but also invented and then produced stationary steam engines that could be harnessed to factory machinery. Before the 1830s, steam engines were almost exclusively used to power river craft. By 1845, steam-powered factories were becoming the rule."

Id., pp..312, 323.

"In 1860, on the eve of what we call the Civil War, the four million enslaved Americans of African descent were the most powerful force in the country. ...Their combined worth of $3.5 billion made Black bodies the single largest asset in the national economy, ...eight of the ten wealthiest states held slaves."

Michael Harriot, *Black AF History: The Un-Whitewashed Story of America* (2023). p.160.

Perhaps. But, by 1865, it was gone.

The Net?

It seems clear that slavery simply was not the source of America's twentieth century prosperity. Baptist suggests that the drive for territorial expansion was caused by slavery. I think that is incorrect. The treaties with the European powers were good deals and generated wealth, independent of slavery. The Native American problems were separate from slavery. Cotton-mania certainly created wealth that was then mostly lost in the crash of 1837-40 and in the Civil War. Expanding trade, new financial instruments, the expansion of banks and of credit, awakened entrepreneurial spirits and the free markets resulted in America's economic wealth. Cotton and slavery were incidental.

"Re-Enslavement" and "The 272"

In December 2023, I read two more books about slavery, one new and one not so new. I have favorable things to say about both. They each contain sensitive, balanced and judicious accounts of their particular subjects.

I.

The older book—Douglas A. Blackmon, *Slavery by Another Name: The Re-Enslavement of Black Americans from the Civil War to World War II* (2008)—includes a strikingly empathetic account of the period immediately following the Civil War, depicting the circumstances of both the defeated Southern whites and of the newly freed Blacks.

He describes the white Southerners as frightened, disoriented and desperate, having lost their fortunes and livelihoods. Their industrial capacity was destroyed, the regional infrastructure severely damaged and the labor and skills for agricultural production (the slaves) gone. It was a time of despair and deprivation. Moreover, a substantial number of whites were illiterate and living in severe poverty. Crime committed by returning soldiers created fear and insecurity.

"African Americans, by the most critical economic measures, were not significantly disadvantaged in comparison to the great mass of poor whites that surrounded them in the South. Of 4.4 million black southerners, poverty was abject and daunting. But millions of white southerners shared the same

---

plight. And while more than half of southern blacks—about 2.5 million—could not read, there were 1.3 million whites among their neighbors who also were illiterate."

Id., p.85.

"...[A] spreading wave of internecine violence and thievery by returning Confederate soldiers, particularly against those southerners who had doubted the war. Deserters, who had been far more numerous than southern mythology acknowledged, began settling old scores. ...The increasing lawlessness of the postwar years was, rather than a wave of crime by freed slaves as so often claimed, largely perpetrated against whites by other whites."

Id., pp.25, 26.

Blacks were euphoric, but disoriented. The community was convulsed by wild, fanciful expectations and speculation. Yet, many were homeless and most were destitute.

"[T]he following year, in 1868, during a period of intense speculation among freed slaves that land was soon to be provided to them, many blacks purchased boundary markers to be prepared for the marking off of their forty-acre tracts." *Id.*, p.19.

"The war years were a conflicted period of confused roles for slaves. They were the subjects of the Union army's war of liberation, and the victims of the South's economic system.Yet at the same time, slaves were also servants and protectors of their white masters. ...[T]he extraordinary events in the aftermath of emancipation—no matter the deprivation or arduousness—must have been bathed in a glow of wonder and astonishment." *Id.*, pp.22, 31.

It was a situation ripe for conflict and tragedy. Indeed, one could have predicted disastrous results from the volatile circumstances. absent a comprehensive plan to address the challenges and rebuild the South, something like the Marshall Plan following World War II. There was no plan, and with Lincoln's assassination, no likelihood of one emerging.

With respect to the theme of the book, "re-enslavement" ("[b]y 1900, the South's judicial system had been wholly reconfigured to make one of its primary purposes the coercion of African Americans to comply with the social customs and labor demands of whites"), Blackmon focuses on the subsequent expansion of forced convict labor. He amply conveys the horror and veniality of what occurred through dozens of anecdotes and vignettes, but he fails to establish the conclusion he asserts.

Convict labor had existed for most of human history and was expressly permitted by the Thirteenth Amendment.

"Many states in the South and the North attempted to place their prisoners in private hands during the eighteenth and early nineteenth centuries." *Id.*, p.54.

"Arkansas began contracting out its state convicts in 1867... . North Carolina began 'farming out' its convicts in 1872. ...After white South Carolinians led by Democrat Wade Hampton violently ousted the last black government of the state in 1877, the legislature promptly passed a law allowing for the sale of the state's four hundred black and thirty white prisoners. ...By the early 1880s, twenty-nine of Alabama's sixty-seven counties were leasing their prisoners. ...County prisoners eventually far surpassed the number of men pressed into forced labor by the state." *Id.*, p.65.

There is no suggestion that the new criminal laws concerning vagrantcy and the like, while probably aimed primarily at Blacks, were enacted in order to supply forced labor. Virginia did not authorize convict labor. Many other Southern states restricted the practice (although, it continued at the local and county levels). The total number of persons subject to such treatment between 1890 and 1950 was some 100,000 (*id.*, p.7), a large number but insignificant compared to the 4 million people enslaved as of 1860 or the 10 million Blacks in the U.S. in 1910 or the 15 million by 1950.

"Tennessee eliminated the sale of men into its coal mines in 1893. South Carolina moved to end the state government's direct involvement in selling prisoners by the turn of the century. Louisiana banned the leasing of state prisoners in 1901... . Mississippi's uncouth governor James Vardaman successfully pushed for stopping the lease in 1907... ." *Id.*, p.351.

"Beginning late in July 1908, a commission established by the Georgia legislature convened a series of remarkable hearings into the operations of the state's convict leasing system. ...The architects of the investigation—primarily state senator Thomas Felder—launched the inquiry in hopes of proving corruption in the management of Georgia's extensive system of buying and selling prisoners." *Id.*, p.338.

"As the legislative inquiry progressed into August 1908, the sordid stories of illness and mayhem—coupled with even more voluminous accounts of corruption and payoffs—stirred an outpouring of public condemnation. ...In October 1908, Georgia's nearly all-white electorate voted by a two-to-one margin to abolish the system as of March 1909. ...Within another five years, Arkansas and Texas had abandoned the system as well." *Id.*, pp.350, 351.

"In March 1926, the front page of the New York World featured an exposé on southern slavery. The stories reported that in fifty-one of Alabama's sixty-seven counties, nearly one thousand prisoners had been sold into slave mines and forced labor camps the previous year... . No more men would be sold into slave mines by the state of Alabama." *Id.*, p.369.

But,

"Contrary to the congratulatory pronouncements that followed Georgia's 'abolition' of the practice of selling black prisoners in 1908, the state had more forced labor slaves than ever by 1930." Id., p.371.

Most importantly, the system described was not obviously motivated by racism. Indeed, the facts Blackmon sets forth indicate that the events were largely motivated and influenced by economics. Blacks were primary targets because they were easiest to capture and hold (which was a result of racism).

"A world in which the seizure and sale of a black man—even a black child—was viewed as neither criminal nor extraordinary had reemerged." *Id.*, p.9.

"Unlike the occasional white man thrown into the jail, the black prisoners, nearly all of them itinerants with no local families or white landowners to speak for them, could neither say nor do anything about the scant provisions." *Id.*, p.306.

At the time, law enforcement and judicial processes were paid for through fees levied on persons who were convicted. Thus, a person found guilty or who confessed to a minor crime or an overdue debt would be fined and charged with the expenses of his arrest and prosecution. The poorer defendants would be unable to pay. They would be sentenced to hard labor for a specified period of time. There were no facilities for and no interst in incarceration as punishment. Two types of practice emerged. A person needing manual labor could pay a defendant's fine and fees in exchange for a commitment to perform labor for the specified period during which he would be a prisoner of the payor. Alternatively, the government involved would "lease" the prisoner to a private enterprise for the duration of his term.

The resulting forced labor differed from antebellum slavery in that it was supposedly for a fixed term and was not hereditary. In addition, the "owner" of the laborer had little or no stake in health or wellbeing of the laborer.

"It was a form of bondage distinctly different from that of the antebellum South in that for most men, and the relatively few women drawn in, this slavery did not last a lifetime and did not automatically extend from one generation to the next." *Id.*, p.7.

"The key distinction, however, between the sheriff and the old slave masters was that since these African Americans were not his or anyone else's permanent property, he had no reason for concern about how they were treated by their new keepers or whether they survived at all." *Id.*, p.64.

"An unintended distinction between antebellum slavery and the new forced labor system became increasingly clear—and disastrous for the men captured into it. Slaves of the earlier era were at least minimally insulated from physical harm by their intrinsic financial value. But the convicts of the new system were of value only as long as their sentences or physical strength lasted." *Id.*, p.96.

Under the then existing circumstances, this forced labor was extremely profitable, leading to a strong demand. The payments were very attractive to the public officials personally and to the government entities that were recipients. Rules were bent, procedures ignored and innocent men were ensnared in the system. Intermediaries arose to facilitate the transactions, for a fee.

"Instead of thousands of true thieves and thugs drawn into the system over decades, the records demonstrate the capture and imprisonment of thousands of random indigent citizens, almost always under the thinnest chimera of probable cause or judicial process." *Id.*, p.7.

"[A]n organized market for prisoners began to evolve." *Id.*, p.64.

"Alabama's sheriffs were financially motivated to arrest and convict as many people as possible, and simultaneously to feed them as little as they could get away with. ...The job of a county sheriff became a heady enterprise, often more akin to the business of trading in mules than law enforcement. ...Increasingly, it was a system driven not by any goal of enforcement or public protection against serious offenses, but purely to generate fees and claim bounties." Id., pp.65, 66.

"[L]ocal sheriffs, deputies, and some court officials also derived most of their compensation from fees charged to convicts for each step in their own arrest, conviction, and shipment to a private company. Steady streams of telegrams and letters radiated from sheriffs, labor agents, and company executives in a furious search for additional laborers or to induce men in positions of petty power to arrest ever more men under any circumstances.

...Often the sheriffs' correspondence reflected a simple gamble by some treacherous white man that if he pointed out a promising black laborer, a sheriff or deputy would find a reason to arrest him and share the financial benefits." *Id.*, pp.100, 101.

"Parke's tally of prisoners held at Coalburg in 1895 included at least five hundred workers not accounted for in the state's official records at the time— indicating that hundreds of laborers had been sold into the mine through extralegal systems." *Id.*, p. 109.

"Across the South, despite claimed reforms in many states, more prisoners than ever before were pressed into compelled labor for private contractors— but now almost entirely through local customs and informal arrangements in city and county courts." *Id.*, p.375.

The practice, in fact, fluctuated with the demand for forced labor. It finally began to diminish as the costs of forced labor approached that of free labor and as technology and market change reduced the need for and value of the type of manual services that could be extracted by force.

"[T]he timing and scale of surges in arrests appeared more attuned to rises and dips in the need for cheap labor than any demonstrable acts of crime." *Id.*, p.7.

"Arrests surged and fell, not as acts of crime increased or receded, but in tandem to the varying needs of the buyers of labor." *Id.*, p.66.

"[T]he difference in the costs of legally enslaved and free, but impoverished, labor narrowed dramatically. The cost of buying prisoners from state governments had risen substantially—while the cost of 'free labor' available from hundreds of thousands of essentially indentured black laborers working on southern farms was flat or declining." *Id.*, p.352.

"[T]he economic logic of the system weakened. ...Crude industrial enterprises to which slave labor lent itself so effectively for fifty years were being eclipsed by modern technologies and business strategies. ...When cotton prices fell drastically after World War I, and the new scourge of the boll weevil ravaged millions of acres of cotton fields, depression set in across the rural landscape. The cost of labor plunged. ...In even the most notorious states, public cries to end the leasing of convicts to private contractors arose for the first time." Id., p.366.

Thus, this is really a sordid, tragic tale of greed and corruption, made worse by individual acts of cruelty and sadism (partly a result of racism). Public officials, like sheriffs and justices of the peace, made money through fees and bribes; unscrupulous entrepreneurs made money as facslitators; enterprises and their owners made money by having cheap labor and the public authorities wre to fund their budgets through the revenue from leasing out the prisoners.

"The leasing of convicts soon was generating in excess of $120,000 a year for the state of Alabama, an extraordinary sum for a state whose total general tax revenue—and budget—at the time barely exceeded $1 million." *Id.*, p.95.

"Payments to the state that year [1903] exceeded a half million dollars, the equivalent of $12.1 million a century later and a figure nearly equal to 25 percent of all taxes collected in Alabama." *Id.*, p.112.

"Nearly every sheriff and town marshal in southern Alabama made his primary living in some variation of this trade in human labor—some through formal contracts between the counties or towns and the big mining companies and timber and turpentine operations." *Id.*, p.127.

"Arresting, convicting, and transporting these prisoners was Eddings's primary livelihood. His and Sheriff Fulton's entire compensation came from an assortment of fees charged for every action taken by the office... ." *Id.*, p.306.

And, the Federal government?

From 1903 through 1906, the U. S. Attorney in Alabama (Warren S. Reese Jr.), assisted by agents of the Secret Service and with the support of the Attorney General (Philander C. Knox) and the encouragement of the President (Teddy Roosevelt), vigorously pursued illegal forced labor in the state, securing dozens of indictments, obtaining multiple guilty pleas and exposing the corruption and savagery of the system, as well as the identities of the principle participants. The crusade was hampered by judicial limitations on Federal jurisdiction under the Constitution.

"Roosevelt was also at least nominally concerned about the chasm between blacks and whites, and the gap between the conditions of African Americans and the promises made to them at the end of slavery." *Id.*, p.159.

"[T]he attorney general wished [Reese] to personally deliver his report to Washington. President Roosevelt had been briefed on the investigations and directed that a legal attack be fully pressed. ...After the meeting, the attorney general authorized what amounted to the most sweeping federal investigation into the working conditions of southern blacks since the Civil War. ... By late June, sixty-three indictments had been returned by the Montgomery grand jury, and locals expected as many as twenty more white men to be arrested.": *Id.*, pp.210, 211.

"Alabama newspaper editors, embarrassed by national reports about the investigation, excoriated the accused slave dealers." *Id.*, p.192.

"[I]n the three months since Reese began his slavery investigation, the guilt of every defendant called to court had in one manner or another been established. He'd won the personal attention and support of the U.S. attorney general and of President Roosevelt himself." *Id.*, p.233.

"[A]n internal review of all peonage prosecutions in Alabama in the first decade of the century found that of forty-three indictments issued..., all ended in acquittals, dismissals, suspended sentences, or presidential pardons. A total of $300 in fines had been collected from the defendants; four of those convicted served short periods in jail.". *Id.*, p.355.

II.

The newer book—Rachel L. Swarns, *The 272: The Families Who Were Enslaved and Sold to Build the American Catholic Church* (2023) —tells the story of the relationship between slavery and Georgetown College.

That story is rather more nuanced and much more complex than the recent media accounts suggest. In Swarns' telling, there are bad guys—Thomas Mulledy, William McSherry, Father Joseph Mobberly— and good guys—Father Patrick Smyth, Father Giovanni Grassi, Father Joseph Carbery, Father Maximilian Rantzau, Father Robert Fenwick, Father Fidèle de Grivel—and some who were probably just overly ambitious or overwhelmed—Father John Carroll, Father Peter Kenney, Father Jan Roothaan, Henry Johnson. But, the roles of the institutions involved are ambiguous.

The Jesuits in Maryland mainly inherited their plantations and slaves from members of their congregations; although, there is record evidence of some purchases (and sales) of individual slaves.

"Lord Baltimore would allocate more than twenty thousand acres of the colony's land to the early Jesuits. In order to work the land, they planned to rely on indentured servants... ." *Id.*, p.4.

"James Carroll, a merchant, landowner, and slave trader who came from a devout Catholic family. ...[I]n 1728, when Carroll wrote his will, he bequeathed more than a thousand acres of land in Anne Arundel and Prince George's counties to the Jesuit superior, George Thorold. The Jesuits also inherited his human property, who would become the nucleus of the slave community on a large Jesuit plantation in Prince George's County known as White Marsh." *Id.*, pp.14, 15.

"In 1756, the Jesuits purchased 'a Negro man called Tom' for the Bohemia plantation in Cecil County. Five years later, the Jesuits at Bohemia paid cash for 'a Negro-man named Charles' ... By the mid-1700s, the Jesuit order had become one of the largest enslavers in Maryland. ...In an accounting sent to their leaders in London in 1765, the priests reported that they owned eight plantations with a total of 12,677 acres, 192 slaves, and a total income of £696 for the year. ...The flurry of sales initiated by the priests in the 1790s would ultimately tear more than two dozen enslaved people from their homes on the Bohemia estate." *Id.*, p.15.

"By 1793, the enslaved people at Bohemia had fallen under the control of the priests in charge of the nation's first Catholic seminary, St. Mary's, which opened its doors in Baltimore in 1791, the same year that George-town received its first students. The French priests took stock and over the next four years sold at least eleven people (men, women, and children)." Id., pp.23, 24.

"'The sale of a few unnecessary negroes' would help cover some of the estates' expenses, Bishop John Carroll wrote in 1805." Id., p.32.

"At St. Inigoes, sometime in 1809 or 1810, the priests decided to sell eleven people, including a thirty-four-year-old man named Peter and his entire family... ." Id., pp.14, 15.

The plantations provided most of the revenue that supported the Order, especially after the Order was suspended by Pope Clement XIV in 1773.

During the latter eighteenth century, "[Father John Carroll] viewed the plantations and enslaved workers, which had already financed the livelihoods of a generation of priests, as a critical funding stream for the Church as it began to grow and extend its influence." Id., p.20.

"Father Patrick Smyth, an Irish priest who had spent time in Maryland, assailed the former Jesuits and their slavehthholding in a pamphlet that circulated in Europe in 1788, just as Carroll was trying to raise funds from friends and supporters there. ...The priests had hoped to raise money for the college in Europe, but given Smyth's allegations against them, Catholic leaders in Rome had decided, at least for a time, against funding Carroll's new academy. ...[T]he lion's share of the financing for the new college would have to come from the priests' plantations and the labor of their enslaved workers." Id., p.21.

"[In 1790,] [t]he clergy directed the managers of the plantations to 'determine on each plantation or settlement what is a sufficient number of slaves for the use & service of the said plantation, & that they be empowered, & are thereby directed to sell to the best advantage all that shall exceed that number.' The managers were told to conduct a similar inventory every three years... . ...In addition to paying off plantation debt and covering the cost of any needed repairs, the profits generated from the sale of human property were intended to flow into the province's general fund... . ...They had decided to allocate any profits generated by the estates over the next three years to cover the costs of building a hall, a 'study-place' and dormitories at Georgetown." *Id.*, p.23.

"Enrollment at Georgetown College had plummeted [by 1804]. Economic woes in the capital, along with a shortage of qualified faculty and the implementation of strict rules and moral codes that made the school less appealing to non-Catholics, were all contributing to the college's decline. To compensate, the Corporation of Roman Catholic Clergymen, the body established to manage the vast plantations, had given Georgetown's president direct control of the Bohemia plantation to ensure that more income and produce would flow into the college." *Id.,* p.31.

The position of the Catholic Church on slavery generally was disapproval, but the official pronouncements were rather equivocal.

"[A]t first, Church leaders frowned on the enslavement of Christians, regardless of whether they were African converts or Europeans. In 1435, Pope Eugene IV condemned the enslavement of the peoples of the Canary Islands since many of them had converted—or seemed likely to convert—to Christianity. ...In a series of papal bulls, Pope Nicholas V made it clear that nonbelievers were fair game. In 1452, the pope explicitly gave the king of Portugal the right to 'invade, search out, capture, vanquish, and subdue all Saracens (Muslims) and pagans whatsoever...[and] to reduce their persons to perpetual slavery... .'" *Id.*, p.9.

"When explaining his rationale to the church, Prince Henry would argue that, technically, he wasn't an 'enslaver' because true Christians would never do that. Instead, he allowed Portuguese 'missionaries' to 'save' Africans by converting them to Christianity. The argument worked. By 1446, more than thirty Portuguese ships had filed applications with Prince Henry for people-stealing licenses. In 1455, Pope Nicholas V granted Henry a monopoly on the African human market—as long as they baptized their cargo." Michael Harriot, *Black AF History: The Un-Whitewashed Story of America* (2023),. pp.31-2.

"In 1493, just one year after Christopher Columbus landed in Hispaniola, the Spanish monarchs successfully pressed Pope Alexander VI for a similar dispensation, this time in the American 'Indies.'" Swarns, *The 272*, p.10.

"In 1537, Pope Paul III condemned the notion that 'Indians...should be treated as dumb brutes created for our service, pretending that they are incapable of receiving the Catholic Faith' ...On the question of freedom and liberty for Africans, however, the Church's supreme leader remained silent." *Id.,* pp.10, 11.

"Rome finally addressed the question later that year [1864], focusing on Bishop Martin's pastoral letter proclaiming that American slavery had God's divine imprimatur. Father Vincent M. Gatti ... dissected the bishop's arguments one by one, issuing a report that amounted to Rome's most pointed and forceful critique of American slavery. ...Gatti acknowledged that the Church had tolerated slavery in the past but said it could not condone a form of systemic bondage based solely on race. ...Gatti's conclusion, which would be supported by Pope Pius IX, marked a profound shift in the Church's position." *Id.,* pp.199-200.

The slaves on the Jesuit plantations enjoyed relative privileges compared to the norm, especially with respect to freedom of movement.

"The enslaved laborers tended the wheat and corn that they worked for the priests and the small vegetable gardens that they grew for themselves." *Id.*, p.28.

"The enslaved families they knew tended their own gardens, which were filled with sweet potatoes, cabbages, and cotton. They raised chickens and sold oysters, eggs, and cabbages to passing sailors and others to earn some cash of their own. In good years, women sometimes saved enough to purchase a hat or a dress for Sunday church services... ." *Id.*, p.58.

"At St. Inigoes, enslaved families raised chickens and, in defiance of Mobberly's orders, harvested oysters on weekends and holidays." *Id.*, p.64.

"[T]he enslaved community at St. Inigoes ... now consisted of forty-one people, most of them children. Many of the older men and women suffered from injuries or illnesses accumulated over a lifetime of servitude." " *Id.*, p.32.

"Ninety enslaved people lived on the plantation, and only forty-three could work, he said. The rest were too old or too young," " Id., p.88.

The College was founded by Father John Carroll in 1789. By 1810, Carroll, now Archbishop, was considering closing it down. The next president of the College, Father Giovanni Grassi, who was to become referred to as the "second founder," turned things around. However, he came to argue that the Order should not continue to own slaves on moral and spiritual grounds. Starting with Father Grassi in 1812, there appeared pressures to terminate the Jesuits' slave ownership on the grounds that it was unseemly and uneconomic. Various officials advocated such an action and proposed plans of implementation over the following 25 years.

"[Father Grassi] wanted the Jesuits to 'take possession' of those cities, establishing a network of schools across the Northeast that would expand the order's reach and influence. To accomplish that, he made a bold proposal: The Church should sell its plantations and the enslaved people whose work had financed the Jesuits' mission since the early 1700s.." *Id.*, p.42.

"The Jesuit leadership ... embraced the idea of divesting itself of 'the greatest part of the blacks on the different plantations... . ...Under the plan, which was debated in 1813 and adopted a year later, the men, women, and children enslaved on Jesuit plantations across Maryland would be sold for 'a term of years after which they should be entitled to their freedom,' and the profits from the mass sale would be vested in 'some safe fund,' for the benefit of the plantations and for other purposes." *Id.*, p.42.

"In August 1820, they formally rescinded their earlier plan to free the Black people they held captive after selling them to buyers who could use their labor for a term of several years." Id., p.70.

"[Mulledy] was determined to attack what he viewed as one of the biggest problems facing the Jesuits in the United States: their reliance on the planta- tion economy and enslaved labor. 'Would it not be better to sell these farms and to invest the money in banks?' he asked. Mulledy suggested selling them all, at least for a term of several years, after which they might be freed... . ...Mulledy was calling for nothing less than the dismantling of the plantation system that had supported the Jesuits for more than a century. He was not alone." *Id.*, pp.72, 73.

"Mobberly was voicing what would become a familiar refrain among some Jesuits, that the Black people owned by the priests were draining the mis- sion's coffers, even though the Maryland mission continued to rely on their labor and the sale of their bodies to expand the Church mission, to cover expenses, and to pay down debt." *Id.*, p.61.

"...Mulledy and his supporters had been unable to persuade Rome to sell off all the nearly three hundred Jesuit slaves. ...But [Father] Kenney, who had begun prodding the Jesuits to divest themselves of their enslaved labor force back in the 1820s, seemed determined to move forward, even if it meant selling one handful of human beings at a time." *Id.*, p.77.

"Most important, Mulledy and his supporters argued, the future of Catholicism lay in the cities, not in the countryside. A mass slave sale would enable the Jesuits to establish colleges in Philadelphia, Richmond, and beyond." *Id.*, p.96.

"The most pressing question, whether to sell the plantations and the enslaved, left the men deeply divided." Id., p.95.

Finally, Rome approved the action subject to substantial conditions designed to keep families together and provide for the continued practice of the Catholic faith.

"In early July [1835], Mulledy and his allies finally had the opportunity to force a decision about the fate of the enslaved. ...The meeting lasted about six days, with the priests fiercely debating the issues on the table. In the end, Mulledy and McSherry emerged victorious. 'The Provincial Congress decided that the project,' the proposal to sell the plantations and the enslaved, 'should be recommended,' Grivel wrote in his report." *Id.*, pp.94, 97.

"...Roothaan [head of the Jesuits worldwide] had decided that the mass sale could take place only if a series of conditions—twenty in all—were met. ...Families should be kept together. ...In instances where enslaved people had spouses owned by neighboring planters, the Jesuits would need to purchase those spouses so that the couples could be sold together as part of the mass sale or sell the Jesuit slave to the neighboring planter so that the couple could remain together in Maryland. ...[A]ny buyer would have to commit to providing the enslaved people with 'every convenience for practicing' their faith... ." *Id.,* pp.106, 107.

But, the officials in the U.S. did not even wait for the formal approval nor implement fully the conditions.

"The proposal was sent to Rome along with a series of others for approval. But McSherry and Mulledy, buoyed by their success at the meeting, had no intention of waiting. Within days, McSherry had begun selling enslaved people." *Id.,* p.97.

"Rome had yet to respond to the province's proposal, but McSherry made it clear that he was just getting started. Outraged, Grivel wrote to Rome and described his concerns about the sales, including the earlier sales at St. Thomas Manor." *Id.,* p.99.

"The enslaved people McSherry sold from St. Inigoes ended up on the plantation of Henry Johnson. Johnson had a foot in two worlds: the elite Catholic circles in the Chesapeake and the wealthy planter community in Louisiana. He had won a seat in the US House of Representatives and had served in the US Senate and as governor of his home state." *Id.,* p.101.

The negotiated sale was to a wealthy Catholic plantation owner under terms that would tend to preserve families and locate them in Catholic regions. The buyer, Henry Johnson (with "a foot in two worlds: the elite Catholic circles in the Chesapeake and the wealthy planter community in Louisiana..."), however, encountered financial difficulties which hindered the realization of the plan and resulted in his default on later payments to the Jesuits.

"The three men—Mulledy, Johnson, and Batey—had come to an agreement. They met in Washington, to put the deal into writing: 272 men, women, and children—many of whom belonged to families that had been enslaved by the Jesuits for generations—were to be sold for the sum of $115,000, roughly $422 per person. The men agreed that $25,000 would be paid on the delivery of the first group of fifty-one people, who were to be shipped to the port of Alexandria, Virginia... ." *Id.*, p.121.

Georgetown College experienced booms and crises, as did the U.S. economy generally and cotton production specifically, over the next 100 years.

"By 1813, the mission's leaders, desperate to revive their flagship institution, had given Georgetown's president complete control over St. Inigoes and all of the enslaved people who lived there. Still, it was not enough. Georgetown's deficit stood at $ 3,000 a year, even with the income streaming in from the St. Inigoes and St. Thomas Manor plantations. It was clear that the Jesuits could not support two schools while simultaneously reviving their religious order in the United States." *Id.*, p.38.

"Father Giovanni Grassi, an Italian-born priest who would become the college's next president... . ...[H]e ... persuaded the Jesuit leadership to close its school in New York City and send its talented faculty ... to Georgetown. ...Grassi's decision to reduce tuition led to a surge in enrollment that wiped out the school's debts. ...Soon the school, which increasingly attracted Protestants as well as Catholics, was drawing students from New York, Pennsylvania, South Carolina, Louisiana, and beyond, in addition to the children of Washington's elite." *Id.*, pp.38, 40.

"Slaveholders all across the Chesapeake were struggling... . Earnings from the sale of tobacco, the region's staple crop, had slumped after the

war. Meanwhile, two years of drought had resulted in severe shortages...
." *Id.*, p.61.

"[Then] the Panic of 1819, and the republic was reeling. Banks failed, and property values plunged in New York, Pennsylvania, and Virginia. The prices of agricultural goods dropped by half. Poverty spread across the country, from the eastern seaboard to towns out west. ...Georgetown, which had enjoyed an economic and intellectual renaissance in the eighteen-teens, was once more in crisis, as was the Jesuit mission itself." *Id.*, p.47.

"Thomas Mulledy ... assumed Georgetown's presidency in 1829... . ...As the new head of Georgetown, he was inheriting a debt of $47,654.54. He managed to bring that down to $23,857.36 with the help of a large donation and other funds. But even that debt left the Jesuits' leadership uncertain as to whether the college could survive." *Id.,* p.116.

Contrary to the theme of the book, the recited facts do not reveal a special connection between the 272 slaves that were sold and Georgetown College.

"By 1793, the enslaved people at Bohemia had fallen under the control of the priests in charge of the nation's first Catholic seminary, St. Mary's, which opened its doors in Baltimore in 1791, the same year that Georgetown received its first students." *Id.*, p.24.

"Using the cash raised by slave labor on plantations, the former Jesuits had already established the nation's first archdiocese, in Baltimore, and helped to finance St. Mary's Seminary." *Id.*, p.37.

"The records ... show that the buyers, who included local farmers, continued to send payments to the Jesuits in the 1840s, the 1850s, and even the 1860s. ...had received more than $130,000 from the 1838 sale, about $4.5 million in today's dollars. The money enabled Georgetown to survive and thrive and helped stabilize the Maryland province's precarious finances. ...Income from the Maryland province had already helped finance the school that would become St. Louis University in Missouri and established the Washington Seminary, which later became Gonzaga College High School, in the nation's capital. ...Over the next decade, the Maryland Jesuits funneled more than $30,000 to [Worcester College, now Holy Cross] to cover construction costs, books, and travel expenses for faculty journeying to Boston....In 1852, the Jesuits established Loyola College in Baltimore, now known as Loyola University Maryland, allocating more than $40,000 by 1860 to support its operations." *Id.*, pp.207, 208.

There were staunch supporters of the wellbeing of the slaves who opposed the sale of the Order's slaves. Even if the Order did not want to be a slave owner, there were disagreements over what to do with the slaves that it held, especially those that were old or infermed.

"By 1817, a new priest had arrived at St. Inigoes. His name was Joseph Carbery. ...Carbery would become known as a champion of the enslaved and a sharp critic of the Jesuit leadership's treatment of the people it owned." *Id.*, p.63.

"'[We] were surprised and mortified to learn that in direct contradiction to the humane decision of the Corporation, sales of Negroes for life have been made and are making from the estate of the White-Marsh,' Archbishop Carroll wrote to a fellow priest in October 1815. Carroll wasn't the only Catholic priest raising questions about the legitimacy of slave sales." *Id.*, p.59.

"The Church frowned on splitting up families and separating spouses, and there is evidence that some of the priests took this into account in managing their estates." *Id.*, p.24.

"[I]n September 1819, Father Peter Kenney, Rome's emissary, ... told the Jesuit leaders in Maryland that they needed to change their ways. ...Even though Kenney was willing to listen to the enslaved men and women on the plantations and to press the Jesuits to improve their living conditions, he wasn't primarily interested in their general welfare. ...[H]e believed that all the enslaved on the plantations should be sold, whether or not it tore families apart." *Id.*, pp.68, 69, 70.

"Father Fidèle de Grivel ... and his allies said that a mass sale would amount to nothing less than a betrayal of the Jesuit mission in the United States... ." *Id.*, pp.96, 97.

"Before the Movement"

"In 1866, 'civil rights' 'had meant rights of contract
and property, and the right to go to court.
By 1954, civil rights meant ending
racial discrimination on the job, at school, in voting,
and an end to lynching... ."

Dylan C. Penningroth
Before the Movement

A contrast with several of the books I discuss is Dylan C. Penningroth's *Before the Movement: The Hidden History of Black Civil Rights* (2023), released in late September 2023. It reflects serious, labor-intensive research, lots of it. Using U.S. Census data to identify the races of litigants, the author and his assistants studied the court records of thousands of cases. The results depict real, authentic three-dimensional Black individuals who took responsibility for their lives and exercised agency, despite the formidable obstacles, some winning and some losing. Moreover, the stories are presented objectively. I make significant use of this book in several chapters.

Perhaps too objectively. Some advocacy would make the book more engaging.

The author has prejudices and is judgemental. But, we get glimpses only. He references "the liberal individualism that this book critically examines" (p.xxviii), but any actual critique is hard to discern. His observation that the Lincoln Republicans emphasized civil rights, and a distinction between slavery and freedom based thereon, seems to be presented as some sort of criticism, as if there were some ulterior motive or secret plan. Should they have done otherwise? He seems to be suggesting that developments in the twentieth-century could have been better if a different approach had been followed by the Republican Party and the abolitionists generally, but he does not suggest what alternatives might have been available then nor even how the outcome might have been different now.

"[D]uring the 1840s and 1850s, white northern leaders like Abraham Lincoln invented a worldview where a small bundle of prerogatives called 'civil rights' marked the fundamental difference between freedom and slavery."

...

"In the 1850s, antislavery politicians took the vast array of practices that made up the slave system—the horrific violence, including sexual violence and family separation, the task and gang systems, the hiring and trading and bargaining and property ownership—and boiled them down to one essential idea: 'the chattel principle.' **All of slavery's cruelties, they insisted, flowed from this principle of treating a person like a thing, deprived of fundamental rights.**"

...

"The Oregon dustup showed that standing up for fundamental civil rights could dovetail with a kind of least-common-denominator racial politics, and it was this combination that powered the Republican Party to the White House in 1860."

...

"[R]emember what "freedom" meant to many of those nineteenth-century Republicans: it meant the bare fact of not being a slave, the freedom to sell one's own labor."

...

"To understand why the Supreme Court's Republican justices believe that the Constitution requires government to be color-blind, we must remember how the party of Lincoln replaced the complicated world of privileges and 'community opinion' with the seductively simple principle of equal civil rights... ."

Id., pp.5, 83, 86, 350.

Yet, he claims that: "This book is not a lament for the path not taken; it is not about the lost promise of private-law civil rights." *Id.*, p.349.

The foremost issue at that time was legally authorized slavery, not discrimination nor "second class" citizenship. The objective was to eliminate actual slavery, and slavery was seen as a matter of civil rights. Also, civil rights were deemed to be within the province of the Federal government. What he refers to as "social rights" were matters for the states, matters of state law.

"Slowly, the high courts converged on the idea that there were a few privileges and immunities that were more fundamental than the rest: 'natural, inherent and inalienable rights of man,' as the Supreme Court put it in 1795, beyond the power of any state to interfere with."

In fact, at that time, there was a presumption of the right to discriminate; no notion of a right not to be discriminated against. English society was based upon segregation by class, as captured by George Eliot in *Middlemarch* (1872), describing the society of rural England in the 1820s/1830s. The community pressures were against egalitarianism, supporting discrimination, separation and exclusivity. So to in the United States.

"The [Supreme] Court had to answer two questions in *The Civil Rights Cases* [1883]: which rights were 'fundamental,' and what could be done when white southerners took away those fundamental rights. [Justice Joseph] Bradley answered the first question bluntly: 'It would be running the slavery argument into the ground' to say that a cabdriver or theater owner was violating a fundamental right when he chose not to welcome someone into his taxicab or theater. Bradley was just as emphatic about the second question: Congress could not protect people's 'social rights' with a nationwide law. It could only counteract 'state action.' ...Justice John Marshall Harlan's dissent revived the Black abolitionists' idea that denying any fundamental rights on the basis of race was tantamount to slavery."

Id., p.147.

There is one theme that peeks out several times, that is, that the free market system based on private property and "freedom" of contract is a sham. He even suggests, implausibly, that the Republican movement to limit slavery was part of an effort to "enslave" poor and working class whites.

" By widening the definition of 'slavery' to include racial discrimination against people who were not slaves, activists like Frederick Douglass and Martin Delany developed a critique of what we now call 'second-class citizenship.' ...These activists insisted that having rights did not necessarily make you free unless you had the same rights, on equal terms with everyone else. So long as Black people were not 'entirely free,' said Douglass and Delany in 1848— free 'to the full enjoyment of all those rights and privileges common to American citizens'—then they were 'slaves.'

Id., p.36.

"[M]ore and more white people nevertheless felt that it was money, not civil rights, that made a person free. America was becoming divided between a few rich families and 'a permanent factory population' living in bondage, they said." *Id.*, p.83.

Ignoring the suggestion of motivation, this is an issue discussed a bit above, in Chapters 8-10. At a minimum, one has to remember that until the nineteenth century, the vast bulk of mankind lived at the bare subsistence level. The first necessary objective was to create a surplus over which people could argue. Economic progress to escape the Malthusian trap requires saving, capital investment, entrepreneurship, ingenuity and risk taking.

History tells us that private profit opportunities coupled with individual freedom are the best catalysts for that behavior. Force, violence, terror and torture are effective means of acquiring power but have consistently proven incompatible with economic growth and prosperity. So, it maybe that inequalities and the appearance of exploitation are necessary to the creation of surpluses sufficient to permit significant increases in standards of living.

Without details of the arrangements Penningroth would put in place, one cannot assess whether his alternative world is viable or is simply Utopian dreaming. The disclosure of biases and reasoning invites evaluation on the merits, if the real world consequences are deemed relevant.

"Caste" and "Money"

I.

Isabel Wilkerson
Caste: The Origins of Our Discontent
(2020, 2023).

This book is very well written, quite vivid and engrossing. The stories she introduces in Part 1—the re-emergence in the Arctic of anthrax from the frozen carcasses of poisoned reindeer that began to defrost, the rapid spread of the Corona virus, silent earthquakes—are suggestive of important lessons, of insightful analogies, of game-changing analyzes, promising a fascinating adventure.

But, then she introduces "caste," a supposedly ubiquitous structural element of various societies including, notably, America. On its face, her theory of caste would seem not to reflect any of the interesting implications of her opening stories. Caste does not seem to have been just resurrected from dormancy, to be spreading virulently or to have crept unnoticed throughout society. In contrast, one might argue that racism is like the Arctic anthrax, that anti-immigration sentiments are like the Corona virus and that moral bankruptcy has slowly overwhelmed us like silent earthquakes. A missed opportunity to develop some meaningful observations about MAGA and Trumpism based on these gripping analogies. Now, that would have been an interesting book.

Her theory of caste is contrived. The caste system in India is very different from racism in the United States (or Great Britain). There have been millions of oppressed people in both countries, and there are similarities in the methods and forms of exploitation and discrimination, just as there are similarities between behavior in these countries and the treatment of women in parts of the Middle East and Africa or the treatment of minority groups in parts of Asia and Northern Africa. Otherwise, the origins, history and structure are quite distinct. *See, e.g., id.*, p.68.

The comparison with Nazi Germany (*id.*, pp.78-88) is silly. The fact that some Nazi social planners looked to laws that had existed in various states in America designed to promote racial purity by outlawing interracial marriages and criminalizing interracial sex does not establish a common system. There is no American parallel to the Nazis' Final Solution. The observation that the Nazis concluded that the definitions of Negro in some states was too inclusive (like "a single drop of blood") for their purposes establishes nothing relevant and is obviously stressed in an effort to engender outrage and prejudice. Such "grandstanding" has no proper role in a scholarly study. (I discuss some other examples in a later essay).

"While the Nazis praised 'the American commitment to legislating racial purity,' they could not abide 'the unforgiving hardness under which "an American man or woman who has even a drop of Negro blood in their veins" counted as blacks,' Whitman [Yale legal historian James Q. Whitman] wrote 'The one-drop rule was too harsh for the Nazis.'" *Id.*, p.88.

Wilkerson provides numerous gripping, powerful stories of horrific violence by whites against Blacks. They are stories that should be told and should be remembered, but they are not evidence supporting her thesis. Analyses of how such things could happen would be valuable, but they are not found here. She quotes characterizations and colorfully worded comments by historians and other writers. These are not evidence of anything other than the views of those quoted. The analysis of the elements ("pillars") of caste is, to me, rather obvious and repetitious.

She prompts readers to infer that the strikingly strange fact that mortality rates for white American men began to rise in the early 2020s was the consequence of the progress being made by Blacks.

"[S]tarting just before the turn of the twenty-first century, the death rates among middle-aged white Americans, ages forty-five to fifty-four, began to rise, as the least educated, in particular, succumbed to suicide, drug overdoses, and liver disease from alcohol abuse393.. ...In a psychic way, the people dying of despair could be said to be dying of the end of an illusion, an awakening to the holes in an article of faith that an inherited, unspoken superiority, a natural deservedness over subordinated castes, would assure their place in the hierarchy." *Id.*, pp.179, 181.

Why? What is the point? If she wants to makes such a claim, she should do so and attempt to demonstrate it.

Wilkerson observers that demographic trends in the United States indicate that in the next 20 years the "white population" will become the minority. This prospect has supposedly caused a panicked response from the dominant caste causing the War on Drugs, bans on abortion, efforts to curtail immigration and discrimination against LGBTQ citizens.

"Mass incarceration for nonviolent crimes, often on charges for which the dominant caste receives lesser sentences, keeps a disproportionate share of black men from the reproductive pool for long periods of time. ...All of these factors, undergirded by caste, keep the black birth rate structurally under assault." *Id.*, pp.393, 394.

Really? Does anyone actually believe that the disproportionate (based on population) incarceration of Black men is part of a scheme, or is motivated by a desire, to reduce the Black birthrate? Do you? And, how can restrictions on abortion, disproportionately occurring among Black woman, be intended to decrease the birthrate among Blacks?

Wilkerson recognizes the illogic and offers an "explanation":

> "Bans on abortion would seem to open the door to a disproportionate number of black and brown births, but the caste system, throughout our history, has shown that it can mutate to sustain itself when under threat. ...[S]ome Latinos, the white-adjacent middle-caste subgroups already being courted by conservative elites, could conceivably be folded into the white population to shore up dominant caste power, as with the Italians and Irish in previous generations."

Id., pp.392-3.

And, incredibly, "forced reproduction suggests an underlying will to curate the American population to forestall the day that the dominant caste might be in the minority... ." *Id.*, p.395.

So, the nefarious plan is to ban abortion, increasing the Black birthrate, but offseting that by incarcerating Black men and making certain Latinos "white," while reducing immigration of Latinos and restricting gay marriages. The grand plan to preserve the white majority. This may seem delusional; but, instead, it is deceitful. The issue is not about caste or a white majority; it is about partisan politics: it is about the supposed efforts "to enshrine the objectives of a conservative minority..." (*id.*, p.392).

Finally, notice her subtitle: "Origins of Our Discontent." Whose discontent? And, of what does it consist? We need to know before we can identify the origins. The "discontent" seems to be rather mercenary, actually, and its origin covetousness.

In the end, this is a remarkably unsatisfying and unsatisfactory book.

II.

Mehrsa Baradaran
The Color of Money:
Black Banks and the Racial Wealth Gap (2017).

"[A] story of economics, politics, and laws that
sowed the seeds of injustice
into the soil of the American economy."

...

"There are certainly stories of inspiration to be found,
but the overemphasis onHoratio Alger tales of success
can lead to distraction."

Id., p.7.

This book is quite frustrating. It could have told one or both of two important stories: one of the economic, political and legal forces that impeded Black economic progress and/or one of the heroic struggles of Blacks to get ahead. Neither quite makes it. The reasons are suggested by the quotations above. The analysis of the obstacles is tainted by the injection of moral characterizations like "injustice" throughout. The stories of the struggles and successes are viewed as a "distraction." (A distraction? To me, they are the real story, the meaningful and important story.)

Baradaran presents vivid, detailed accounts of examples of Blacks' thrift, initiative, entrepreneurship and resilience. ("Between 1867 and 1917, 4,000 black-owned businesses grew to 50,000. By 1930, the number of black businesses had grown to 70,000." *Id.*, p.51.) These accounts would make a powerful and constructive book. But, her stories are interspersed with what can most succinctly be called whining. Nothing is ever right. Always too much or too little.

- Black banks were essential/Black banks ruined Black lives;
- Black banks were too conservative/Black banks took too many risks;
- Black businesses were successful because of Black customers/ Black businesses suffered because their customers were Black;
- Black businesses suffered because they had higher costs/Black consumers paid higher prices;
- Blacks had too little access to mortgage financing/Blacks had too much access to mortgage financing;
- Blacks had too little access to revolving credit (credit cards)/Blacks had too much access to revolving credit;
- Jim Crow laws stifled Black businesses/The end of the Jim Crow laws did not eliminate the disadvantages.

Of course, all of these things are true, because the world is complex and messy. But, Baradaran seems to forget that. She seems to forget that people make mistakes, that capitalism is risky, that businesses fail, that luck can be bad, that the future is uncertain, that shit happens. She bemoans the mistakes and misfortunes that befell the Black businesses and communities. She seems to think that, in contrast, everything went well and easily for white businesses and communities. She ignores the white failures and setbacks.

"Such was the allure of counterfeit capitalism—it had such a convincing semblance to the real thing that it was able to conceal the fact that blacks were still being consumed by capitalism as opposed to fully participating in capital production." *Id.*, p.35.

She sidesteps the implications of the fact that many of the problems were the result of nationwide economic disruptions that affected all businesses. And, of error, mismanagement, unintended consequences, all with respect to government policy, legislation and regulation. Just the normal types of things that routinely go wrong.

- "The scheme began to unravel following the Panic of 1873, when railroad investments failed." *Id.*, p. 29.
- "The hardships caused by cotton and debt almost erupted into a revolution during the depression of the 1880s and 1890s." *Id.*, p. 34.
- "Many of these banks fell, just like their white counterparts, under the stress of the Panic of 1893." *Id.*, p.44.
- "The Great Depression brought down both the titans of black finance and the budding shoots of smaller black banks." *Id.*, p. 86.
- "By 1970, the country was in a recession. Jobless numbers were so bad by 1971 that the Nixon administration decided to stop reporting them. The new aspiring entrepreneurs in the ghetto suffered most acutely as inflation soared and banks closed the credit pipeline." *Id.*, p. 184.
- "Maggie Walker's bank endured the Great Depression and two world wars, but it could not survive the 2008 financial crisis." *Id.*, p. 44.

- "The financial crisis of 2008 disproportionately affected segregated black communities and turned the persistent racial wealth gap into a chasm. ...The financial crisis wiped out 53 percent of total black wealth." Id., p.249.
- Also, the Panics of 1890 and 1907.

Baradaran then concludes each example with accusations about the motives of other groups and of conspiracies supposedly underlying the outcomes.

- "Support for black banking and black capitalism have been consistent **policy band-aid** solutions, **a decoy response** to the fundamental challenge of overcoming America's legacy of slavery." *Id.*, p.4 (emphasis added).
- "The idea of community self-help, valuable as it was when there was no other choice, has been **deployed cynically** at several pivotal historical moments **to thwart** other, more direct answers to the racial wealth gap." *Id.*, p. (emphasis added)
- "The moment the war ended, **nervous cotton interest**s worked in local, state, and national courthouses and legislatures to restore a cotton-growing system as quickly as possible and as close to slavery as permissible. **Across the globe**, cotton traders and capitalists agreed that blacks needed to grow cotton." *Id.*, p.19 (emphasis added).
- "They could not be plantation labor if they had capital, which meant that **they were prevented from accruing capital**. Had they had land, they could not have been so easily conscripted back into cotton labor." *Id.*, p.21 (emphasis added).
- "Just as the Reconstruction reformers had failed to break the cotton oligarchy and achieve black equality, so too did the Populists. ...They failed because **the established political parties of the**

> **North and South** had already understood that **sowing animosity between poor whites and poor blacks** was the easiest way to maintain the status quo and to reject the costly and disruptive demands of a coalition of the poor." *Id.*, p.35 (emphasis added).
>
> - "Southern planters and northern industrialists **joined forces** in maintaining a racial hierarchy that benefited both by preserving the status quo. ...The U.S. Supreme Court **also fell in line...** ." *Id.*, pp.36, 37 (emphasis added).
> - "Hemmed in by the walls of Jim Crow, black communities had to create their own financial institutions, but **the injustice of segregation that created these banks** also made them weak." *Id.*, p.46 (emphasis added).

Perhaps, the most striking such assertion is the claim that somehow the pursuit of civil rights for Blacks after the Civil War represented a reversal or betrayal of the goals of the antislavery movement. Clearly, such a view mischaracterizes the objectives of the Abolitionists and antislavery proponents and distorts the nature of the subsequent efforts by Black leaders. There is no promise of economic equality in the Nation's founding documents. I think that almost everyone of any race in the last quarter of the nineteenth century would have been puzzled by the assertion that the struggles were really about property, not freedom. (Other books I have discussed make similar arguments that it was a mistake, presumably an innocent one, to have pursued legal emancipation and civil rights rather than compensation.)

> "Moderate northern Republicans began to pivot away from the fight for racial equality and began to see equal citizenship as an end goal to be attained by blacks gradually over time through increased education, work, and the accumulation of property. ...But even as reformers abandoned land and economic reform, they fought for civil rights for blacks in form if not in

function. ...The legal right to participate in democracy could not overcome the legal prohibition against engaging in the free market or the gaping gap in wealth. ...**Instead of land, freed slaves got rights that they could not use** due to their economic and political status at the bottom rung of society."

Id., pp.21, 22 (emphasis added).

Similarly, Baradaran seems to be claiming that President Nixon's promotion of Black capitalism, affirmative action in employment and government contracting and jobs was a complex and successful ruse, whether intentional or fortuitous:

"An expert in political détente, Nixon used black capitalism to let out just enough steam from the pent-up pressure cooker of rage in the poverty-stricken ghetto to squelch the brewing revolution. ...With this one move, Nixon took the sting out of the black radicals' demand for black power, jettisoned Johnson's antipoverty programs, maintained his opposition to integration, and even won the support of many black leaders. Checkmate."

Id., p.191.

Baradaran also attacks the wars on drugs and crime as part of a scheme to emasculate the Black community. I think that accusation is ridiculous. These efforts, in fact, backfired in that the tougher criminal penalties failed to deter young Black men from drug use and related criminal acts. There is no evidence that that result was foreseen, let alone intended.

> "The weeds that grew ...
> did not need to be fed with racism.
> It [*sic*] used the materials available
> —commerce, credit, money, and segregation—
> to regenerate inequality."

Id., p.7.

Baradaran provides clear descriptions of the economic challenges facing Black businesses. There was a role for Black banks because many Black communities were not being served by the existing banks. The Black banks customer base was dominated by small depositors, and the customers were likely to withdraw deposits frequently. The consequence was that the Black banks had to hold larger reserves than other banks meaning higher costs and less money available for loans.

The Black banks faced difficult decisions with respect to their lending practices. They were pressured to lend locally to Black businesses and individuals, but these loans carried greater than average risks. To the extent that the banks sought more secure investments, the money saved within the Black communities would flow out into the broader economy and its productive use would occur elsewhere. Much of the need within the communities was for the funding of mortgages, but again the mortgages tended to be of greater risk levels because of the volatile nature of housing prices in the segregated neighborhoods. The conflicts between service to the community and profitability.

"However, these banks also faced specific challenges. When they began to offer loans, there was often a dangerous conflict of interest. Successful banking relies on good underwriting, or the ability to choose between a profitable loan and a losing loan or a creditworthy borrower and one who is likely to default.

...

"[T]hey often made loan decisions based on factors having less to do with good underwriting and more to do with community need or pressure... ."

Id., p.42.

"Concentrated populations of black wage workers proved to be a bounty for the black banks. But that same concentration also created special vulnerabilities." *Id.*, p.70.

"Although Chelsea Exchange Bank took all of Harlem's deposits, it did not make loans to Harlem. ...The Chelsea bank manager responded that the bank's refusal to extend credit to African Americans was not due to prejudice, but rather to the bank's strictly conservative policies." *Id.*, pp.77, 78.

"Black bank deposits differed from those in white banks—they were smaller and were more frequently withdrawn, which made them more risky. ...In order to minimize the risks presented by their small and fickle deposits, bank managers held more capital, cash reserves, and liquid assets. All of this meant that they could make fewer loans and thus were not able to fully enjoy the benefits of fractional reserve lending." *Id.*, pp.88, 89.

"Home loans were inherently risky, but the key problem for black banks was not the proportion of these loans they held, but their nature. ...Members of the black middle class moving into a neighborhood were seen as harbingers of a neighborhood being swallowed by the ghetto. ...These fears turned into self-fulfilling prophesies, because once a neighborhood 'tipped' and was seen as a 'black neighborhood,' whites fled and the neighborhood declined... . ...Data also revealed what was already obvious to the black middle class: that the first blacks to own a home in a formerly white neighborhood paid a premium to buy the home to break the color barrier. So values rose slightly, and then, as more blacks entered the neighborhood, home values suffered a drastic decline." *Id.*, pp.90, 91.

"The crucial difference, one that would perpetually prove insurmountable, was that black banks' assets, loans on black properties, were not appreciating in value. ...The irony is that black banks, which were created to control the black dollar, were the very mechanism through which black money flowed out of the community." *Id.*, pp.95, 96.

"The decision to favor small community banks over larger bank networks was not racially motivated, but it did negatively affect the prospects for black banking." *Id.*, p.124.

"[T]hey had to make sure that a majority of their shareholders were black. This limited their pool of potential investors and diminished their ability to attract capital." *Id.*, p.244.

In the twenty-first century, the trend in Harlem is reversed and rising prices are the problem.

"Indeed, Harlem is experiencing something of a real estate renaissance, which looks more like a transformation. Instead of a smattering of small-scale businesses, Harlem now has large retail outlets, hotels, and businesses that have followed the wave of more prosperous residents. ...[R]esidents are being priced out of Harlem as Manhattan's booming population begins to overflow uptown."

Id., p.270.

Black businesses selling to Black customers often lacked the scale achieved by white businesses, leading to higher costs and, therefore, higher prices. The higher prices were a source of discontent among Black consumers.

Baradaran blames the reliance on installment purchases for greater costs for Black consumers, asserting that whites benefited economically from the availability of credit cards as an alternative to installment purchases. ("The consumer credit market shifted from the rigid and expensive installment lending model to the flexible and less expensive 'revolving credit' enabled by the credit card. ...This was another instance in which the **New Deal credit reforms created** an abundant and low-cost credit market for whites and **an extractive and inescapable debt trap for blacks.**" *Id.*, p.113, emphasis added.) I am not convinced. Credit card debt can be very expensive, and credit cards can tend to lead to excessive spending and ruinous debt. Indeed, she observes that:

"Consumer loans also came flooding into the ghetto. Where credit card issuers had been avoiding the zip codes where blacks lived, by the 1980s they joined the mortgage lenders and began looking for them. With the usury cap lifted and the general aversion to risk abated, lenders went looking for higher profits on high-risk borrowers. They found their ideal customers in the credit—and wealth—starved ghetto. And when they did, these revolvers, who paid interest each month, began to subsidize the credit cards of the wealthy. Credit issuers pulled on blacks to borrow so that they could profit from the attendant fees and interest. At the same time, blacks were being pushed to borrow by their low and volatile wages."

Id., p.238.

In addition, the exploitation of captive customers is a widespread problem regardless of race, as evidenced by company towns and company stores or the common practice in human trafficking of using debt as chains to ensnare people.

She offers no solutions to these challenges. She attributes them to segregation. They are apparently the inevitable consequences of segregated communities. They presumably would be removed only by complete integration, by the elimination of Black communities, of Black banks. Such a result could not easily be achieved, even if it were determined to be desirable. It would require rather extreme coercion and disregard of individual choice.

Otherwise, Baradaran suggests that compensation, the reallocation of wealth, would be just and a solution to the perceived problems, but she fails to indicate how it would change things going forward, what would be different apart from a sudden, temporary reduction in inequality of wealth. How, if at all, would the dynamics of the country change? What, if any, structural changes would occur? We are left with nothing more than a lengthy complaint about how things are.

"The wealth gap is where historic injustice breeds present suffering." *Id.*, p.1.

What does this statement mean or reveal? "The wealth gap ... breeds present suffering"? Why? Envy? Manipulation? Who is sowing the seeds of discontent?

It is correct that the government policies implemented with the New Deal and thereafter disproportionately benefited white Americans and failed to benefit Blacks. That fact can be reasonably labeled unfair. However, the repeated assertion that these government benefits or subsidies came "at the expense of" Black Americans is unsupported. (*E.g.*, "Yet this was a manufactured prosperity that left blacks out. **It was achieved at their expense.**" *Id.*, p. 107 (emphasis added).) There is no basis for a claim that these policies made Blacks worse off than they were or otherwise would have been

She sharply criticizes the arguments that welfare dependency was a cause of the deterioration of Black communities. Okay. Let's leave that hypothesis aside. We do all agree, however, that, first, the programs of President Johnson's Great Society did not solve the problems that Baradaran highlights and, second, the problems of the Black communities have gotten far worse since the 1960s, despite the welfare programs.

So, what is the explanation?

Baradaran argues that the amounts spent were too little, especially since much of the assistance went to poor whites. But, what evidence is there that more public assistance would have altered behavior? I note that a recent study concluded that the discharge of huge medical bills did not lead to greater happiness or, even, improved economic situations. *See* Raymond Kluender, Neale Mahoney, Francis Wong and Wesley Yin, "The Effects of Medical Debt Relief: Evidence from Two Randomized Experiments," *NBER*, April 2024 ("we find no impact of debt relief on credit access, utilization, and financial distress on average ... we find no effect of medical debt relief on mental health on average, with detrimental effects for some groups in pre-registered heterogeneity analysis").

The fundamental flaw and source of misdirection in the "wealth gap" analysis is its underlying conceptualization of the issue as a competition or race. Of course, anyone with a "headstart" will have an advantage in a race, but why is the essence of the matter how one stacks up against another? That seems to place envy as the central fact of life. I suggest, instead, that a fair opportunity to improve one's situation or circumstances is the key to satisfaction and that the appropriate comparison is not to others, but to one's past, one's heritage. I am not asserting that under that standard, all is well; only that the problems and solutions should be assessed within that framework.

"Beloved Community"

Because it was discussed in a series at my church, The Old Presbyterian Meeting House, I read *A More Perfect Union: A New Vision for Building the Beloved Community* (2022) by Adam Russell Taylor. I write about it here, because it is in front of me and because it wass the most expensive Kindle book I had bought.

Taylor begins by noting the importance of "framing," how the way a question or issue is presented or framed can affect how it is answered or perceived. Then, he goes on to frame his discussion quite aggressively to create his narrative. His thesis is that "America can never fully thrive as an idea or a shared political, social, and economic project without us choosing to become one people." He says, "The pressing question is this: Is America truly a people in addition to being a nation? Or do our ethnic and racial identities and divisions make it impossible to identify as a common people with shared values, aspirations, and experiences?"

One people? That sounds good, but what does it mean in practice? One, homogenious community? One culture? One reiigion?

"Cultural appropriation" poses a knotty issue for the "woke" orthodoxy. Compelled to challenge anything done by the white dominant society, one needs to accommodate the equally necessary commitment to a world of harmonious, if not homogeneous, views and values. How does one reconcile the preservation of minority differences while promoting uniformity? Well, one response is to make profit the key. It is wrong to appropriate something from a marginalized culture if one does so for economic benefit.

Is it permissible to do so for emotional or psychic benefit or for physical pleasure? What about for getting attention? *See, e.g.*, Ligaya Mishan, "What Does Cultural Appropriation Really Mean? And as accusations of improper borrowing increase, what is at stake when boundaries of collective identity are crossed?" *The New York Times Style Magazine*, September 30, 2022 ("[W]hat most people think of today as cultural appropriation is the opposite: a member of the dominant culture — an insider — taking from a culture that has historically been and is still treated as subordinate and profiting from it at that culture's expense. The profiting is key. ...The harm in appropriation comes when a culture is shrunk in possibility, reduced to a set of disembodied gestures — style without substance, which can verge on blasphemy, as when a non-Indigenous person speaks of having a spirit animal").

There are some specific points I feel are worth addressing.

1. Taylor cites approvingly the argument from Ibram X. Kendi's book *How to Be an Antiracist* that the opposite of racist is not non-racist but antiracist.

> "What's the difference?" Kendi asks. "One endorses either the idea of a racial hierarchy as a racist, or racial equality as an antiracist. One either believes problems are rooted in groups of people, as a racist, or locates the roots of problems in power and policies, as an antiracist. One either allows racial inequities to persevere, as a racist, or confronts racial inequities, as an antiracist."

Thus, it is not sufficient not to discriminate and not to feel prejudice; not to be racist requires that one be opposed to and seek to eliminate racism. Activism is required. We must not just be good, but must make others good too. That seems like a prescription for meddling and for coercion: we should all be part of a kind "Neighborhood Watch" to keep an eye on each other. That is not a very Christian idea.

2. Then, Taylor goes on to explain, "one of the most challenging aspects of building the Beloved Community is repenting and making amends for the deep wounds. ...This necessarily includes intentional amends through **some form of reparations** for the legacy of slavery." (Emphasis added.)

Reparations?

Certainly, the victims who were enslaved deserved some compensation, but it is too late for that. Would reparations or amends today be made as penance or recompense?

Taylor notes:

> "The case for reparations is often tied to all the ways in which 246 years of legal slavery served as the backbone in building America's wealth, as well as to the specific promise made by General William T. Sherman at the end of the Civil War to grant "forty acres and a mule" to every surviving family of slavery, a promissory note... ."

But,

- The first reason might have been persuasive in 1850, when the factual assertion would have been accurate, but that wealth was destroyed in the Civil War. Slavery was not the source of the wealth of the United States in 1920 or in 2022. There may be some property that was taken from or is attributable to slaves, but that is very case specific.

- The alleged "promissory note" never existed. Such a long-term commitment could not have been validly created by General Sherman as a war time executive order, only by an act of Congress. The "40 acres and a mule" was proposed as a means of assisting the former slaves to become self sufficient and independent. It is a tragedy that it did not happen. We would likely have had a stronger country if it had. (The equivalent today would be education.)
- As a matter of compensation, it could never be enough to eliminate the resentment or quell demands for more.
- If the goal is restitution (to put the descendants of slaves in the position that they would have been in but for slavery), few of them would agree to be so treated today. Many would have descended from slaves anyway, slaves in Africa. They would be living in Africa or the Caribbean with average incomes of about 10% of what they earn here or receive in government benefits. Indeed, there are billions of people in the world world who eagerly change places with them and millions who would risk their lives to do so.

"[T]he large medieval West African states of Mali, Ghana, and Songhai made heavy use of slaves in the government, the army, and agriculture, adopting organizational models from the Muslim North African states with whom they traded. ...Many African states had become organized around slaving... . ...[S]lavery had become much more prevalent within Africa itself. ...After 1807, ...slaving and slavery did not end. Rather, slaves were settled on large plantations ... spread throughout the empire (corresponding to most of the interior of Ghana). ...[T]he abolition of the slave trade, rather than making slavery in Africa wither away, simply led to a redeployment of the slaves, who were now used within Africa rather than in the Americas."

Daron; Acemoglu and James A. Robinson, *Why Nations Fail: The Origins of Power, Prosperity, and Poverty* (2012), pp.251, 256, 257.

- Or, penance? Was not the Civl War penance on an unprecedented scale? The Christian thing would be to forgive, especially the "sins of the fathers."

3. Taylor invokes the early Church, presumably as an example to follow: "In scripture there are countless glimpses into God's preferred future. In Acts 2 and 4, the Apostle Paul paints a picture of the Beloved Community in the early church, where resources are shared, everyone is cared for, and multiethnic, multilingual, and multinational community takes shape." However, the earliest Christians believed that the world was about to end, that Judgment Day was at hand. People behave differently when they think they are about to die. Watch the movie *On the Beach* (preferably the 1960 version in black and white). Of course, the Church then struggled when confronted with the lack of the imminent end.

4. Taylor discusses the founding myths of America and how to change them. Referencing Richard T. Hughes, Taylor states:

> "Hughes identifies five myths that emerged in specific periods of American history; to varying degrees, each flourishes today, often in combination with others. While most of these myths hold a kernel of truth and offer the potential for good, in the absolutizing and distorting of them, Americans have often undermined the potential virtues that otherwise stood at their *respective* cores."

These myths are:

- "The Myth of a Chosen Nation—the notion that God Almighty chose the United States for a special mission in the world.

- The Myth of Nature's Nation—the conviction that American ideals and institutions are rooted in the natural order, that is, in God's own intentions first revealed at the dawn of civilization.
- The Myth of the Millennial Nation—the notion that the United States, building on that natural order, will usher in a final golden age for all humankind.
- The Myth of a Christian Nation—the claim that America is a Christian nation, consistently guided by Christian values.
- The Myth of the Innocent Nation—the conviction that, while other nations may have blood on their hands, the nobility of the American cause always redeems the nation and renders it innocent."

The difficulties here are that while each of these myths appeared with some force in the course of our history (from the first Puritans in the 17th century to Woodrow Wilson in 1917), none has much of any traction today. They are a part of our history, a part of which we should be aware. But, ask people today is America the nation "that God Almighty chose ... for a special mission in the world", how many would say yes? "Manifest destiny"? The same.

5. Astonishingly, Taylor argues that stigmatizing certain other nations as evil can blind us to our own shortcomings, but there are in fact differences in the moral status of nations. Some are imperfect but striving to be better; some are evil and revel in being so. The world may now be starting to recognize that it may not be possible to be neutral, that one may have to choose. Can we simply tolerate Russia, Iran, North Korea?

6. Taylor recognizes that there are different points of view, but he recognizes only one as correct.

> "While history is always told from a particular vantage point, if every American were able to receive a more accurate and honest baseline understanding of our nation's history, our conversations around who we are, what we value, and who we want to be would have common ground and be much less contentious."

"[A] more accurate and honest baseline understanding"?

Really?

And,

7. Taylor says that our politics are corrupted today by identity politics, by seeing the other as evil, by attributing motives.

> "Polarization—so often driven and exacerbated by distrust, anger, grievance, contempt, and vitriol—has poisoned our politics and public discourse. It has become one of the greatest threats to our democracy and civic health....[He claims to admire] deep commitment to disagree without impugning other participants' motives or character and to engage in ways that enable us to learn from and be changed by each other's perspectives, expertise, and convictions."

Yet, like any typical conspiracy theorist, he sees the motive of racial discrimination in virtually every Republican legislative action, Federal or state, in the last 50 years. Do you really think that the War on Drugs and the War on Crime were plots designed in order to incarcerate more

Black males and weaken the Black community? Do you really think that voter fraud ended with Lyndon Johnson and Richard Daly (giving the presidency to JFK)? That we no longer need any election safeguards? Attributing motive is a dangerous game.

For me, Taylor's book does not advance the discussion or shed light on the issues. It certainly fails to offer meaningful solutions.

"What Kind of Christianity"

A new book by theology professor William Yoo examines the relationship between the Presbyterian Church in America and slavery up to the Civil War. *What Kind of Christianity: A History of Slavery and Anti-Black Racism in the Presbyterian Church* (2022). (It now has the distinction of being the most expensive Kindle book that I have purchased. The two most expensive are also the two shortest, but the length is not relevant for pricing ebooks since the production cost is zero. Both books concern religion and race.)

The reviewers all praise Yoo for confronting or exposing the "complicity" of the Presbyterian Church in the U. S. with the existence of slavery in this country. Curiously, Yoo himself never explicitly asserts that the Church was "complicit," though he undoubtedly thinks so.

He says, rather indirectly, that White Christians were complicit in Black slavery. For example:

- "[T]he need to identify and confront the sinfulness of white Christians in their active participation and **intentional complicity** in Black enslavement." *Id.*, p.28.

- "A plethora of white individuals and institutions in the northern states made moral compromises to accommodate enslavers and thusly **exhibit their complicity** in Black enslavement." *Id.*, p.173.

And, he quotes many others who made the accusation. *See, e.g., Id.,* pp.36, 41. Not that this curious circumstance makes any real difference to my discussion below. I looked at the evidence he collected, not his conclusory characterizations.

THE OFFICIAL POSITION

Yoo's discussion of the official position of the denomination is relatively brief but scattered. Here are the basic points:

> "In 1815, the PCUSA General Assembly commissioners affirmed an earlier resolution from twenty years prior that Black enslavement was a complicated matter requiring a charitable spirit of peace because of the great diversity of viewpoints within their denomination, but they added to their resolution a note stating that the 'buying and selling of slaves by way of traffic' was 'inconsistent with the spirit of the gospel.'"
>
> ...
>
> "[T]he General Assembly in 1818 declared 'the **voluntary enslaving of one part of the human race by another'** was a 'gross violation' of human **rights and 'totally irreconcilable with the spirit and principles of the gospel of Christ,** [but, the inclusion of] the exhortation to '**forbear harsh censures' toward enslavers** in the same resolution resulted in **no concrete** actions toward Black liberation. ...[It] **denounced [slavery] in principle but recommended no disciplinary action against enslavers.**"
>
> ...

"In 1836, approximately 250 commissioners from across the northern and southern states gathered in Pittsburgh for the annual meeting of the General Assembly of the Presbyterian Church in the United States of America (PCUSA), the largest Presbyterian denomination in the nation with over 2,800 congregations and nearly 220,000 members. One of the matters these Presbyterians would grapple with was their church's position on the enslavement of more than two million Black persons."

Id., pp.50, 14, 13 (emphasis added).

But, Yoo reports, "the 'subject of slavery' was introduced at one session with a majority report comprising a mere 211 words, postponed in two other sessions, and then indefinitely postponed by a vote of 154 in favor, 87 in opposition, and 4 abstentions." *Id.*, p.17.

Remember, the importation of slaves into the U.S. was suspended from the early 1770s until 1800, then banned in 1807, effective 1808. Between 1774 and 1807, most northern states had banned slavery.

In the end, his principal criticism of the official position is that it permitted slave owners to be Church members and to participate in the Sacraments. He seems to believe that the only proper Christian thing to have done is banish them (and their families?) from the congregation and refuse them Communion, rather like some Catholics today think should be done to President Biden because of his advocacy of abortion.

(Apparently, the Church had some 60,000 members in 1837 because they disavowed "original sin." *Id.*, p.184.) Was there a moral imperative to deny slave owners and supporters of slavery participation in the church community? Is that the Christian way? It certainly was not Christ's approach to sinners.

Yoo is obviously highly critical that Church leaders gave any weight to the facts that the future of slavery was a political matter, that it was very "complicated" or that there was widespread disagreement over what should be done. (And, all three were facts in the nineteenth century prior to the Civil War, especially with respect to what should happen to the people that had been enslaved.) Every one and all are to him irrelevant or only pretense. (Yoo notes that the two largest national denominational organizations both fell apart in the mid-nineteenth century (1857 for the new PCUSA and May 1861 for the original PCUSA), leaving just regional Presbyterian organizations until 1983. *Id.*, p.29. The splintering of the Church was largely due to disagreements related to slavery.)

A FALSEHOOD?

Yoo identifies what he considers a falsehood about the Presbyterian Church and slavery: that people did not know the realities of slavery. If they were not fully informed, it was a conscious choice they made to be ignorant. Yet, Yoo's lengthy (and very informative and moving) summaries of a relative handful of largely autobiographical books published between 1836 and 1860 disclosing the truth about slavery belies his assertion.

The information was not widely available, only the pamphleteering. Indeed, *Uncle Tom' Cabin* in 1851/1852 was met with charges of exaggeration, causing Harriet Beecher Stowe to publish a companion guide (a "Key") setting out evidence supporting her descriptions in 1853. *Id.*, pp.83-4.

"At the time of publication the book's portrayal of the sheer brutality of slavery proved revelatory to many readers and added fuel to the already surging antislavery movement. ...In book form, it sold three hundred thousand copies in just the first three months after its publication. In the North, [*Uncle Tom' Cabin*] confirmed readers' worst imaginings about the true nature of slavery... ." Erik Larson, *The Demon of Unrest: A Saga of Hubris, Heartbreak, and Heroism at the Dawn of the Civil War* (2024), pp.45, 46.

In addition,

> "Over one hundred ... survivors published their autobiographies during the nineteenth century. As time went on, such memoirs found a market, in no small part because escapees from southern captivity were changing the minds of some of the northern whites about what the expansion of slavery meant for them."

Edward E. Baptist, *The Half Has Never Been Told: slavery and the making of American capitalism* (2014, 2016) (Kindle), loc.404.

And, of course, "normal conditions" were quite different then. Corporal punishment, including flogging, was commonplace in the nineteenth century. It was employed in schools, the military, the criminal justice system and in private homes. As another example, many immigrants had experienced very difficult trans-Atlantic crossings. Also, all the colonies had had indentured servitude, where the right to an individual's labor could be sold to another. *See* Note on Slavery, below. I do not mean to minimize the sufferings of slaves, but I think it creditable that many Americans did not appreciate the extent or severity of the abuses, attributing the worse incidents reported as the doings of a relative few "monsters".

As to the evidence of Church "complicity," Yoo cites the fact that many Presbyterians were slave holders, including several Presbyterian ministers; that there were reports that some Presbyterian slave holders engaged in physical abuse of slaves; and that many ministers preached biblical interpretations that portrayed slavery as God's will (the mark of Cain, the curse of Ham, various versions of Manifest Destiny). *See id.*, pp.189-95.

Certainly, there were many Presbyterian slave owners. Yoo cites estimates that 80,000 slaves were owned by Presbyterians in the 1850s, when Presbyterians numbered almost 400,000. But, Yoo estimates the number of Presbyterian slave owners as 50,000 to 75,000 in 1860 (averaging 1.1 to 1.6 slaves per owner?). *Id.*, pp.22-4. In the U. S. at the time, about 1.5% of the population owned slaves (averaging about 10 slaves per owner). Could it be that proportionally more Presbyterians owned slaves but far fewer than other groups? (No.) ** Yoo does not make that claim. Nor does he suggest that Presbyterians were more abusive than others. As for the biblical interpretations, absent evidence that they were advanced in bad faith, I fail to see that as immoral or complicit.*** So, we are left with the affirmative acts of individuals in their own lives. And, "guilty bystanders who chose to be complicit through inaction and indecision." *Id.*, p.29.

Perhaps, most striking to me is Yoo's reaction to what he perceives as greater attention being paid by many Presbyterians to the consequences of the rupturing of the denomination over slavery than to the consequences of slavery. He utilizes his strongest critical language in discussing that perceived error of priorities.

"I find it **deeply troubling** that the withering of Presbyterianism **is attributed to these ecclesial schisms and not the active participation of white Presbyterians in slavery.** It is also infuriating that Black enslavement is presented as a barrier to church unity rather than a tragedy. ... [T]he terrible result is that some white Presbyterians today **feel more remorse for church disunity** than the oppressive abuse and reprehensible violence that their Presbyterian predecessors inflicted upon enslaved persons."

Id., p.30 (emphasis added).

And,

"...one struggles to find **the requisite anger** over the pain and torture that millions of enslaved persons suffered from white Presbyterian enslavers, supporters of Black enslavement, and **guilty bystanders who chose to be complicit through inaction and indecision.**"

Id., p.29 (emphasis added).

This obsession is odd. The state of the Church is clearly an appropriate concern of its members and is something that can be addressed currently.

And, what about "forgive and forget"?

> "For I will forgive their iniquity,
> and their sin I will remember no more."

Jeremiah 31:33-34

There is no doubt that after the Civil War, Presbyterians, like other white Americans, were strongly racist. The debates over what should be done with the freed slaves had focused on whether to send them back to Africa or to settle them in a new, separate territory in North America. (Since the vast preponderance of ex slaves had been born here and had no connections with Africa, the first option seemed cruel and highly coercive.) Few people then thought full integration was desirable or even feasible.

I think that slavery presented levels of moral culpability. The most evil were the owners or masters who engaged in sexual or severe physical abuse of enslaved persons. The sins of these persons was not directly tied to slavery, but slavery dramatically opened up opportunities for persons inclined to sadism and violence. The next would be those who directly participated in and profited from the slave trade. The moral culpability of slave ownership, to me, depends upon how the ownership came about and how the owner thereafter behaved. But, the guilt of the "bystanders who chose to be complicit through inaction and indecision"?

Complicity by "Indecision"?

An important part of the Reformation was that the church would no longer tell people what to think or do. People would be reasoned with, guided, persuaded, but look to their own conscience. I know that in the Reform tradition, there are differences in view as what the church should do to bring about social reform and a better world, but I am one who thinks that the Gospel emphasis is on the individual, on oneself and one's role as a stewaed and an example to others. We are not the judge and certainly not the enforcer (or executioner).

I do not intend to suggest that our Church history on this issue is something of which we should or could be proud or something that should be ignored. To the contrary, that history is something we should study and contemplate. Soberly. Not with outrage nor condemn with sanctimonious rhetoric. We should strive to understand, to place ourselves in our predecessors' shoes. Examine the positions taken and arguments made, on all sides of the issues, with empathy, not scorn, recognizing that the Presbyterian Church was and is made up of people, people with all of the human strengths and weaknesses, qualities both good and bad, the capacity for good and evil. We can learn about ourselves from such an examination.

But, remember:

"When they kept on questioning him, he straightened up and said to them, 'Let any one of you who is without sin be the first to throw a stone at her.'"

John 8:7.

I suspect that the things that I find most objectionable about this book are the result of someone's efforts to make the book sell better, to attract more attention. That is unfortunate. There is a story that needs to be told. It should be told well.

ENDNOTES

* We can do better. The U.S. Census data provides the best available information, and there was a census in 1860. The 1798 Census reported that slaves then represented about 18% of the population. Thereafter, even though the importation of slaves had been suspended since the 1770s and the slave trade banned in 1808, the slave population increased, but not as rapidly as the total population. By 1860, slaves constituted some 12.6% of the total. About 1.4% of the persons in the U. S. owned slaves, and about 7.4% of the families either owned slaves or used slave labor in their homes. In six Southern states, such family percentages approached or exceeded 50%. So, we may assume that Yoo's data mixes up counting by persons with counting by families and that Presbyterians were pretty similar to the rest of the country. *See, e.g.,* Louis Jacobson, "Viral post gets it wrong about extent of slavery in 1860," *POLITIFACT,* August 24, 2017.

** To be "fair," Yoo does impugn the motives of the Church clergy, accusing them of being swayed by economic concerns, due in part to their very low pay. They allegedly tailored their messages to please members who owned slaves and to increase their chances of being called by larger, wealthier congregations. Those who owned slaves, often by marriage to wealthy women, were unwilling to give up through emancipation the wealth that the slaves represented. *Id.,* pp.223-32. However, he presents no evidence in support of his accusations, simply quoting similar unsupported accusations made in the nineteenth century. (And, he does not try to explain how so many men strongly motivated by money world have chosen such a poorly paid profession.)

"The South Won" and "Awakening"

Yeoman Farmer to Cowboy
...To Donald Trump??

I want to offer some comments on two books by Heather Cox Richardson: *How the South Won the Civil War: Oligarchy, Democracy, and the Continuing Fight for the Soul of America* (2020) and *Democracy Awakening: Notes on the State of America* (2023). Both books contain interesting historical details, some of which I have incorporated in other chapters. But, here I focus on the themes of the books, the propositions that are used to construct the narrative. I should acknowledge that I struggled a bit in trying to understand her arguments. It is quite apparent who Richardson views as the "bad guys," of which there are many. As an historian, Richardson starts with historical details then begins layering interpretation and inference, until she has created the stories, purportedly from the ground up. But, I kept getting lost. So, I have reconstructed her stories from the top down.

I.

Here is my top-down summary of the first book:

1. The South "won" the Civil War because the particular political philosophy that the slaveholders embraced and advocated (along with the Democratic Party) and opposed by the North, Abraham Lincoln and the Republican Party, was adopted by westerners, then by Teddy Roosevelt and, finally, by the Republican Party generally, becoming (briefly) the governing view.

"The parallels between the antebellum Democrats and the modern-day Republican Party were clear. ...This was **the narrative an elite group of slaveholders used to take over the government in the 1850s.** They were defeated on the battlefields, but their vision of America moved West after the Civil War, where it gathered the strength to regain power."

...

"The resurrection of antebellum southern ideology through the rise of the western individualist rewrote American history. ...Thanks to the American West, the ideology of the Confederacy had regained a foothold in national politics."

...

"[William F. Buckley Jr.] insisted that **the government must be limited solely to protecting life, liberty, and property.** Only if individuals were allowed to organize their lives as they saw fit would they be able to advance the cause of freedom and spread prosperity spread across the nation. ...**This was precisely the argument slaveholding Democrats had made in the 1850s ... .**"

How the South Won the Civil War, pp.28, 186, 217, 205 (emphasis added).

The maintenance of law and order (personal security), the enforcement of contracts and the protection of private property are traditional and essential functions of government, enabling urban living, civilization and economic progress. These functions ought not to be disparaged or minimized. The only question is what other functions are appropriate and desirable.

---

2. That political philosophy was that of oligarchy, the belief that a few "elite" individuals should rule over the masses.

> "Like elite slaveholders before the Civil War, they believed in a world defined by hierarchies, where most people—dull, uneducated, black, female, weak, or poor—needed the guidance of their betters."
>
> ...
>
> "...*How the South Won the Civil War* tells the story of **the second rise of American oligarchy....**"
>
> ...
>
> "[I]n much the same way, it would permit the rise of oligarchy...."

Id., pp.12, 28, 205 (emphasis added).

"[A] very different set of principles that lay at the heart of American democracy: equality and self-determination. Those who embraced this vision believed that society moved **forward because self-reliant individuals produced and innovated far more effectively than a small group of elites,** whose wealth insulated them from the need to experiment." *Id.*, p.13.

---

3. America has embraced heroic idols, starting with the yeoman farmer, supplanted by the cowboy, and the supporters of oligarchy utilized these idealized images to gain support.

> "[T]he image of the cowboy helped spur **a return to a caste system....**"
>
> ...

"The cowboy era and Reconstruction overlapped almost exactly, and to oppose Republican policies, **Democrats mythologized the cowboy, self-reliant and tough, making his way in the world on his own.**"

...

"The image of the western individualist offered status to white men, as **it set them above people of color and above women,** who in the western vision could be either wives and mothers, dependent on their men, or sex objects."

...

"Thus, at times when it seems as if people of color or women will become equal to white men, oligarchs are able to court white male voters by insisting that universal equality will, in fact, **reduce white men to subservience.**"

...

"To sell to voters a program that hurt most of them, **the new Republicans deliberately shaped popular culture to bolster their ideology. ...[C]ulture swung away from inclusion and toward western individualism** even as most Americans still embraced the liberal consensus. **Western clothing and culture moved from the ranch into the mainstream.**"

Id., pp.22, 127, 243, 14, 228 (emphasis added).

"In the world that I inhabit today, however, nothing is cooler than dressing like a cowboy. My fashionable friends and normies alike have adopted the look in various forms." Chris Black, "Why We're Dressing Like Cowboys Now," *GQ*, October 26, 2023.

---

4. The American West was racist, sharing the views of the former slave owners during Reconstruction.

"[T]he racism and sexism that were always inherent in the idea of a white man taking on the wilderness became a primary part of a western individualist's identity."

...

"Western legislators interpreted the Fourteenth Amendment, adopted in July 1868, to include only African Americans. The amendment itself excluded Indians, and westerners argued that Chinese and other immigrants fell under a law passed in 1802 that established that enslaved immigrants were different from white immigrants. The 1802 law said only 'free white' people could be citizens. ...American settlers in the West had written racial hierarchies into their laws before the Civil War... ."

...

"[In the West,] the hierarchical lines were as crucial to the image of the prosperous white western individualist as they had been to the image of the rising yeoman farmer in the East after the American Revolution. And just as **the image of the farmer had helped pave the way for the rise of wealthy southern planters, so the image of the independent rising westerner helped pave the way for the rise of industrialists.**"

...

"Crucially, however, [Teddy] **Roosevelt's definition of hardworking Americans in the western mold excluded people of color,** many immigrants (including Asians), organized workers, and independent women, all of whom had come to be seen as 'special interests' wanting government benefits. He kept America from turning into an oligarchy at the beginning of the twentieth century, but he did so the same way the Founders had: by **creating an ideological underclass.**"

Id., pp.97, 19-20, 133, 174.

5. In its competition with the Democrats for national political control, the Republican Party courted the West, coming to adopt the westerners' political philosophy.

> "In 1882, a Republican Congress bowed to pressure to recognize racial distinctions and inscribed them back into American law with the Chinese Exclusion Act, the first federal law in history that restricted immigration."
>
> ...
>
> "[Teddy] Roosevelt and his fellow progressives called for a very specific kind of reform. They did not want to protect everyone. Rather, they wanted to make it possible for those they saw as true Americans to succeed."
>
> ...
>
> "[The nomination of Barry Goldwater in 1964] marked the resurrection of an old political movement by a modern political party. A century before, their predecessors had called themselves **'Confederates.' Like elite slaveholders before the Civil War, they believed in a world defined by hierarchies... .**"
>
> ...
>
> "The nomination ... marked the ideological **shift by the larger Republican Party toward the hierarchical ideology of the West.**"

Id., pp.21, 173, 12, 25 (emphasis added).

She claims: "These themes came together in the blockbuster 1977 film Star Was, which was the classic western story mythologized into space, with Luke Skywalker and the Resistance taking on the Empire by rejecting expertise and relying on 'the Force.'" *Id.*, p.229. How can anyone who has seen the barroom scene where Luke selects a crew call Star Wars racist? On the subject of people who do not believe in experts, it is rather ironic that the group claiming to oppose governance by elites embraces governance by the "experts." I guess it depends on the political views of the experts.

There are important things to say about each of these propositions, some of which I note below; but, I must observe that, even on their face, these propositions do not hold together in a persuasive narrative. Richardson writes (pp.14-5) of "the extraordinary strength of the ideology of American freedom":

> "[T]he profoundly exciting, innovative, and principled notion that has been encoded in our national DNA since Englishmen first began to imagine a New World in the 1500s. That ideology asserts that individuals must have control of their own destiny, succeeding or failing according to their skills and effort. It speaks directly to the fundamental human condition, and rather than bowing to the dictates of religion or tradition, it endows us all with the ability to control our own fate. **This ideology is the genius of America,** and we have embodied it in two distinctive archetypes: that of the independent yeoman farmer before the Civil War and that of the western cowboy afterward."

So, is the ideology that "endows us all with the ability to control our own fate ... [i] the genius of America" or did it [ii] bring a "world defined by hierarchies, where most people—dull, uneducated, black, female, weak, or poor—needed the guidance of their betters," that is "the second rise of American oligarchy"?

In any event, I have several specific issues with this narrative.

First, without qualification, Richardson expounds the supposed motivations and viewpoints of the key players. I have no problem with assertions about the consequences of acts, decisions or policies; but, I do find suspect assertions about the intentions of the participants. Intentions are difficult, if not impossible, for the observer to know. Here, moreover, the players are large groups defined by geographical location: Southerners, Westerners and Northerners. It is inconceivable that there were motivations and viewpoints shared by everyone in any particular group, and unlikely that there were even broad consensuses. Moreover, she attributes longterm strategies to groups, presuming degrees of foresight, tactical sense, competence and discipline highly unlikely to be achievable. Thus, I reject all such assertions, of which there are many.

Second, her thesis is based on the proposition that a unique element in the mindset of Southern slave owners was the belief in an oligarchical political structure, *i.e.*, governance by an elite. There was the touch of an aristocracy in the South; but in the early nineteenth century, no government allowed all its people to vote or participate in governing. "Elites" ruled every where. ("In 1776, it seemed self-evident to leaders that not every person living in the British colonies was capable—or worthy—of self-determination." *Id.*, p. 13.) The slave owners' perspective on slavery certainly was not focused on the right to vote.

- Africans were inferior;
- the ownership of slaves represented significant economic value;
- for certain types of labor, slaves were highly profitable and
- the potential for a slave rebellion was a constant threat to the safety of their families.

The right to vote was not a question until Reconstructuon. So, it is rather meaningless to say that Southerners (or westerners) were especially attached to oligarchy, while Northerners believed in democracy, or that the essense of the motivations among slave owners was social or political—it was economic.

"Southerners and westerners discovered that they shared common ground, objecting both to Republican racial policies and to fiscal policies that favored the Northeast. In the 1890s, westerners of both parties joined with southern Democrats to demand silver coinage, which would boost the western economy, where the silver mines were located, and spark inflation, which would help the struggling South." *Id*, p.182.

Third, I do not see how the image or mystique of the yeoman farmer or of the cowboy are dependent on or presume, or support, racism or elitism. Richardson asserts that both are defined in contrast to their perceived inferiors. "Just as the prewar eastern independent farmer had depended on slavery, the cowboy depended on racial and gender hierarchies. In the mythologized West, Americans who were increasingly defined as 'white' stood against the 'other.' *Id*, p.132. (*Also*, p.139.) But, I do not think that "whiteness" was a defining characteristic in either case. Things can be defined in terms of their opposites, but I do not think that the idolization of the yeoman farmer or the cowboy implies anti-democratic tendencies.

Fourth, the racism in the West was essentially defensive, to protect jobs and economic opportunities for Americans by restricting the access of the Chinese and Mexicans, rather like some of the concerns today over illegal immigration. Slavery in the South was exploitative, extracting labor by force. During Reconstruction, the interests of the West and South were more similar, but the South was more focused on limiting political participation, while in the West, the concerns again were essentially economic.

"[I]n the summer of 1890, a new political movement began, quietly, to take shape. In western towns, workers and poor farmers and entrepreneurs shut out of opportunities by monopolies began to talk to one another. Westerners suffering in the new economy began to come together. Reviving older social organizations, they distributed literature across the country explaining how tariffs worked and how railroad monopolies jacked up prices. ...The new western movement also reflected the community focus of marginalized Americans, redefining what it meant to be a success in America."

Democracy Awakening, p.224.

The alleged result ?

"Once in office, Reagan began to shape policy according to the Movement Conservative view, a process that would gradually concentrate wealth at the top of society. ...Americans of color, workers, and women fell far behind white men economically; they also suffered disproportionately from the structure of criminal laws and policing."

...

"Once in office, President Trump and his allies in Congress reinforced this ideology by slashing taxes for the rich while gutting health care and government regulations. ...[T]he Trump administration **reflected the ideology of oligarchy**. Government was not designed to promote equality of opportunity by guaranteeing equality before the laws. Rather, such meddling interfered with **the ability of a few to arrange society as they saw fit; they, and they alone, truly understood what was best for everyone**"

...

"[T]akers belonged at the bottom of society and should have no say in government."

...

"Movement Conservatives had taken over the Republican Party with the intention of destroying the liberal consensus. Wealth was moving upward, and women and minorities were headed toward positions of subordination. America was on its way to becoming an oligarchy."

How the South Won, pp.27, 28, 256, 253, 240 (emphasis added).

Thus, the images of the Yeoman Farmer and the Cowboy brought us Donald Trump.

I note that Richardson also views the cowboy image as detrimental to the interests of women. In that world, all women allegedly are either mothers and wives or prostutes.

"The image of the western individualist offered status to white men, as it set them above people of color and above women, who in the western vision could be either wives and mothers, dependent on their men, or sex objects."

...

"If Movement Conservatives were right that women and minorities were dangerous to democracy, it was imperative to remove them from positions of influence in the government, the same way elite slaveholders had sought to take the government out of the hands of their opponents a century and a half earlier."

Id., pp.243, 248.

But, to my recollection, they were also business owners, shopkeeprs, courageous settlors, equal partners in adversity and strong parents. (She is particularly offended by *Little House on the Prairie*, for reasons I do not comprehend. See *id.*, p.227; *Democracy Awakening,* p.51.) Today's Westerns certainly portray women with great diversity (*see Yellowstone, 1887* or *1923*, for example).

She concludes: 'The world of 2018 looked a lot like that of 1860." *Id.*, p.258. Really? That is ridiculous.

II.

Her book three years later repeats much of content of her 2020 book, but the yeoman farmer is gone, as is the theme of oligarchy. She no longer tries to connect the Republicans to the Southern slaveholders, asserting that the key commonality emerged from resentful Southerns in 1871, during Reconstruction.

> "In America the use of the word socialism came long before the Bolshevik Revolution. In 1871, during the period of Reconstruction after the Civil War, white supremacist southerners seized on a word that had been a general term for utopian communities and gave it a political definition that was specific to the United States. ...The next year, in 1871, unreconstructed white southerners began to argue that they objected to Black rights not on racial grounds—which now was unconstitutional and ran the risk of jail time from a Department of Justice prosecution—but rather on economic grounds. ...Thus, they said, Black voting amounted to a re-distribution of wealth from white men to Black people, who wanted something for nothing."

Democracy Awakening, p.27.

In the first book, the thesis was clear; it was the supporting arguments that required some effort to understand. In this second book, I cannot even find the arguments. Only the prejudices. The "bad guys" are castigated; the "good guys" are lavishly praised. She says: "This is a book about how a small group of people have tried to make us believe that our fundamental principles aren't true." *Id.*, p.xvii. But, where is the analysis?

"They have made war on American democracy by using language that served their interests, then led us toward authoritarianism by creating a disaffected population and promising to re-create an imagined past where those people could feel important again. As they took control, they falsely claimed they were following the nation's true and natural laws." *Id.*xvii.

The thesis is that today's supposed movement toward more democracy, toward popular government, is a return to or "reawakening of" the Founders' vision.

Okay.

But, the Founders were opposed to democracy, which they saw as just another type of tyranny. The carefully constructed system of checks and balances was expressly designed to prevent the consolidation of power anywhere, including with a popular majority. Indeed, Richardson explains that the "liberal consensus" began to emerge in the 1930s with FDR and the New Deal. And, now President Biden and "the Democrats managed to pass historic legislation that echoed that of FDR and LBJ... . ...Biden and his administration centered liberalism not around nuclear families headed by male breadwinners, as had always been the case before, but around children and their caregivers." *Id.*, pp.247, 248.

"Desperate to break out of the Depression, Americans embraced FDR's promise to use the federal government to protect ordinary Americans. In 1932 they elected him president and put Democrats in charge of Congress. In place of businessmen, Democrats brought into the government new voices like law professors and economic advisors—a so-called Brain Trust." *Id.*, p.4.

"Ironically, the restriction of immigration after 1920, based partly on bigotry, was one reason why Franklin D. Roosevelt and the Democrats could unite the working class behind the New Deal during the 1930s." John B. Judis and Ruy Teixeira, "How the Democrats Lost the Working Class on Immigration," *WSJ.com*, November 3, 2023.

A sub-theme is that the working class "need" someone below them and the "elite" (first, the wealthy Southern planters, then the wealthy Northern industrialists) have been able to manipulate that need to retain their control by promoting racism and insecurity.

I do not find either prong of that theme persuasive.

Another sub-theme is that the advocacy for "states' rights" was introduced in the last third of the nineteenth century in an effort to extend the elites' control of state governments to the Federal government by reducing and limiting the role of the Federal government. Surely, there is something backwards here. The States were first, evolving from the colonies. The country started as a confederation of states. The evident inadequacies of that structure gave rise to the Constitution, granting only limited powers to the Federal government. The radical position was that the Federal government had the authority and responsibility to address the new concerns. Therein lay the dramatic transfer of power. Moreover, there is nothing inherently anti-democracy about states' rights.

If the state government accurtely represents the will of the people, then so be it. If it does not, then the remedy lies in improving the representativeness of the state political system, not in the removal of decision-making from the state to the Federal government. If the problem is that one does not like the states' chosen policies, then we are not talking about democracy. Practically speaking, those who disagree with Federal policies will favor states' rights; those who disagree with a state's policies will advocate Federal control. Another thing, in addition to history, that supports states' rights is the the theory behind decentralized decision-making: minimization of the consequences of mistakes, greater opportunities for creativity and innovation, better and quicker access to relevant information and responsiveness to local conditions.

But, the cowboy still features prominently and still ambiguously.

"Seeking a contrast to the government action they called socialism, southern Democrats after the Civil War celebrated the American cowboy, who began to drive cattle from the border of Texas and Mexico north across the plains to army posts and railheads in 1866. In their view, **cowboys were real Americans who wanted nothing from the government but to be left alone.** ...That mythological cowboy caught the nation's imagination in the 1870s as the antithesis of what southern Democrats insisted was government-backed socialism in the East. ...**The cowboy would be an effective propagandist for those standing against the liberal consensus in the 1950s and 1960s.**

...

"After the Civil War, Democrats had created the cowboy to represent a white man who worked hard, stood alone, and dominated those around him. **The Spanish-American War redefined the image of the cowboy as a man who represented a brotherhood and who valued fairness for all. Any man who was hardworking and independent, who 'demanded only to . . . be judged on [his] merits,'** could represent America as one of Roosevelt's cowboys. The new cowboy seemed to represent a new America, and Roosevelt took that image into government."

...

"But the 1954 *Brown v. Board* decision resurrected the mythological cowboy, now backed by the extraordinary power of television, as a brilliant vehicle for Movement Conservatism. By 1959, there were twenty-six Westerns on TV, and in one week of March 1959, eight of the top shows were Westerns. September 1959 introduced viewers to Bonanza, the first television show filmed in color, which sprinted up the charts and went on to run for fourteen seasons. ...Westerns like Bonanza showed a male world of hardworking cowboys protecting their land from evildoers. The cowboys didn't need help from their government; they made their own law with a gun. They even helped keep order in nearby towns that had a government."

Id., pp.28, 227, 31 (emphasis added).

So, Ben Cartwright is a reflection of Jim Crow murderers, terrorists and rapists? And, as channeled through Luke Skywalker, the predecessor to Donald Trump? I do not think so.

I would happily vote for a Ben Cartwright (or a Teddy Roosevelt).

So?

Something more is going on, but it is disguised by Richardson's desire to have a catchy title supported (sort of) by a compelling narrative. I think her anger actually is with some twentieth-century phenomena which she projects back to the nineteenth century to tie them to acknowledged "bad guys," the Southern slaveowners.

It seems focused, first, on the promotion of a distinction between the "self-reliant" and those who rely on government benefits and, second, on a growing inequality in weealth and income.

"As had been the case a century and a half before, the program of keeping capitalists free from regulations and taxes moved wealth upward. Beginning in 1981, tax cuts, the destruction of social welfare spending, and hostility to unions reversed the Great Compression of the liberal consensus and replaced it with what economists call the Great Divergence."

...

"By 2016, Republican leaders **sounded eerily like antebellum slaveholders** in their defense of a system in which wealthy elites ruled over the masses. Presidential candidate Mltt Romney and his running mate, future Speaker of the House Paul Ryan of Wisconsin, talked vaguely in 2012 about **"makers and takers.. ."**

...

"The story they told of an **America under siege by 'takers' was not based in fact**. Rather, it followed a formula that rewrote history in order to divide voters and win election by turning their supporters against minorities and women. To sell to voters a program that hurt most of them, the new Republicans deliberately shaped popular culture to bolster their ideology."

Id., pp.173, 171, 253 (emphasis added).

As to the first matter, the yeoman farmer and the cowboy were self reliant by necessity—there were no government benefits or government assistance available. It is not as if they turned help down. But, they managed to survive. As she observes, "The reality was that power in the West came from social networks and kinship ties rather than from individual prowess, but these men saw the West as a land of unparalleled opportunity, where a man willing to swing a pick could make a fortune literally out of the dirt. It was the stuff of hope and legends... ." *Id.*, p.97.

The issue of government benefits arose seriously only in the last 60 years, starting with President Johnson. Moreover, self-reliance, independence, stoicism, hard-working and individuality seem like desirable qualities to have in one's citizenry. Richardson's objection is that that the image is used in contrast to people who are dependent on government, who are "takers," who cannot cope on their own. Yes, well. But, desirable qualities can be aspirational, too. Certainly, the world would not be improved by the banning or the denial of good qualities. And, I do not see the connection except in the generally applicable sense that the concept of a "good citizen" presupposes the possibility of a "bad citizen."

As to the second, growing inequality in wealth and income was simply not a nineteenth century phenomenon. "[A]t least since the end of the eighteenth century there has been a historical movement toward equality. The world of the early 2020s, no matter how unjust it may seem, is more egalitarian than that of 1950 or that of 1900, which were themselves in manyer respects more egalitarian than those of 1850 or 1780." Thomas Piketty, *A Brief History of Equality* (2022), pp. 1-2. Indeed, in her later book, Richardson notes that the increase in inequality began with Ronald Reagan in 1981. *Democracy Awakening*, p.52.

Richardson proffers some fanciful stories based on wishful thinking laced with inflammatory rhetoric and extensive repetition. There are two glaring problems with her themes.

First, she does not show that the common or dominant philosophy among Southern slave owners was a belief in oligarchy. In fact, it was just a commitment to the preservation of slavery. Similarly, she does not demonstrate that the nineteenth century Westerners were believers in oligarchy. Instead, they were defenders of freedom from government interference. She does not establish that Teddy Roosevelt, Barry Goldwater, or Ronald Reagan were believers in oligarchy. They were committed to limited government. And, she cannot claim that Donald Trump is a would-be oligarch. For him, she switches to the word authoritarianism, but even that is not right. He is a would-be tyrant or dictator with no respect or concern for legal institutions or the law. So, the supposed connection on which she bases the first book just does not exist.

Second, the Founders and the founding principles were not supporting democracy. So, the theme of the second book is simply incorrect. And, as for the ideology that was the "genius of America"—

- "the profoundly exciting, innovative, and principled notion that has been encoded in our national DNA since Englishmen first began to imagine a New World in the 1500s ... [t]hat ... asserts that individuals must have control of their own destiny, succeeding or failing according to their skills and effort,
- "[that] speaks directly to the fundamental human condition, and rather than bowing to the dictates of religion or tradition, it endows us all with the ability to control our own fate,
- "[that believes that] an independent man who worked in his own fields, supported his wife and children, and promoted good policies when he voted to advance his own interests,
- "[that believes in] a brotherhood and who valued fairness for all. Any man who was hardworking and independent, who 'demanded only to ... be judged on [his] merits,'

- "[that believes that] society moved forward because self-reliant individuals produced and innovated far more effectively than a small group of elites, whose wealth insulated them from the need to experiment,
- "[that believes that] cowboys were real Americans who wanted nothing from the government but to be left alone"

—, where does that stand?

Certainly, it is not represented perfectly by the Republican Party. But, it is clearly rejected by today's Democratic Party—today's advocate for governance by the elite (the "self-anointed"), by "experts" and by the highly educated. Therein, there is no faith in the wisdom of the common man. And, Donald Trump is not the heir to the tradition of Teddy Roosevelt, Barry Goldwater, Ronald Reagan and Mitt Romney. Indeed, he has more in common with Joe Biden—both populists courting the lowest common denominator, they simply have different views of what appeals to the populous. Neither are leaders of the people, just manipulators, with popular support being bought by "bread and circuses."

A Note on Lincoln and the Workingman

Both Heather Cox Richardson and Dylan Penningroth reference Lincoln's 1860 campaign appeal to the working class male. But, while Richardson lauds it, Penningroth suggests tht it was a strategem in support of capitalism's exploitation of labor.

Richardson: "[Lincoln's] centering of the Declaration of Independence led the Republican Party to create a new, active government that guaranteed poorer men would have access to resources that the wealthy had previously monopolized." *Democracy Awakening*, p.9.

"On September 30, 1859, ... Lincoln explained that Hammond... divided the world into permanent castes: capitalists driving the economy and workers stuck at the bottom. But there was another theory: that workers, not capitalists, drove the economy, and hardworking men could—and should—rise. **This latter 'free labor' theory articulated the true meaning of American democracy for northerners and for the non-slave-holding southerners,** who, as Lincoln reminded his listeners, made up a majority in the South. ......**[T]hose at the bottom were there not because of a caste system, but because of improvidence, folly, or singular bad luck.**"

How the South Won the Civil War, p.77 (emphasis added).

Penningroth:

"The Republican Party won the White House in 1860 largely because its leaders told a compelling story about why the sixteen-hour-a-day factory worker ... was still, fundamentally, a free man. And it won by deflecting northern voters' rampant racism ... onto what Republicans contemptuously called 'the Slave Power,' the southern plot to dominate the national government... ."

Before the Movement: The Hidden History of Black Civil Rights (2023), p.83.

Go figure.

"Advisory Group on the Legacies of Enslavement"

In reaction to well-publicized events at American universities, the University of Cambridge, in England, established a multidisciplinary Advisory Group to undertake an in depth investigation of the University's involvement with slavery and the slave trade (the "Advisory Group on the Legacies of Enslavement").

> "The scope of their research was to encompass both (a) historical (including archival) research into the ways in which the University may have been involved financially and otherwise in the slave trade or other historical forms of coerced labour connected to colonialism, and (b) the University's contribution to knowledge that may have supported the validation and dissemination of racialised and racist social structures and beliefs. Within their work, they were also asked to consider broader context, and especially the prominent place of Cambridge in the anti-slavery movement."

The report overview is now available (late summer 2022).

The Group acknowledges that:

"Cambridge University played an important role in the effort to end the slave trade and Caribbean slavery, and it is well-known that abolitionists pivotal to this movement, such as Thomas Clarkson, William Wilberforce, and Peter Peckard, once called Cambridge home. The abolition of the slave trade was one of the few issues that the City of Cambridge and University officials—racked by political, religious, and intellectual disagreements throughout the early modern period—had some degree of unity about. The University Senate sent petitions to the House of Commons in 1788 and again in 1792. Colleges, Masters, and Fellows also sent money to the Society for Effecting the Abolition of the Slave Trade."

Indeed, Clarkson performed a remarkable feat:

"In 1785, Thomas Clarkson, a son of an Anglican clergyman in England, won an essay contest at Cambridge University with the prompt 'Is it right to make slaves of others against their will?' Clarkson ... had given little thought to the international slave trade and Black enslavement."

William Yoo. *What Kind of Christianity*, p.53 (discussed below).

His essay, published in 1786, debunked several the prevailing myths about the slave trade, for example, that most captives were prisoners of war, that the traders simply bought people that had already been enslaved by African kings, that European traders played a passive role as mere intermediaries and that the enslaved were largely docile and reconciled to their fate.

Then, the Group attempted to identify every benefit that the University derived from the existence of slavery, directly or indirectly, and every connection. But, the decision was made not to quantify them.

"While we consider financial connections in the form of donations and investment, the report also tries not to make the research principally about numbers. There can be no doubt that collectively the collegiate University gained economic benefit from colonial exploitation, which was itself based on the labour of enslaved people, as did the country as a whole, and the economic legacy of that gain has continued to the present day."

They found the following:

1. Several alumni became slave owners. (A very, very small percentage.)
2. Some Colleges held stock or bonds in companies that participated in the slave trade. "Cambridge Colleges (those that have come to our attention being Corpus Christi, Gonville & Caius, Jesus, King's and Pembroke) directly purchased South Sea Company shares and annuities during the years of the company's major participation in the Atlantic Slave Trade." And, "East India bonds were owned by several Cambridge institutions, including Trinity College, although they do not seem to have reached the same extent as investments in the South Sea Company." (Likely, these investments constituted relatively modest amounts of the Colleges' wealth and of the companies' capital.)
3. The Colleges had many students who were the sons of slave holders and even actively recruited such sons. The Report says that the Colleges were "enriched" by the fees paid on behalf of those students. (The necessary implication is that the Colleges were in those days making a profit from the student fees over the costs of

educating the students; but, that is not explicitly stated and not demonstrated.)

4. Substantial gifts were received from benefactors who made some of their fortunes from slavery.

5. Some large gifts were received from benefactors whose wealth had largely derived from the slave trade or from slave labor. "In certain prominent cases donations came in the form of South Sea capital itself."

6. "As slavery and the slave trade came under scrutiny, some Cambridge intellectuals actively defended them while others passively accepted their continuation. ...Throughout the period under discussion individuals at Cambridge were writing about race, and presenting ideas that were used to justify the enslavement and colonisation of other people."

7. "Key institutions within Cambridge like the Fitzwilliam Museum memorialise those linked to slavery ... College benefactors ... whose wealth derived from slavery ... are memorialised in a variety of forms."

That is it.

The receipt of wealth directly connected to slavery seems to be the only one to single out criticism. All of the others are the "connections" that one would expect any institution of the size and prestige of Cambridge to have had. Indeed, most of us would be shocked or highly skeptical to be told that it had not. Moreover, many of us would question the wisdom or appropriateness of most conceivable actions or policies that would have attempted to prevent those connections. How would one control the future behavior of one's graduates? Do we want censureship of academic research? Of speech? Should one have attempted to monitor all the activities of any company in which one invested or all the sources of a benefactor's wealth (or tried to trace the sources of specific funds)? Would it have been right to refuse admission to a child based upon the business of the father?

The Group made no such distinctions. Its recommendations are rather benign, but I think it should have issued a commendation rather than an indictment. But, in fact, the recommendations were probably inevitable as a minimum, even if nothing had been found.

I have no problem with a conclusion that certain gifts or bequests ought to have been turned down or returned, but I consider that to be a decision for the recipient to make. I have no objection to returning works of art to the country of origin if there are reasonable assurances that the works can be protected. Otherwise, I do not think that statues, portraits and building names can be said to "memorialize" the subject for more than a generation, maybe two. Thereafter, they become simply a reminder that we have a past or just a name.

Finally, I think that the Group cast the net too broadly by including colonialism with slavery. There is an historical connection, of course, but colonialism had a separate existence and its own consequences, not all bad. For what it is worth, I rank the Opium Wars as the most disgraceful of British acts of the nineteenth century.

"Limitarianism"

"I became convinced that we must create a world
in which no one is super-rich—that there must
be a cap on the amount of wealth any
one person can have. I call this limitarianism."

...

"Occasionally, someone will agree that
inequality is a bad thing while also saying that
putting a limit on how much we can have is
too drastic a measure. Such a claim is puzzling.
How could that be the case?"

Ingrid Robeyns
Limitarianism:
The Case Against Extreme Wealth
(2024), pp.xiv, xviii.

I skimmed a review of this book that caused me mistakenly to expect sophisticated arguments and some penetrating analyses. I was intrigued, because I feel some sympathy for the general proposition being advanced.

I was disappointed.

I promptly realized that the book would not be what I was looking for when I saw her definition of "super rich" and her proposed caps on individual wealth ($5 million). I think of the "super rich" as those whose wealth enables a lifestyle that differs in kind, not just degree, from that of the upper middle class. People in the world of private jets, super yachts, large staffs, exotic cars and multiple mansions. Not that one necessarily has all of that, but could comfortably afford to. I used to view $100 million as the threshold, but times have changed. Luxury properties sell for $40 to $80 million, lottery jackpots frequently are in the hundreds of millions and now occasionally break a billion dollars. So, I would now place the threshold for being "super rich" at $500 million.

There apparently are close to 3,000 (2,668 on the Forbes list for 2022) billionaires in the world today, holding about $13 trillion. Robeyns, *Limitarianism,* p.xii. There are some 7,070 individuals with wealth of more than $500 million. Credit Suisse Research Institute, *Global Wealth Report 2022.* That group holds roughly $20 trillion out of a global total of $463.6 trillion. *Id.* (About 4%.) This is the group to which I will apply Robeyns' arguments. (There are almost 30,000 individuals with at least $100 million.)

"Dirty Money"

Robeyns argues first that certain categories of the super rich should have their wealth confiscated because it is "dirty money." Robeyns, pp.41-71. That is certainly correct with respect to dictators and oligarchs ("kleptocrats and public officials engaging in corruption ") who looted their countries, to criminals who profited through illegal activities and to those holding the proceeds of tax evasion. But, that is an objective of law enforcement, not tax policy. Whether we have significantly reduced the number of people of interest is unclear, because many of these individuals were unlikely to have been included in the initial count since their illegally obtained wealth would have been undisclosed.

However, I think she defines "dirty money" far too broadly. For example, she includes conscious tax avoidance, even though it is legal. She expresses clear distain for the "wealth-defense industry," the accountants and lawyers and bankers who provide tax advice and services. But, if one decides to use an ethical concept of "dirty" tax strategies rather than a legal definition of tax evasion, then there will be little agreement or consistency of results. Similarly, she categorizes as "dirty" wealth derived from "unethical activities" (child labor, exploitative trade, unfair labor practices, slavery) at any time in the past. Now, this is surely a standard that could never practically be implemented. But, Robeyns, has no intention that "dirty money" actually be identified. The point of her discussion is to claim that most of the wealth of the super rich (or of anyone else) is not "deserved"—that it is not something to which anyone is "entitled."

> "It is rather to show that, for a significant proportion of super-rich individuals, we do not even have to ask about the negative consequences of their having so much money—a question reserved for the next two chapters. They simply should not have had that money in the first place, full stop."

Id., p.43.

Robeyns challenges the view that large incomes are the result of superior performance, skill, effort or ingenuity. I think that she significantly underestimates the role and impact of such individual qualities, but she also misses a fundamental point. She is correct that much of the extraordinary earnings are "economic rent," but she forgets that rents play a central role in the allocation of desired goods and services. The highest bidder gets the concert ticket, the painting, the center fielder, the quarterback, the waterfront property, the proven CEO. The alternative is to allocate by lottery or by fiat.

"It follows that the more unequal a society is, the more important it is to have government rationing rather than relying on the price mechanism." *Id.*, p.112.

Inequality is detrimental

In my earlier writings on inequality, I reviewed arguments that had been made as to why inequality was detrimental and found them strikingly unimpressive. I hoped to find something better here. Disappointment. Her principal argument is premised on the supposed bad effects of inequality, but she fails to establish any.

> "Inequality, by contrast, is only ever instrumentally important. In other words, inequality is bad because it **has bad consequences**. It produces **differences in social status** and thereby **creates stigma and undermines social cohesion**. It leads to the **abuse of power and domination of the political process** by the elite, which then results in unfair policies that help the rich more than the poor. It undermines equality of opportunity. It **generates stress** and has negative effects on people's mental health."

Id., p.36 (emphases added).

"So here we are, with this long list of ways that wealth undermines democracy." *Id.*, p.94. But, the alleged adverse impact on social cohesion is based on a belief in the power of envy. (I discuss that last.) The alleged distortion of the political process from money is based on the mere conviction that money must make a difference. ("[I]t seems very unlikely that the funds available to lobbyists would not translate into political influence." *Id.*, p.84.) The claim of reduced opportunities is totally unsupported.

> "By now, it should be abundantly clear that the economic elite have too much political power, and that they are making things worse for ordinary people." *Id.*, p.93.

> "When money can be used to buy votes, those who funded the elected politician will see their interests protected in the policies that are implemented—but a large part of the costs of those policies will be borne by everyone else. Vote-buyers are, in a certain sense, free-riding on the spending of society as a whole."

Id., p.82.

Robeyns is highly critical of the inheritance of wealth, declaring that no one deserves to inherit. "Perhaps the most obvious case of unde-served wealth is that of inheritance. Inheritances are a significant source of extreme wealth, sometimes making individuals very rich indeed." *Id.*, p.121. Ultimately, she acknowledges that the issue in not the right to inherit, but the right to bequeath. It is the interests of the wealthholders that is at stake. (She almost, but not quite, recognizes that the concept of family is implicated.) She concludes that these interests are valid but outweighed by other considerations.

> "[I]nheritances of a significant size do indeed have negative effects on other people—on society at large. They undermine equality of opportunity. They undermine social mobility. They provide negative incentives... ."

> ...

"It would be a cruel society that punished this family-oriented idea of a good life in favor of the consumerist idea of one. So, in principle, the lawmaker should not disregard this aspiration. But there are other factors to take into account, such as whether the inheritance ... is so large as to threaten the common good."

Id., pp.123, 124.

Of course, she is partially correct. The matter at issue is one of degree. The bigger problem is that she fails to appreciate the impact of current estate taxes. For wealthy families in the United States, for example, the inheritance (through lifetime gifts and bequests) by family members will be taxed at 40% above a specified amount (currently about $13 million per estate). The tax can be avoided primarily only by gifts to charities. Now, one might argue for a higher or lower exemption or a higher or lower tax rate, but it is error to claim that large inheritances escape taxaion.

Robeyns devotes the most words to the assertion that inequality contributes to climate change.

"Can we avert the climate crisis from within a system that creates such extreme wealth inequality? Can environmental safety and stability go hand in hand with the lifestyles of the super-rich?" *Id.*, p.97.

"[W]e also need to do something about extreme wealth concentration, because it is translating into lifestyles that are ecologically unsustainable." *Id.*, p.109.

Apart from her mischaracterization of the threat ("[s]cience tells us that we are turning the Earth into a place that will become uninhabitable

for most humans, and indeed for many other living species" *id.*, p.112),
her identification of inequality as a cause is illogical.

Greenhouse emissions are due to activities like the production of
concrete and steel, the transportation of goods and flatulence of cows
and sheep. How much of any of those activities are attributable to the
super rich? To the top .01 or top .0001 % of the world's population?
Suppose the super rich generate on average 200 tons of CO^2 per person
per year and everyone else generates on average 1 ton (the 1 percent ...
emit a staggering 101 tons per person per year. ... In North America,
the richest 10 percent emit 69 tons of CO^2 per person each year... "*id.*,
p.100). Then, the 7,000 super rich will be responsible for 1.4 million
tons of CO^2 while the other 8 billion people will cause the emission of
8 billion tons.

Indeed, her own data reveals the fallacy: "In 2019, ... the global
bottom 50 percent of the income and wealth distribution ... contribute
... 11.5 percent of the total emissions" (*id.*, p.100); yet, "their wealth
ranges between 2 percent and 10 percent" (*id.*, p.26). Similarly, "the top
10 percent ... hold 50–70 percent of all wealth (*id.*, p.26), but "emit ...
48 percent of total global emissions" (*id.*, p.100). It seems clear that the
poor are responsible for a greater percentage of greenhouse emissions
than their percentage of total wealth. And, the rich are responsible for a
smaller percentage than their share of total wealth—the exact opposite
of the assumption on which Robeyns's argument is based. So, it is likely
that a more equal distribution of income and wealth would result in
greater, not lesser emissions. (This conclusion is consistent with common experience. The lower income households invariably spend a much
higher percentage of their resources on current consumption than do
the richer households. The rich are responsible for more emissions per
capita, but less per dollar of wealth.)

"[T]he wealth share of the bottom 50% of households in the United States increased from 1.84% to 2.65% in 2021... ." Credit Suisse Research Institute, *Global Wealth Report 2022.*

The super rich have not caused the climate change crisis. Robeyns real complaint again comes down to the envy she feels that other people must feel: "The 90 percent will resent having to make sacrifices if the 10 percent keep emitting so intensively; they will resent even more that the 1 percent are emitting many times what the 90 percent emit." *Id.*, p.115.

Envy

Interestingly, Robeyns recognizes that many people do not actually share her feelings of envy and outrage, contradicting her claim that inequality diminishes social cohesion. That she views as an undesirable state of affairs, which she blames on "neoliberalism," a philosophical view that she condemns.

> "Conceived as **a deliberate attempt by certain right-wing ideologues to dominate governance and policy-making,** this ideological revolution began gradually and was ultimately successful. It was most visible in the US under President Ronald Reagan and the UK under Prime Minister Margaret Thatcher."

Id., p.33 (emphasis added).

"It starts from the belief that, outside their families, humans are **motivated by selfishness**, and that we would all be better off if we arranged our societies accordingly. It asks us to believe that **human beings are not intrinsically motivated to work hard**, and so we should be extensively monitored **and held accountable**, even if that leads to huge bureaucracy. It asks us to believe that, in order to arrange an economy efficiently, we need to put people in competition with each other. ... And it asks us to believe that, within this system, **individuals should be held fully responsible** for their failures and given sole credit for their success."

Id., p.34 (emphasis. added).

What is wrong about neoliberalism? The alleged source of the model and her disagreement with it. I believe, however, that a theoretical model should be assessed on its merits—the validity of its assumptions, the soundness of its inferences and the accuracy of its predictions—and not by who its proponents are.

Robeyns, however, simply presumes that her readers share her biases and need no evidence or analysis. She asks:

"So why, then, do they not vote for more redistribution? There are many possible explanations. One is that they believe in the existence of social mobility—in the American Dream.... . Another possible explanation [is that] [t]he participants dramatically underestimated how unequal the distribution of wealth in their country was."

Id., p.205.

A third possibility, one she does not recognize, is that many people view what is theirs (how ever great or small) as theirs and consider personal property as an important safeguard for their families. They rely on government to protect their rights and property but recognize that government can also be a threat to those rights and property. History and experience tells them that if government is allowed to take from one's neighbor today, one's own might be at risk tomorrow. The view of government as a threat against which people need and want protection, while contrary to Robeyns's philosophy, is very much part of the American heritage and a pillar supporting the American Dream.

The real irony, almost too painful to discuss, is that while the principle alleged adverse impact of inequality of wealth is the undermining of social cohesion, the principle exhortation in the book is to become activists. Activists to what end? To undermine social cohesion by convincing the currently complacent citizenry that they are victims.

"The first and perhaps most important action limitarianism requires is one that we've already touched on: to dismantle neoliberal ideology, because it is at the heart of the problems we are facing. ...As long as neoliberalism is our dominant ideology, fighting its consequences will be insufficient. We must therefore attack the root cause and replace neoliberalism with something more humane... ." *Id.*, pp. 215-216.

"We must share this critique with everyone." *Id.*, p.217.

"I have dedicated this book to all activists who are fighting against injustice. ...[N]ot only to those who are on the barricades, but also to those writing pieces for newspapers, setting up organizations, and trying in other ways to mobilize people and power for the good." *Id.*, p.235.

She bases this call to activism on the assertion that the regular people are ignorant of the facts and fail to see their self-interests accurately.

> "To what extent are ordinary people aware of today's immense economic inequality? Do they know that this inequality is not 'natural,' by any means? Do they know that the dominant classes have quietly established a set of global economic rules that favor their own interests, that they have influenced national decisions on taxes and spending, and that ... they have largely sought to improve their own financial position? ...I'd venture that many people have no idea how deep the problem goes. Such ignorance applies to everyone—the rich, the poor, and the middle classes."

Id., p.204.

"Why does this matter? Well, if people perceive or believe that inequalities are high, they might well make stronger demands for redistribution. If, as is the case, they are mistaken in believing that inequalities are smaller than they really are, their demands for redistribution will be more timid." *Id.*, p.206.

Robeyns claims that the disrepute of Communism is used (unfairly) to discredit limitarianism. She acknowledges the widespread rejection of Communism, describing it as follows:

> "[T]he dominant view has been that the communist experiment failed. Some citizens had spent years trying to escape these countries, but by that point the majority had decided they had had enough of living in repressive regimes while across the border people were living much better lives.
>
> ...

"There was severe political repression that infiltrated all levels of society; you could not be sure that your aunt or friend wasn't a spy for the state. In several countries, the state made important personal decisions for its citizens, such as who could study and what subject."

Id., p 207.

Yet, she identifies the reason for the rejection is the dislike of "despotic central planning of the economy" by the government, a feature to which she herself objects. Thus, she argues that since limitarianism does not necessarily require central planning, the attack based upon characterizing it as similar to Communism is a devious ploy to misled the masses. Indeed,

"...the suggestion that limitarianism is akin to communism is also very sad, perhaps even maddening, since it indicates that, all too often, the opponents of progressive ideas are not really interested in having a genuine discussion about these proposals. Instead, they want to caricature them in a way that they know will put many people off the discussion entirely. "

Id., p.208.

She totally disrards the issue of the loss of freedoms.

That omission is extraordinarily telling as she proceeds to set forth tte necessary first six steps in the implementation of limitarianism:

- Change how people think. "[D]ismantle neoliberal ideology... ." *Id.*, pp. 215-216.
- Alter where and how the people live. "The second thing limitarianism requires is that we reduce class segregation. We must do so because it will directly help to restore and nurture democracy, in particular democratic citizenship. ...Alas, relying on voluntary action will not do the trick. If class desegregation is made voluntary, then we can expect that many very rich and privileged people will not join in." *Id.*, pp.217-8.
- Revise our economic institutions. "The third action limitarianism requires is for us to establish a balance of economic power." *Id.*, p.219.
- Strengthen government revenue raising. *Id.*, p.221.
- Confiscate "dirty" money and pay reparations. *Id.*, p.222.
- Stop the transfer of wealth within families. "[T]he most urgent of all... ." *Id.*, p.226.

That is for starters.

Whose happiness is Robeyns seeking to promote?

Her own and of those who share her political values. It makes me want to cry.

Probably my greatest divergence in views is with respect to the societal consequences of having significant assets in the hands of governments rather than of private individuals. Robeyns clearly, longingly perceives that prospect as the benefit propelling her policy recommendations.

> "We need limitarianism because there is a clear case to be made against extreme wealth concentration. But we also need limitarianism because there is so much good that money above the riches line could do, if only it were used for addressing collective problems." *Id.*, p.117.

> "The bottom line is simply this: there is so much good our governments could do with the excess money of the super-rich. And taking it from them would probably not affect their welfare at all—not in any meaningful sense. If there is a slight drop in the luxury of their lifestyles, it would be massively outweighed by the gains to others, and the gains to the common good." *Id.*, p.159.

I, in contrast, see it as a great uncertainty. Undoubtedly, very good and desirable things could conceivably be realized, but what is most likely to happen?

There are two different types of concerns about transferring assets to government. The first is government inefficiency, waste and corruption. The problem is the inherent lack of accountability compared to the private sector. There exists everywhere temptations inviting laziness, inattention and corruption. There will everywhere incompetence, misjudgements, errors and accidents; but, the private sector has an impersonal, ruthless and tireless overseer—competition—that the public sector lacks. The second is that decisions as to the use of the assets will be made through the political process run by politicians. Experience demonstrates how treacherous reliance on politicians is likely to be. I simply do not think it accurate to claim that political spending decisions reflect the will of the people or tend to promote the general well being.

Robeyns is critical of private philanthropy where there is significant inequality because it is "undemocratic." I, however, am severely disappointed in the political process' handling of budgeting and spending.

One should recognize that governments have played a significant role in increasing inequality over the last 50 years. Governments own more than $100 trillion of assets consisting of land, infrastructure and natural resources, in addition to financial assets. That wealth can be attributed to their citizens per capita—roughly $12,000 per person. However, over the last 50 years, public debt has soared, largely spent on current consumption rather than invested in public assets, thus reducing public net worth.

In effect, governments borrowed against public assets, giving the proceeds to only some of their citizens who then spent it. The result is that in much of the world, including the U.S. And the U.K., the public net worth is now negative. There is per capita public debt rather than public wealth.

"The total public sector assets in the [38] countries covered are worth $103 trillion. ... These assets consist of public infrastructure such as bridges and roads, financial assets such as bank deposits, as well as natural resource reserves in the ground. Total liabilities stand at $93 trillion. This comprises some $44 trillion of general government debt, but also includes $22 trillion of current pension obligations and the debt of state-owned enterprises. Net worth—assets minus liabilities—comes to $10 trillion ... ."

Jason Harris, Abdelhak Senhadji, "A Global Picture of Public Wealth," *IMF Blog*, June 18, 2019.

"In advanced economies, fiscal deficits soared as countries saw revenues collapse due to the recession and put in place sweeping fiscal measures as COVID-19 spread. Public debt rose 19 percentage points of GDP, in 2020, an increase like that seen during the global financial crisis, over two years: 2008 and 2009." Vitor Gaspar, Paulo Medas, Roberto Perrelli, "Global Debt Reaches a Record $226 Trillion," *IMF Blog*, December 15, 2021.

> "Global debt has hit a record $300 trillion, or 349% leverage on gross domestic product. This translates to $37,500 of average debt for each person in the world versus GDP per capita of just $12,000. Government debt-to-GDP leverage grew aggressively, by 76%, to a total of 102%, from 2007 to 2022." Terry Chan, "Global Debt Leverage: Is a Great Reset Coming? Rising rates and slowing economies mean the world's high leverage poses a crisis risk," *S&P Global Ratings*, January 13, 2023.

The relationship between income broadly defined (including unrealized appreciation) and wealth is current consumption. Thus, it is safe to bet that the result of a significant transfer of wealth from the super rich to the bottom half, directly or through governments as intermediaries, would quickly result in the reduction in total wealth and an increase in current consumption. Remember that the total wealth of the households with at least $500 million is around $20 trillion. Divided among roughly 3 billion households in the world, that amount would provide about $6,700 per household, and that would be a one-time payment. How much of that do you think would be saved and invested? And, what would be the impact of the sudden increase in consumer demand? Well, we have just been experiencing a trial run. The result is inflation.

The fact is that inequality assists the creation of wealth and economic growth.

Robeyns is correct that property, wealth and markets depend upon, are created by, organized society and government. Thus, each person's rights are defined by and subject to the rules of that society and government. "Limitarianism rests on the fundamental philosophical insight that markets and property are social institutions. ...[I]n the world as it is, there is no property, and there are no markets, outside the social context... ." *Id.*, p.118.

Robeyns seems to like island hypotheticals. "[P]ut them on a desert island. They still have all the same talents and personal traits as before. How rich could they become? Not very rich, obviously. ...[W]ithout collective institutions, public goods, basic infrastructure, and collaboration with other people, it would be impossible for anyone to become rich—in other words, that we all rely on the social contract." *Id.*, pp.135, 137. It is probably correct that no one would become super rich stranded on an island, but hierarchies based on individual strengths would probably still arise. *See, e.g.*, James Matthew Barrie, *The Admirable Crichton,* (1902).

At the same time, the authority of that government and the society to impose burdens on or require sacrifices from its citizens is constrained by those rules. The balance between the individual's rights to pursue his own self interest and the individual's obligations to society will be a defining feature of that society.

ABOUT THE AUTHOR

Born in Columbus, Ohio, and raised in Northville, Michigan, John majored in economics at Amherst College (Class of 1970), graduating *summa cum laude*, and received his J.D., *magna cum laude*, from The Harvard Law School in 1973. Following law school, he did post-graduate research at the University of Cambridge (Trinity College). In late 1974, John began a 37-year career as a commercial litigator with a major law firm in New York City. He retired from the practice of law in 2011 and, shortly thereafter, located just outside of Cambridge, England. In March 2015, however, he was diagnosed with ALS. So, he returned to the U.S., settling in Alexandria, Virginia. In 2016, he finished the book on science that he had been working on during his retirement.

Confined to a wheelchair in 2018, he wrote his first collection of essays, entitled *Wanderings of a Captive Mind*. The next set, *The Eyes Have It*, was written entirely using his eyes. And, so on.

Other Books

Important Things We Don't Know: About Nearly Everything

Wanderings of a Captive Mind (Wanderings Part 1)

The Eyes Have It (Wanderings Part 2)

All that Is Gold (Wanderings Part 3)

Still Wandering: Still Wondering (Wanderings Part 4)

Disappointments: Books Not Written, ... (Wanderings Part 5)

On Living While Dying: A Decade with ALS

Imaginings: An Addendum to Important Things

Matter, Life, etc.: A Second Addendum to Important Things